THE LEADERSHIP CHALLENGE

FOREWORD BY
TOM PETERS

THE LEADERSHIP CHALLENGE

How to *Keep* Getting Extraordinary Things
Done in Organizations

JAMES M. KOUZES

BARRY Z. POSNER

JOSSEY-BASS PUBLISHERS / *San Francisco*

Substantial discounts on bulk quantities of Jossey-Bass books are available to corporations, professional associations, and other organizations. For details and discount information, contact the special sales department at Jossey-Bass Inc., Publishers. (415) 433–1740; Fax (800) 605–2665.

For sales outside the United States, please contact your local Paramount Publishing International Office.

Manufactured in the United States of America on Lyons Falls Pathfinder Tradebook. This paper is acid-free and 100 percent totally chlorine-free.

Library of Congress Cataloging-in-Publication Data
Kouzes, James M.
    The leadership challenge: how to keep getting extraordinary things done in organizations / James M. Kouzes, Barry Z. Posner.—2nd ed.
        p.   cm.— (The Jossey-Bass management series)
Includes bibliographical references and index.
ISBN 0-7879-0110-5
    1. Leadership. 2. Executive ability. 3. Management. I. Posner, Barry Z. II. Title.
III. Series.
HD57.7.K68 1995
658.4'092—dc20   95-11314

SECOND EDITION
HB Printing   10 9 8 7 6 5 4 3 2 1

The Jossey-Bass Management Series

Consulting Editors
Organizations and Management

WARREN BENNIS
University of Southern California

RICHARD O. MASON
Southern Methodist University

IAN I. MITROFF
University of Southern California

CONTENTS

PART I

When Leaders Are at Their Best

PART 2

Challenging the Process

PART 3

Inspiring a Shared Vision

PART 4

Enabling Others to Act

PART 5

Modeling the Way

PART 6

Encouraging the Heart

PART 7

Beginning the Journey

FOREWORD

The airport bookshop shelves are the acid test. Here today, gone tomorrow. That's the story of most faddish management texts. A couple of Druckers hang in there. Steve Covey has staying power . . . and so does *The Leadership Challenge,* which I saw in London's Heathrow Airport in December 1994, seven years after initial publication.

Of course, leadership is fundamental. Always has been. But leadership books are a dime a dozen—and most don't last for seven weeks, let alone seven years. Why this one? And if it's hanging in there, why update it?

The Leadership Challenge has lasted, I believe, because (1) it is research-based, (2) it is practical, and (3) it has heart.

Jim Kouzes and Barry Posner now have data in their files, stretching back eleven years, from ten thousand leaders and fifty thousand constituents. The five fundamental practices of successful leaders (at *all* levels) that you'll read about in these pages were carefully teased from, literally, a mountain of data. Believe me, this is "hard" evidence about what we ordinarily think of as a "soft" topic.

The real trick, of course, is turning these very human practices (such as challenging the process, inspiring a shared vision) into something that we ordinary folks can, well, *practice* on a moment-to-moment basis. This is where the book really shines.

Jim and Barry are both master teachers. Their seminars, it's fair to say, are works of art. (The *Wall Street Journal* in September 1993 ranked Jim Kouzes as one of the top-twelve leadership trainers in the country.) Both authors are also leaders in their own right—which doesn't hurt a bit.

And the book has heart. Leadership, many have said, is different from management. Management is mostly about "to do" lists (can't live without them!). Leadership is about tapping the wellsprings of human motivation—and about fundamental relations with one's fellows. Jim (whom I've known for over a decade), like Winston Churchill, cries easily; he cares. And he and Barry aren't afraid to admit that caring (heart) is the essence of leading in semiconductor companies as well as in the theater.

But why the revision, when the original is continuing to do so well? Practically speaking, the authors have a ton more data than in 1987. The good news for old fans: the basic findings have stayed put. The better news (for all of us): each finding (each practice, for example) has been fine-tuned again and again. As a result, this is basically a new book.

The more fundamental reason for the revision is that the world has changed so much more than Jim or Barry or I would have imagined eight years ago. The Berlin Wall has fallen since the first edition of *The Leadership Challenge* appeared; and the global village, with all virtually linked to all, has arrived with a vengeance. Oddly (or perhaps not so oddly!), this plays directly into Jim and Barry's hands. For the practices they espouse are now "musts," not "nice tos," in a world where hierarchies have been flattened, old command-and-control structures are not possible (let alone desirable), and knowledge (and the creative power of knowledge workers, all of us) is the new basis for economic value.

I highly recommended *The Leadership Challenge* in 1987. I do so even more in 1995. And I expect to find *this* edition on the Heathrow bookstall shelves in 2002!

Palo Alto, California   Tom Peters
May 1995

PREFACE

Everyone's Business

The New Realities of Leadership

The Leadership Challenge is about how leaders get extraordinary things done in organizations. It's about the practices leaders use to turn challenging opportunities into remarkable successes.

There's no shortage of challenging opportunities to radically alter the world in which we live and work. The opportunities for leadership are available to all of us every day. Yet today's challenges seem so daunting. They make us wonder: "Are we up to the task?"

The New Realities

The cynics are winning. People are fed up. They're angry, disgusted, and pessimistic about their future. Alienation is higher than it's been in a quarter-century. Our loyalty to institutions—and institutions' loyalty to people—is sinking like a stone. No longer would we rather fight than switch; we just switch. Nearly half the population is cynical, and cynics don't participate in improving things. In such a climate, how can a leader possibly mobilize a seemingly unwilling constituency?

Power has shifted. Today there's more computing power in your car than there was on the first manned space flight. Your home video camera has more processing power than an IBM 360. There's more power in the personal computers we used to write this book than existed on earth before 1950. We once called the mainframes in the glass houses "masters" and the terminals on our desks "slaves." In the computing world of today, the new relationship is described as client-server. Power *has* gone to the people—the clients. With access to information only a keystroke away, power has shifted from those with titles to those with technology and the skills to use it. More than any other force, this power shift is responsible for the flattening of hierarchies and the movement of the center of organizational gravity away from the powerful boss to empowered people. How do you lead in a client-server world when the so-called modern management techniques were designed to support a master-slave world?

We're all connected. While Jules Verne may have dreamed of going around the world in a balloon in eighty days, with a modem you can circumnavigate the globe from your desktop in eighty seconds or less. Technology has transformed us into an interconnected global village. You wake up in Tokyo knowing that you can tune in to CNN to find out what's happening in Toronto. And because of these electronic links, you can send an electronic order today to your factory half a world away and workers can manufacture and ship that order tomorrow. How do you lead in a wired world, where information is instant and news is old instantly?

Knowledge is the new currency. Knowledge has replaced land and capital as the new economic resource. *Knowledge-added* is the new *value-added*, whether in goods or services. How else can you explain why software producer Microsoft's stock trades at a higher price than that of car maker General Motors? This is good news and bad news. For those with degrees, it means higher incomes and more opportunity. For those who haven't graduated from high school, much less college, it means a reduced standard of living. For organizations and nations, it also means that fitness to compete is dependent upon the mental fitness of the workforce. How do you lead in a world in which your most important resources go in and out the front door every day?

The world is fragmented. Despite the electronic linkages—or perhaps because of them—the world, while connected, is far from a community. For all the talk of the global economy, the world is a pretty parochial place. There are more countries in the world today than a decade ago. Fierce tribal rivalries threaten domestic and international peace, and special-interest lobbying tears at our sense of community. There are more products and services than a decade ago, breaking the marketplace into ever smaller pieces. The new marketing segment has become a segment of one. How can a leader unite such a diverse and disparate constituency?

There's a new social contract on the table. The largest organizations have shed jobs at a record pace, shrinking in size and focusing their businesses in fewer industries. The contingent workforce is on the rise, while the permanent workforce is on the decline. More people are now self-employed— by choice or not—than twenty years ago. Project teams of specialists are recruited to produce a product, provide a service, or make a movie, and they're disbanded and reformed when the project is over. Students readying themselves for the workforce are told to expect to change their career many more times in their lives than their counterparts of a generation earlier and to not be with the same employer as long as their parents were. Loyalty and job security, we're told, have gone the way of the dodo bird. Instead, we have a new social contract that promises interesting work and greater employability in exchange for commitment to excellence. But how do leaders create commitment in a virtual organization? Can there be such a thing as virtual commitment? How capable are leaders of delivering on the promises implicit in the new contract?

There's a renewed search for meaning. With today's cynicism, fragmentation, and shifting relationships has come a yearning for a greater purpose in our lives. The best-seller lists now include books on spirituality, civility, and community. Values and virtues are discussed more openly, and people worry about the legacy they're leaving. While we may now have more experts on every conceivable subject, whether it's health care or computers, family and friends are still the most trusted sources of information. As the world erupts with the quakes of change, we seek to calm our fears by searching our souls and reaching out to our companions. How can leaders close the credibility gap and become more like trusted friends in this increasingly cynical world?

In the face of these new realities, there are countless opportunities to make a difference. Opportunities to restore hope and create a sense of meaning in our lives. Opportunities to rebuild a sense of community and increase understanding among diverse peoples. Opportunities to turn information into knowledge and, by doing so, to improve the collective standard of living. Opportunities to apply knowledge to products and services, creating extraordinary value for the customer.

More than ever, there's a need for people to seize these opportunities to lead us to greatness. *The Leadership Challenge* is about those who do. It's about how traditional systems of rewards and punishments, control and scrutiny, give way to innovation, individual character, and the courage of convictions. It offers a set of leadership practices that are based on the real-world experiences of thousands of people who have answered the cry for leadership.

Based on what we've observed in our research, we expect to rejoice in the outcome as more and more people answer that cry. For what we've discovered, and rediscovered, is that leadership isn't the private reserve of a few charismatic men and women. It's a process ordinary people use when they're bringing forth the best from themselves and others. Liberate the leader in everyone, and extraordinary things happen.

Who Should Read This Book?

The fundamental purpose of *The Leadership Challenge* is to assist people—managers and individual contributors alike—in furthering their abilities to lead others to get extraordinary things done. Whether you're in the private or public sector, whether you're an employee or a volunteer, whether you're on the front lines or in the senior echelon, whether you're a student or a parent, we've written this book to help you develop your capacity to guide others to places you (and they) have never been before. We believe that you're capable of developing yourself as a leader far more than tradition has ever assumed possible.

This book isn't about being in a leadership *position* (as if leadership were a place) but about having the courage and spirit to move from whatever place you're in to make a significant difference. This book isn't about leaders per se. It's about leadership and how ordinary people exercise it—and in the process become leaders. This book presents stories of regular people, from all walks of life, who got bigger-than-life results; it's not about bigger-than-life celebrities and corporate saviors.

The leaders we've worked with and learned from have asked and been asked many questions such as these on the road to enhancing their leadership capabilities:

- What are my strengths and weaknesses as a leader?
- Where do I need to improve my leadership ability?
- What's required to recognize opportunities and put risk in perspective?
- How can I inspire and motivate others toward a common purpose?
- What skills are needed to build a cohesive and spirited team?
- What's the source of the self-confidence required to lead others?
- How can I put more joy and celebration into our efforts?

This book is designed to help anyone—anyone who has the desire to lead, that is—to answer these questions.

Doing Our Best as Leaders

While *The Leadership Challenge* was written to strengthen your abilities and uplift your spirits, the principles and practices described in it are based solidly on research. The book has its origins in a research project we began in 1983. We wanted to know what people did when they were at their "personal best" in leading others. We wanted to hear about experiences in which, in their own perception, people set their individual leadership standard of excellence. We started with the assumption, however, that we didn't have to interview and survey star performers in excellent companies to discover best practices. We assumed that by asking ordinary people to describe extraordinary experiences, we would find patterns of success. And we surely did.

The personal-best leadership experience survey that we compiled consists of thirty-eight open-ended questions such as these: Who initiated the
project? How were you prepared for this experience? What special techniques and strategies did you use to get other people involved in the project?
How would you describe the character or feel of the experience? What did
you learn about leadership from this experience? The survey generally
requires one to two hours of reflection and expression. More than 550 of
these surveys were collected for our first edition, published in 1987. A short-
er, two-page form was completed by another group of 780 managers. In
addition, we conducted forty-two in-depth interviews. Since that time, we've
collected thousands of additional cases. In our initial study, we examined the
cases of middle- and senior-level managers in private- and public-sector
organizations. Over the last eight years, we've expanded our research to
include community leaders, student leaders, church leaders, government
leaders, and hundreds of others in nonmanagerial positions.

Every person we spoke with had at least one leadership story to tell.
Many had several. And those stories seldom sounded like textbook management. They weren't logical cases of planning, organizing, staffing,
directing, and controlling. Instead, they were tales of dynamic change and
bold action.

In one case, for example, manufacturing productivity was improved
over 400 percent in one year; in another, quality improvements moved
products from last to first on a customer's vendor list in three months; in
yet another, the company grew fivefold in sales and 750 percent in profits
over six years. In the not-for-profit and public sectors, we learned of a
school system that went from student performance in the lowest percentile
to performance in the sixty-eighth percentile in two years, an award-winning U.S. Army unit, and an organization that fought for and won the passage of legislation to protect abused and battered children.

From an analysis of the personal-best cases, we developed a model of
leadership. We then developed a quantitative instrument—The Leadership
Practices Inventory—to enable us to measure the leadership behaviors we
uncovered. Finally, we put all this to the test by initially surveying over
three thousand leaders, and their constituents, to assess the extent to
which these leaders exemplified the practices. We've since expanded that
sample: there are now more than ten thousand leaders and fifty thousand
constituents in our database.

The results of our research have been striking both in their refutation of the leader stereotype and in their consistency. Leaders do exhibit certain distinct practices when they're doing their best. And this behavior varies little from industry to industry, profession to profession, community to community, country to country. Good leadership is an understandable and a universal process.

A Field Guide for Leaders

Think of *The Leadership Challenge* as a field guide to take along on your leadership journey. We've designed it to describe what leaders do, explain the fundamental principles that support these leadership practices, provide actual case examples of real people who demonstrate each practice, and offer specific recommendations on what you can do to make these practices your own and to continue your development as a leader.

The first two chapters introduce you to our point of view about leadership. In Chapter One, we describe the five fundamental practices of exemplary leadership revealed in our research. Through examples, we discuss the actions that leaders take to get extraordinary things done. We conclude Chapter One with the Ten Commitments of Leadership—ten behaviors our research shows you can put to use in your organization.

The leader's tale, however, is only half the story. To be a leader, you have to have constituents. In Chapter Two, we describe the results of our survey of the characteristics that people most admire in their leaders. It turns out that constituents are also in agreement about the essentials of leadership.

In Chapters Three through Twelve, we explore the five fundamental practices of exemplary leadership, each in a pair of chapters. Within each of those ten chapters, we discuss one of the ten commitments. The discussions are built on the results of our research, and we expand our understanding of leadership by drawing on the research of other scholars. We also illustrate each practice and commitment with case examples that exemplify it. Each chapter then concludes with a set of recommended actions to help you put both the practice and the commitment to use in your organization.

When successful leaders talk about their personal-best achievements, they talk about searching for opportunities to innovate and change things. As we see in Chapter Three, the real motivator is the challenge of the adventure, not the material rewards. In Chapter Four, we learn that the source of most innovation is external to the leader's organization; therefore, the leader must keep the lines of communication open. We find that innovation also brings risk, so leaders accept the mistakes that result from experimentation and make every effort to learn from them.

In Chapter Five, we talk about how leaders look beyond the horizon of present time and imagine how things could ideally be several years ahead. Leaders have a sense of direction and a purpose beyond the moment. Yet even the clearest vision isn't enough to transform organizations. Unless the vision can be effectively communicated, people won't enlist in making the dream a reality. In Chapter Six, we see how leaders are positive and expressive in their presentations and are able to forge a shared agenda.

The leaders we studied are involved and in touch with those they lead. They care deeply about others, and they often refer to those with whom they work as family. We explore these ideas in Chapter Seven, as we examine how leaders foster collaboration and build effective teams. In Chapter Eight, we see how leaders create a climate in which it's possible for others to do their best. We see what leaders do to enable others to be in charge of their own lives. Leaders turn constituents into leaders.

As Chapter Nine unfolds, we see how personal clarity around values and principles is necessary for leaders to serve as models for what constituents are expected to be and do. In Chapter Ten, we discuss how leaders build commitment through a process of incremental change and small wins; they make it easy for others to say yes.

In Chapters Eleven and Twelve, we discuss how leaders sustain the commitment to achieve excellence by recognizing individuals, building social support, and celebrating team successes. Leadership is hard work, but it's also great fun—an effort of love.

Finally, in Chapter Thirteen, we discuss how, in order to lead others, we must first learn to lead ourselves. We treat leadership as a learnable set of practices. In so doing, we hope to demystify it and show how each of us has the capacity to lead. In this concluding chapter, we discuss how people learn to become leaders. We also offer guidance on how you can continue your own growth and development.

Those who wish to know more about how we conducted this research will find information on our research methodology, statistical data, and highlights of validation studies by other scholars of this leadership paradigm included in the Appendix.

The Future of Leadership

The domain of leaders is the future. The leader's unique legacy is the creation of valued institutions that survive over time. We hope this book will contribute to the revitalization of organizations everywhere, to the creation of new enterprises, and to the renewal of healthy communities. The most significant contributions leaders make are not to today's bottom line; they are to the long-term development of people and institutions who adapt, prosper, and grow.

More than that, we want to convince you that leadership is important not just in your own career and within your organization; it's important in all of your dealings with other people. Leadership is everybody's business, and the leadership challenge is everyone's challenge. The next time you say to yourself, "Why don't *they* do something about this?" look in the mirror. Ask the person you see, "Why don't *you* do something about this?"

More than ever, this society needs you to say, "Okay, I'll accept the challenge. I'll take the lead on this." And in so doing, we'll all come to realize that the leadership challenge is a personal—and a daily—challenge. And that the only limits are the limits we place on ourselves. We sincerely hope that this book will enable you to unleash more of your own courage and more of your own talent to *keep* getting extraordinary things done in organizations.

Santa Clara, California   James M. Kouzes
May 1995   Barry Z. Posner

PART I
When Leaders Are at Their Best

- ➤ **Challenge the Process**
- ➤ **Inspire a Shared Vision**
- ➤ **Enable Others to Act**
- ➤ **Model the Way**
- ➤ **Encourage the Heart**

1

The Practices and Commitments of Exemplary Leadership

The greatest rewards come only from the greatest commitment.
—ARLENE BLUM
Mountain Climber, Leader
American Women's Himalayan Expedition

Employees at Synergistic Systems, Inc. (SSI), located in Los Angeles's San Fernando Valley, have always known Jean Campbell, founder and CEO, to be positive, organized, enthusiastic, personable, caring, and unflappable. Campbell's leadership has been tested many times since 1984, when she started and began growing this computer-based medical billing company. The company is now a trusted firm that employs 200 people and handles over $200 million in charges for more than 1,200 physicians in 84 medical groups nationwide. Yet never has Campbell been as challenged as she was on the days following Monday, January 17, 1994, when at 4:31 A.M. a major earthquake rumbled through the San Fernando Valley, shaking her world to its very foundation.

On that Monday afternoon, as she worked her way to the damaged SSI building, located uncomfortably close to the hard-hit Northridge Mall and the campus of California State University, Northridge, Campbell was already formulating alternatives for keeping clients apprised of the company's status. Her primary concerns were to keep the revenues flowing for her clients and to be operational within two weeks. She also knew her employees would need money; she didn't want anyone to go without a paycheck any longer than was absolutely necessary. Yet as she inspected the SSI facility— its 25,000-square-foot tile ceiling lying collapsed on the floor, its twenty-eight-foot-high south wall pulled ten inches off its concrete base, its desks overturned, its files scattered, and its ceiling pipes leaking—she saw that she had a "no-business business." Her earlier goal of being fully operational within two weeks might have seemed impossible to some, given the extent of the destruction. Not to Jean Campbell: to her it became a mission.

Working closely with IBM Business Recovery Services, Campbell began going through a review of critical business requirements. With her business initially in shambles, Campbell organized, planned, listened, reassured, and motivated Syners (as the SSI employees call themselves) and contractors alike to restore essential services within forty-eight hours and full services in less than ten business days. How did Campbell and her team restore services so quickly and so smoothly?

As IBM's Larry Meyer recalls, "Jean knows her business inside out and could make quick decisions. She could formulate contingency plans in her head. She knows her people and what each of them do. Jean listened to the recommendations provided by the recovery experts and accepted their counsel, even when it was not in accordance with her first instinct. When people came back to work, Jean was there to greet them. Loyalty goes both ways."[1]

As IBM recovery crews worked, curbside management offices were moved back into the building and employees were called back to work to resume essential services in temporary but safe areas. So that billings and collections could proceed uninterrupted, the conference room adjacent to Jean Campbell's office became "Deposits R Us." The parking lot became the communal lunch room, with local caterers contracted to provide meals for Syners and invited guests: the IBM contractors and construction workers who were restoring the building. According to construction contractor Jim Long, "Without a doubt, the heart of SSI lies in the camaraderie that's fostered by the care and concern Jean Campbell sincerely has for her employees. It's felt throughout the company, and it flowed over the construction workers who were happy to be on this job and part of this project. Sometimes it seemed they were here in part because of the emotion almost as much as for the paycheck. The rebuilding process evoked such positive emotion, which in turn created enormous energy to get the job done."

Little things, such as hard hats worn by all Syners and construction workers, changed the mood from that of a building under siege to that of a building under construction. People customized their hard hats and color-coordinated their outfits to match the hats; some even attached Mickey Mouse ears. Deposits R Us staffer Kristy Bowler recalls, "Jean made it a lot easier by taking care of the necessities—water, food, comfort—and checking on us after each aftershock." Campbell took care in other ways too. Since she knew many employees had major cleanups to finance at home, she stipulated that employee paychecks be issued every week instead of every other week as usual.

Finally, with reconstruction complete, Jean Campbell held a Town Hall meeting (an SSI phrase for a special meeting) on February 2, declaring, "It's time to celebrate our victory with all those who helped to bring it about and to give heartfelt thanks to so many." In introducing the guests who had been an integral part of SSI's recovery, Campbell spoke with great pride as she recalled those early postquake days: "We have become a highly collaborative organization. There were no boundaries, except for the yellow [construction zone] ribbons. There was a determination for survival; the whole organization was at stake. The lives that Synergistic Systems affects are thousands: physicians and their families, patients, families within our own organization. Customer service could not and would not be compromised."

Her concern for her customers and her pride in the team's accomplishments were clear as she recalled a particular incident: "Isi Russ, M.D., called on the evening of January 17 inquiring about personnel and property and found himself answering my question, 'What will bring the clients comfort?' His reply was, 'Keep the courier going and keep making deposits.' And as you all know, that's exactly what we did!"

When the Northridge quake struck, Campbell energized a partnership of employees, suppliers, and customers so powerful that it overcame the forces of devastation unleashed by nature. Campbell demonstrated exemplary leadership skills, and she showed how to guide a talented and committed team in accomplishing exceptionally challenging goals. Campbell serves as a model for how other leaders can get extraordinary things done in a world of constant chaos and change.

While Campbell is truly a remarkable person, her story is not. We've found such achievements to be commonplace. We've discovered that there are myriad success stories in virtually every arena of organized activity—in profit-based firms and nonprofits, manufacturing and services, government and business, education and entertainment, work and community service. Leaders reside in every city and every country, in every position and every place. They're employees and volunteers, young and old, women and men. Leadership knows no racial or religious bounds, no ethnic or cultural borders, as the following example demonstrates.

The shakeup at Metalsa, an automotive metal stamping company in Monterrey, Mexico, came not from an earthquake but from Antonio Zárate. To the outside world, he is the chief executive officer, but internally he goes by "coordinator of the guiding team." Zárate's title says a lot about both his values and the company's. One immediately begins to understand that at Metalsa all people are the same; only what they do is different.

The turnaround at Metalsa began in earnest after Zárate, then director of operations, visited Japan in 1985. "The Japanese firms were a little bit different from Metalsa not only in tools but also in *values,*" observes Zárate. "The people I saw seemed to care for each other; the team was more important than the individual, and the people were very honest." Zárate knew that Mexican people shared these values but felt that they were somehow inhibited from expressing them at work. He suspected that the bureaucratic and autocratic nature of traditional Mexican business practices prevented organizations from tapping into the best efforts and the will of the people. This would have to change if Metalsa was to become competitive in world markets.

The change started with a change in values. In 1986, Zárate started promoting a new philosophy within operations at Metalsa. In 1987, when he was appointed CEO, he started spreading that new credo to other parts of the company as well. Zárate summarizes the Metalsa way with this formula:

$$QWL = TPQ + TQC + LDS$$

And everyone at Metalsa knows what it means: "Quality as a way of life" results from "total personal quality" plus "total quality control" plus "leadership." As Zárate says, "We believe that quality products and services can be produced only by quality people."

This overarching philosophy is elaborated in a set of corporate-wide cultural values—values such as trust, solidarity, service, and training—and a set of individual personal values, including responsibility, punctuality, honesty, humility, austerity, patience, service, and the search for "total personal quality."

To spread the change, Zárate knew he had to take his message directly to each member. "I felt the people needed to see that I was taking time to talk to them personally about quality, philosophy, and how we were going to go ahead," explains Zárate. Zárate implored employees to concentrate on improving the quality of the person within. He knew that if they did so, and if they adopted a high spirit of service, their actions would surely reflect their own quality as persons. He also assured them that if they practiced the right attitude every day on little things, *all* things would get a little better every day.

In all discussions about the new philosophy, Zárate also conveyed his belief that service to the customer was as important as the physical quality of the product. He believed that "if we improve on service, our profits will improve; not the opposite." Zárate was equally adamant about solidarity, asking rhetorically, "When you want to conquer your enemy, you try to divide them; so why divide our own company?"

Things began to change. Executives started serving the customer and stopped being bureaucrats. They stopped wasting time on needless paperwork. Time clocks were ripped out, and work teams began to keep their own attendance records. Quality control inspectors and supervisors were eliminated; their roles were assumed by team members. In the process, Metalsa went from seven layers of management to only four levels—including Zárate's.

Beyond layers of management, social layers were eliminated as well. Status is central to all hierarchies, and it is quite pronounced in Mexican society. Thus the first division Zárate eliminated was status. It was typical, for instance, that attendance at a meeting held under the old order was recorded according to position. Now everything is alphabetical. There are no reserved parking spots for executives any longer; all parking spaces are open to everyone. People don't have job titles; everyone is a coordinator.

Upon this new foundation of clear values, Zárate has guided Metalsa's workers from a questionable future into worldwide recognition as a manufacturer of quality products for the automotive industry and a model of an enlightened Mexican employer. When Antonio Zárate joined on as a manager in 1978, Metalsa operated just one plant, had $23 million in domestic sales, had sales per employee of only $23,000, produced no exports, employed 1,000 workers, and had a 10 percent rejection rate. By 1994, after seven years under Zárate's leadership, Metalsa operated 6 plants, had increased sales to over $140 million (with 40 percent exports), had over 2,000 employees, had sales per employee of up to $70,000, had improved productivity by 200 percent, had reduced the rejection rate to .1 percent, and had won numerous supplier awards for quality, including the prestigious QSP award in 1994, awarded by General Motors to only 171 out of its 30,000 suppliers worldwide.

The future of Metalsa is far brighter today than a decade ago, and the company is clearly positioned to compete in the global marketplace. "Quality at Metalsa is a way of life," Zárate boasts proudly, "based upon the conviction that in order to compete in the marketplace, it is necessary to serve. We say that people have to live to serve instead of living to be served."

Faced with different cultures and difficult circumstances, Jean Campbell and Antonio Zárate each seized the opportunity to lead. They chose a pioneering path and led their organizations to new summits of excellence. And while their cultures and circumstances are distinct, we can learn some important lessons about leadership from Campbell, Zárate, and the thousands of others who told us their personal-best experiences. From them we can learn what it takes to mobilize other people—by the force of their own free will and despite hard work and potential risk—to want to climb to the summit.

Through our studies of personal-best leadership experiences, we've discovered that ordinary people who guide others along pioneering journeys follow rather similar paths. While each case we looked at was unique in expression, each path was also marked by some common patterns of action. We've forged these common practices into a model of leadership, a route for leaders to follow as they attempt to keep their own bearings and guide others toward peak achievements.

The Five Fundamental Practices of Exemplary Leadership

As we looked deeper into the dynamic process of leadership, through case analyses and survey questionnaires, we uncovered five fundamental practices that enable leaders to get extraordinary things done. The individual stories of how ordinary people got extraordinary things done brought the leadership model to life for us, giving it character and color. When they were at their personal best, the leaders we studied were able to

➤ Challenge the process
➤ Inspire a shared vision
➤ Enable others to act
➤ Model the way
➤ Encourage the heart

These practices, which we discuss briefly in this chapter and elaborate on in later chapters, aren't the private property of the people we studied or of a few select shining stars. They've stood the test of time, and they're available to anyone, in any organization or situation, who accepts the leadership challenge.

CHALLENGING THE PROCESS

Leaders venture out. While many people in our studies attributed their success to "luck" or "being in the right place at the right time," none of them sat idly by waiting for fate to smile upon them. Those who lead others to greatness seek and accept challenge. Jean Campbell, for instance, rose to the occasion when nature jolted SSI off its foundations. In the process, she also found innovative ways to run the business. Antonio Zárate caused a quake of his own by confronting a traditional culture with some radical new ideas.

Every single personal-best leadership case we collected involved some kind of challenge. The challenge may have been an innovative new product, a cutting-edge service, a groundbreaking piece of legislation, an invigorating campaign to get adolescents to join an environmental program, a revolutionary turnaround of a bureaucratic military program, or the start-up of a new plant or business. Whatever the challenge, all the cases involved a change from the status quo. Not one person claimed to have done his or her personal best by keeping things the same. *In short, all leaders challenge the process.*

Leaders are pioneers—people who are willing to step out into the unknown. They're willing to take risks, to innovate and experiment in order to find new and better ways of doing things. But leaders need not always be the creators or originators of new products, services, or processes. In fact, it's just as likely that they're not. Product and service innovations tend to come from customers, clients, vendors, people in the labs, and people on the front lines, while process innovations tend to come from the people doing the work. Sometimes a dramatic external event thrusts us into a radically new condition.

The leader's primary contribution is in the recognition of good ideas, the support of those ideas, and the willingness to challenge the system in order to get new products, processes, services, and systems adopted. It might be more accurate, then, to say that leaders are early *adopters* of innovation. Leaders know well that experimentation, innovation, and change all involve risk and failure, but they proceed anyway.

It would be ridiculous to assert that those who fail over and over again eventually succeed as leaders. Success in any endeavor isn't a process of simply buying enough lottery tickets. The key that unlocks the door to opportunity is learning. In his own study of exemplary leadership practices, University of Southern California professor Warren Bennis writes that "leaders learn by leading, and they learn best by leading in the face of obstacles. As weather shapes mountains, problems shape leaders. Difficult bosses, lack of vision and virtue in the executive suite, circumstances beyond their control, and their own mistakes have been the leaders' basic curriculum."[2] In other words, leaders are learners. They learn from their failures as well as their successes.

INSPIRING A SHARED VISION

When people described to us their personal-best leadership experiences, they told of times when they imagined an exciting, highly attractive future for their organization. They had visions and dreams of what *could* be. They had absolute and total personal belief in those dreams, and they were confident in their abilities to make extraordinary things happen. Every organization, every social movement, begins with a dream. The dream or vision is the force that invents the future. In the rubble, Campbell saw a new and even more responsive Synergistic Systems; Zárate imagined a company of total quality people producing total quality products.

Leaders inspire a shared vision. They gaze across the horizon of time, imagining the attractive opportunities that are in store when they and their constituents arrive at a distant destination. Leaders have a desire to make ✓ something happen, to change the way things are, to create something that no one else has ever created before.

In some ways, leaders live their lives backward. They see pictures in their mind's eye of what the results will look like even before they've started their project, much as an architect draws a blueprint or an engineer builds a model. Their clear image of the future pulls them forward. Yet visions seen only by leaders are insufficient to create an organized movement or a significant change in a company. A person with no constituents is *not* a leader, and people will not follow until they accept a vision as their own. Leaders cannot command commitment, only inspire it.

To enlist people in a vision, leaders must know their constituents and ✓ speak their language. People must believe that leaders understand their needs and have their interests at heart. Only through an intimate knowledge of their dreams, their hopes, their aspirations, their visions, their values is the leader able to enlist support. Leadership is a dialogue, not a monologue.

Leaders breathe life into the hopes and dreams of others and enable them to see the exciting possibilities that the future holds. Leaders forge a unity of purpose by showing constituents how the dream is for the common good.

Leaders can't ignite the flame of passion in others if they don't express enthusiasm for the compelling vision of their group. Leaders communicate their passion through vivid language and an expressive style.

Without exception, the people in our study reported that they were incredibly enthusiastic about their personal-best projects. Their own enthusiasm was catching; it spread from leader to constituents. Their belief in and enthusiasm for the vision were the sparks that ignited the flame of inspiration.

ENABLING OTHERS TO ACT

The individuals in our study recognized that grand dreams don't become significant realities through the actions of a single leader. Leadership is a team effort. After reviewing over 2,500 personal-best cases, we developed a simple test to detect whether someone is on the road to becoming a leader. That test is the frequency of the use of the word *we*.

Exemplary leaders enlist the support and assistance of all those who must make the project work. This sense of teamwork goes far beyond a few direct reports or close confidants. In today's "virtual" organization, cooperation can't be restricted to a small group of loyalists; it must include peers, managers, customers and clients, suppliers, citizens—all those who have a stake in the vision. Leaders involve, in some way, all those who must live with the results, and they make it possible for others to do good work. *They enable others to act.* Leaders know that no one does his or her best when feeling weak, incompetent, or alienated; they know that those who are expected to produce the results must feel a sense of ownership.

David Butler, controller at Plextor, told us the following: "As a society and global economy, we've progressed beyond the industrial revolution. The control-oriented structures and management techniques of that era don't apply anymore. . . . You need to give people on the front lines proper vision and proper training, and then follow that up with responsibility so they can act on decisions." Leaders recognize the validity of Butler's statement and work to make people feel strong, capable, and committed. Leaders enable others to act not by hoarding the power they have but by giving it away. When people have more discretion, more authority, and more information, they're much more likely to use their energies to produce extraordinary results.

In the cases we analyzed, leaders proudly discussed teamwork, trust, and empowerment as essential elements of their efforts. For constituents, too, a leader's ability to enable others to act is essential; in fact, from the constituents' vantage point, this is the most significant of the five practices. Leadership is a relationship, founded on trust and confidence. Without trust and confidence, people don't take risks. Without risks, there's no change. Without change, organizations and movements die.

MODELING THE WAY

Titles are granted, but it's your behavior that wins you respect. As Gayle Hamilton, a division manager with Pacific Gas & Electric Company, told us, "I would never ask anyone to do anything I was unwilling to do first."

Leaders go first. They set an example and build commitment through simple, daily acts that create progress and momentum. *Leaders model the way through personal example and dedicated execution.*

To model effectively, leaders must first be clear about their guiding principles. Leaders are supposed to stand up for their beliefs, so they better have some beliefs to stand up for. Eloquent speeches about common values aren't nearly enough. Leaders' deeds are far more important than their words and must be consistent with them. Toni-Ann Lueddecke knows that there are no unimportant tasks in an organization's efforts at excellence. She demonstrates this to her associates in her seven Gymboree Play Centers in New Jersey by her daily actions. As just one example, she scrubs floors just as often as she teaches classes.

At a faculty convocation at Santa Clara University several years ago, the Reverend William J. Rewak, S.J., then president, spoke eloquently about changes anticipated for the campus. After showing slides of the planned new buildings and gardens, he said, "Vision needs management, electricity, and concrete." Grand dreams, he reminded us, can't become significant realities with élan alone. New tomorrows aren't realized without hard work and persistence. The personal-best projects we heard about in our research were all distinguished by relentless effort, steadfastness, competence, and attention to detail.

Leaders need operational plans. They must steer projects along a predetermined course, measure performance, give feedback, meet budgets and schedules, and take corrective action. Yet the personal-best cases we examined included very little about grand strategic plans and massive organizational changes; they sounded more like action adventure stories. They were about the power of little things piled one on top of the other until they added up to something big. Concentrating on producing small wins, leaders build confidence that even the biggest challenges can be met. In so doing, they strengthen commitment to the long-term future.

ENCOURAGING THE HEART

The climb to the top is arduous and long. People become exhausted, frustrated, and disenchanted. They're often tempted to give up. *Leaders encourage the heart of their constituents to carry on.* If people observe a charlatan making noisy pretenses, they turn away. But genuine acts of caring can uplift the spirits and draw people forward. Jean Campbell held a Town Hall meeting when reconstruction was complete to "celebrate victory," you'll remember; at Metalsa, Antonio Zárate "encourages self-esteem."

Encouragement can come from dramatic gestures or simple actions. When he was plant manager of the Wire and Cable Division of Raychem Corporation, Phil Turner would occasionally put on a clown costume and give out balloons to employees. He still enjoys celebrating milestones in various ways, and people get a good laugh from his playful acts. Heather Gioia, president of TPG/Learning Systems, is a master of recognition. She gives out stickers, stuffed animals, masks, buttons, toys, and every other conceivable award to people when they achieve a milestone.

It's part of the leader's job to show people that they can win. In the cases we collected, there were thousands of examples of individual recognition and group celebration. You can use marching bands, bells, T-shirts, note-cards, personal thank-yous, and a host of other awards to offer visible signs of encouragement to keep on winning. Recognition and celebration aren't about fun and games, however. Encouragement is curiously serious business. It's how leaders visibly and behaviorally link rewards with performance. When striving to raise quality, recover from disaster, start up a new service, or make dramatic change of any kind, leaders make sure people benefit when behavior is aligned with cherished values.

In the cases we examined, we saw evidence not only of the encouragement leaders give to others but of the encouragement that leaders give themselves. When we asked George Gananian, owner of Star Graphics, why he worked so hard, he said, "I love to turn the key in the door and put on the coffee pot." Love—of their products, their services, their constituents, their clients and customers, and their work—may be the best-kept leadership secret of all.

Myths, Traditions, and Realities

These fundamental leadership practices, revealed in our examination of personal-best leadership experiences, offer hope. More than ever, there's need for people to seize opportunities to lead us to greatness. Our neighbors, friends, and colleagues have shown us how. Yet people increasingly ask us, "Why aren't there more leaders?" Why *are* people reluctant to answer the cry for leadership?

We believe this cautiousness results not from a lack of courage or competence but from outdated notions about leadership. Just about everything we were taught by traditional management prevents us from being effective leaders. And just about every popular notion about leadership is a myth.

Our first leadership challenge is to rid ourselves of these traditions and myths. They foster a model of leadership antithetical to the way real-life leaders operate. They also create unnecessary barriers to the essential revitalization of our organizations.

Traditional management teaching implies that the ideal organization is orderly and stable, that the organizational process can and should be engineered so that things run like clockwork. Yet when ordinary people talk about their personal-best leadership achievements, they talk about challenging the process, about changing things, about shaking up the organization.

At the same time, one popular leadership myth portrays the leader as a renegade who magnetizes a band of followers with courageous acts. In fact, leaders attract constituents not because of their willful defiance but because of their deep faith in the human capacity to adapt and grow and learn.

Traditional management teaching focuses our attention on the short term, the Wall Street analysts, the quarterly statement, and the annual report. Yet all the effective leaders we've seen have had a long-term, future orientation. They've looked beyond the horizon of the present.

A new and equally fictitious folklore developing about leadership suggests that leaders are prescient visionaries with Merlin-like powers. To be sure, leaders must have a vision, a sense of direction, but the vision need not reveal any psychic foresight. It can spring from original thinking or represent the inspiration of someone else. It can be celestial or mundane.

Traditional management teaches that leaders ought to be cool, aloof, and analytical; they ought to separate emotion from work. Yet when real-life leaders discuss what they're the proudest of in their own careers, they describe feelings of inspiration, passion, elation, intensity, challenge, caring, and kindness—and yes, even love.

Another leadership myth says that leaders are "charismatic," that they possess some special gift. At best, this distorts our appreciation of leaders.

At worst, it can lead to hero worship and cultism. To be sure, leaders must be energetic and enthusiastic. But a leader's dynamism doesn't come from special powers. It comes from a strong belief in a purpose and a willingness to express that conviction.

Traditional management teachings suggest that the job of management is primarily one of control: the control of resources, including time, money, materials, and people. Flesh-and-blood leaders know, however, that the more they control others, the less likely it is that people will excel. They also know that the more they control, the less they'll be trusted. Leaders don't command and control; they serve and support.

Another generally accepted leadership myth tells us that it's lonely at the top. Not so. The most effective leaders we know are involved and in touch with those they lead. They care deeply about others, and they often refer to those with whom they work as family.

Tradition suggests that the job of leaders is to detach themselves from mundane, day-to-day work and invent a grand strategic plan. Tradition would have us believe that great policy promotes progress. But we know that leaders' deeds are far more important than their words. Credibility of action is the single most significant determinant of whether a leader will be followed over time.

Still another myth associates leadership with superior position. It assumes that *leadership* starts with a capital L and that those who are on top are automatically leaders. But leadership isn't a place; it's a process. It involves skills and abilities that are useful whether one is in the executive suite or on the front lines, on Wall Street or Main Street.

And the most pernicious myth of all is that leadership is reserved for only a very few of us. That myth is perpetuated daily, whenever anyone asks, "Are leaders born or made?" Leadership is certainly not conveyed in a gene, and it's most definitely not a secret code that can't be understood by ordinary people. Contrary to the myth that only a lucky few can ever decipher the mystery of leadership, our research has shown us that leadership is an observable, learnable set of practices. In over ten years of research, we've been fortunate to hear and read the stories of over 2,500 ordinary people who have led others to get extraordinary things done. And there are millions more. The belief that leadership can't be learned is a far more powerful deterrent to development than is the nature of the leadership process itself. If there's one singular lesson about leadership that can be drawn from all of the cases we've gathered, it's this: *leadership is everyone's business.*

The Ten Commitments of Leadership

Embedded in the five fundamental practices of exemplary leadership discussed above are behaviors that can serve as the basis for learning to lead. We call these the Ten Commitments of Leadership. These ten commitments, as shown on the following page, serve as the guide for our discussion of how leaders get extraordinary things done in organizations and as the structure for what's to follow.

We'll fully explore each of these commitments in Chapters Three through Twelve. Before delving into the practices and commitments further, however, let's consider leadership from the vantage point of the constituent. What do people look for and admire in leaders? What do people need to willingly continue on the journey?

Ten Commitments of Leadership

PRACTICES	COMMITMENTS
Challenging the Process	**1.** *Search out* challenging opportunities to change, grow, innovate, and improve.
	2. *Experiment*, take risks, and learn from the accompanying mistakes.
Inspiring a Shared Vision	**3.** *Envision* an uplifting and ennobling future.
	4. *Enlist* others in a common vision by appealing to their values, interests, hopes, and dreams.
Enabling Others to Act	**5.** *Foster* collaboration by promoting cooperative goals and building trust.
	6. *Strengthen* people by giving power away, providing choice, developing competence, assigning critical tasks, and offering visible support.
Modeling the Way	**7.** *Set* the example by behaving in ways that are consistent with shared values.
	8. *Achieve* small wins that promote consistent progress and build commitment.
Encouraging the Heart	**9.** *Recognize* individual contributions to the success of every project.
	10. *Celebrate* team accomplishments regularly.

Source: The Leadership Challenge by James M. Kouzes and Barry Z. Posner. Copyright © 1995.

2

What Constituents Expect of Leaders

Knowing the Other Half of the Story

Without credibility, you can't lead.
—BRIAN CARROLL
Head of Retail Banking
Challenge Bank, Australia

Challenging the process, inspiring a shared vision, enabling others to act, modeling the way, and encouraging the heart: these are the practices that emerge from personal-best leadership cases. But they paint only a partial picture. The portrayal can be complete and vivid only when constituents see their own views represented, because leadership is a reciprocal process between those who choose to lead and those who choose to follow. Any discussion of leadership must attend to the dynamics of this relationship. Strategies, tactics, skills, and practices are empty unless we understand the fundamental human aspirations that connect leaders and constituents.

To balance our understanding of leadership, we investigated the expectations that constituents have of leaders. We asked constituents to tell us what they look for and admire in a leader. Their responses affirm and enrich the picture that emerged from our studies of personal bests. Clearly, those who aspire to lead must embrace their constituents' expectations.

Leader Characteristics That Constituents Admire

We began our research in the early 1980s by surveying several thousand business and government executives. We asked the following open-ended question: "What values (personal traits or characteristics) do you look for and admire in your superiors?"[1] (As you can see, our perspective and choice of metaphors has changed since then.) In response to that question, the managers identified more than 225 different values, traits, and characteristics. Subsequent content analysis by several independent judges reduced these items into fifteen categories. In later studies, we elaborated on several categories and added a few new characteristics not originally included. The current version contains a list of twenty characteristics. We've administered this questionnaire, in its final form, to over 20,000 people on four continents. We ask participants to imagine they're electing a leadership council of seven members and that there are twenty candidates in the running; these candidates, however, represent ideal qualities, not specific individuals. We then ask respondents to select the seven qualities that they "most look for and admire in a leader, someone whose direction they would *willingly* follow."

The results from these surveys, shown in Table 2.1, have been striking in their regularity over the years we've been conducting this research. It appears that a person must pass several essential tests before others are willing to grant the title *leader.*

To understand more fully, from the perspective of the constituent, the actions through which leaders demonstrate these leadership characteristics, in the 1990s we began expanding our study to include written case studies of admired leaders. People responded to questions about leaders with whom they had had personal experience and for whom they had great admiration and respect, and their responses were fleshed out into

Table 2.1.   Characteristics of Admired Leaders.

Characteristics	1995 Respondents: Percentage of People Selecting	1987 Respondents: Percentage of People Selecting
HONEST	88	83
FORWARD-LOOKING	75	62
INSPIRING	68	58
COMPETENT	63	67
Fair-minded	49	40
Supportive	41	32
Broad-minded	40	37
Intelligent	40	43
Straightforward	33	34
Dependable	32	32
Courageous	29	27
Cooperative	28	25
Imaginative	28	34
Caring	23	26
Determined	17	20
Mature	13	23
Ambitious	13	21
Loyal	11	11
Self-Controlled	5	13
Independent	5	10

Note: These percentages represent respondents from four continents: America, Asia, Europe, Australia. The majority, however, are from the United States.

case studies. From these case studies (now numbering over 400), we collected specific examples of actions of respected leaders, information on the affective nature of admired leader–constituent relationships, and details about the types of projects or programs involved. These data came from sources in North America, Mexico, Western Europe, Asia, and Australia. Focus groups conducted subsequent to the collection of early cases further enabled us to determine the behaviors of admired leaders. Additionally, we conducted in-depth interviews with more than forty respected leaders and asked them to comment as constituents on the actions they believed exemplified quality leadership. Through a series of quantitative studies, we gained further insight into the leadership actions that influence people's assessments of credibility. We analyze these findings and discuss their implications in detail in our book *Credibility: How Leaders Gain and Lose It, Why People Demand It.*[2] In this chapter, we briefly summarize the results of these various studies and their relationship to the five fundamental practices of exemplary leadership.

As Table 2.1 suggests, the majority of us admire and willingly follow leaders who are

- Honest
- Forward-looking
- Inspiring
- Competent

These themes are woven into the text in subsequent chapters, as they are in the workplace. Here, however, let's focus on the meaning and implications of these most frequently selected leadership qualities.

BEING HONEST

In every survey we conducted, honesty was selected more often than any other leadership characteristic; it consistently emerged as the single most important ingredient in the leader-constituent relationship. It's clear that if we're to willingly follow someone—whether it be into battle or into the boardroom, into the classroom or into the back room, into the front office or to the front lines—we first want to assure ourselves that the person is worthy of our trust. We want to know that the person is being truthful, ethical, and principled. We want to be fully confident of the integrity of our leaders, whatever the context. That nearly 90 percent of constituents want their leaders to be honest above all else is a message that all leaders must take to heart.

Just how do constituents measure a characteristic as subjective as honesty, though? In our discussions with respondents, we learned that the leader's *behavior* provided the evidence. In other words, regardless of what leaders say about their own integrity, people wait to be shown; they observe the behavior. Consistency between word and deed is how we judge someone to be honest. If leaders espouse one set of values but personally practice another, we find them to be duplicitous. If leaders practice what they preach, we're more willing to entrust them with our career, our security, and sometimes even our life. This expectation directly corresponds to the practice of *modeling the way*, which we'll discuss in Chapters Nine and Ten.

Honesty is also related to values and ethics. We appreciate people who take a stand on important principles. We resolutely refuse to follow those who lack confidence in their own beliefs. Confusion over where the leader stands creates stress; not knowing the leader's beliefs contributes to conflict, indecision, and political rivalry. We simply don't trust people who won't tell us their values, ethics, and standards.

BEING FORWARD-LOOKING

Fully 75 percent of our respondents selected the ability to look ahead as one of their most sought-after leadership traits. We expect our leaders to have a sense of direction and a concern for the future of the organization. This expectation directly corresponds to the ability to envision the future that leaders described in their personal-best cases. But whether we call that ability vision, a dream, a calling, a goal, or a personal agenda, the message is clear: leaders must know where they're going if they expect others to willingly join them on the journey.

Two surveys that we conducted with top executives reinforce the importance of clarity of purpose and direction. In one study, nearly 300 senior executives rated "developing a strategic planning and forecasting capability" as their most critical concern. When asked to select the most important characteristics in a CEO, these same senior managers ranked "a leadership style of honesty and integrity" first and "a long-term vision and direction for the company" second.[3] Our own research is confirmed by a joint Korn/Ferry–Columbia University study. Seventy-five percent of respondents in that assessment ranked "conveys a strong vision of the future" as a very important quality for CEOs *today;* it was so ranked by an almost unanimous 98 percent for the year 2000.[4] The desirability of this ability didn't vary by more than three percentage points across the regions studied (Japan, Western Europe, Latin America, and the United States).

By the ability to be *forward-looking*, people don't mean the magical power of a prescient visionary. The reality is far more down-to-earth: it's the ability to set or select a desirable destination toward which the company, agency, congregation, or community should head. Vision is the magnetic north that provides others with the capacity to chart their course toward the future. As constituents, we ask that a leader have a well-defined orientation toward the future. We want to know what the organization will look like, feel like, be like when it arrives at its goal in six months or six years. We want to have it described to us in rich detail so that we'll know when we've arrived and so that we can select the proper route for getting there.

BEING INSPIRING

We also expect our leaders to be enthusiastic, energetic, and positive about the future. We expect them to be inspiring—a bit of the cheerleader, as a matter of fact. It's not enough for a leader to have a dream about the future. A leader must be able to communicate the vision in ways that encourage us to sign on for the duration. In the personal-best cases, *inspiring a shared vision* was a common practice; when leaders breathe life into constituents' dreams and aspirations, constituents are much more willing to enlist in the movement.

In his book *Working,* Studs Terkel quotes Nora Watson, an editor: "I think most of us are looking for a calling, not a job. Most of us . . . have jobs that are too small for our spirit. Jobs are not big enough for people."[5] Her words underscore how important it is to find some greater sense of purpose and worth in our day-to-day working life. While the enthusiasm, energy, and positive attitude of a good leader may not change the context of work, they certainly can make work more meaningful.

Some react with discomfort to the idea that being inspiring is an essential leadership quality. One chief executive officer of a large corporation even told us, "I don't trust people who are inspiring." No doubt this is a response to past crusaders who led people to death or destruction. Others told us they were skeptical of their own ability to inspire others. This lack of faith in others and in ourselves is a terrible mistake. In the final analysis, leaders must inspire our confidence in the validity of the goal. Enthusiasm and excitement are essential and signal the leader's personal commitment to pursuing that goal. If a leader displays no passion for a cause, why should anyone else?

BEING COMPETENT

To enlist in another's cause, we must believe that the person is competent to guide us where we're headed. We must see the leader as capable and effective. If we doubt the leader's abilities, we're unlikely to enlist in the crusade. As Ken Nissley of James River Creative Expressions put it, "You can't give credibility to people without a record of achievements."

Leadership competence doesn't necessarily refer to the leader's abilities in the core technology of the operation. In fact, the type of competence demanded seems to vary with the leader's position and the condition of the organization. For example, those who hold officer positions are expected to demonstrate abilities in strategic planning and policy making. If a company desperately needs to clarify its core competence and market position, a CEO with savvy in competitive marketing may be perceived as a fine leader. But in the line function, where people expect guidance in technical areas, these same strategic marketing abilities will be insufficient. A leader on the line or at the point of customer or client contact will typically have to be more technically competent than someone less engaged in providing services or making products. Yet it's not necessary that the leader have the same level of technical competence as constituents. Much more significant is that the leader takes the time to learn the business and to know the current operation before making changes and decisions that affect everyone in the organization.

We are, however, noticing a trend toward requiring more technical competence of leaders. The age of the generalist manager may be coming to a close, especially in the knowledge industries. Although an effective leader in a high-technology company may not need to be a master programmer, that leader must understand the business implications of electronic data interchange and networking. A good leader in a professional services firm may have little direct client responsibility but must have towering competence as a consultant.

We've come to refer to the kind of competence needed by leaders as *value-added competence*. Functional competence may be necessary, but it's insufficient; the leader must bring some added value to the position. Having a winning track record is the surest way to be considered competent. Expertise in leadership skills themselves is another dimension of competence. And the abilities to challenge, inspire, enable, model, and encourage must be demonstrated as well, if leaders are to be seen as capable.

Putting It All Together: Credibility

Honest, forward-looking, inspiring, and competent: these characteristics have, over the last two decades, been consistently selected by all respondent groups as the four most essential leadership prerequisites. While these four qualities have remained at the top of the list over all the years of our studies, the relative importance of forward-looking and inspiring have increased over time. More people now want their leaders to provide future direction and show enthusiasm than in years past. These times of transition require leaders with the vision and the energy to sustain hope.

Whatever the order, these characteristics make up what communications experts refer to as "source credibility." In assessing the believability of sources of communication—whether newscasters, salespeople, managers, physicians, politicians, or priests—researchers typically evaluate people on three criteria: their perceived trustworthiness, their dynamism, and their expertise. Those who are rated more highly on these dimensions are considered to be more credible sources of information.

Notice how strikingly similar these three characteristics are to honest, inspiring, and competent—three of the four most frequently selected items in our survey. What we found in our investigation of admired leadership qualities is that more than anything, we want leaders who are credible. Above all else, we must be able to believe in our leaders. We must believe that their word can be trusted, that they'll do what they say, that they're personally excited and enthusiastic about the direction in which we're headed, and that they have the knowledge and skill to lead. We have come to refer to this as The First Law of Leadership: If we don't believe *in* the messenger, we won't believe the message. This is a principle that every leader must acknowledge.

As part of our quantitative research, we used a behavioral measure of credibility and asked organizational members to think about the extent to which their immediate manager exhibited credibility-enhancing behaviors.[6] We found that when people perceive their immediate manager to have high credibility, they're significantly more likely to

- Be proud to tell others they're part of the organization
- Feel a strong sense of team spirit
- See their own personal values as consistent with those of the organization

- Feel attached and committed to the organization
- Have a sense of ownership of the organization

When people perceive their manager to have low credibility, on the other hand, they're significantly more likely to

- Produce only if they're watched carefully
- Be motivated primarily by money
- Say good things about the organization publicly but criticize it privately
- Consider looking for another job if the organization experiences problems
- Feel unsupported and unappreciated

These differences certainly provide clear reasons for organizational leaders to seriously consider how their constituents perceive their credibility. Loyalty, commitment, energy, and productivity depend upon it.

But much as we demand that people be credible in order for us to accept what they're saying, credibility alone doesn't satisfy us; we demand something more. As we've noted, we demand that leaders be forward-looking: that they have a sense of direction, a vision for the future. We expect credible newscasters, for example, to be independent when reporting what's happening today; however, we expect leaders to have a point of view on today's events and to also be firm about the destination of our national, organizational, or civic journey. We may want certain people to be cool and objective, but we want leaders to articulate the exciting possibilities. Leaders don't just report the news; they make it.

Leaders who are forward-looking are biased—biased about the future. They aspire to change the way things are and guide us to a better tomorrow. But this very admirable and desirable leadership quality means that leaders often become the target of those who propose an alternative future. Thus when a leader takes a position on issues—when that leader has a clear point of view and a partisan sense of where the country, community, or company ought to be headed—that individual will be seen as less believable than someone who takes no stand. Consequently—ironic as it might seem—by the very nature of the role they play, leaders will always have their credibility questioned by those who oppose them.[7]

What does this mean for aspiring leaders? First, we place leaders in an awkward situation. We demand that they be credible, but we also contribute to undermining their credibility by expecting them to focus on a clear direction for the future. Leaders must learn how to balance their personal desire to achieve important ends with the constituents' need to believe that the leader has others' best interests at heart.

Second, because of this balancing dilemma, leaders must be ever diligent in guarding their credibility. Their ability to take strong stands—to challenge the status quo, to point us in new directions—depends upon their being perceived as highly credible. If leaders ask others to follow them to some uncertain future—a future that may not be realized in their lifetime—and if the journey is going to require sacrifice, isn't it reasonable that constituents should believe in them? To believe in the exciting future possibilities leaders present, constituents must first believe in their leaders' trustworthiness, expertise, and dynamism.

This is not to suggest for one second that leadership is a popularity contest. It's totally unrealistic for any leader to expect 100 percent of potential constituents to willingly enlist. Leaders have to learn to thrive on the tensions between their own calling and the voice of the people.

Opinions about those in leadership positions also tend to rise and fall with events.[8] When times are good, people exhibit more confidence in their leaders; when times are bad, they show less. The more severe the events and the more compressed the time frame, the more cynical people are likely to become. And cynics have significantly less trust in their management than those who are upbeat. Nearly half of the cynics doubt the truth of what management tells them, and only a third believe management has integrity. Three-quarters believe that top executives do pretty much what they want to no matter what people think.[9]

It's thus understandable that in a drastic restructuring, with attendant layoffs and shrinking family incomes, the credibility of business, labor, church, and government leaders has declined. A natural suspicion of power and the confluence of events (such as the financial and political scandals of the 1980s and 1990s) certainly explain a great deal about why leaders have lost credibility. Bad timing can often ruin credibility as much as bad actions.

Yet credibility problems aren't simply a function of the times. In any circumstance, credibility is one of the hardest attributes to earn. And it's the

most fragile of human qualities. It's earned minute by minute, hour by   ✓
hour, month by month, year by year. But it can be lost in very short order
if not attended to. We're willing to forgive a few minor transgressions, a
slip of the tongue, a misspoken word, a careless act. But there comes a time
when enough is enough. And when leaders have used up all of their credibility, it's nearly impossible to earn it back.

The Essence of Leadership

Most of us can agree on what we want from our leaders. We want them to
be credible, and we want them to have a sense of direction. Leaders must
be able to stand before us and confidently express an attractive image of
the future—and we must be able to believe that they have the ability to
take us there.

There are many striking relationships between what leaders say they do
when at their personal best and what people say they admire and look for
in their leaders. Clearly, the leadership practice of inspiring a shared vision
involves being forward-looking and inspiring. By challenging the process,
leaders enhance the perception that they're dynamic. The practice of modeling the way includes the clarification of a set of values and being an
example of those values to others. This consistent living out of values is a
behavioral way of demonstrating honesty and trustworthiness. We trust
leaders when their deeds and words match. Trust is also a major element   ✓
of enabling others to act. In their descriptions of their personal bests, leaders said that they trusted others, which fostered others' trust in them.
Likewise, encouraging the heart—the recognition and celebration of significant accomplishments—contributes to perceptions that one is just, fair,
and sincere.

The quality of competence or expertise is more difficult to ascertain
from leaders' descriptions of their personal bests. They didn't talk about
this element directly. We can infer, however, that since they were talking
about a time when they did their best, they were also talking about a time
when they felt competent. Competence is determined largely by track
record, as we noted earlier. If we succeed at something over time, we can
assume some expertise in that area. The cases in our research are examples
of competent (and then some) performance.

When leaders demonstrate the practices described in the personal-best cases, they attract others to what they represent. In a certain sense, they "manage" their credibility. They're conscious of how their behavior shapes the impressions others have of them, and so they take charge of how others come to see them. If this is done with sincerity and integrity—and not with the unethical manipulation of the con artist—leaders earn credibility in the eyes of their constituents. This credibility establishes the foundation upon which dreams for the future can be built.

Defining Leadership

The portrait of leadership that emerges from both the personal-best cases and the survey of constituents' expectations is a study in relationships. Without constituents to enlist, a prospective leader is all alone, taking no one anywhere. Without leaders, constituents have no energizer to ignite their passions, no exemplar to follow, no compass by which to be guided. Essential to the definition of leadership is an understanding of this relationship.[10]

Also embedded in our findings is the consensus that leaders must appreciate and articulate a shared vision of the future. Leadership is also a performing art—a collection of practices and behaviors—not a position. Constituents don't willingly follow positions; they follow people engaged in a process. And people don't get extraordinary things done unless they have the will to do so. Excellence rises from within; it can't be imposed from without.[11] Thus we define leadership as *the art of mobilizing others to want to struggle for shared aspirations.*

Two words in this definition stand out for us as most significant: *want to.* Without *want to* in the definition, the meaning of leadership is significantly altered. Choice, internal motivation, and inner desire disappear. Leadership then implies something less than voluntary involvement on the part of constituents.

It's a fairly easy task to get people to do something. Promise them a favorable review, a promotion, or a bonus if they perform exceptionally well. Or if incentives don't work, threaten to report them, demote them, fire them, or punish them in some other way. With these extrinsic rewards and pressures, we can get most people to act. Managers have been proving this for years. But what of those who have no bonuses to give, no promotions to offer, and no performance reviews to write? What of those who can't pay any compensation and yet ask us to contribute our time, our resources, our services, our energies, even our lives? What of those who must rely upon our willingness, our internal motivation, to give of ourselves for some just cause? Do they not lead?

To get a feel for the true essence of leadership, assume that everyone who works with you is a volunteer. Assume that your employees are there because they want to be, not because they have to be. (In fact, they really are volunteers—especially those upon whom you depend the most. The best people are always in demand, and they can choose where they lend their talents and gifts. They remain because they volunteer to stay.) What conditions would need to exist for your staff to want to enlist in your "volunteer" organization? Under volunteer conditions, what would you need to do if you wanted people to perform at high levels? What would you need to do if you wanted them to remain loyal to your organization?

If there's a clear and distinguishing feature about the process of leading, it's in the distinction between mobilizing others to do and mobilizing others to *want* to do. People in positions of authority can get other people to do something because of the power they wield, but leaders mobilize others to *want* to act because of the credibility they have. There are monumental differences between enlisting support and giving orders, between gaining commitment and commanding obedience. Leaders sustain the requisite credibility by their actions—by challenging, inspiring, enabling, modeling, and encouraging. In the next ten chapters of this book, we'll describe how leaders engage in each of these practices. We'll support these practices with our own research and with that of other leadership scholars. In addition, we'll offer suggestions and practical ideas on how you can put these to use in your everyday endeavors.

PART 2

Challenging the Process

- ➤ **Challenge the Process**
- ➤ **Inspire a Shared Vision**
- ➤ **Enable Others to Act**
- ➤ **Model the Way**
- ➤ **Encourage the Heart**

3

Search for Opportunities

Confronting and Changing the Status Quo

Leadership is getting people to look beyond their own job description for ways to improve and challenge the process.
—MAUREEN FRIES
Administrator
Los Olivos Women's Medical Group

Take out a piece of paper and draw a line down the middle. Now think about the people you consider exemplary leaders, whether contemporary or historical. Think about the men and women who you believe have led organizations, communities, states, nations, or the world to greatness. Write their names in the left-hand column. In the right-hand column opposite each name, record the events or actions with which you identify each of these individuals.

Now review the list. Is there any pattern in the leadership situations? What do they have in common? We predict that if some of the leaders on your list are businesspeople, you've associated them with the turnaround of failing companies, the start-up of entrepreneurial ventures, the development of new product lines or services, or other business transformations.

For those on your list who are leaders in government, the military, the arts, the community, or the church, we predict a similar kind of association; most likely you identify these leaders with the creation of new institutions, the resolution of serious crises, the winning of wars, the organization of revolutionary movements, protests for improving social conditions, political change, innovation, or some other social transformation.

When we think of leaders, we recall times of turbulence, conflict, innovation, and change. We think of people who triumphed against overwhelming odds, who took initiative when there was inertia, who confronted the established order, who rose to the challenge of adversity, who mobilized people and institutions in the face of strong resistance. We think of people who generated momentum in society and then guided that energy toward a more fulfilling future.

Throughout this book, we use the metaphor of the journey when discussing the work of leaders. We find it to be the most appropriate metaphor, because the word *lead,* at its root, means "go, travel, guide."[1] Leadership has about it a kinesthetic feel, a sense of movement. Leaders "go first." They're pioneers. They begin the quest for a new order. They venture into unexplored territory and guide us to new and unfamiliar destinations.

In contrast, the root origin of *manage* is a word meaning "hand."[2] At its core, managing is about "handling" things, about maintaining order, about organization and control. The critical difference between management and leadership is reflected in the root meanings of the two words—the difference between what it means to handle things and what it means to go places. The unique role of leaders is to take us to places we've never been before.

Now, the path out of crisis and into peace, or out of the familiar and into the novel, is full of ghostly unknowns. It often winds through the wilderness, blocked repeatedly by the barriers of convention. The study of leadership is the study of how men and women guide us through empty and frightening expanses of uncharted territory.

The appropriate place to begin our detailed discussion of leadership practices is with leaders' search for opportunities. Leaders look for ways to radically alter the status quo, for ways to create something totally new, for revolutionary new processes, for ways to beat the system. Whether leaders are selected for projects or initiate them, they always search for opportunities to do what has never been done.

The Challenge of Change

The first thing that struck us as we analyzed the personal-best cases was that they were about significant change. Regardless of function, field, economic sector, organizational level, or national boundary, the leaders in our study talked about times when they led adventures into new territory. They told us how they turned around losing operations, started up new plants, installed untested procedures, or greatly improved the results of poorly performing units. And these weren't 10, 25, or even 50 percent improvements in products and processes; in many cases, the magnitude of changes was in the *hundreds* of percent. The personal-best leadership cases were about firsts, about radical departures from the past, about doing things that had never been done before, about going to places not yet discovered.

What's surprising about the emphasis on innovation in these leadership cases is that we didn't ask people to tell us about change; we asked them to tell us about *personal-best leadership experiences.* They could discuss any leadership experience they chose: past or present, unofficial or official; in any functional area; in any community, voluntary, religious, health care, educational, public-sector, or private-sector organization. Participants chose to talk about times of change, not stability and the status quo. Their stories reflect the idea that leadership requires changing the business-as-usual environment. Patricia M. Carrigan is a leader who did just that.

Carrigan faced a significant challenge of change as she became the first female assembly plant manager in the history of General Motors. Educated as a clinical psychologist, prior to that promotion she had spent more years in public education than in the auto industry. The task before her was awesome—the turnaround of the Lakewood assembly plant outside of Atlanta. Soon after Carrigan began her tenure at Lakewood, the plant was shut down for a year and a half due to declining car sales. "The fact that the plant was out of production so long that its workers scattered to other plants across the country gave strong impetus to change," said Carrigan. Under Carrigan's leadership in the two years after the plant was reopened, it became an entirely different place. Its successes were evidence of a phenomenal change.

Here are a few of Lakewood's extraordinary successes during Carrigan's tenure (as described by Carrigan):

Lakewood became the first plant in GM history to attain a widely
accepted corporate standard for high quality in the first published
audit after start-up and the first to repeat that performance just after
the second shift started up.

Grievances fell to and remained at or near zero, and discipline incidents
declined by 82 percent since the plant began operating on two shifts.
There were no cases of protested discipline after the plant reopened.

Despite the addition of heavy daily and Saturday overtime since production resumed, absenteeism declined from 25 percent to 9 percent, saving more than $8 million.

Sickness and accident costs were cut by two-thirds. A jointly established five-year goal for reduction in sick-leave costs was attained in
the first year (netting a $1.3 million credit).[3]

These results are testimony to the unprecedented cooperation between
management and labor at Lakewood. Jointly, they accomplished what few
have ever been able to do, in any industry: they completely transformed
an organization, and they made it work.

Getting these results required a totally new approach to working
together. The strategy had three main ingredients. First, labor and management jointly structured and presented a two-week pre–start-up training class for all employees. The training involved the presentation of
detailed business information and of jointly developed plans for improving plant business performance. That same training was then conducted
for all new employees after start-up. Both hourly and salaried people
served as facilitators.

Second, labor and management jointly and successfully encouraged
Lakewood employees to participate more fully in the business. There were
133 planning/problem-solving workgroups (involving over 90 percent of
the workforce) functioning on a voluntary basis a year and a half after the
plant's reopening.

Third, an extensive ongoing training program was established for
Lakewood employees. At the time of Carrigan's departure, labor and management had jointly enhanced the skills of over 3,000 people in a total of
over 360,000 hours of training.

All of these actions flowed directly from the jointly developed plant philosophy, whose essence is contained in the following four principles:

To change, take risks, accept responsibility, and be accountable for our actions.

To respect all people, promoting unity, trust, pride, and dedication to our mission.

To achieve a high quality of work life through involvement of all our people in an environment of openness and fairness in which everyone is treated with dignity, honesty, and respect.

To promote good communications among all employees by operating in an open atmosphere with freedom to share ideas and speak one's mind without fear of reprisal.[4]

Carrigan gave credit for these achievements to a "partnership with people." Those people, the employees at the plant, recognized her contribution as well. When she left, the union local honored her with a plaque commemorating "her leadership, courage, risk-taking, and honesty."[5]

More than anything else, leadership is about creating a new way of life. And to do that, leaders must foster change, take risks, and accept the responsibility for making change happen. But Carrigan went beyond that. As she says, "The challenge is posed by what's out there and by our need to survive. The ability to participate in that challenge and to make it a shared challenge in the organization is an incredible task for a leader. The question is, 'How are you going to do that?' If you're going to expect an organization to take some risks, you have to show some willingness to do that too."[6]

Carrigan and the other leaders in our study accepted the challenge presented by the shifts in their industries or the new demands of the marketplace. In finding opportunities to get extraordinary things done, they made use of three *essentials:*

- Arousing intrinsic motivation
- Balancing the paradox of routines
- Using outsight: looking outside for stimulation and information

By their actions, these leaders showed the willingness to take risks for the sake of changing the business-as-usual environment. They demonstrated what social psychologists have documented empirically: challenge raises motivational and performance levels.[7]

Arousing Intrinsic Motivation

Leaders search for opportunities for people to exceed their previous levels of performance. They regularly set the bar higher. However, leaders also appreciate that the challenge shouldn't be so great as to be discouraging. This awareness of the human need for challenge and this sensitivity to the human need to succeed at that challenge are among the critical balancing skills of any leader.

According to a traditional organizational cliché, what gets rewarded gets done. So organizations generally offer a lot of extrinsic rewards—money, stock options, bonuses, perks, prestige, and position—to get people to perform. Carrigan's success at the Lakewood plant, however, didn't involve a huge financial payoff for the employees involved. True, her situation involved survival of the organization, and that's a significant economic benefit. But the typical survival strategy would have been for the organization to slash and trash its way out. That's not what Carrigan and the Lakewood people did. So why did they go so far beyond survival expectations? Why did they set such incredible goals for themselves? For that matter, why do people do things for nothing? Why do they volunteer to put out fires, raise money for worthy causes, or help children in need? Why do people sign up for the Peace Corps or join Mother Teresa in caring for the poorest of the poor? Why do they risk their careers to start a new business or risk their security to change the social condition? If extrinsic rewards explained all our behavior, we would be hard pressed to find an explanation for any of these actions. How do people find satisfaction in efforts that don't pay a lot of money or provide a lot of prestige?

We believe that intrinsic motivation must be present if people are to do their best. And contrary to the hierarchical theory of motivation, we believe that it's possible to excel even when fighting for survival. We believe that what is rewarding gets done. We can never pay people enough to care—to care about their products, services, communities, or families, or even the bottom line. True leaders tap into peoples' hearts and minds, not merely their hands and wallets.

But if external rewards and punishments are successful, why should leaders concern themselves with these intrinsic rewards? After all, people in the workplace *aren't* volunteers; they're getting paid.

It's precisely because people *are* getting paid, because people *are* eligible for bonuses and other awards, that a leader ought to be concerned. If work comes to be seen solely as a source of money and never as a source of fulfillment, organizations will totally ignore other human needs at work—needs involving such intangibles as learning, self-worth, pride, competence, and serving others. Employers will come to see people's enjoyment of their tasks as totally irrelevant, and they will structure work in a strictly utilitarian fashion. The results will be—in fact, have already been—disastrous for many organizations. In *Reinvention of Work: A New Vision of Livelihood for Our Time,* Matthew Fox explains that there are vast differences between a job and work. A job is about economics, while "work comes from the inside out; work is an expression of our soul, our inner being. It's unique to the individual; it's creative. Work is an expression of the Spirit at work in the world through us."[8] Without employing people's hearts, organizations lose precious return on their investment in people.

People who justify their employment on solely economic grounds will never contribute more than the minimum. They will also tend to feel alienated and may leave when another job—one that pays equally well or better—becomes available. Pay and other external rewards can significantly lower intrinsic motivation and can create dependence upon expensive reward systems.[9]

Absolute dedication to extrinsic motivators severely limits an organization's ability to excel and to use the full potential of its employees. It wastes human talent and drains away organizational resources. Certainly, we should pay people fairly and provide equitable benefits; ours isn't an argument for exploitation. However, reliance upon external incentives and pressures doesn't liberate people to perform their best, and it constrains leaders from ever learning why people *want* to excel. If we don't learn that, we'll never learn to lead.

What makes something intrinsically motivating—a reward in itself? And what can we learn from this that might make us better leaders? University of Chicago professor Mihaly Csikszentmihalyi and his colleagues have conducted intensive studies to explore the nature of activities that contain rewards within themselves.[10] They first analyzed such activities as rock climbing, dance, chess, and high school basketball. But since none of these is a so-called productive pursuit, they bridged the gap between leisure and work by also studying the work activities of people from all walks of life—composers of music, scientists, surgeons, teachers, and others. They wanted to know what made an activity or a job enjoyable. What they discovered was that people enjoyed their chosen activity because of the pleasure they derived from the experience and the pleasure they derived from using their skills. These reasons are purely intrinsic: we enjoy doing something because the doing of it is enjoyable. In contrast, the reasons that were most extrinsic—power, prestige, glamour—ranked last in the Csikszentmihalyi study.

What is it about the structure of these activities that produces the intrinsic motivation? The researchers found the answer to be surprisingly consistent: "Whatever the specific structure of an autotelic [rewarding in and of itself] activity is like, it seems that its most basic requirement is to provide a clear set of challenges."[11] The challenges that ranked highest among respondents were "designing and discovering something new," "exploring a strange place," and "solving a mathematical problem."[12] These aren't the only challenges in life, but they do suggest that the key to intrinsic motivation is getting involved in something that requires us to look at a situation in new ways.

Whether it's doing our best as leaders or simply enjoying what we do, answering the summons of adventure lifts our spirits. Being invited to do better than we've ever done before compels us to reach deep down inside and bring forth the adventurer within. The lessons for leadership are clear: for leaders to perform at their personal best, they must

- Believe that the project requires full use of skills and talents.
- Experience the project itself as enjoyable and challenging.

And if leaders wish to get the best from others, they must

- Search for or create opportunities for people to outdo themselves.
- Find opportunities for people to solve problems, make discoveries, explore new ground, reach difficult goals, or figure out how to deal with some external threat.
- Make work responsibilities fun.

To find the proper balance between action opportunities and individual skills, leaders must know the abilities of their constituents. They must

- Know what others can do.
- Recognize what others find personally challenging.

It's important that leaders have challenges, but it's even more important that they know what it is that challenges others and what others are capable of performing.

Balancing the Paradox of Routines

We've argued, on the basis of the personal-best cases, that the opportunity to change the business-as-usual environment is fertile soil for leadership. The challenge of creating a new way of life is intrinsically motivating to leaders and constituents alike. Routines, on the other hand, can be the enemies of change. They can stifle the very adventure that leaders seek to create.

Warren Bennis, distinguished professor at the University of Southern California and leadership scholar, describes how routines prevented change when he was president of the University of Cincinnati:

> My moment of truth came toward the end of my first ten months. . . .
> The clock was moving toward four in the morning, and I was
> still in my office, still mired in the incredible mass of paper
> stacked on my desk. I was bone weary and soul weary, and I found
> myself muttering, "Either I can't manage this place, or it's
> unmanageable." I reached for my calendar and ran my eyes down
> each hour, half-hour, quarter-hour to see where my time had gone
> that day, the day before, the month before. . . . My discovery was
> this: *I had become the victim of a vast, amorphous, unwitting,
> unconscious conspiracy to prevent me from doing anything whatever
> to change the university's status quo.*[13]

He coined Bennis's First Law of Academic Pseudodynamics to describe this phenomenon: "Routine work drives out nonroutine work and smothers to death all creative planning, all fundamental change in the university—or any institution."[14]

Everyone we know can relate to Bennis's dilemma. Situations and people seem to conspire to make leaders into bureaucrats. Organizations do this through established procedures and demands—all those memoranda, telephone calls, reports, meetings, plans, speeches, letters, and so on. Bennis found himself caught up in the routine and the trivial. Others have told us that they get so busy in the day-to-day details of their work that they become ensnared in an activity trap. The only thing that gets crossed off their daily "to do" list is the day at the top of the week!

So leaders must challenge the process precisely because any system will unconsciously conspire to maintain the status quo and prevent change. But leaders live with a paradox when fighting against the routines of organizational life. They must destroy routines because routines get us into ruts, dull our senses, stifle our creativity, constrict our thinking, remove us from stimulation, and destroy our ability to compete. Once-useful routines sap the vitality out of an organization and cause it to atrophy. Yet some routines are essential to a definable, consistent, measurable, and efficient operation. We get annoyed when we can't figure out who reports to whom. We get confused when our employers keep changing the strategy. We get absolutely livid when we're taken off one project and put on another just when we're beginning to get the hang of it. There are no economies in *always* changing; constant changes in direction and in the ways things are done are confusing to everyone.

It seems that we can't live with routines and routine work—but we can't live without them either. Established procedures annoy us, and yet we're glad we have them when we expect trains to run on time. Repetitious work is definitely tedious. Yet if we never did anything the same way twice, we would rarely make any return on our investments or provide quality services and products. The critical issue for leaders isn't whether to have routines but which routines to have. Those few essential routines that serve the key values of the organization should be worshiped. Those that don't should be rooted out. Those routines that help the organization to change—routines such as customer satisfaction surveys—should be promoted. Those that are excuses—the "always done it that way around here" routines—should be exposed for the injury they do to the welfare of the organization and its people.

If organizations and societies are to make progress, then, leaders must be able to detect when routines are becoming dysfunctional. They must be able to see when routines are smothering creative planning and blocking necessary advancement.

Russell L. Ackoff, professor emeritus at the University of Pennsylvania's Wharton School, offers one way out of this dilemma. "If I could add only one subject to business-school curricula," writes Ackoff, "it would be on how to beat the system. Beating the system means making a well-designed system work poorly or a poorly designed system work well."[15] Sharon Kneeland, founder of H-R Solutions, clearly understands Ackoff's point. One of the things she learned from her personal-best leadership experience was that "it's easier to ask forgiveness than permission." Kneeland is an old hand at beating the system, and she knows that leaders have to go for it at first—and confess later. Leaders may be rule makers, but they're also clearly rule breakers. Furthermore, they know that beating the system sometimes means looking into new areas, looking outside.

Using Outsight

Leaders can expect demand for change to come from both inside and outside the organization. Customers and clients are generally the source of demand for product and service innovation, while requests and suggestions for process innovation generally come from the people doing the work (that is, those outside the ranks of management). But organizational leaders are likely to cut themselves off from critical information sources over time, whether because they're too busy, because they think that they've heard it all before, or because of cuts to travel, phone, and conference budgets. However, unless external communication is encouraged and supported, people interact with outsiders less and less over time and new ideas are cut off.

If leaders are going to detect demands for change, they must use their *outsight*. They must stay sensitive to the external realities, especially in this networked, global world. They must go out and talk to their constituents, be they citizens, customers, employees, stockholders, students, suppliers, vendors, business partners, managers, or just interested parties. They must listen and stay in touch.

EXTERNAL AND INTERNAL COMMUNICATION

James M. Utterback of Massachusetts Institute of Technology is one of this country's leading authorities on innovation. He has studied thousands of innovations in processes and products and has found that "market forces appear to be the primary influence on innovation. From 60 to 80 percent of important innovations in a large number of fields have been in response to market demands and needs."[16] In a separate study of the introduction of 224 new electronics products—half successes and half failures—entrepreneur and University of Miami professor Modesto Marquis found that the key success factor was the development team's interaction with the customer.[17] Very few innovations emerge because someone in the organization says, "Aha, maybe we can find a user for this technical idea."[18]

Research by Ralph Katz and Tom Allen of the MIT Sloan School of Management gives additional evidence to support these claims. Katz and Allen conducted a field study of research and development teams over a number of years. As one aspect, they examined the relationship between the length of time that people had been working together in a particular project area—what they called "group longevity"—and the level of communication of project groups at various stages of their lives. Three areas of interpersonal oral communication were examined for each team: (1) intraproject communication, (2) organizational communication, and (3) professional communication. Each team's technical performance was also measured by department managers and laboratory directors.[19]

The higher-performing groups had significantly more communication with people outside their labs, whether with organizational units such as marketing and manufacturing or with outside professional associations. Those groups with the highest longevity index reported lower levels of communications in all three areas. As a result, they "were significantly more isolated from external sources of new ideas and technological advances and from information within other organizational divisions, especially marketing and manufacturing."[20] The low-performing teams cut themselves off from the kind of information they needed the most. Katz concludes that less effective project performance stems not from a reduction in project communication per se but from "an isolation from sources that can provide the most critical kinds of evaluation, information, and new ideas."[21]

The message here is that there just aren't enough good new ideas floating around the lab when people don't listen to the world outside. As Rebecca Henderson's studies of U.S. and European pharmaceutical companies attest, the most successful companies make certain that they're efficiently connected to the scientific community and to their peers *outside* of their own firm.[22]

Extending the implications of these research studies beyond technical functions, we can understand how some workgroups and organizations become myopic and unimaginative. The people themselves aren't dull or slow-witted; they've just become too familiar with their routines and too isolated from outside influences. To infuse fresh ideas into an organization, a leader needs to shake it up periodically. That can be done by adding new members to the group, sending existing ones off on a tour, or holding a seminar. Whatever the technique, the leader must keep communication pathways open and vital.

OUTSIGHT AND INSIGHT

On a recent visit to the coast of Northern California, we came across some important advice for leaders. Printed at the top of a pamphlet describing a particular stretch of the Pacific Ocean was this warning: "Never turn your back on the ocean." Why can't we turn and look inland, to catch a view of the town? A rogue wave may come along when our backs are turned and sweep us out to sea, as it has many an unsuspecting traveler. This warning holds good advice for travelers and leaders alike. When we take our eyes off the external realities, turning inward to admire the beauty of our own organization, we may be swept away by the swirling waters of change.

So too with innovation: we must always scan the external realities. If creative ideas come from outside our own group, innovation requires the use of outsight, whether directed to pricing in the marketplace or diversity in the workforce. Outsight is the sibling of insight—the ability to apprehend the inner nature of things—and the awareness and understanding of outside forces comes through openness. It's by keeping the doors open to the passage of ideas and information that we become knowledgeable about what goes on around us.

Thus leaders must destroy confining barriers. Those who enclose themselves, who shut the doors to the world outside, will never be able to detect change. And worse, they may be overtaken by it. Over and over again, those we interviewed told us that leaders keep their eyes and ears open. They permit passage of new ideas into the system. They remain receptive and expose themselves to broader views.

Leaders remove the protective covering in which organizations often seal themselves. Leaders are willing to hear, consider, and accept ideas from sources outside the company. As Irwin Federman, venture capitalist and former CEO of Monolithic Memories, noted as he reflected on the lessons from his own personal best, "Leaders listen, take advice, lose arguments, and follow."[23] At first, Federman's comment seems counter to our traditional assumptions about leadership. Our initial reaction is that leaders are supposed to tell other people what to do, give advice, win arguments, and be directive. But Federman knows that if leaders were to behave like that, their organizations would never succeed.

Innovation requires even more listening and communication than does routine work. Change and innovation can be effectively led only through human contact; leaders guiding a change must therefore establish more relationships, connect with more sources of information, and get out and walk around more frequently. Successful innovations don't spring from the fifty-second floor of the headquarters building or the back offices of City Hall. It's only by staying in touch with the world around them that leaders can ever expect to change the business-as-usual environment. Therefore, they stay in touch with trends in the marketplace, with the ideas and advice of people from a variety of backgrounds and disciplines, and with social, political, technological, economic, and artistic changes.

Conditions That Foster Leadership

We had never seen a recruiting poster for leaders—not until we saw a poster for Operation Raleigh (now called Youth Service International). At the top of the poster was printed, in big, bold letters, "Venturers Wanted!" Below the headline was a photograph of a group of people neck deep in a swamp with broad smiles on their faces. The recruiting copy read as follows:

Join the Voyage of Discovery
For 1500 young Americans between the ages of 17 and 24, it will be the
adventure of a lifetime. Underwater archaeology on sunken ships, aerial
walkways in tropical rainforests, medical relief for remote tribal villages—
innovative, exciting, worthwhile projects. . . .
   The selected applicants will join fellow venturers from many
nations for three-month periods. They will work alongside an expert
expedition staff under rigorous conditions in over 40 countries
worldwide.
   Science and service are the themes and leadership development is a
primary goal. It is the pioneer spirit of Sir Walter Raleigh's day rekin-
dled, and you are invited to apply.[24]

   This recruiting poster is the most descriptive statement we've seen of the
conditions that develop leadership abilities. Leadership opportunities are
indeed voyages of discovery and adventures of a lifetime. They're challenging
explorations under rigorous conditions, and they require pioneering spirits.
   Our clue to the conditions that foster leadership came when we
reviewed the answers to this item on our personal-best questionnaire:
"What five or six words would you use to best describe the character (the
feel, the spirit, the nature, the quality) of your personal-best leadership
experience?" The answers suggested a highly spirited outlook, one that
viewed the white waters of change as a personal challenge. All of the
descriptions given by the respondents are vibrant and full of life. They res-
onate; they pulse and throb. As the below samples illustrate, the personal
bests were times when people felt fully alive:

- David Arkless described the spirit of his international
  diplomacy mission for Hewlett-Packard, S.A., as
  "challenging, tough work, fun, daunting, unusual, uplifting."
- Saffrona Alexander described her experience as chair of
  the CITIES scholarship program as "exciting,
  demanding, positive, rewarding, inspirational, discovering."
- Julie Marshall talked about starting up a store for
  Nordstrom in these terms: "demanding, exciting, stimulating,
  stressful, whole-hearted, fun."

- Jeff Crosby recalled his experience as a counselor for Project 50, which brought underprivileged students to Santa Clara University for a combination summer school and summer camp: "uplifting, developmental, challenging, fun, spiritual."
- Gale Kingsbury led a project to improve financial systems at Tektronix and found it "energizing, rewarding, motivating, strengthening, exciting, challenging."
- Richard Namm described his work with the National Weather Service Regional Forecast Office—on the evening lightning knocked out the power—as "exciting, demanding, exhausting, rewarding, and thrilling."
- Ann Marie Dockstader recalled her experience as an officer of her sorority during a time of fiscal and academic crisis as "challenging, daunting, stimulating, empowering, dynamic."

The words most frequently used by leaders in our study in describing the character of their personal bests were *challenging, rewarding,* and *exciting.* Words signifying passion—*dedication, intensity, commitment, determination*—and inspiration—*inspiring, uplifting, motivating, energizing*—also appeared regularly. *Unique, important, proud,* and *empowering* got their fair share as well. Fully 95 percent of the cases were described in the above terms.

But leadership bests can also be filled with stress. Of the 95 percent of the men and women we studied who said their projects were exciting, 20 percent also described their projects as frustrating, and 15 percent said that they aroused fear or anxiety. But instead of being debilitated by the stress of a difficult experience, they were challenged and energized by it. Stress always accompanies the pursuit of excellence, but when we're doing our best it never overtakes us. The positive feelings generate momentum that enables us to ride out the storm.

It's also instructive to observe how people chose *not* to describe their personal bests. In no single instance did anyone use the word *boring.* Neither did anyone use *dull, unsatisfying, ordinary, indifferent, impassive, apathetic,* or *routine.* Humdrum situations aren't associated with award-winning performances. Starting a new organization, turning around a losing operation, installing a new system, greatly improving the social condition, enhancing the quality of people's lives—these are all uplifting human endeavors. They're also endeavors that demand much of leaders as agents of change.

BEING AGENTS OF CHANGE

In reviewing the literature for this book, we discovered a very useful reference in *The Change Masters,* by Rosabeth Moss Kanter, a Harvard Business School professor. In her classic research, Kanter investigated the human resource practices and organizational designs of innovation-producing organizations. She wanted to know what fostered and what hindered innovation in the U.S. corporation.

Our study and Kanter's were done quite independently of each other, at different periods in time, and with different purposes. We were studying leadership; Kanter was studying innovation. Yet when we compared Kanter's cases with ours, we were struck by their similarity. In some instances, Kanter's innovators and our leaders talked about nearly identical projects, yet they were in completely separate organizations in vastly different regions of the country. We and Kanter arrived at a similar conclusion in analyzing our respective cases: leadership is inextricably connected with the process of innovation, of bringing new ideas, methods, or solutions into use. To Kanter, innovation means change, and "change requires leadership . . . a 'prime mover' to push for implementation of strategic decisions."[25] Like hers, our cases are evidence of that.

Similarly, James MacGregor Burns, professor emeritus of government at Williams College and author of *Leadership,* concludes his probing analysis of the subject by saying, "The ultimate test of practical leadership is the realization of intended, real change that meets people's enduring needs."[26] We agree.

Consider the case of Marion Krause, who made some lasting changes at The Tom Peters Group (TPG). A devoted environmentalist, Krause believes strongly in recycling and other citizen actions that make the world a cleaner, more beautiful place for her son, Benjamin, and for the rest of us. When she arrived at TPG, she noticed that the office didn't recycle paper, bottles, cans, or plastic products. Had there been a poll, people would have agreed that they *should* recycle; the trouble was, no one had taken the initiative to do anything about it. Krause did. She gathered all the necessary bins and boxes, demonstrated what and how to recycle, and persisted in carrying the banner for this change until it became a daily habit. Krause has since moved on, but her legacy remains. To this day, people at TPG recycle, saving money and the environment.

The real result of Krause's work (or Carrigan's work, or the work of any of the other leaders with whom we talked) was that the organization was substantively improved. There was a real difference that could be seen, felt, and measured. It wasn't just that a new system was installed but that the new system was in use and making things better for everyone. It wasn't just that there was a reorganization but that the new structure made a difference. It wasn't just the formulation of a creative solution for the organization's problems but the implementation of that solution.

LEADING THROUGH ASSIGNED WORK

Leaders must be change agents and innovators. But they need not be entrepreneurs, if by that term we mean those who actually initiate and assume the risk for a new enterprise. Neither must they be "intrapreneurs"— entrepreneurs within a corporation. In fact, we maintain that the majority of leadership in this world is neither entrepreneurial nor intrapreneurial.

In our research, we asked people to tell us who initiated the projects that they selected as their personal bests. We assumed, when we formulated our question, that the majority of people would name themselves. Instead, we found that more than half the cases were initiated by someone other than the leader—usually the leader's immediate manager.

Some see this finding as discouraging news, demonstration of a lack of initiative on the part of managers and nonmanagers alike. We see it otherwise. Much of what people do is assigned; few of us get to start everything from scratch. As organizational members, we seldom get to choose all our colleagues or decide on many (if any) of the organization's products and services. That's just a fact of organizational life.

We were actually encouraged to find a substantial number of examples of exceptional leadership in situations that weren't self-initiated. Were that not the case, there would be cause for terrible pessimism. Consider this: if the only times people reported doing their best were when they got to be the founder, CEO, county supervisor, police chief, agency director, or "head honcho," the majority of leadership opportunities would evaporate. Carrigan, for example, didn't found General Motors or start the plant; she was selected to be plant manager. But when she arrived at Lakewood, she took it upon herself to excel. She challenged the process in order to achieve what had never before been done in the automotive industry. Marion Krause wasn't a founder, officer, or manager of TPG, yet her effect is still felt there.

In considering people's personal-best leadership experiences and their roles in them as agents of change (whether or not they initiated the project discussed), we see three important lessons:

1. People who become leaders don't always seek the challenges they face. Challenges also seek leaders.

2. Opportunities to challenge the status quo and introduce change open the door to doing one's best. Challenge is the motivating environment for excellence.

3. Challenging opportunities often bring forth skills and abilities that people don't know they have. Given opportunity and support, ordinary men and women can get extraordinary things done in organizations.

Whether one is an entrepreneur, an intrapreneur, a manager, a community activist, a volunteer, or an individual contributor, the leadership attitude is what makes the difference. That attitude is characterized by a posture of challenging the process—of wanting to change the business-as-usual environment. A sense of adventure, whether in overcoming adversity or creating something unique and new, contributes to our doing our best as leaders. Enterprising situations contribute to a sense of personal achievement and self-worth. They promote leadership and high performance.

Committing to the Challenge: Moving Toward Opportunities

Let's pause and review our leadership journey so far. In this chapter, we've observed how closely associated leadership is with change and innovation. When people talk about their personal-best leadership experiences, they talk about the challenge of change. When we look at the research on innovation, we see the presence of leaders. When we review the events involving people we consider to be leaders, we see that they're associated with transformations, whether small or large. Leaders don't have to change history, but they do have to make a change in "business as usual."

The quest for change is an adventure. It tests our skills and abilities. It brings forth talents that have been dormant. It's the training ground for leadership. And while the challenge of change is tough, it's also stimulating and enjoyable. For leaders to get the best from themselves and others, they must find their task intrinsically motivating.

Leaders always seem to be present when there's a search for opportunities to introduce the new and untried. Studies of product and process innovations teach us that most ideas for improvement come from people other than leaders. So leaders use their outsight—their ability to perceive external realities—to discover these useful ideas for themselves. These findings bring us to our first commitment and to the action-steps that leaders can take to move themselves and others along the path to getting extraordinary things done.

Commitment Number 1

Search Out Challenging Opportunities to Change, Grow, Innovate, and Improve

➤ Treat every job as an adventure.

Even if you've been in your job for years, treat today as if it were your first day. Ask yourself, "If I were just starting this job, what would I do?" Chances are you would do some things differently. Begin doing those things now.

Think of your leadership assignment as an exciting adventure through unexplored wilderness. Think of your constituents and colleagues as pioneers. Set your sights on discovering new territory together. Identify those projects that you've always wanted to undertake but never have. Ask your team members to do the same. Pick one major project per quarter. Implement one smaller improvement every three weeks. Figure out how to do all of this within the budget you now have (or using the money you'll save or earn when your project succeeds). If you still need more money, go out and raise it from your supporters, as other adventurers do.

Your new projects don't have to change the world. Perhaps they'll simply get your organization moving on the road to ever greater heights. Early in her tenure as plant manager of Apple Computer's Macintosh factory, Debi Coleman had the floors cleaned, the walls painted, and the employee washrooms fixed up—mundane stuff, but it hadn't been done before, and the employees responded to this beginning effort.

➤ Treat every new assignment as a start-over, even if it isn't.

Stay alert to ways to constantly improve the organization. There's no magic to making a previously poor-performing unit a high-performing one. The talent and resources for excellence are there, dormant in your organization; all you have to do is unlock them. Often the critical difference is a leader who sees within the existing group untapped energy and skill and who assumes that excellence can be achieved. It's that old pioneering spirit reawakened.

Ask for a tough assignment. Volunteer to take on that losing operation. Challenge calls forth leadership. There's no better way for you to test your limits than to voluntarily place yourself in difficult jobs. Researchers have found a "strong and statistically highly significant relationship between ratings of job challenge and advancement."[27]

➤ Question the status quo.

Make a list of all the practices in your organization that fit this description: "That's the way we've always done it around here." For each one, ask yourself, "How useful is this in helping us become the best we can be? How useful is this for stimulating creativity and innovation?" If your answer is "absolutely essential," then keep it. If not, find a way to change it. Review all the policies and procedures. For each one, ask yourself the same question and take the same action. Vow to eliminate every stupid rule and every needless routine within the next month. At Wal-Mart they call this ETDT: "Eliminate the Dumb Things."

Clearly, some standard practices and policies are critical to productivity and quality assurance. On the other hand, many are simply matters of tradition. Take corporate dress, for instance. Are those suits and ties, dresses and high heels, really adding to innovation, creativity, and productivity?

Hold a meeting with employees and ask them what really bugs them about the organization. Ask them what gets in the way of doing the best job possible. Promise to look into everything they bring up and get back to them with answers in ten days. Commit yourself to removing three frequently mentioned organizational roadblocks that stand in the way of getting extraordinary things done.

➤ Send people shopping for ideas.

Since external and internal communication are keys to innovation, one of your top priorities ought to be finding more ways to gather suggestions and innovations from constituents, such as customers, employees, suppliers, and other key stakeholders.

As one example, at Chef Allen's, a $3 million restaurant in North Miami Beach, owner Allen Susser runs a "Chow Now" program. Susser gives servers and cooks $50 each to dine at any restaurant with cuisine similar to that of Chef Allen's. Employees return with short written and oral reports on what they learned. One cook, for example, reported at a staff meeting that he had sampled a competitor's fare and was dismayed to find elegant food being served on cold plates, ruining the meal. Nearly all thirty staffers have participated, at a rate of two or three each month. "They like to laugh at the little mistakes and believe they wouldn't make them," says Susser. And there's no doubt that they now pay more attention to warming plates up—and the hundreds of other details that make a restaurant truly elegant.[28]

Processes for collecting suggestions are abundant: focus groups, advisory boards, suggestion boxes, breakfast meetings, brainstorming sessions, customer evaluation forms, mystery shoppers, mystery guests, visits to competitors, and scores more. Each is a way to open people's eyes and ears to the world outside the boundaries of the organization. They're ways that allow you to become a net importer of new ideas. Be creative about these processes, and make them fun for employees and customers.

➤ Put idea gathering on your own agenda.

Whatever method you use, you must make gathering new ideas a personal priority. If you're serious about promoting innovation and getting others to listen to people outside the unit, make sure that you devote at least 25 percent of every weekly staff meeting to listening to ideas for improving process technologies and developing new products or services. Don't let weekly staff meetings be simply status reports on the present. Invite people from other departments to offer their suggestions on how your unit can improve.

Make idea gathering a part of your daily, weekly, and monthly schedule. Call three customers or clients who haven't used your services in a while and ask them why. Call three customers or clients who have made recent purchases and ask them why. Ride a route with one of your salespeople or delivery people. Work the counter and ask people what they like and don't like about your organization. Shop at a competitor's store. Better yet, anonymously shop for your own product and see what the salespeople in the store say about it. Call your organization and see how the phones are answered and how questions are handled. Mary Ann Corley, branch chief with Maryland's Department of Education, asked both internal and external constituents to complete the TEAM-Leadership Practices Inventory as one mechanism for gaining ideas about how other departments and their clients viewed the leadership being provided by her organization.

If you want to receive weak as well as strong signals from the line or the marketplace, always keep your antenna up. You can never tell where or when you might find new ideas. When he was general manager of the professional photography division of Eastman Kodak Company, Raymond H. DeMoulin got an idea in a Tokyo fish market. He noticed that a photographer who could use only one hand was having trouble getting the lid off a film container and finally had to use his teeth. DeMoulin made a mental note of the incident and had a more flexible lid developed.[29]

➤ Go out and find something that needs fixing.

Nothing can stifle innovation more than the attitude that says, "If it ain't broke, don't fix it." Something always needs fixing in every organization. Go find what needs fixing in yours.

Wander around the plant, the store, the branch, the halls, or the office. Look for things that don't seem right. Ask questions. Probe. When Phil Turner moved from facilities manager to plant manager of the Wire and Cable Division of Raychem Corporation, he spent a lot of time getting accustomed to the sounds and smells of the place. At first he couldn't tell one sound from another; it all seemed like indistinguishable noise. But soon he was able to hear the special music of each machine, much as a conductor gets to know the instruments in an orchestra. Turner discovered that the machines used to spool the wire weren't running at full speed. When he asked why, he was told that people didn't know how to fix them and were afraid that if the machines were run at capacity, they would wear down. Turner went quickly into action and began an employee training program that got the machines up and enabled the operators to fix them whenever they broke.

A new assignment is a perfect opportunity to use your naive understanding of the operation to your advantage. Everyone tolerates your dumb questions. By constantly asking people, "Why do we do this, and why do we do that?" you'll uncover some needed improvements in the organization.

➤ **Assign people to the opportunities.**

Typically, organizations assign their best-performing people to deal with problems—to the main product line that's performing below expectations, to the old technology that's being hammered by some new whizbang innovation, or to the philanthropic foundation that's shifting its funding priorities—and no one is assigned to the "opportunities." Longtime management sage Peter Drucker calls this a "deadly business sin." He says that opportunities produce growth, whereas problem solving is more like damage containment.[30] Draw up a list of the opportunities facing your organization. Make sure that you've assigned yourself, as well as others, to work on these challenges with the same vigor and resources that have been allocated to problems.

For example, Hewlett-Packard challenged the high-tech industry notion that you have to manufacture overseas to be competitive by looking for opportunities in every aspect of operations in their Roseville (California) plant. Nothing was considered sacred; no possibility was left unexplored. The organization worked out one arrangement whereby a supplier shipped parts to Hewlett-Packard in a container that could be reused for shipping the finished product, saving thousands of dollars and avoiding considerable cardboard and plastic waste disposal. By starting fresh and looking for opportunities, people at H-P revamped the way they built everything, from plant to product; they reduced paperwork by 90 percent and labor time needed to build the terminals by 75 percent. Further, thanks to improved product reliability, a mere 4 percent of the workforce now repairs defective parts (versus the 20 percent formerly required). As a result of these changes, H-P's newest terminals cost from 5 to 45 percent less than competitors' products, many of which are made in foreign plants.[31]

➤ **Renew your teams.**

Teams seem to go through life cycles, just as products do. Even the best teams get stale and need to be refreshed.[32] Never let teams get disconnected from outside information. Make sure members attend professional conferences, participate in training programs, and visit colleagues in other parts of the organization. It's tempting to slash the meeting, training, and travel budgets when times get tough, but beware: you could pay the price of falling further behind the competition. Staying ahead of the competition means staying ahead in your knowledge of the technology and the market.

Add a new member or two to the group every couple of years. Rotate some people out and rotate others in. New people—especially those who haven't been socialized into your way of doing things—can help you get a new perspective on the situation. If you can't move people in or out and you have a long-tenured group to lead, be very directive in your insistence that they go out and locate a measurable number of process or product enhancements. Force them to interact with others, and send them as much information as you can about new developments in the field. Put everybody through a creativity course. Give people the knowledge, skills, and tools they need to contribute to the generation of new ideas. Put everyone through a listening course as well. No great idea ever entered the mind through an open mouth.

➤ Add adventure and fun to everyone's work.

Leaders aren't the only ones who do their best when challenged. All of us do. For people to excel, they must find what they do intrinsically motivating—rewarding in and of itself. Look for ways to add challenge to people's work.

You can do this by asking people to join you in solving problems or starting a new service or process, by asking them for creative ideas, or by delegating more than just routine jobs (such as filling out forms). The magic in the total quality management (TQM) arena is challenge. In TQM organizations, people who have never been asked for the time of day are given problem-solving tools and opportunities to contribute.

First, however, be sure to find out what motivates each of your team members. This means that you'll have to spend some time with each person, because different people find different things challenging. Get to know their skill levels. What might be a stretch for one person is too easy for another.

Make the adventure fun. If you—and others—aren't having fun doing what you're doing, chances are people aren't doing the best they can do. We aren't talking about a laugh-a-minute party: every moment can't be fun, but the overall experience should be enjoyable. Humor and laughter shouldn't be confused with frivolity, however. Researchers have found that "appropriate" humor can lead to cohesion and bonding among coworkers.[33]

That work should be fun is one of the key values at the nation's most profitable airline. In fact, having a sense of humor is an explicit hiring criterion at Southwest Airlines. Consider the open house for Southwest's new corporate headquarters building at Love Field in Dallas. The dispatchers, who were the only ones who hadn't moved into the new facility, got there early and screened off part of the parking lot. They then provided their own valet parking—for dispatchers only! Everyone in the headquarters building then got together and retaliated by decorating the dispatchers' offices with wilted flowers, like a funeral parlor. On another occasion, CEO Herb Kelleher gathered 500 employees to cheer him on while he arm-wrestled another CEO for the rights to a marketing slogan (as opposed to settling the matter in a courtroom battle).[34]

Just for the fun of it, make a list of all the activities that are fun for you. Ask your colleagues at work to do the same. Then pick one and figure out a way to integrate it into the work of your organization.

➤ Take a class; learn a new skill.

Enroll in a class, course, workshop, or seminar dealing with a subject you don't know anything about (or know about only vaguely). As you learn some new content, substance, or skill, pay attention to the experience of being a learner. How does it feel to be incompetent (having spent all your life pursuing mastery)? Where does the confidence come from that allows you to acknowledge your inability? How do you deal with these feelings, and how can you help others to learn? After all, education is a leadership concept: the word *education* literally means "to lead from ignorance."[35] You have to keep adding to your own knowledge and skill base. Like capital equipment, these personal resources—if not updated, replaced, or revised—depreciate steadily over time.

The techniques leaders can use in searching for opportunities and confronting the status quo are limitless; we've described only some of them. But because projects that are fun, exciting, and challenging are often risky, finding and grasping opportunities requires that leaders balance innumerable benefits and risks. In the next chapter, we'll examine how leaders appreciate the risks involved in their experiments and innovations.

Commitment Number 1

Search Out Challenging Opportunities to Change, Grow, Innovate, and Improve

➤ Treat every job as an adventure.

➤ Treat every new assignment as a start-over, even if it isn't.

➤ Question the status quo.

➤ Send people shopping for ideas.

➤ Put idea gathering on your own agenda.

➤ Go out and find something that needs fixing.

➤ Assign people to the opportunities.

➤ Renew your teams.

➤ Add adventure and fun to everyone's work.

➤ Take a class; learn a new skill.

Source: The Leadership Challenge by James M. Kouzes and Barry Z. Posner. Copyright © 1995.

4
Experiment and Take Risks
Learning from Mistakes and Successes

If you believe something should change, then you must try to change it, no matter if there are risks.
—JOSÉ LUIS GUERRERO
Local Leader
Unión Nacional Sinarquista, Mexico

The search for opportunities beyond tradition is an exploration of the new. It requires individual creativity and organizational innovation. Leaders are open to ideas and willing to listen; they try untested approaches and accept the risks that accompany all experiments. When people are at their personal best as leaders, their projects involve the type of creative, beyond-the-boundaries thinking that Brian Biro describes in his forthcoming book, *Beyond Success: The Fifteen Secrets of a Winning Life*. Here's an illustrative case that Biro presents (and that we've used in classes and workshops). Imagine that the following figure represents a cake:

Your task is to slice the cake into as many pieces as possible using only four straight cuts. How many pieces of cake can you come up with? Eight? Nine?

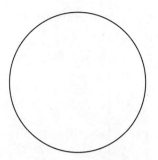

Ten? Eleven? Twelve? If you're a highly efficient one-dimensional thinker, you may have made eleven pieces of cake, as shown in the next figure:

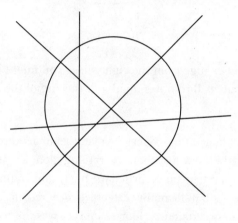

Does a reminder that cakes are three-dimensional alert you to a different approach? If your first three cuts are vertical, as shown, you'll have

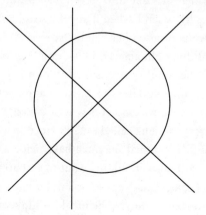

seven pieces. If you then think multidimensionally and make your fourth cut horizontal, you'll have fourteen pieces.

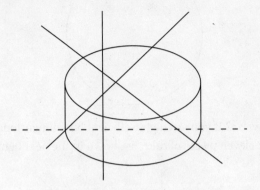

That's quite a change from the eight slices you might have served at the dinner table. But, as Biro notes, that's not the end of the exercise. Listen to what he says:

> I have conducted this exercise in many seminars through the years, and figured I knew just about everything there was to know about it. Recently, a participant surprised me by demonstrating once again how the master skill of flexibility can create new results.
>
> Absolutely certain that fourteen pieces was the "correct" answer, I asked if anyone had sliced the cake into ten pieces and most of the hands in the room went up. Then I asked for the hands of participants who had divided the cake into eleven pieces, and a few more hands went up. Finally, when I asked if anyone had found more than eleven, one young woman raised her hand. Occasionally a participant will come up with the right answer. I love to invite them up on the stage to demonstrate their multi-dimensional thinking. I was just about to congratulate the woman on her flexibility of approach in arriving at the correct answer of fourteen pieces when I asked, "How many slices did you come up with?" She called out, "Sixteen pieces!"
>
> Immediately I assumed she must have made a mistake. After all, I knew the correct answer. I didn't want to embarrass her in front of everyone so I said, "That's amazing, but I'll have to look at how you came up with sixteen during the break. I think you might have misun-

derstood my directions." I then proceeded to demonstrate how to "correctly" slice the cake into fourteen pieces. Once again I enjoyed the surprised reaction from the participants and we proceeded with the seminar.

At the break, the woman came up to talk about her sixteen-piece solution. I had almost forgotten about it by that time. I assumed she had used a curved cut, or inadvertently made five cuts instead of the required four. Very quickly, she proceeded to catch me in the act of inflexible thinking. Using four perfectly straight cuts, she sliced the cake into sixteen pieces, adding a new dimension in approach I had failed to see in the many times I had played the game before: stacking the pieces![1]

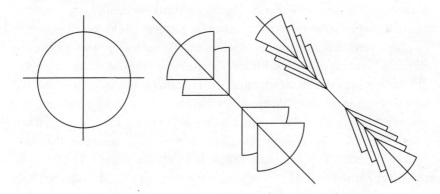

When attempting to solve a puzzle such as this, many people find themselves unwittingly bound by self-imposed constraints that make it impossible to solve the problem. Only when we remove these constraints can we hope to find new ways to slice the cake.

This problem is also a metaphor for the self-imposed constraints of rules, routines, and assumptions that we mentioned at the close of the previous chapter. Standard operating procedures are the "habits" of organizations. Even the loosest of organizations adopt practices that become second nature. These cultural norms operate in subtle but powerful ways to box us in and restrict our thinking. They're especially potent barriers in times when innovation is required.

Creative solutions to difficult problems require identifying and breaking free of self-imposed limitations. We need to look outside the existing way of doing things if we're to be innovative. Innovation requires risk taking, which is critical to an organization's health and development. Without constant innovation in products, services, and work processes, an organization will atrophy. '

The Importance of Taking Risks

Whenever leaders experiment with innovative ways of doing things, they put themselves and others at risk. Yet if we want to lead efforts to improve the way things are, we must be willing to take risks; we must, to paraphrase Eleanor Roosevelt, do the things we think we cannot.

Studies show that the work climate for success is characterized by an equitable reward system that recognizes excellence and by a willingness to take risks and experiment with innovative ideas.[2] One of the most glaring differences between the leader and the bureaucrat is the leader's inclination to encourage risk taking, to encourage others to step out into the unknown rather than play it safe. Leaders get to know the skills and motivating tasks of their constituents. They set goals that are higher than current levels, but not so high that people feel only frustration. Leaders raise the bar gradually and offer coaching and training to build skills that help people get over each new level.

Reno Taini and Randi DuBois know about risk. Their organization, Pro-Action, sponsors executive development programs involving, among other things, outdoor challenges. Through these programs, participants learn about trust, risk taking, group problem solving, and teamwork.

Taini began experimenting with outdoor adventures while educating high school students. As a field biologist who felt that classroom learning was insufficient to give kids a true sense of the wonders of nature, he began taking students on field trips to climb mountains, cross deserts, and raft white waters—a program he dubbed the Wilderness School. Taini also took his students into the urban wilderness—places in the inner city where students confronted the challenges of poverty and homelessness. They served holiday meals to seniors and gathered litter from public streets. In the process, the students did more than learn about nature, humanity, and survival; they also experienced themselves firsthand.

Taini then began working with DuBois, a recreation specialist, to take the Wilderness School into the larger community, first to many of the parents and friends of his students, who wanted to have similar adventures. Taini and DuBois created the Ropes Course on five acres in La Honda, California. It's a maze of ropes, cables, tires, logs, trees, platforms, ladders, and other gear collected from everything from ships to fire stations. Taini, DuBois, and their staff have served over 50,000 people. Executives from some of the country's largest corporations have learned about trust and risk taking through this unusually powerful form of education. Taini and DuBois have also worked with Vietnam veterans in wheelchairs, Amerasians from Vietnam immigrating to the United States, and abused women with emotional scars. Children as young as five and adults as old as seventy have experienced the thrill of shared adventure and the quest for self-discovery through this course.

Taini and DuBois encourage people who go through their program to do things most have never done before, to experiment with themselves, to stretch and break their self-imposed limitations. For example, they invite people to walk a cable stretched thirty-five feet above the ground between two trees or leap for a ring from a platform at thirty feet. Each event is rigged for maximum safety, and no one has ever been injured in any of these events. We use events like these in our leadership development programs as well, to provide leaders with the opportunity to personally experience what it feels like to try something new. It's the first time most participants have ever walked a tightrope or climbed a fifteen-foot-high wall. A lesson that emerges is that our fear and apprehension are greater barriers to success than the actual difficulty or danger of the experiment itself.

DuBois puts it this way:

> Consistently, we observe that the weakest muscle in the body is the one between the ears. Self-imposed limitations and beliefs hold most people back. When individuals feel the surge of adrenalin and the thump of their hearts growing louder, they frequently interpret that feeling as fear. We encourage them to explore and push on their perceived limits. By translating that feeling into excitement, they then discover the elation of victory over crippling doubts—and the tiebacks to their workplace are enormous.

The key to DuBois and Taini's success is in getting people to venture beyond the limitations that they normally place around themselves. They began by seeing the teaching of field biology as an outdoor adventure and recreation as an opportunity for personal growth; they now lead a creative enterprise that enables others to experience victory over doubt. In this enterprise, they demonstrate that all exemplary leaders:

- Learn from mistakes (and encourage others to do the same)
- Promote hardiness and foster risk taking
- Make something happen

Like all leaders, Taini and DuBois use these *essentials* to turn uncertainty into positive results.

Learning from Mistakes

The risks involved in the Ropes Course are like the risks leaders must take when involved in learning and in mastering change: making a mistake—or worse yet, failing. To be sure, failure can be costly. For the individual who leads a failed project, it can mean a stalled career or even a lost job. For an adventurous leader, it can mean the loss of personal assets. For mountain climbers and other physical adventurers, lives are at risk.

It is, however, absolutely essential to take risks. Over and over again, people in our study told us how important mistakes and failure had been to their success. Without those experiences, they would have been unable to achieve their aspirations. It may seem ironic, but many echoed the words of Mike Markkula, chairperson of the board of Apple Computer: "I believe the overall quality of work improves when you give people a chance to fail." Studies of the innovation process make this same point even more strongly: "Success does not breed success. It breeds failure. It is failure which breeds success."[3] If that advice seems patently absurd, think about the careers of many famous winners (as shown in Table 4.1).

Failure plays an important role in success. Recall the times when you tried to learn a new game or a new sport. It might have been skiing, tennis, bridge, hockey, roller blading, or any of a dozen other enjoyable activities. Did you get it perfect the very first day? Not likely. We understand

Table 4.1. Failure as a Precursor of Success.

- Babe Ruth struck out 1,330 times. In between his strikeouts, he hit 714 home runs.
- Martina Navratilova lost twenty-one of her first twenty-four matches against arch-rival Chris Evert. She resolved to hit more freely on the big points and beat Evert thirty-nine out of their next fifty-seven matches. No woman tennis pro has ever won as many matches or as many tournaments, including a record nine Wimbledon singles titles, as Navratilova.
- R. H. Macy failed in retailing seven times before his store in New York became a success.
- Abraham Lincoln failed twice as a businessperson and was defeated in six state and national elections before being elected president of the United States.
- Louisa May Alcott's family encouraged her to find work as a servant or seamstress rather than write. She wrote—and *Little Women* is still popular more than 125 years later.
- Theodor S. (Dr. Seuss) Geisel's first children's book was rejected by twenty-three publishers. The twenty-fourth publisher sold six million copies.

from our own life experiences that nothing is ever done perfectly the first time we try it—not in sports, not in games, not in school, and most certainly not in organizations.

Actually, Urban E. Hilger, Jr., who was then president of the Dalmo-Victor division of the Singer Company, reported to us that he did get one sport right the first time he tried it. Naturally, we asked Hilger to tell us about that experience, and this is what he said:

> It was the first day of skiing classes. I skied all day long, and I didn't fall down once. I was so elated; I felt so good. So I skied up to the ski instructor, and I told him of my great day. You know what the ski instructor said? He told me, "Personally, Urban, I think you had a lousy day." I was stunned. "What do you mean, lousy day? I thought the objective was to stand up on these boards, not fall down." The ski instructor looked me straight in the eye and replied, "Urban, if you're not falling, you're not learning."

Hilger's ski instructor understood that if you can stand up on your skis all day long the first time out, you're doing only what you already know how to do, not pushing yourself to try anything new or difficult. If your objective is to stay upright, you aren't going to improve yourself, because when you try to do something you don't know how to do, you'll fall down. That's guaranteed, as anyone who has ever learned to ski knows very well.

Our point isn't to promote failure for failure's sake, of course. We don't advocate for a moment that failure ought to be the *objective* of any endeavor. Instead, we advocate learning. Leaders don't look for someone to blame when mistakes are made in the name of innovation. Instead, they ask, "What can be learned from the experience?" Indeed, consider the very shape of most learning curves. Whether tracking our own performance or some new product, process, or service, these curves invariably show performance going down before it goes up. Learning doesn't take place in the absence of mistakes.

There's no simple test for determining the appropriate level of risk in a venture. We must weigh costs and benefits, potential losses versus gains. Knowing that one person's risk is another's routine activity, we must factor in the present skills of the team members and the demands of the task. But even if we could compute risk to the fifth decimal place, every innovation would still expose us to some peril. Perhaps the healthiest thing we can do is determine whether what we can learn is worth the cost. And as we shall see, our ability to grow and learn under stressful, risk-abundant situations is highly dependent on how we view change.

Promoting Psychological Hardiness and Fostering Risk Taking

We recognize that uncertainty, risk, and mistakes are part of the price we pay for innovation, change, and learning. But how do we learn to accept the inevitable failures and accompanying stress of innovation, and how do we help others to handle the stress of change?

Many of us associate stress with illness. We've been led to believe that if we experience serious stressful events, we'll become ill. If we adopt this point of view, we might as well sit back in our overstuffed easy chairs, surf through the television channels, and never venture into the world. Fortunately, the reports of illness resulting from stress are seriously misleading. Stress—not even the most strenuous of it—doesn't necessarily contribute to severe illness. After all, many people have experienced life-threatening, even tortuous, circumstances and remained healthy. Indeed, some stress even energizes us. The personal bests shared with us by the leaders in our study are clear examples of difficult, stressful projects that generated enthusiasm and enjoyment. It isn't stress that makes us ill but how we respond to stressful events.

APPROACHING STRESS POSITIVELY

Psychologists Suzanne C. Kobasa and Salvatore R. Maddi have taken a different approach to the study of stress.[4] Intrigued by people who'd experienced a high degree of stress yet had a relatively low degree of illness, they and their colleagues hypothesized that such individuals must have a distinctive attitude toward stress. Kobasa and Maddi originally studied groups of executives at Illinois Bell, who—like employees at all the regional Bell operating companies—were going through the enormous upheaval brought on by the prospect of deregulation. Theoretically, these executives were candidates for stress-related illnesses.

Data were collected on illnesses among these executives over a ten-year period. Although some executives had high stress scores along with high rates of illness, another group of executives with equally high stress scores were below average on incidence of illness. As the researchers had predicted, there was a clear attitudinal difference between the high-stress/low-illness group and the high-stress/high-illness group—a difference that they called *psychological hardiness*. High-stress/low-illness executives had these traits in common:

- They were *committed* to the various parts of their lives.
- They felt a sense of *control* over the things that happened in their lives.
- They experienced change as a positive *challenge*.

The high-stress/high-illness executives, on the other hand, felt alienated and powerless, and they saw change as more of a threat than a challenge.

Recent studies involving such diverse groups as police officers, basketball players, working women, officer candidates in the Israeli military, and city bus drivers report consistent differences between psychologically hardy and nonhardy individuals as well.[5] Furthermore, researchers have continued to find that psychological hardiness is a more important source of resistance to stress than are personal constitution, health practices, or social support.

Maddi and Kobasa describe how this coping process works:

> People strong in *commitment* find it easy to be interested in whatever they are doing and can involve themselves in it wholeheartedly. They are rarely at a loss for things to do. They always seem to make maximum effort cheerfully and zestfully. In contrast, alienated people find things boring or meaningless and hang back from involvement in the tasks they have to do. They are often at a loss for leisure activities. Although they are seldom strongly involved, they often appear taxed.
>
> People strong in *control* believe and act as if they can influence the events taking place around them. They always reflect on how to turn situations to advantage and never take things at face value. In contrast, people who feel powerless believe and act as if they are passive victims of forces beyond their control. They have little sense of resourcefulness or initiative and prepare themselves for the worst.
>
> People strong in a sense of *challenge* consider it natural for things to change and anticipate the changes as a useful stimulus to development. They see life as strenuous but exciting. In contrast, people who feel threatened think it is natural for things to remain stable, and they fear the possibility of change because it seems to disrupt comfort and security.[6]

People with a hardy attitude, then, take the stress of life in stride. When they encounter a stressful event—whether positive or negative—they react predictably:

- They consider the event interesting.
- They feel that they can influence the outcome.
- They see it as an opportunity for development.

Such optimistic appraisals of events reflect what University of Virginia professor Lynn Isabella and colleague Ted Forbes call "learning and challenge mindsets"—ways of framing events that are crucial to executive success. Isabella and Forbes found that managers with a learning mindset "characterized by a continuous sense of ongoing learning and transformation" received the highest job performance ratings of all those they studied. The next-highest performers were those with a challenge mindset "characterized by an overwhelming sense of challenge and adventure."[7]

Isabella and her team observed that the managers they studied who had a learning mindset "were natural questioners. They reported learning early on or learning over time that it is often more important to ask questions than to seek answers. They tended to see their job as a process, not just a series of activities and tasks. . . . They used information from a variety of sources."[8] Executives with this attitude also reported more transformational events—events that altered the very fabric of their lives. These events became catalysts for change, opening up new possibilities for learning and advancement.

Apparently, it isn't just innovation and challenge that play important roles in our personal progress; it's also the way we view the challenges that come our way. If we see them as learning opportunities, we're much more likely to succeed than if we see them simply as checkmarks on a report card. Thus our view of events contributes to our ability to cope with stress: with a positive view, we can transform stressful events into manageable or desirable situations rather than regress or avoid the issue.

FOSTERING HARDINESS

How do we develop the hardy personality? Is it wired in our genes? Do we get it from our parents? Do we learn it in school? In the neighborhood? Just how do people come to have the attitudes of commitment, control, and challenge?

According to researchers, the family atmosphere is the most important breeding ground for a hardy attitude. When there's a varied environment, many tasks involving moderate difficulty, and family support, then hardiness flourishes, regardless of our socioeconomic background. But we shouldn't resign ourselves to a life of illness or unresolved stress if we didn't grow up in the right environment. Maddi and Kobasa point out that "hardiness can be learned at any time in life and, therefore, . . . people are not damned by an unfortunate childhood."[9] Although it's often difficult to overcome a habitual pattern of avoidance, it's possible to learn to cope assertively with stressful events through counseling. Organizations can also help their members cope more effectively; they can do three things to create a climate that develops hardiness:

- Build commitment by offering more rewards than punishments.
- Build a sense of control by choosing tasks that are challenging but within the person's skill level.
- Build an attitude of challenge by encouraging people to see change as full of possibilities.

There are two important implications for leaders from this work on hardiness. First, people can't lead if they aren't psychologically hardy. No one will follow someone who avoids stressful events and won't take decisive action. Second, even if leaders are personally very hardy, they can't enlist and retain others if they don't create an atmosphere that promotes psychological hardiness. People won't remain long with a cause that distresses them. They need to share their leader's sense of commitment, control, and challenge. In short, they need to believe that they can overcome adversity if they're to accept the challenge of change. Leaders must create the conditions that make all of that possible.

The personal-best examples we collected in our research involved stressful events in the lives of leaders; they involved significant personal and organizational change. Yet fully 95 percent of these cases were described in terms consistent with the conditions for psychological hardiness. Participants in these personal-best cases indicated commitment rather than alienation, control rather than powerlessness, and challenge rather than threat.

While our cases are a highly biased sample of only the best of times, it's instructive to know that people associate doing their best with feelings of meaningfulness, mastery, and stimulation, that people are biased in the direction of hardiness when thinking about their best. It's equally helpful to know that people don't produce excellence when feeling uninvolved, insignificant, and threatened. Furthermore, feelings of commitment, control, and challenge provide internal cues for recognizing when we're excelling and when we're only getting through the day. They tell leaders what signs to look for when assessing the capacity of their constituents to get extraordinary things done and give them guidelines to use when creating an environment for success. The relationship of risk and uncertainty to psychological hardiness is illustrated graphically in Figure 4.1; when these two forces are balanced, people feel in charge of change.

Our personal-best cases signify that the vast majority of us can feel in charge of change at least some of the time. They tell us that we have an intuitive sense of what makes us strong and what makes us weak. The challenge is to apply these lessons more rigorously to our daily lives at work. Leaders have a responsibility to create an environment that breeds hardiness on a regular, not an occasional, basis.

Making Something Happen

When times are stable and secure, we're not severely tested. We may perform well; we may get promoted; we may even achieve fame and fortune. But certainty and routine breed complacency. In times of calm, we don't take the opportunity to burrow inside and discover the true gifts buried down deep.

Figure 4.1. Balancing Forces in Change.

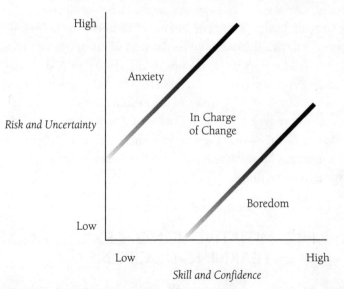

Source: Based on the work of M. Csikszentmihalyi and I. S. Csikszentmihalyi, *Optimal Experience: Psychological Studies of Flow in Consciousness* (Cambridge: Cambridge University Press, 1988), p. 74; and S. R. Maddi and S. C. Kobasa, *The Hardy Executive: Health Under Stress* (Chicago: Dorsey Professional Books/Dow Jones–Irwin, 1984).

In contrast, personal and business hardships have a way of making us come face to face with who we really are and what we're capable of becoming.

Name any great leader, performer, scientist, athlete, activist, citizen. Chances are that the crucible of that person's crowning achievement was some distressing crisis, wrenching change, tragic misfortune, or risky venture. Only challenge produces the opportunity for greatness. And given the daunting challenges we face today, the potential for greatness is monumental. As *Fortune* writer John Huey notes in discussing the crazy corporate maelstrom of the 1990s, "To the survivors, the revolution feels something like this: scary, guilty, painful, liberating, disorienting, exhilarating, empowering, frustrating, fulfilling, confusing, challenging. In other words, it feels very much like chaos."[10]

In the process of transformation, people and their organizations live with a high degree of ambiguity. Innovation upsets the stability we've worked hard to establish; it throws off our equilibrium. As Meg Wheatley points out in *Leadership and the New Science,* "The things we fear most in organizations—fluctuations, disturbances, imbalances"—are also the primary sources of creativity.[11] But how do we get from the scary, painful, and disorienting parts of this process to the liberating, exhilarating, and empowering parts? Fortunately, there are some useful guidelines for crossing the chasm of change.

As we've seen, leaders and constituents alike need psychological hardiness to cope well with the risks and the failures of innovation and the challenge of change. Leaders must also have the ability to make something happen under conditions of extreme uncertainty and urgency. In fact, leadership is needed more during times of uncertainty than in times of stability: when confusion over ends and means abounds, leadership is essential.[12] Leaders master change—and they master uncertainty, seizing the imperative to act. Leaders know that action and flexibility are required to bring people through these times.

TAKING INITIATIVE, BEING FLEXIBLE, AND LEARNING DISCIPLINE

People have a tendency to resort to self-pity when they're hurt by a corporate downsizing, a shift in national policy, or stormy winds of nature. But those who rise through adversity don't allow themselves to be resentful, bitter, or alienated. Instead, they become engaged, involved, and committed. Author and editor Michael Korda recently reported on the legendary Hollywood superagent Irving Lazar, quoting Lazar's reflection on his own success: "Sometimes I wake up in the morning and there's nothing doing, so I decide to *make something happen by lunch.*"[13] Lazar's philosophy is an elegantly simple and extraordinarily powerful view of life—one that enabled him to outfox the competition. Like Lazar, leaders make something happen by lunch; they don't wait for their organization to do something to turn itself around.

People are inspired by those who take initiative and who risk personal safety for the sake of a cause. Only those who act boldly in times of crisis and change are going to succeed. Without courage there can be no hope—and little chance of survival in today's highly volatile economic and social situations. No one can accurately predict what will happen next. Those who are the most agile and flexible—those supple enough to adapt to the shifting conditions—will succeed.

It's quite instructive to note that the newest paradigm in the world of production is called "agile manufacturing." This paradigm allows for more product customization, more rapid introduction of new products, faster response time to customer requests, an increase in upgradeable products, and other improvements. And agile manufacturing is intended not just for the shop floor but for the entire enterprise.

Yet flexibility can increase stress on the system and must be balanced with extreme discipline. Both are essential if we want to experiment and take risks. Imagine calling 911 and hearing, "Thank you for calling. We'll be there when we get our act together." Imagine the emergency crew arriving to reenact a scene from the Keystone Kops. Such behavior wouldn't instill a feeling of security.

When interviewed on public television, Peter Hall, former director of England's National Theatre, observed, "You have to have the discipline and then you'll be liberated by it." One of the paradoxes of urgent situations is that, as Jean Campbell demonstrated in pulling Synergistic Systems through the physical and emotional damage caused by an earthquake, they require relaxed group informality and tight personal discipline—simultaneously.

We'd better hope that our time of need brings out both professionals and professionalism as well. Everyone must have mastered his or her job and must have a total sense of personal responsibility. True freedom is the result of learning discipline first, and then acting with it. Not the other way around.

ACKNOWLEDGING THE FEARS

While leaders must act decisively under urgent and uncertain conditions, they must also acknowledge the fear and doubt that people feel as they face the unknown. Consider, for example, the intense anxiety evoked in many state agencies in the wake of recent successful initiatives to limit governmental authority to raise property taxes—and the concomitant need for positive leadership that was created. Since property taxes are generally the major source of local revenue, these tax limitations have severely restricted the capacity of county agencies to provide health, education, and welfare services, resulting in a good deal of uncertainty.

Along with our colleague Paul Mico, we have helped several agencies deal with the effects of these citizen initiatives. In one series of meetings, we asked county health department employees to divide into three groups: those who knew that they would still have a job if an initiative passed, those who knew that they would have to leave, and those who were uncertain about what would happen to them. Members of each group were asked to discuss how they felt about the situation and how they were personally and professionally coping with it.

The reactions, which were very revealing, demonstrate how people respond to uncertainty. Those who knew that they would have to leave had resigned themselves and were making other plans. Those who knew that they would stay felt a little guilty, but they were otherwise accepting. The people in the uncertain group—those who didn't know what would happen to them—exhibited stress and hostility. They felt stuck, unresolved about whether to stay or leave, and angry at being in the situation. For the uncertains, the old rules had been broken, and there were no new rules in place. They were unclear about their personal goals as well as the goals of the county. They had little or no experience in dealing with that sort of situation, so it was difficult to predict the effects of various alternatives. They were immobilized and unable to decide what to do. These were people who had lost their sense of identity.

Leaders have a responsibility when people feel stuck and stressed, angry and alienated. Those leaders who take the time to listen and offer support will find it easier to mobilize action in the face of such feelings. While change can be extraordinarily disruptive and can tear us from our moorings, it also offers us the chance to sail on to a new opportunity. As author and transitions consultant Bill Bridges says, "Change doesn't destroy opportunities; it relocates them."[14] Leaders enable their constituents to move through fear and risk and find the new opportunities that inevitably arise in times of tremendous change.

There's more to positive change than relocating opportunities, however. It's one thing for citizens to want a change—to foster innovation, if you will—but another to offer a positive new direction. When citizens and their tax-cutting champions tear something apart but offer nothing in its place, they solve one problem only to create another. As with many reengineering efforts, slashing services and cutting costs aren't acts that create the future; they simply deal with the status quo. Responsible leaders can't behave so capriciously. They know that simply challenging the process doesn't make one a leader. There are other essential practices that one must master to guide constituents on a journey to places they've never been.

Committing to the Challenge: Learning the Lessons of Experimentation

Leaders are experimenters: they experiment with new approaches to old problems. A major leadership task involves identifying and removing self-imposed constraints and organizational conventions that block innovation and creativity. Yet innovation is always risky. We may make a mistake when we try something new. Wise leaders recognize failure as a necessary fact of the innovative life. Instead of punishing it, they encourage it; instead of trying to fix blame for mistakes, they learn from them; instead of adding rules, they encourage flexibility.

With an attitude of psychological hardiness, leaders can turn the potential turmoil and stress of innovation and change into an adventure. In discussing our next commitment, we describe ways to establish a climate in which people can take charge of change and turn uncertainty into an opportunity to experiment, take risks, and learn from the accompanying mistakes. With these action-steps, leaders can help ensure that everyone derives the greatest benefit possible from change.

Commitment Number 2

Experiment, Take Risks, and Learn from the Resulting Mistakes

➤ Set up little experiments.

If you're uncertain about the effect of a new idea, experiment with it first. Consumer product companies try out a new product in select locations before launching it in all markets, for example. A word of caution, though: don't wait until you have a perfect product or process before trying it out. The window of opportunity can close very quickly. It's always better to run trials at the early stages of innovation than to wait until thousands, or even millions, of dollars have been spent and possibly wasted.

A rigorous evaluation of your process innovations can be very instructive as well. After alpha (or first) tests have been completed, select a few beta (or second) test sites. Establish ways of quantifying the outcomes, select comparison groups, conduct pretests with your experimental and control groups, run the experiment, and measure the results. While the costs of research evaluation are often as great as the costs of the intervention itself, the learnings are usually worth the expense.

➤ Make it safe for others to experiment.

How do Taini and DuBois get people to go beyond their physical comfort levels? They do it the same way that leaders make it easy for people to experiment: by taking whatever actions are required in order to make people feel safe and secure. Taini and DuBois go to great lengths to demonstrate how the safety systems work, the experience of the spotter, and the strength of the rope; this reassurance helps allay people's anxiety. As a leader, you must make your constituents feel equally safe if you expect them to venture out and take chances.

Gene Calvert, author of *Highwire Management,* offers a number of specific actions that leaders can take to make others feel safe.[15] For example, he suggests verifying whether people feel ready for the new or challenging assignment, asking them how best to support their management of the risks involved, and encouraging them to ask for help whenever they need it. Calvert also suggests holding informal, face-to-face update sessions and implores, "Resist the well-meaning tendency to snoop." Another valuable suggestion he offers is to provide others the flexibility to handle any risk in their own way—unless this sets them up to fail in ways you find unaffordable or that are detrimental to them. It's also important to keep your word about not punishing people when they've done their best under the circumstances, regardless of how the situation turns out.

In making it safe for people to experiment, you must also make sure it's safe for them to challenge authority. In airline safety, there's something called the Muser Principle, after Swissair's former chief of air safety, Hugo Muser. Said Muser, "Modern aircraft and operational techniques have become dangerously safe. Therefore safety needs a healthy dose of disagreement in the cockpit."[16]

Even the most sophisticated electronic equipment can't prevent pilot error, and one of the most dangerous errors is hubris. Our safety in the air depends a lot on whether those in the cockpit can talk back to the boss. One might say that the modern corporation and its operational techniques have also become dangerously safe. We've been lulled into a false sense of security. We've become highly vulnerable to corporate captains who interpret healthy disagreement as mutiny. So if you want people to act with a shared sense of urgency, be sure they feel safe in challenging authority. Everyone's ultimate survival may depend on it.

➤ Eliminate firehosing.

It's altogether too easy to put down new ideas: "It's not in the budget." "It'll never work." "We've never done that before." "How about quality assurances?" Too often, write Robert Kriegel and Louis Patler in *If It Ain't Broke . . . Break It!* people cling to the familiar and play it safe when confronted with change by responding like firefighters hosing down a fire—dousing ideas and extinguishing enthusiasm and spirit.[17] In order to move us out of our comfort zones, leaders should instead be on the lookout for ways to eliminate firehosing.

Maureen Fries, administrator of Los Olivos Women's Medical Group, knew that before she could motivate the staff to find and implement more cost-effective processes, she would have to break the atmosphere of negativism hanging over the department. Discussing how negativism was draining the department of the energy needed to actively meet new challenges, Fries introduced the staff to the idea of firehosing at a meeting. One staff member suggested that anyone heard firehosing should be required to contribute twenty-five cents to a fund. Everyone agreed, and the policy went into effect immediately.

As this meeting (and subsequent meetings) progressed, Fries listened with amazement as staff members began to think more carefully about what they were saying in order not to either be—or sound—negative. Team members policed each other on a daily basis. Comments such as, "You owe me a quarter!" could be overheard across the department; collection jars could be found everywhere. Morale improved noticeably, as did the number of innovative ideas. The jars were a physical reminder of the importance of eliminating firehosing and keeping a positive attitude about new possibilities.

Tackle firehosing at your next meeting and determine how best to eliminate it within your group.

➤ Work even with ideas that sound strange initially.

An addendum to eliminating firehosing is working with and being tolerant of ideas that sound strange or even stupid initially. Caleb Atwood, president of a Houston management consulting firm, reminded us during our research that ideas don't appear magically, fully created and ready to implement. They almost always require nurturing. If, as is usually the case, ideas that sound strange are rejected or ridiculed, two things generally happen:

- Potentially good ideas are lost.
- People stop offering ideas—no matter how often they're asked for them.

Instead of rejecting ideas that sound off-the-wall or bizarre, Atwood suggests saying, "Yes, if . . . " Here's his example of how this might work at a utility company:

Team Member: Let's train bears to climb utility poles in winter to shake off the ice that breaks transmission wires. [Guess how long a suggestion of this nature would survive in most companies?]

Leader: Yes, if you can explain how we could get bears to climb the poles.

Team Member: We could put pots of honey on top of them.

Leader: Yes, if you can come up with a way to get the honey up there.

Team Member: We could use helicopters.

Leader: Wouldn't the downdraft from the helicopters blow the pots off the poles?

Team Member: Yes. It would also blow the ice off. Forget the bears; let's use helicopters to clear the lines.

An added advantage of this approach is that you don't have to say no to ideas. If people have trouble handling the "if" questions, they arrive at the "no" by themselves. Of course, if they can respond effectively, you've arrived at the best of all possible situations: solutions suggested (owned) by your constituents are ones they can live with!

➤ Honor your risk takers.

Every organization should have an Innovators' Hall of Fame.[18] We have one in our business school at Santa Clara University. Students, parents, administrators, executives, guests, and faculty members all stop to read it. The contributors stop by too. It's a great boost to morale and a helpful reminder.

In developing your Hall of Fame, include every business function, from research and development to marketing, and make sure inventors of big and small innovations, as well as those whose role is simply to support innovation, are represented. Put a glass case in a prominent place in the hall for employees and visitors to see. Fill it with trophies, plaques, pictures, and the paraphernalia of innovation.

Make sure to reward good attempts, not just successes. Well-intentioned efforts that don't work out are just as important as those that do.

Many, if not most, innovations fail. If people are going to continue to contribute new ideas, they need to see that failure doesn't result in banishment to Siberia.

➤ Debrief every failure as well as every success.

We frequently suggest that participants in our training programs write a case on their personal-worst leadership experience, for many important lessons are learned from failure. Although it's tempting to let painful memories fade, the lessons are too precious to go unrecorded.

At the completion of a project, or at periodic intervals during it, take the team off-site on a review retreat. Build the agenda around four questions:

- What did we do well?
- What did we do poorly?
- What did we learn from this?
- How can we do better the next time?

Make sure that everyone contributes. Record all the ideas visibly on chart paper and then type up the notes and make them available to everyone. Take immediate action as needed when you return, and begin the next project with a review of any lessons learned.

That's exactly what Boeing did in response to scheduling difficulties with the 737 and 747 plane programs. To ensure that problems weren't repeated, senior managers commissioned a high-level employee group to compare the developmental processes for these planes with earlier, more profitable programs. Project Homework, as the group was called, developed a set of "lessons learned" that could be used for future projects. After working for three years, they produced hundreds of recommendations in an inch-thick booklet. Several members of the team were then transferred to the 757 and 767 start-ups; and, guided by experience, they helped produce the most successful, error-free launch in Boeing's history. British Petroleum has gone even further, establishing a postproject appraisal unit that reviews major investment projects, writes up case studies, and derives lessons that are then incorporated into updates of the company's planning guidelines.[19]

➤ Model risk taking.

Encourage others to take risks by doing so yourself. We've been part of several programs in which the leader was an active participant in challenging physical tasks, such as the Ropes Course. In these activities, the leader would often step aside and let an associate guide the group. Rather than sitting on the sidelines and watching, however, the leader became vulnerable by trying (and often failing) in front of all the others.

Whether you choose to participate in an organized expedition, make house calls, or make a sales call on a tough customer, showing others that you're willing to risk is essential to getting others to do the same.

➤ Encourage possibility thinking.

To build an attitude of challenge, encourage people to see change as full of possibilities. As we've discussed, this requires making people feel safe and reducing the costs of failure. But beyond this, people are unlikely to show much interest in making new solutions work if they don't fully understand the problem in the first place. Build time and dialogue into the change process so that everyone involved can develop a personal stake in the idea's success. Be willing to put yourself in the other person's shoes and speak to the question, "What's in it for me?" Make certain that people see the benefits.

If people are mired in the status quo, discourage "rearview mirror thinking." You can tackle this problem head on by reviewing some of your organization's earlier strategic plans. Chances are excellent that a critique of these documents will demonstrate that your organization is constantly in the midst of internal and external change. The ancient saying, "You can never step into the same river twice, because the water is always flowing," illustrates the constancy of change.

➤ Maximize opportunities for choice.

Innovation and change must be perceived as opportunities rather than threats if your constituents are to feel strong and efficacious. Employee suggestion programs and quality circles are formal ways to increase choice. On a one-on-one basis, or with small groups, always ask for a second alternative to the first suggestion made. People have a tendency to satisfice when it comes to making decisions, and with proper encouragement they can always come up with another alternative. More important, research indicates that in nearly two-thirds of the cases, the second alternative will be superior to the first one generated.[20]

When people feel they have choices, they're less likely to feel that they've been forced to take a particular action against their will. In addition, if the path taken is their choice, not management's, they're less likely to blame someone else in the organization for any negative outcomes of that decision. In a more positive vein, by giving people alternatives, you set in motion a self-fulfilling process of commitment: "This was my choice, and I'll make it work!"

➤ Make formal clothing and titles optional.

During the 1989 earthquake in the San Francisco Bay Area, ordinary citizens on their way home from work grabbed firehoses and scaled bridges to help. No one cared what your title was or what clothes you wore. Emergencies can't be handled according to the old formalities of business. The hierarchy is the *worst* possible organizational design in urgent times.

When the global marketplace quakes, creating turmoil inside an organization, reliance on the routine bureaucracy—with its scheduled meetings, reporting relationships, and other formalities—is a sure way to hasten the organization's demise.

Research validates what we've all learned from our personal experience with emergencies. When uncertainty increases, impersonal, bureaucratic forms of coordination quickly give way to more personal and group approaches. Rules, plans, and vertical channels of coordination all dramatically decline; unscheduled meetings and horizontal, peer-to-peer coordination go way up.[21]

There's a strong pull to create order during chaotic times; but if you want a strong sense of urgency to pervade your organization, the right order is informality. If you want to get things moving quickly and smartly, tear down the functional walls, break that chain of command, ditch those strangulating neckties and uncomfortable shoes, get out from behind the desk, and let people talk face to face.

As we've seen, leaders have a hardy attitude about change. They see change as an opportunity to innovate. They venture outside the constraints of normal routine and experiment with creative and risky solutions. Their first act during times of adversity is to create a climate in which organizational members can also accept the challenge of change.

To create purposeful movement out of uncertainty, leaders must also guide and channel the often frenetic human motion of change toward some end. When things seem to be falling apart, leaders must show us the exciting new world we can create from the pieces. Out of the uncertainty and chaos of change, leaders rise up and articulate a new image of the future that pulls the organization together. Through efforts such as the action-steps we've highlighted here, leaders show how accepting the present challenge will actually help shape a better tomorrow. This is critical to commitment levels, since we need to believe that we're dedicating ourselves to the creation of a noble and meaningful future. We must feel that what we've committed ourselves to is worthy of our best efforts.

In the next chapter, we discuss at length how leaders do this—how they *inspire a shared vision* of the future and enlist others in it. In subsequent chapters, we discuss how leaders mobilize others to make the new vision a reality.

Commitment Number 2

Experiment, Take Risks, and Learn from the Resulting Mistakes

➤ Set up little experiments.

➤ Make it safe for others to experiment.

➤ Eliminate firehosing.

➤ Work even with ideas that sound strange initially.

➤ Honor your risk takers.

➤ Debrief every failure as well as every success.

➤ Model risk taking.

➤ Encourage possibility thinking.

➤ Maximize opportunities for choice.

➤ Make formal clothing and titles optional.

Source: The Leadership Challenge by James M. Kouzes and Barry Z. Posner.
Copyright © 1995.

PART 3

Inspiring a Shared Vision

- ➤ Challenge the Process
- ➤ **Inspire a Shared Vision**
- ➤ Enable Others to Act
- ➤ Model the Way
- ➤ Encourage the Heart

5

Envision the Future

Imagining Ideal Scenarios

No dream is too old to redeem.
—Sharon Williams
Executive Director
Opportunities Industrialization Center West

At first glance, there seems to be little relationship between Arlene Blum's desire to have a team of women scale Annapurna and Phil Turner's desire to give the people of Raychem's facilities department a real purpose. What could possibly be less similar than climbing a mountain and fixing a toilet?

At 3:29 P.M. on October 15, 1978, a team of ten women accomplished something that no other group had ever done. The American Women's Himalayan Expedition was the first American climbing team to reach the summit of Annapurna I, the tenth-highest mountain in the world. Arlene Blum was the leader of the expedition. Her stirring account of that adventure, *Annapurna: A Woman's Place*, is a highly acclaimed adventure story.[1] But why should someone, whether man or woman, want to do something like that?

91

"For us, the answer was much more than 'because it is there,'" says Blum. "We all had experienced the exhilaration, the joy, and the warm camaraderie of the heights, and now we were on our way to an ultimate objective for a climber—the world's tenth-highest peak. But as women, we faced a challenge even greater than the mountain. We had to believe in ourselves enough to make the attempt in spite of social convention and two hundred years of climbing history in which women were usually relegated to the sidelines."[2] Blum talks about how women had been told for years that they weren't strong enough to carry heavy loads, that they didn't have the leadership experience and emotional stability necessary to climb the highest mountains. After a climb of Mount McKinley in 1970, her personal faith in the abilities of women climbers was confirmed.

No woman had ever attempted a climb of Annapurna, and this fact provided Blum with yet another opportunity for further confirmation. "Our expedition would give ten women the chance to attempt one of the world's highest and most challenging peaks, as well as the experience necessary to plan future Himalayan climbs. If we succeeded, we would be the first Americans to climb Annapurna and the first American women to reach eight thousand meters (26,200 feet)."[3]

When we interviewed Phil Turner, he was facilities manager of Raychem Corporation. He described for us the daily life of the people who work in facilities. A typical day might begin with a phone call like one of these: "Phil, the toilet is overflowing in the men's room. Would you send somebody over to fix it?" Or "Phil, the air conditioner is broken in our building. It feels like it's 100 degrees in this place. Can't you send someone over to fix it?" Or "Phil, when are the plans for the new plant going to be done? We're already six months behind schedule."

One could get the impression that the people who work for Raychem are ungrateful, that they don't appreciate the hard work of the men and women in facilities. "But," Turner said, "I don't think that's what they're trying to tell us at all. I think they're trying to tell us that they care about their space. I have a vision for this department. I got the insight from Bob Saldich [then senior vice president of Raychem]. The other day, Bob came by my office. The door was open and he walked in. He put his hand on my shoulder and said, 'Phil, I want to thank you for planting those flowers outside my office window. They make me feel good.' So I think our job is to make people feel good," declared Phil. "Our job is to lift people's spirits through beauty, cleanliness, and functionality, enthusiasm, good cheer, and excellence."

The Importance of Having a Vision

These two leaders, Blum and Turner, saw what others had not seen. They both imagined something for their groups that went far beyond the ordinary, far beyond what others thought possible. For Blum, it was proving that women are capable of doing things that others had thought impossible. For Turner, it was showing that there's a special purpose to work that others had thought ordinary. Blum and Turner, and hundreds of other leaders in our study, share the characteristic of "envisioning the future," of gazing across the horizon of time and imagining that greater things lie ahead. They saw something out there, vague as it might appear from a distance, that others did not. They imagined that extraordinary feats were possible or that the ordinary could be transformed into something noble.

The leaders we interviewed echoed the perspective that making life better in the long run is a key element in getting extraordinary things done. The overwhelming consensus was that, without vision, little could happen. All enterprises or projects, big or small, begin in the mind's eye; they begin with imagination and with the belief that what's merely an image can one day be made real.

Vision hasn't always been part of the management lexicon. In years past, we sometimes heard it uttered by human potential psychologists or bandied about by community activists, but it didn't often pass easily from the lips of businesspeople and management scholars. Even today some senior executives belittle the concept, referring to it as the "vision thing." But recently, in detailing what was described as the "biggest turnaround in American corporate history," *Fortune* magazine pointed out that General Motors's CEO Jack Smith hadn't been shy about using the V word. In fact, establishing a vision was at the top of his list of leadership tips.[4] Current scholarly work also documents the importance of leadership vision.[5] In looking into the lives of ninety leaders, for example, professors Warren Bennis and Burt Nanus found that "attention through vision" was one of their key strategies.[6]

It's not just academics who have brought leadership vision out of the dark shadows. A few years ago, the magazine *Esquire* devoted an entire issue to "50 Who Had Made the Difference." Lee Eisenberg, contributing editor, wrote the following in his introduction to the section on nine "visionaries": "While their contemporaries groped at the present to feel a pulse, or considered the past to discern the course that led to the moment, these nine squinted through the veil of the future. Not that they were mystics. They were much more worldly than that. For most of them, reality was pure and simple; what set them apart was the conviction that a greater reality lay a number of years down the pike."[7]

Not everyone we interviewed used the term *vision* in describing leadership practices. Some referred instead to *purpose, mission, legacy, dream, goal, calling,* or *personal agenda.* No matter what the term, though, the intent was the same: leaders want to do something significant, to accomplish something that no one else has yet achieved.[8]

Recall that the constituents in our studies expected leaders to be "forward-looking." In a 1994 *Industry Week* study, "management taking a long-term view" was rated as the most important of eight organizational issues.[9] And in another study, the personal behavior trait most frequently mentioned as desirable in a CEO by 1,500 senior leaders from twenty different countries (including Japan, the United States, Western Europe, and Latin America), both for the present and for the year 2000, was a "strong sense of vision of the future."[10] And in a recent study by Shareholders Surveys Inc., long-term vision was at the top of traits desired in companies in which they would invest.[11]

If leaders are going to take us to places we've never been before, constituents of all types demand that they have a sense of direction. Leaders develop this capacity to envision the future by mastering the *essentials* of

- Imagining the ideal
- Intuiting the future

It's their sense of vision and their ability to look ahead that distinguishes credible leaders.

Imagining the Ideal

In referring to the ability to imagine the ideal, we prefer to use the term *vision,* because it's the most descriptive term we've found for leaders' foresightedness. Consider the following:

- *Vision* derives from a word literally meaning "see."[12] What better word than *vision* to describe the capacity to be forward-*looking* and fore*sighted*?
- *Vision* suggests a *future* orientation.
- A vision is an *image*, a picture of what could be. Visual metaphors are very common when we're talking about the strategic intent of an organization.
- *Vision* connotes a standard of excellence, an *ideal*. It implies a choice of values.
- *Vision* also has the quality of *uniqueness*. It hints at what makes something special.

Therefore, we define a vision as *an ideal and unique image of the future*.

Think about it in another way. Suppose you feel a strong desire to go on a challenging expedition to a place you've never been. It's a desire that you can't shake, something that you think about day and night. You wake up thinking about it; you go to bed thinking about it. It becomes an obsession.

At first, your desire for challenge is quite vague; you don't have a specific destination in mind. But soon you feel a need to decide on the kind of challenging journey that you want for yourself. You look at some alternatives: trekking through the mountains, sailing an ocean, hiking across a desert, going on a safari. Whether through conscious thought or unfocused meditation, you discover what appeals to you the most: you decide, for example, that you've always wanted to take a trek through the Himalayas.

So what do you do now? More than likely, you consult a travel guide, study maps, look at photographs. You talk to people who have climbed the Himalayas, read adventure stories by those who have done it before. You begin to get a real sense of the place—the weather, the dress, the customs, the food, the travel conditions—all those impressions that clarify your understanding of your destination. Not wanting your trip to be just like others you've heard about, you decide that you'll make this something special. You decide that your expedition will be unique, one that no one else has ever undertaken—perhaps even one *National Geographic* would want to cover.

Then you set a date many months or even years in the future. (Your destination being the Himalayas, your trip requires considerably more preparation time and complex thinking than a day's drive to the nearest beach would.) You know such arduous journeys aren't done alone, so you determine who else might share your desire for challenge and how those people would benefit from the experience. You recruit some colleagues, selling them on the benefits of high adventure. Then the planning begins in earnest.

Discovering a vision for your organization is similar in many ways to these initial stages of preparing for an expedition. You feel a strong inner sense of dissatisfaction with the way things are in your community, congregation, or company and have an equally strong belief that things don't have to be this way. Envisioning the future begins with a vague desire to do something that would challenge yourself and others. As the desire grows in intensity, so does your determination. The strength of this internal energy forces you to clarify what it is that you really want to do. You begin to get a sense of what you want the organization to look like, feel like, and be like when you and others have completed the journey. You may even write down your image of the future or draw a model of it.

Because you want what you create to be unique, you differentiate your organization or cause from others that produce the same product, provide the same service, or make the same promise. Yours is a distinctive vision, you believe. And it's also ideal. After all, you want to set a new standard of perfection, beauty, or excellence. You want yours to be a model for others. Yours is an ideal and unique image of the future.

Visions for organizations or reformations or movements, as well as visions for journeys, are more complex than this, of course. And we don't necessarily follow such a sequential process for clarifying our visions—especially if we're attempting to achieve what no one has ever achieved before.

The pioneers in any endeavor have no maps to study, no guidebooks to read, no pictures to view. They can only imagine all the possibilities. As it was with the Vikings preparing for their first voyage, explorers can only dream. Without any previous experience for guidance, the first ones to explore may find that their dreams are fantasies or that their visions are much more difficult to attain than they had expected. On the plus side, however, the lack of previous experience means that pioneers can make up the kind of future that they wish to create or discover. Those in previous centuries who set out in search of new lands were often not very realistic:

their boats were small, provisions meager. But that lack of realism didn't deter them from making the journey; in fact, it helped. Their dreams of what was possible fueled their enthusiasm and better enabled them to persuade others that many interests would be served.

In early 1992, the Avionics and Surveillance Group at TRW systematically involved all of their 3,400 employees in "creating the future from the future," soliciting ideas about what and where their business would be in the future. The goal was to "create a new future for ourselves and then look back to the present to find our way." The results were presented in the form of an annual report for the year 2003. In his introduction to the annual report, Robert Kohler, executive vice president and general manager, pointed out, "Although we have definitely inserted a strong element of reality, this report is neither fact nor fiction: it is an invention. Our future cannot be predicted; it must first be imagined. Let's not be afraid to imagine what the future for us and those who follow us could look like. Will it look exactly this way? Certainly not. Could it look like this? Definitely yes. Join me in envisioning the future of our organizations in the year 2003, and let that be the foundation and inspiration for doing extraordinary work today."[13]

Let's take a closer look at the four attributes of vision as we've defined it: *an ideal and unique image of the future*. We'll discuss another attribute—the collective nature of visions—in the next chapter.

IDEALITY: THE PURSUIT OF EXCELLENCE

Visions are about possibilities, about desired futures. They're ideals, standards of excellence. As such, they're expressions of optimism and hope. A mode of thinking based on visions opens us up to considering possibilities, not simply probabilities. *Probabilities* must be based upon evidence strong enough to establish presumption. *Possibilities* need not be. All new ventures begin with possibility thinking, not probability thinking. After all, the probability is that most new businesses will fail and most social reforms will never get off the ground. If entrepreneurs accepted this view, however, they'd never start a new business. Instead, they operate from the assumption that anything is possible. Like entrepreneurs, leaders also assume that anything is possible. It's this belief that sustains them through the difficult times.

Indeed, this is exactly the belief that sustains Nolan Dishongh and helps him spark possibility thinking in students otherwise at risk. Many of the fourteen- to sixteen-year-olds in Dishongh's construction trades class at Alice Johnson Junior High, twenty-five miles east of Houston, have well-earned reputations as troublemakers, as students with short attention spans, low grades, and little interest in learning. Many are from broken or abusive homes; some are known gang members.

Dishongh sets the tone at the start of each school year by asking his students to lay their heads on their desks. Then, in his deep, soothing voice, he instructs them to think about their mother, to feel her loving them even before they were born—think about her holding them close as infants, feeding them and singing to them. He asks them to try to remember how that felt. He encourages them to think about how proud she was when they said their first word and took their first step. "See her smiling," he implores; "see her eyes shining as she claps her hands with joy and hugs you." Dishongh asks them to think about what they've done to repay their mother for all that she's done to raise them: cooking their food, washing their clothes. He says, "She *loves* you, no matter what, but what makes her happy is being proud of you." He tells the students to be very still and breathe deeply, saying, "Imagine now that you're dying, that the next four or five breaths will be your last. As you call out her name with your last breath, are you calling out to a mother you've made proud by the things you did in your life or to a mother who will always feel sorrow for the life you led? I believe each and every one of you *wants* your mother to be proud of you. I know I do. And that's what we're doing here. It's not about grades. It's about your mother being proud."

At this point, it's not unusual to see a boy or two wipe tears from his eyes. Dishongh promises to start them on a journey of self-discovery, to help them find a sense of their own self-worth and their ability to change—a journey that will permanently affect their lives, not just one year at school. The youths quickly realize that this isn't a "normal" classroom and Dishongh isn't a "normal" teacher. He cares. He believes his students can become people to be proud of—not at risk but full of possibilities.

It's instructive to recall that all the personal-best cases we collected, like Dishongh's, were about possibilities. They were about improving upon the existing situation or creating an entirely new state of existence. The leaders who shared their experiences were characterized by a dissatisfaction with the status quo and a belief that something better was attainable. In other words, those personal-best leadership experiences are examples of possibility thinking. They represent the choice of an ideal.

Ideals reveal our higher-order value preferences. They represent our ultimate economic, technological, political, social, and aesthetic priorities. The ideals of world peace, freedom, justice, a comfortable life, happiness, self-respect, and the like are among the ultimate strivings of our existence—the ones that we seek to attain over the long term. They're statements of the idealized purpose that we hope all our practical actions will enable us to attain.

UNIQUENESS: PRIDE IN BEING DIFFERENT

Visions communicate what makes us singular and unequaled; they set us apart from everyone else. Visions must differentiate us from others if we're to attract and retain employees, volunteers, customers, clients, donors, or investors. There's no advantage in working for, buying from, or investing in an organization that does exactly the same thing as the one across the street or down the hall. Only when people understand how we're truly distinctive, how we stand out in the crowd, will they want to sign up with us. After all, how would you like to go to work every day if the sign over the front door read, "Welcome to our place. We're just like everyone else"?

Uniqueness fosters pride. It boosts the self-respect and self-esteem of everyone associated with the organization. The prouder we are of the place we shop, the products or services we buy, the school we (or our children) attend, the community in which we live, or the place we work, the more loyal we're likely to be. One of the best ways to discover the uniqueness in your organization's vision is to begin by asking why your customers, internal or external, would want to buy your particular service or product, attend your program, or listen to your sermon.

One of our favorite answers to that question is this simple yet eloquent statement from Edward Goeppner of the Podesta Baldocchi chain of flower shops: "We don't sell flowers, we sell beauty." While customers of a florist do exchange money for a dozen roses, what they're really buying is something more than that: they want to beautify their homes, or express their love for others, or brighten the day. It doesn't take vision to sell a flower on a street corner, but it does take vision to sell beauty.

Uniqueness also enables smaller units within large organizations, or neighborhoods within large cities, to have their own vision while still being encompassed by the collective vision. While every unit within a corporation, public agency, religious institution, school, or volunteer association must be aligned with the overall organizational vision, it can express its distinctive purpose within the larger whole. Every function and every department can differentiate itself by finding its most distinctive qualities. Each can be proud of its ideal and unique image of its future as it works toward the common future of the larger organization.

FUTURE ORIENTATION: LOOKING FORWARD

As we've seen, constituents want their leaders to be "forward-looking," to have "a long-term vision or direction." Despite the necessity of a future orientation, however, strategy scholars Gary Hamel and C. K. Prahalad observe that less than 3 percent of senior management's energy is typically devoted to building a collective perspective on the future, and they warn that this is woefully inadequate.[14] Leaders need to be proactive in thinking about the future, and this imperative increases with one's scope and level of responsibility. Naturally, all roles require attention to the present and the future; it's only the ratio that varies. As illustrated in Figure 5.1, when a leader's role is strategic (as it is for a CEO, president, or research scientist, for example), the time orientation is longer-term and more future-oriented than the time orientation of a leader whose role is more tactical (for example, a production supervisor or operations manager). As a rule of thumb, we believe that leaders should set for themselves the goal of developing their abilities to envision the future at least three to five years ahead.

Visions are statements of destination, of the ends of our labor; they are therefore future-oriented and are made real over different spans of time. It may take three years from the time we decide to climb a mountain until we actually reach the summit. It may take two to three years before a new car is ready for production. It may take a decade to build a company, a century to grow a forest, and generations to set a people free. For leaders of a

Figure 5.1. Mix of Present-Future Orientations of Leaders.

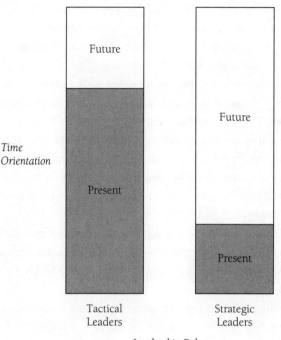

community who envision neighborhoods so safe from crime that little children might once again walk alone to the corner store, aspirations may take a lifetime to achieve. The point is that leaders must occupy themselves with thinking about the future and become able to project themselves ahead in time. The result of their thinking ahead is what we call a "vision."

IMAGERY: PICTURES OF THE FUTURE

Leaders often talk about future issues in terms of foresight, focus, forecasts, future scenarios, points of view, and perspectives. These are all *visual* references. Isn't it striking how our language reveals the visual nature of our thoughts about the future state of affairs?

Try this experiment. Stop reading for a moment and think about the city of Paris, France. What immediately comes to mind? When we do this exercise with groups, people typically tell us that they think of the Eiffel Tower, the Arc de Triomphe, the Seine, Notre Dame, good food, wine, romance. These are images of real places and real sensations. Note that people do *not* mention the square kilometers, population, or gross domestic product of Paris. Numbers aren't what first comes to mind. Why? Human memory is stored in images and senses, not in numbers. We recall the images of reality, not abstractions from reality.

So what does this mean for leaders? It means that to envision the future, we must be able to draw upon that very natural mental process of creating images. When we invent the future, we need to get a mental picture of what things will be like long before we begin the journey. Images are our windows on the world of tomorrow. When talking about going places we've never been—whether to the top of an unclimbed mountain or to the pinnacle of an entirely new industry—we imagine what they'd look like. We picture the possibilities. Those who are more auditory by nature talk about a "calling."

All of us make efforts to see the future—not in some mystical sense but in a cognitive sense. We do it every time we plan a trip for the summer or put a little money in the bank for our retirement. While some of us may have greater creative imagination than others, it's a more common skill than some have assumed.

Visions, then, are conceptualizations. They're images in the mind, impressions and representations. They become real as leaders express those images in concrete terms to their constituents. Just as architects make drawings and engineers build models, leaders find ways of giving expression to their hopes for the future.

BRINGING IT ALL TOGETHER

Maureen Saltzer Brotherton provided us with an example of how a leader can skillfully merge all of these various elements into an eloquent vision statement. When she was at the *Valley Times* in Pleasanton, California, she was the youngest general manager of a daily newspaper in the country. Prior to that job, she had orchestrated the profitable start-up of a tabloid weekly with a circulation of 6,500. (This is especially notable since profitable newspaper start-ups are uncommon.) "We had an opportunity to create something out of nothing," Brotherton explained in discussing the start-up of the paper, "and I got the staff to believe in themselves and the project and to see that others believed in their ability as well."

Here are a few excerpts from what she told her co-workers at the *Valley Times* when they had reached a significant circulation milestone:

> I want to see us truly *be* the winning team. Be the First Choice, the *only* good local choice. Be the heartbeat of the Valley.
>
> When we win, our *readers* win—they'll get *more* of everything, because we will have the space to give it to them. When we win, our *advertisers* win—they'll get results, because we will have the loyal readers to bring them those results. When we win, our *carriers* and *circulation staff* win—because routes will be lucrative enough that we will have a carrier waiting list in *every* district. When we win, our *editorial staff* wins—because they'll have space for *all* their meaningful, in-depth, and exciting stories. Our *photographers* will have room to truly showcase their art. When we win, our *salespeople* win—because these business emissaries will have happy customers, and more customers. When we win, we will even find the time to thank those who usually go thankless, our *support staffs*. When we win, we will *be* the pulse of the Valley—with the image, market share and financial rewards that come to *winners*.
>
> And we *will* win. We *will* be the Valley's heartbeat. But only because of *you*. . . . *You* already offer so much. And you can offer more to hurry us on the way: Sell that extra ad, get all the papers out on the customers' porches, scramble for those award-winning photos and stories. Keep on scooping the *Herald*. Most of all, help each other on the way. I'll be there with you, every step of that way—listening to your frustrations, acting on your requests, backing up your needs with concrete support, keeping your paths as clear as I possibly can.
>
> *Together, we* are the winning team that will make *The Valley Times* the heartbeat of the Valley.

In creating this vision statement, Brotherton made clear and tangible her ideal and unique image of the future for the people who made up the *Valley Times*. With it, she helped them see the future.

Intuiting the Future

Intuition is the wellspring of vision. In fact, by definition, intuition and vision are directly connected. Intuition has as its root the Latin word meaning "to look at."[15] Like vision, then, intuition is a "see" word: it has to do with our ability to picture and to imagine.

Despite the fact that vision and intuition are identified by leaders as important, they haven't been subjects of serious study in business. As McGill University management scholar Henry Mintzberg notes, "There will be little headway in the field of management if managers and researchers continue to search for the key to managing in the lightness of ordered analysis. Too much will stay unexplained in the darkness of intuition."[16] Mintzberg bases this assertion upon his seminal research into the nature of managerial work, concluding that "the key managerial processes are enormously complex and mysterious (to me as a researcher, as well as to the managers, who carry them out), drawing on the vaguest of information and using the least articulated of mental processes. These processes seem to be more relational and holistic than ordered and sequential, and more intuitive than intellectual; they seem to be most characteristic of right-hemispheric activity."[17]

Envisioning and intuiting aren't logical activities. They're extremely difficult to study, explain, and quantify. Many researchers either ignore them or don't take them seriously. Those who have addressed them, however, have found that senior executives generally report that their intuition has been a guide in most of their important decisions.[18] Yet even many executives who commonly use intuition are reluctant to talk about it, considering it too "soft" and mystical a process to openly acknowledge. Intuition is like that big elephant in the middle of the room: everybody can see it, but since it isn't supposed to be there, no one will talk about it. Let's examine it for a bit.

ACCEPTING EXPERIENCE AS THE BEST TEACHER

Despite the reservations of many executives, intuition isn't some mystical process. Rather, it's a clearly understandable phenomenon. As we acquire experience in an organization and in a profession or an industry, we acquire information about what happens, how things happen, and who makes things happen. The longer we spend in an organization, profession, or industry, and the more varied our experiences, the broader and deeper our understanding is likely to be.

When we're presented with an unfamiliar problem in our work, we consciously (or unconsciously) draw upon those experiences to help us solve it. We select relevant information, make relevant comparisons, and integrate experience with the current situation. For the experienced leader, all of this may happen in a matter of seconds. But it's the years of direct contact with a variety of problems and situations that equip the leader with unique insight. Listening, reading, smelling, feeling, and tasting the business—these tasks improve our vision.

Intuition is the bringing together of knowledge and experience to produce new insights. It's being able to fully participate in life's trial and tributions, mentally sift through the facts or events, and apprehend what has been experienced. It's being able to distinguish successful from unsuccessful experiences and developing an understanding of that sorting process.

Many of the people we interviewed mentioned that the exercise of analyzing their personal-best leadership experiences was enlightening for them: by highlighting key lessons from the past, respondents generated an insightful roadmap for leadership highways still to be explored. Direct experience with the organization, the industry, or the profession is a critical source of knowledge regarding how the organization or field operates. That's why, when senior managers are given a list of twenty-three competencies used in selecting a CEO and asked to rank them by importance, they place "knowledge of how the company operates" third and "knowledge of the industry" seventh; it's why they rank "academic training in business" and "knowledge of management science" as sixteenth and seventeenth.[19] Knowledge gained from direct experience and active searching, once stored in the subconscious, becomes the basis for leaders' intuition, insight, and vision.

USING PAST KNOWLEDGE

The research reported by Omar A. El Sawy of the University of Southern California extends our understanding of the relevance of past experience in planning for the future.[20] El Sawy studied thirty-four chief executive officers, dividing them into two equal groups. Among the tests that he administered to the two subgroups was the Vista Test, a test he devised to measure their time orientation. In one part of this test, the CEOs were asked to look ahead into their personal future—to "think of things that might (or will) happen to you in the future." In another part, they were asked to look into their personal past—to "think of the things that have happened to you in the past." In each case, they were asked to list ten events and to date each event.

One group listed the past events first; the other group listed the future events first. El Sawy then compared the length of the past and future time horizons for the two groups. As illustrated in Table 5.1, the CEOs who listed their past events first had significantly longer future time horizons— over four years longer—than the CEOs who listed future events first. The two groups had similar past time horizons, both with a maximum of about twenty years. El Sawy refers to the difference in future horizons as "the Janus Effect," after the two-faced Roman god of beginnings.

Of several plausible explanations for the Janus effect, El Sawy believes his research supports the "one-way-mirror hypothesis." This hypothesis states, "We make sense of our world retrospectively, and all understanding originates in reflection and looking backward. . . . We construct the future by some kind of extrapolation, in which the past is prologue, and the approach to the future is backward-looking."[21] It appears that when we gaze first into our past, we elongate our future. We also enrich our future and give it detail as we recall the richness of our past experiences.

Table 5.1. The Janus Effect.

	Looked Toward Future First	Reviewed Past First
Mean time in future	1.8 years	3.2 years
Maximum time in future	5.1 years	9.2 years
Minimum time in future	0.2 years	0.4 years

In other words, reflecting upon our past may enhance our ability to be forward-looking. As El Sawy comments, "If we want to plan for the distant future, and we want the participants to elongate their time horizons in their image of future, let them talk about history first. Let them look into the past and deliberate about it, before looking into the future."[22]

None of this is to say that the past *is* our future. Adopting that extremely dangerous perspective would be not unlike trying to drive to our future while looking only in the rearview mirror. If that were our point of view, we'd drive ourselves and our organizations right off a cliff. What the Janus effect *does* tell us is that our memories are stored images of our experiences. It's difficult, if not impossible, for us to imagine going to a place we've never experienced, either actually or vicariously. Therefore, leaders would be well advised to avail themselves of the richest set of experiences possible. The broader their experiences and the vaster their network of connections, the longer their time horizons are likely to be.

MINING THE PRESENT

Visions don't leap out of our past wholly formed. While knowledge and experience are the resources of intuition, they aren't by themselves enough to produce an ideal image of the future. Like all raw materials, they must first be extracted, refined, and processed; then they can produce usable ideas.

While the past is the prologue, the present is the opportunity. The past gives us knowledge and experience from which to draw; the present offers the chance to apply them. The past is our source of light (think of sunlight, which is really "old" by the time it gets to earth); the present is the opening in the door through which the light is able to shine. The essential executive action, then, is opening that door. Opportunity knocks often but never waits long. If we keep shut our various doors of opportunity, the light can never shine on us. Opening those doors is what many people describe as "trusting your intuition."

Don Bennett, a Seattle businessperson and the first amputee to climb Mount Rainier's 14,410-foot volcanic summit, describes how he came up with the idea for the Amputee Soccer League and about his sense of where visions come from:

When I got off the mountain, I was in top shape. The best shape I'd ever been in my life. And so right away, because I'm doing one thing on the positive, my mind is thinking, "What can I do to stay in shape?" So where does it come from? I think there is a bolt of lightning in the middle of the night. All I had was the inspiration. I didn't know that much about soccer. I didn't know there were even two sizes of soccer balls. . . . So the next thing with the inspiration is "get out and start doing something." The doing part of it is picking up a phone, calling a few friends, and saying, "Why don't you meet me over on Mercer Island? I've got an idea here. I really feel it." So when they come over, I pull out a soccer ball. They already have their crutches, and we start kicking it. . . . Then things start happening.

Bennett's description of the process that he went through in starting his unique soccer team is typical of other descriptions we heard in our study. There was a moment of inspiration—a bolt of lightning—and then action (not planning, but action) to test out the idea. As Bennett said, "You've got to kick the ball around to get a feel for it. To see if you like it. . . . The inspirations come with kicking the ball."

And what gets the action started? You have to feel strongly about your idea. Whether your inspiration has come in a bolt of lightning or has crystallized over time, you must feel its worth. Unless you firmly believe that your idea has value, that you *must* do something with it, you won't act on it. If you say, "Oh, no one would ever buy that," you'll be right. People won't buy it because you aren't likely to sell it! As we'll see in the next chapter, people won't follow those who lack conviction for their own ideals.

APPLYING VISION TO THE FUTURE

Visions are reflections of our fundamental beliefs and assumptions about human nature, technology, economics, science, politics, art, and ethics. Two leaders within a single organization may have identical experiences and identical opportunities and yet have completely different visions of the organization's future. The reason for their divergence may be that they operate under fundamentally different premises. They may have very different visions of the way the world works.[23]

Our fundamental beliefs all influence what we foresee for our groups and organizations. Those who see unlimited potential around them (as Dishongh does in his students) will have a very different vision of the future from that of those who see limitations and constraints. Before an opportunity can be seized, leaders must assume that something will come of the seizing; and the "something" that each person expects—that is, the vision—is dependent on that person's fundamental beliefs. What, then, is the source of our visions? They flow from the reservoir of our knowledge and experience. They mix with our conviction and are filtered through our assumptions. They take form when we open the doors of opportunity.

The most important role of visions in organizational life is to give focus to human energy. Visions are like lenses that focus unrefracted rays of light. To enable everyone concerned with an enterprise to see more clearly what's ahead of them, leaders must have and convey a focus.

John Cardozo made sure his vision for a new product was crystal clear from the outset. Cardozo had been at Power Up, a small software development company, for six years when he took on the Calendar Creator for Windows project. He envisioned a product that was far more than a simple Windows version of the existing successful DOS program. He dreamed of creating a top-selling, high-quality product that included all the features needed to help people create, manage, and publish calendars. He believed that the product could be hugely successful, both in terms of actual utility offered customers and in terms of sales for the company. His biggest challenge would be to get his development team to envision the project with the same sense of the possible and with the same sense of excitement as he did.

Cardozo made sure that anyone walking into his area would be able to see what the team was working on. He also posted a copy of the latest industry best-seller list, with Calendar Creator for DOS highlighted, in the workstation of new team members. This list provided new and old members alike with a strong and constant reminder of what they could achieve. In addition, he took every opportunity to discuss with team members the product's many potential applications and the value it could provide future users. To make these discussions tangible, Cardozo accumulated a huge collection of calendars (from conventional twelve-month calendars to church newsletters to a nearby gym's aerobics schedule) and displayed them in a highly visible location. He sent his team members to visit bookstores and office supply stores to study types of calendars not in his collection and to think about how people actually used them. He also arranged numerous usability tests for the evolving Windows calendar (in which engineers observed potential customers actually using the product) to help the team get a sense of exactly how their product would be used.

Given Cardozo's strong convictions and his ability to envision the future, it's not surprising that Calendar Creator for Windows quickly made it to the top of the industry best-seller list. Upgrades from the previous DOS version exceeded expectations, and all development expenses were recouped in the first three months of the product's sales. Cardozo had seen what others could not—and was able to make his vision so tangible to others that they willingly made that vision their own.

In contrast, imagine watching a slide show when the projector is out of focus. How would you feel if you had to watch blurred, vague, and indistinct images for an entire presentation? We've experimented with this in some of our leadership programs. The reaction is predictable. People express frustration, impatience, confusion, anger, even nausea. They avoid the situation by looking away. When we ask them whose responsibility it is to focus the projector, the vote is unanimous: "the leader—the person with the focus button." Some people get out of their chairs, walk over to the projector, and focus it themselves, but this doesn't change how they feel: they're still annoyed that the person with the button—the leader—wouldn't focus the projector.

Committing to the Challenge: Focusing the Vision

The leader's job is to keep the projector focused. No matter how much involvement other people have in shaping the vision, we expect that the leader will be able to articulate it. What we refer to as the jigsaw puzzle principle helps illustrate the need for leadership around vision issues: it's easier to put a jigsaw puzzle together if you can see the picture on the box cover. In any organization, people have different pieces of the organizational puzzle. Members may have detailed descriptions of their roles and responsibilities, but very often they lack information about the "big picture"—about the overall purpose or vision of the organization.

While people may be able to work on the puzzle anyway, randomly sticking their pieces here and there in an attempt to make them fit, they lack the essential information that will enable them to contribute to the whole. It's possible that after many random tries, the persistent few will eventually assemble the puzzle. What's more likely is that many other participants will become frustrated, lose interest, and quit. The leader's job is to paint the big picture, to convey the vision, giving people a clear sense of what the puzzle will look like when everyone has put the pieces in place.

A vision is a mental picture of what tomorrow will look like. It expresses our highest standards and values. It sets us apart and makes us feel special. It spans years of time and keeps us focused on the future. And if it's to be attractive to more than an insignificant few, it must appeal to all of those who have a stake in it.

Whether you're leading a small department of fifteen, a large organization of fifteen thousand, or a community of one hundred fifty thousand, your vision sets the agenda and gives direction and purpose to the enterprise. As a leader, you must create a vision for your organization—one based on ideal and unique images of a common future.

Visions spring forth from our intuition. If necessity is the mother of invention, intuition is the mother of vision. Experience feeds our intuition and enhances our insight. Our past is prologue to our future, and leaders who are students of their own and the organization's history are better able to see into the future.

Organizational visions are influenced by our assumptions about people and the world in which we live. No matter how grand the opportunity, if a leader isn't open to it, the vision for developing that opportunity will be constrained. In the next commitment, we offer some practical guidance in developing your vision and preparing to move with it into the future. With the action-steps we suggest, you can enhance your own capacity to envision the future.

Commitment Number 3

Envision an Uplifting and Ennobling Future

➤ Think first about your past.

As we saw, leaders with the longest time horizons are those who understand their past. Before you attempt to write your vision statement, we recommend that you write down significant past events. We especially like the "lifeline" exercise developed by Herb Shepard and Jack Hawley.[24] Here's an abbreviated version:

- Draw your lifeline as a graph, with the peaks representing the highs in your life and the valleys representing the lows. Start as far back as you can remember and stop at the present time.
- Next to each peak, write a word or two identifying the peak experience. Do the same for the valleys.
- Now go back and think about each peak, making a few notes on why each was a high point for you.
- Analyze your notes. What themes and patterns are revealed by the peaks in your life? What important personal strengths are revealed? What do these themes and patterns tell you about what you're likely to find personally compelling in the future?

Participants in our leadership workshops have found this exercise extremely revealing and useful as they prepare to clarify their visions of the future.

We've also applied the process to the organization rather than the individual. By looking over the history of their organization, members begin to see the organizational strengths and weaknesses, the patterns and themes that have carried them to the present. They're then better informed about the foundation on which they're building the organizational future.

➤ Determine what you want.

Are you in your job *to do something,* or are you in your job *for something to do?* If your answer is "to do something," take out a sheet of paper and at the top write, "What I want to accomplish." Now make a list of all the things that you want to achieve on the job. For each item, ask yourself,

"Why do I want this?" Keep on asking why until you run out of reasons. By doing this exercise, you're likely to discover those few higher-order values that are the idealized ends for which you strive.

Here are some additional questions that you can use as catalysts in clarifying your vision:

- How would I like to change the world for myself and my organization?
- If I could invent the future, what future would I invent for myself and my organization?
- What mission in life absolutely obsesses me?
- What's my dream about my work?
- What's the distinctive role or skill of my organization (department, plant, project, company, agency, congregation, community)?
- What's my burning passion?
- What work do I find absorbing, involving, enthralling? What will happen in ten years if I remain absorbed, involved, and enthralled in that work?
- What does my ideal organization look like?
- What's my personal agenda? What do I want to prove?

Jack Haderle's personal best clearly reflected his desire to do something. In discussing his role as a U.S. Forest Service ranger responsible for the reforestation of Forest Hill (in the Tahoe National Forest) after a fire, he said that the work was about a "great cause. It's not about getting some product out. It's not about fixing something in a company that will only break again sometime in the future. It's about helping future generations, making life better for others in the long run." Haderle knew what he wanted to do.

➤ Write an article about how you've made a difference.

Your responses to the questions just posed should give you some clues to what you would like to accomplish in your life (and why). Now take it a step further. Imagine that it's the year 2005 and you've been selected to receive an award as one of the fifty people who have made a difference in this century. Imagine that a national magazine has put together an article about the difference that you've made to your organization, family, or community. Write that article.

Don't censor yourself. Allow yourself this opportunity to record your hopes and dreams even if you find the process somewhat embarrassing. The more comfortable you are in discussing your innermost wishes, the easier it will become to communicate a vision to others. In writing your article, ask yourself the following questions:

- What are you most proud of?
- What's your greatest contribution to your community's or organization's growth?

Then, once you've answered these and similar questions, project your answers into the future.

Writing such an article—and then reading it to your colleagues—is a very powerful way to clarify what's truly important to you. By looking back over your life and its potential, you come face to face with the legacy you want to leave. Your article should bring that legacy into clearer focus.

➤ Write a short vision statement.

Take all the information you've just gathered and write your ideal and unique image of the future for yourself and for your organization. We recommend that this statement be short, because you ought to be able to tell it to others in about five to seven minutes. Any longer than that, and people are likely to lose interest.

Once you've written it, try drawing it, finding a picture that resembles it, or creating a symbol that represents it. Finally, create a short slogan of five to nine words that captures the essence of your vision. Something similar to Edward Goeppner's "We don't sell flowers, we sell beauty" is what we have in mind. A brief slogan is very useful in communication. It's not a substitute for a complete statement, but it does help others to remember the essential reason for the organization's existence.

➤ Act on your intuition.

Visions often take a while to take shape in the mind. We need even longer before we can formulate them into articulate statements. Instead of struggling with words on paper, do something to act on your intuition. Do as Don Bennett did when he acted immediately on his inspiration to start the Amputee Soccer League. If you're inspired to do something, go try it. Go kick the ball around. Then you'll see whether you really believe that you're on the right track. You'll also see whether others are as enthusiastic about the idea as you are. Visions, like objects in the distance, get clearer and clearer as we move toward them. Talk to people. Share your thoughts with others. Do some homework. Write your congressional representative or local newspaper. Kick the tires. Challenge the process!

➤ **Test your assumptions.**
Our assumptions are mental screens that expand or constrain what's possible. To determine their validity in regard to your vision, take the following steps:

- Make a list of the assumptions underlying your vision.
- Flesh out each assumption: ask yourself what you assume to be true or untrue about your constituents and your organization, about science and technology, about economics and politics, about the future itself.
- Ask a few close advisers to react to your assumptions. Do they agree or disagree with you? Why or why not?
- Ask people who you think might have different assumptions to respond to yours.
- Test your assumptions by trying an experiment or two. Don Bennett assumed amputees could do more than they might think—like play soccer—so he tested his assumption by kicking the ball around one day. Now there's a world cup of amputee soccer each year.

Keep in mind that your assumptions may blind you to new solutions. Take a lesson from Brian Biro, who was surprised to learn of an entirely new way of slicing the cake. Take those blinders off.

➤ **Become a futurist.**
Ask yourself what's driving your organization's agenda (or that of your congregation, community, department, or agency). Is it your own view of the future or someone else's perspective (such as the competition's)? Does the organization have a clear and shared understanding of how the field or industry will be different ten years from now?[25]

Make it your business to spend some time studying the future. There are dozens of books and other sources of information. Listed below are a few classics you might start with:

- John Naisbitt, *Megatrends* (New York: Warner Books, 1988).
- Alvin Toffler, *The Third Wave* (New York: Morrow, 1980), and *Powershift* (New York: Bantam, 1990).
- For an excellent collection of articles on the use of "future search conferences" for bringing people together to achieve breakthroughs in shared vision, see M. R. Weisbord and others, *Discovering Common Ground: How Future Search Conferences Bring People Together to Achieve Breakthrough Innovation, Empowerment, Shared Vision, and Collaborative Action* (San Francisco: Berrett-Koehler, 1993).

Our colleague Jim Smith, from the Business Futures Network, recommends the following books:

- Sheila Moorcroft, ed., *Visions for the 21st Century* (England: Adamantine Press, 1992).
- Peter Schwartz, *The Art of the Long View* (New York: Doubleday, 1991).
- John Stoffels, *Strategic Issues Management: A Comprehensive Guide to Environmental Scanning* (Elmsford, N.Y.: Pergamon Press, 1994).
- Howard Rheingold, *The Virtual Community: Homesteading on the Electronic Frontier* (Reading, Mass.: Addison-Wesley, 1993).
- Michael Rothschild, *Bionomics: Economy as Ecosystem* (New York: Henry Holt and Company, 1990).

In addition, the following magazines address the future: *American Demographics* provides demographics on the present and into the future, *Utne Reader* offers a digest of the alternative press, *Scientific American* covers scientific developments, and *Wired* serves up hip, hop, and hype on the leading edge of info-land. Thoughtful commentary on important cultural and social issues by thinkers around the world is included in *New Perspectives Quarterly*, while the *Economist* provides comprehensive coverage of world events, along with periodic surveys on a variety of topics.

The following organizations periodically publish reports about likely trends that are relevant to business. We recommend that you look into them:

- Business Futures Network (San Francisco/London)
- Global Business Network (Emeryville, Calif.)
- Weiner, Edrich, Brown, Inc. (New York City)
- SRI International Business Intelligence Center (Menlo Park, Calif.)
- The Futures Group (Glastonbury, Conn.)
- Institute for the Future (Menlo Park, Calif.)
- The World Futures Society (Washington, D.C.)

"Organizations" such as Prodigy, CompuServe, America On-Line, and The WELL also provide access to many on-line electronic conferences dealing with a number of future-oriented subjects.

Set up a futures research committee in your organization to study developing issues and potential changes in areas affecting your business. A few years ago, the American Life Insurance Council established the Trend Analysis Project. A team of more than 100 people began continually tracking more than sixty publications that represented new thoughts on trends in American society and abstracted the articles. A smaller team then pulled the abstracts into reports for use in planning and decision making. You could adapt this methodology, or a similar one, to your setting. Have all the people in your organization regularly clip articles from the newspapers and magazines they subscribe to. Surf the Internet. Circulate the ideas generated by this tracking and discuss trends and impacts on your product, service, technology, department, agency, company, and/or community. Use these discussions to help you and your organization develop the ability to think long-term.

➤ Rehearse with visualizations and affirmations.

Once you've clarified your vision, one of the most effective things you can do to help you realize it is mental rehearsal—the act of mentally practicing a skill, sequence of skills, or attitude using visual imagery or kinesthetic feelings. Mental rehearsal is used extensively in sports training to improve athletic performance. By visualizing yourself doing a move perfectly or reaching a desired goal, you increase your chances of making imagination become reality. Don Bennett told us that he imagined himself on the top of Mount Rainier a thousand times a day before his climb. Adapt this technique to your situation: imagine what it will be like when you and your organization attain your vision. Rehearse this scenario over and over again.

Another practical technique is affirmation—a positive assertion that something is already so. It's a way of making firm that which you imagine for the future. An affirmation, sometimes called positive self-talk, can be made in writing, made silently, or spoken aloud. Whatever the mode, it's most effective in the present tense, as if the desired state already existed.

Write several affirmations about the ideal and unique image of your organization. Phrase your affirmation positively in terms of what you want. Make it short, and repeat it over and over to yourself. As a start, here are a few leadership affirmations:

- I'm confident that I'm finding exciting opportunities as I accept these new challenges.
- I'm learning from my mistakes as I experiment with new ideas and methods.
- I'm creating enthusiasm as I communicate my vision of the future.

You might use these affirmations, and others, as part of a meditation for self-improvement.

The techniques we've presented should help you focus your vision and create positive expectations about the future. These techniques, and others like them, aren't substitutes for personal conviction and a vision of substance, but they're extremely useful in keeping you focused on what you want to create. The more positive you feel about the future you envision, the better able you'll be to communicate positively with others.

But even armed with techniques, leaders find that there's no freeway to the future, no paved highway from here to tomorrow. Nor are there roadmaps or signposts. Instead, the explorer must rely upon a compass and a dream. The vision of an organization acts as its magnetic north. It possesses the extraordinary ability to attract human energy. It invites and draws others to it by the force of its own appeal.

Leadership vision is necessary if an organization is to move forward with purpose toward a common destination, but it isn't sufficient. As important, if not more so—because envisioning the future isn't a solo act—is the ability to communicate that vision so that others come to see what the leader sees. After all, constituents have no idea what a leader's vision is until the leader describes it. As an assembly worker once told us, "One of the jobs of a leader is to have a vision. But sometimes top management sees an apple. When it gets to middle management, it's an orange. By the time it gets to us, it's a lemon."

The image that constituents develop in their minds is highly dependent upon the leader's ability to describe an apple so that it appears as an apple in the minds of others. That ability is an integral part of enlisting others in a vision of the future. The dreams and aspirations of a leader's constituents must be inherent in that leader's vision of the future, for a shared vision is possible only if constituents find the purpose appealing. Even when the leader is a master communicator, constituents won't bite from the apple if they prefer oranges—or anticipate lemons.

In this chapter, we've defined a vision as an ideal and unique image of the future. In fact, however, we should add one more phrase to our definition to make it complete, to make it inclusive: a vision is an ideal and unique image of the future *for the common good*. In the next chapter, we'll discuss that common good and examine how leaders define a common purpose and then effectively communicate a vision so that others come to share it as their own.

Commitment Number 3

Envision an Uplifting and Ennobling Future

➤ Think first about your past.

➤ Determine what you want.

➤ Write an article about how you've made a difference.

➤ Write a short vision statement.

➤ Act on your intuition.

➤ Test your assumptions.

➤ Become a futurist.

➤ Rehearse with visualizations and affirmations.

Source: The Leadership Challenge by James M. Kouzes and Barry Z. Posner.
Copyright © 1995.

6

Enlist Others

Attracting People to Common Purposes

*Leaders must communicate the vision in a way that
attracts and excites members of the organization.*
—DAVID E. BERLEW
President
Rath & Strong

On August 25, 1993, a new Kroger food store opened its doors for the first time in the small river town of New Albany, Indiana, directly across the Ohio River from Louisville, Kentucky. It proved to be a historic day in the life of 110-year-old The Kroger Co., one of the largest grocery chain operations in America. Store manager Thurman Conrad and his team of assistant managers, department managers, and 250 associates blew away previous company sales records for both opening day and the first week. The sales total for the initial seven days far exceeded what the "experts" had predicted and what history had suggested: for example, over 116 tons of meat, 301,500 pounds of fresh fruit and vegetables (including 24,000 ears of corn), and 3 tons of salad from the salad bar were sold! According to Conrad, "It shows what happens when the team rallies around an inspiring vision of what they want to accomplish and works together."

Grocery store departments, such as meat, grocery, produce, and front-end operations, don't always communicate well or work toward common goals. But for the New Albany crew, that changed when they participated in a team-building event several months prior to the opening.[1] Two days of studying leadership in a team environment, Conrad explained, "really jelled the management team [store manager and assistant managers] and the department heads into a more trusting, supportive, and enthusiastic group with shared objectives."

Conrad described New Albany's store opening as the smoothest opening in which he had taken part. Department managers "rose to the occasion" as the unexpected business started to hit, bringing with it tremendous resupply problems. Conrad said the leadership team avoided the usual stress of such a situation and pulled together the entire week of the opening. He cited the leadership workshop as accounting for the difference, explaining that the management team and department heads, in addition to building trust and a better understanding of how to enable their associates, had created a vision of how they wanted to distinguish their new store as *the* place to shop and work in New Albany.

As team members talked at the workshop, they tried to sketch pictures and symbols for their ideas. When someone drew the Sherman-Mitten Bridge, a local landmark connecting New Albany and Louisville, everyone got excited; group members knew they were on the right track. Together, using newsprint, colored construction paper, felt pens, glue, and glitter, they created a picture of a large bridge beneath a starry sky. The bridge was holding aloft a company logo, and beneath the bridge was the slogan "Bridging New Albany into the Future." This was a tangible image of how their new Kroger store could make a difference in the community, and it gave them a theme to rally around as they tackled the challenge of opening a new market.

But they weren't finished yet with this "vision of an ideal and unique image of the future for the common good." One store associate created an oil painting depicting the bridge and slogan; it was beautiful and inspiring—but still not enough, as far as the group was concerned. Gary Hettinger, deli department manager, coordinated the construction of an eight-foot-long, four-foot-high replica of the Sherman-Mitten Bridge. It included a miniature neon logo, lampposts, and cars. Hettinger kept enthusiasm high at the store by bringing in photos of the replica's progress.

When the entire store leadership team went to Louisville for the traditional new-store planning meeting with the divisional president and headquarters staff, the new bridge made the journey too, complete with special lighting, smoke machine, and theater curtains. At the right moment, members of the store team proudly and dramatically unveiled the embodiment of their vision to a duly impressed senior management team, which quickly decided to incorporate the bridge theme into the print media promoting the store opening. The store team had enlisted the solid support of upper management.

The pace quickened as opening day drew near. Deciding to share their vision with the community, team members put the bridge on prominent display in the new store's lobby, complete with starry sky, neon sign, and slogan. The display became a sort of shrine, reminding the team of its commitment to leadership, teamwork, and bringing the future to New Albany's grocery shoppers. (The bridge subsequently became a regular part of new-employee orientation—a way to share the vision.)

When opening day arrived, it was the customers' turn to appreciate what the bridge and the vision it represented meant to them and to their community. The bridge remained on display, customer service employees wore shirts with the bridge and slogan colorfully printed on the back, and the scene in the lobby was reproduced in brochures given to each customer. Response was overwhelming: positive customer comments, offers to buy the bridge, requests from the mayor's office to display the bridge in the town library—and food sales in record numbers!

While the "bridge shrine" has since been replaced, the vision of leadership, teamwork, and community and customer service lives on. The store leadership firmly believes that the right vision empowers positive change by focusing the collective energy of store associates and by building commitment and a willingness to take personal responsibility for the enterprise's success.

Developing a Shared Sense of Destiny

In the personal-best cases that we collected, people frequently talked about the necessity to get "buy-in" on the vision, to "enlist others" in the dream.

People talked about how they had to communicate the purpose and build support for the direction. As Barry Mitchelson, a professor in the Department of Physical Education and Sport Studies at the University of Alberta, Edmonton, said to us, "It isn't enough for a leader to have a vision; for an organization to approach its potential and successfully implement change, its members must understand, accept, and commit to the vision."

Barbara Brodsky Jungert, associate director of Big Brothers/Big Sisters, says simply, "You have to teach others your vision." But teaching a vision—and confirming that the vision is shared—isn't a one-way process; on the contrary, it's a process of engaging constituents in conversations about their lives, about their hopes and dreams. Remember that leadership is a dialogue, not a monologue. Leadership isn't about imposing the leader's solo dream; it's about developing a *shared* sense of destiny. It's about enrolling others so that they can see how their own interests and aspirations are aligned with the vision and can thereby become mobilized to commit their individual energies to its realization. A vision is *inclusive* of the constituents' aspirations; it's an ideal and unique image of the future for the *common* good.

When leaders effectively communicate a vision—whether it's to one person, a small group, or a large organization—that vision has very potent effects. We've found that when leaders clearly articulate their vision for the organization, constituents report significantly higher levels of the following:

- Job satisfaction
- Motivation
- Commitment
- Loyalty
- Esprit de corps
- Clarity about the organization's values
- Pride in the organization
- Organizational productivity

Clearly, teaching others about the vision produces powerful results.

Yet this competency isn't always effectively utilized. We found in our research, for instance, that inspiring a shared vision is the least frequently applied of the five fundamental practices of exemplary leadership. People also report that inspiring a shared vision is the leadership practice with which they feel the most uncomfortable. And when we ask people whether they consider themselves to be inspiring, only 10 percent say that they are.

People just don't see themselves as personally uplifting, and they certainly receive very little encouragement or training to be that way at work. What might have come naturally in youth has been dampened in adults. But perhaps people underestimate themselves in this area: we've found that people's common perception of themselves as uninspiring is in sharp contrast to their performance when talking about their personal-best leadership cases or about their ideal futures. When relating hopes, dreams, and successes, people are almost always emotionally expressive. Expressiveness comes naturally to people talking about deep desires for the future. They lean forward in their chairs, they move their arms about, their eyes light up, their voices sing with emotion, and a smile appears on their faces. In these circumstances, people are enthusiastic, articulate, optimistic, and uplifting. In short, people *are* inspiring!

This contradiction is most intriguing. Why is it that people seem to see no connection between the animated, enthusiastic behavior they use in describing their dreams and the ability to lift others' spirits? We believe that most people have attributed something mystical to the process of inspiring a shared vision. They seem to see it as supernatural, as a grace or charm that comes from the gods. This assumption inhibits people far more than any lack of natural talent for being inspirational. We believe that it's not necessary to be a famous, charismatic person to inspire a shared vision. It *is* necessary to believe, however—and to develop the skills to transmit that belief. This enthusiasm is what mobilizes movements and energizes enterprises. It's this enthusiasm, genuinely displayed, that brings the vision to life for all of us. In learning how to reach people as leaders do, to move our souls and uplift our spirits, we look to a master of that art: the Reverend Dr. Martin Luther King, Jr.

On August 28, 1963, on the steps of the Lincoln Memorial in Washington, D.C., before a throng of 250,000, Martin Luther King, Jr., proclaimed his dream to the world. It was, he said that day, "a dream deeply rooted in the American dream." As he spoke, and as thousands clapped and shouted, a nation was moved. That speech is among the most instructive of inspiring public presentations because of the speaker's skill, his success in moving his listeners. King's uplifting speech also illustrates how the ability to exert an enlivening influence is rooted in fundamental values, cultural traditions, and personal conviction.

We play an audiotape of King's address in all of our leadership development programs. As participants listen, we ask them to imagine that they're communication researchers studying how leaders enlist constituents. We ask them to listen to the content as well as to the delivery and to notice the use of various rhetorical techniques. We ask them to place themselves on the steps of the Lincoln Memorial and attempt to get a feel for how the audience reacted as they listen to these words from King's "I Have a Dream" speech:

> I say to you today, my friends, that in spite of the difficulties and frustrations of the moment I still have a dream. It is a dream deeply rooted in the American dream.
>
> I have a dream that one day this nation will rise up and live out the true meaning of its creed: "We hold these truths to be self-evident; that all men are created equal."
>
> I have a dream that one day on the red hills of Georgia the sons of former slaves and the sons of former slaveowners will be able to sit down together at the table of brotherhood.
>
> I have a dream that one day even the state of Mississippi, a desert state sweltering with the heat of injustice and oppression, will be transformed into an oasis of freedom and justice.
>
> I have a dream that my four little children will one day live in a nation where they will not be judged by the color of their skin but by the content of their character.
>
> I have a dream today.
>
> I have a dream that one day the state of Alabama, whose governor's lips are presently dripping with the words of interposition and nullification, will be transformed into a situation where little black boys and black girls will be able to join hands with little white boys and white girls and walk together as sisters and brothers.
>
> I have a dream today.
>
> I have a dream that one day every valley shall be exalted, every hill and mountain shall be made low, the rough places will be made plains, and the crooked places will be made straight, and the glory of the Lord shall be revealed, and all flesh shall see it together.
>
> This is our hope. This is the faith with which I return to the South. With this faith we will be able to transform the jangling discords of our nation into a beautiful symphony of brotherhood. With this faith we

will be able to work together, to pray together, to struggle together, to go to jail together, to stand up for freedom together, knowing that we will be free one day.

This will be the day when all of God's children will be able to sing with new meaning, "My country 'tis of thee, sweet land of liberty, of thee I sing. Land where my fathers died, land of the pilgrim's pride, from every mountainside, let freedom ring."

And if America is to be a great nation this must become true. So let freedom ring from the prodigious hilltops of New Hampshire. Let freedom ring from the mighty mountains of New York. Let freedom ring from the heightening Alleghenies of Pennsylvania!

Let freedom ring from the snowcapped Rockies of Colorado!

Let freedom ring from the curvaceous peaks of California!

But not only that; let freedom ring from the Stone Mountain of Georgia!

Let freedom ring from every hill and molehill of Mississippi. From every mountainside, let freedom ring.

When we let freedom ring, when we let it ring from every village and every hamlet, from every state and every city, we will be able to speed up that day when all of God's children, black men and white men, Jews and Gentiles, Protestants and Catholics, will be able to join hands and sing in the words of that old Negro spiritual, "Free at last! Free at last! Thank God almighty, we are free at last!"[2]

Here are some of the observations that participants have made in commenting on King's speech:

- "It was vivid. He used a lot of images and word pictures. You could *see* the examples."
- "People could relate to the examples. They were familiar to them—for example, the spirituals."
- "His references were credible. It's hard to argue against the Constitution and the Bible."
- "He talked about traditional values of family, church, country."
- "He mentioned children—something we can all relate to."
- "He appealed to common bonds."
- "He knew his audience."

- "He made geographical references to places the people in the audience could relate to."
- "He included everybody: different parts of the country, all ages, both sexes, major religions."
- "He used a lot of repetition: for example, 'I have a dream,' 'Let freedom ring.'"
- "He said the same thing in different ways."
- "He began with a statement of the difficulties and then stated his dream."
- "He was positive and hopeful."
- "He talked about hope for the future, but he also said people might have to suffer in order to get there. He didn't promise it would be easy."
- "There was a cadence and a rhythm to his voice."
- "He shifted from 'I' to 'we' halfway through."
- "He spoke with emotion and passion. It was deeply felt."
- "He was personally convinced of the dream."

After going through this process of hearing and then commenting on King's speech, participants in our leadership development programs recognize the ease with which they're able to identify what makes the speech so uplifting. They see that it's easy to decipher the code and that there's no mystery to its power.

We then take the next step: going down the list of observations, we ask, "Can *you* do this in presentations to your own group?" We discuss with participants which of the these things they feel they could do:

- Use images and word pictures.
- Use examples that people can relate to.
- Talk about traditional values.
- Appeal to common bonds.
- Get to know your audience.
- Use repetition.
- Be positive and hopeful.
- Shift from "I" to "we."
- Speak with passion and emotion.
- Have personal conviction about the dream.

As we work our way through the list, participants say yes to nearly every question. When the "magic" of inspiration is revealed, most say that they could do more than they now do to awaken passion in others.

Fortunately, oratory skills as fine as King's are by no means necessary to enlist others. What matters isn't the eloquence of the speech but the appeal of the message to the audience. For that appeal to exist, we have to understand others' dreams, and we have to find common ground on which we can build a shared dream. We must believe in our own dreams—and in the collective dream. To move others to share the vision, leaders must

- Discover and appeal to a common purpose
- Communicate expressively, thereby bringing the vision to life in such a way that people can see themselves in it
- Sincerely believe in what they're saying and demonstrate their personal conviction

Whether they're trying to mobilize a crowd in the grandstand or one person in the office, leaders must practice these three *essentials* to enlisting others.

Discovering a Common Purpose

The first task in enlisting others is to identify our constituents and find out what their common aspirations are. No matter how grand the dream of an individual visionary, if others don't see in it the possibility of realizing their own hopes and desires, they won't follow. Leaders must show others how they, too, will be served by the long-term vision of the future, how their specific needs can be satisfied.

If leaders need one special talent, it's the ability to sense the purpose in others. By knowing their constituents, by listening to them, and by taking their advice, leaders are able to give voice to constituents' feelings. They're able to stand before others and say with assurance, "Here's what I heard you say that you want for yourselves. Here's how your own needs and interests will be served by enlisting in a common cause." In a sense, leaders hold up a mirror and reflect back to their constituents what they say they most desire. When the constituents see that reflection, they recognize it and are immediately attracted to it.

Harlan Cleveland, a former U.S. ambassador and respected university dean, once observed that "decision making proceeds not by 'recommendations up, orders down,' but by development of a shared sense of direction among those who must form the parade if there is going to be a parade."[3] Cleveland illustrated his point with an excerpt from the columnist Russell Baker:

> What does this country need today?
> Leadership. . . . The country yearns for new leadership for a new era.
>   If led, will the country follow?
> If given the right kind of leadership, the country will surely follow.
>   But what kind of leadership is the right kind?
> The leadership that leads the country in the direction it wants to take.
>   And what specific direction does the country want to take?
> Who knows? That's for the leader to figure out. If he is the right kind of leader, he will guess correctly. . . .
>   Am I wrong in concluding that it isn't leadership the country wants in a President but followership?[4]

Cleveland adds, "Russell Baker was not wrong. High policy—that is, major change in a society's sense of direction—is first shaped in an inchoate consensus reached by the people at large."[5] What's true for the society at large is also true for organizations. Leaders know very well that the seeds of any vision are those imperfectly formed images passed on from volunteers or frontline personnel about what the clients or customers really want or those inarticulate mumblings from the manufacturing folks about poor product quality—not crystal-ball-gazing in upper levels of the organization's stratosphere. The best leaders are the best followers. They pay attention to weak signals and quickly respond to changes in the marketplace, whether overseas or just around the corner.

Leaders find the common thread that weaves the fabric of human needs into a colorful tapestry. They develop a deep understanding of the collective yearnings; they seek out the brewing consensus among those they would lead. They listen carefully for quiet whisperings in dark corners and attend to subtle cues. They get a sense of what people want, what they value, what they dream about. Sensitivity to others is no trivial skill; rather, it is a truly precious human ability. But it isn't a *complex* skill. It requires only a receptiveness to other people and a willingness to listen. It means getting out of the office and spending time with people out in the field or on the factory floor or in the showroom or warehouse or back room. It means being delicately aware of the attitudes and feelings of others and the nuances of their communication.

And what do leaders discover when they listen with sensitivity to the aspirations of others? What do they discover about the common values that link us together? Psychologist David E. Berlew, now president of Rath & Strong, believes that what really excites people, what really provides meaning and generates enthusiasm, are these value-related opportunities:[6]

- A chance to be tested, to make it on one's own
- A chance to take part in a social experiment
- A chance to do something well
- A chance to do something good
- A chance to change the way things are

After sifting through mountains of numbers, dozens of surveys, and years of research studies, *Inc.* magazine's researchers determined that people "want the same things they've always wanted."[7] Even though job security is increasingly tenuous, regardless of industry or location, "interesting work" has a dramatic twenty-two-point lead over "high income" when it comes to importance to workers.[8] A survey of *Industry Week* readers found that quality of leadership ("working for a leader with vision and values") means more than dollars ("pay raises and bonuses") as a source of motivation for today's workforce.[9] *The National Study of the Changing Workforce* reports that "personal satisfaction for doing a good job" is the most frequently mentioned measure of success in worklife—cited nearly two to three times more often than "getting ahead" or "making a good living."[10]

These findings suggest that there's more to work than is commonly assumed. There's rich opportunity for leaders to appeal to more than just the material rewards. Great leaders, like great companies and countries, create meaning, not just money. The values and interests of freedom, self-actualization, learning, community, excellence, uniqueness, service, and social responsibility truly attract people to a common cause.

There is a deep human yearning to make a difference. We want to know that we've done something on this earth, that our life means something. We want to know that there's a purpose to our existence. Work can provide that purpose, and increasingly work is where men and women seek it. Work has become a place where we pursue meaning and identity.[11]

The best organizational leaders are able to bring out and make use of this human longing for meaning and fulfillment by communicating the meaning and significance of the organization's work so that the individual understands his or her own important role in creating it. When leaders clearly communicate a shared vision of an organization, they ennoble those who work on its behalf. They elevate the human spirit.

Leaders speak to people's hearts and listen to their heartbeats because, in the final analysis, shared visions are simply about common caring. That's how David Clancy explains what Westpac's Commercial Banking organization is trying to accomplish by focusing on the question, "What does it mean to work here?" As head of that organization's Learning Resource Centre, which used to be called the Corporate Training Department, Clancy—along with his colleagues—has a vision: for individuals to take responsibility for their own learning requirements and, in so doing, to discover what it is that they really care about—individually, as a team, and as an organization. John Evans, a partner in Cultural Imprint and an outside consultant with Westpac, reports that most corporate "statements of vision" generally fail to compel people to action or personal responsibility. Based on his research in Australia, he contends that if people are to become committed to their organizations, they need a cause to work for and a clear picture of what it means to work at those organizations. Our own research on what people expect from their leaders echoes this perspective: leaders uplift people's spirits.

In today's world, when books like M. Scott Peck's *The Road Less Traveled* can remain on the best-seller list for more than eleven years, we know that people are searching for a deeper meaning to their lives.[12] A shared vision meets this longing because, as Peter Senge explains in *The Fifth Discipline*, it "is a force in people's hearts, a force of impressive power. . . . [F]ew, if any, forces in human affairs are as powerful as shared visions."[13] People really do want to make commitments; and united in a common cause, calling, mission, purpose, or vision, they can get extraordinary things accomplished.

Visions are not strategic plans. Henry Mintzberg's recent analysis demonstrates that *"strategic planning* is not *strategic thinking.* Indeed, strategic planning often spoils strategic thinking, causing managers to confuse real vision with the manipulation of numbers. And this confusion lies at the heart of the issue: the most successful strategies are visions, not plans."[14] Mintzberg goes on to articulate that planning represents a "calculating" style, while leaders employ a "committing" style—one that, as he explains it, "engage[s] people in a journey. They lead in such a way that everyone on the journey helps shape its course. As a result, enthusiasm inevitably builds along the way. Those with a calculating style fix on a destination and calculate what the group must do to get there, with no concern for the members' preferences. But calculated strategies have no value in and of themselves. . . . [S]trategies take on value only as committed people infuse them with energy."[15]

Leadership that focuses on a committing style is what leadership scholars now refer to as "transformational leadership." As James MacGregor Burns says, transformational leadership occurs when, in their interactions, people "raise one another to higher levels of motivation and morality. Their purposes, which might have started out as separate but related, as in the case of transactional leadership, become fused. . . . But transforming leadership ultimately becomes moral in that it raises the level of human conduct and ethical aspiration of both the leader and the led, and thus it has a transforming effect on both."[16]

The most admired leaders speak unhesitatingly and proudly of mutual ethical aspirations. They know that people aspire to live up to the highest moral standards. So the first essential for enlisting others is to find and focus on the very best that the culture—group, organizational, or national—shares in common and what that means to its members. This communion of purpose, this commemoration of our dreams, helps to bind us together. It reminds us of what it means to be a part of this collective effort. It joins us together in the human family.

Giving Life to a Vision

The second essential requirement for enlisting others is to bring the common vision to life. Leaders animate the vision and make manifest the purpose so that others can see it, hear it, taste it, touch it, feel it. In making the intangible vision tangible, leaders ignite constituents' flames of passion. By using powerful language, positive communication style, and nonverbal expressiveness, leaders breathe life (which is the literal definition of the word *inspire*) into a vision.

POWERFUL LANGUAGE

Leaders make full use of the power of language to communicate a shared identity and give life to visions. Successful leaders use metaphors and figures of speech; they give examples, tell stories, and relate anecdotes; they draw word pictures; and they offer quotations and recite slogans.

Review again the words of Martin Luther King, Jr. Notice his use of visual and aural images: "the red hills of Georgia," "the prodigious hilltops of New Hampshire," "the heightening Alleghenies of Pennsylvania," "the jangling discords of our nation," and "a beautiful symphony of brotherhood." Read the specific examples: "where little black boys and black girls will be able to join hands with little white boys and white girls and walk together as sisters and brothers" and "a dream that my four little children will one day live in a nation where they will not be judged by the color of their skin but by the content of their character."[17] Notice the references to the Constitution and the quotations from anthems and spirituals. All these skillful uses of language give the listener a visceral feel for King's dream. They enable us to picture the future in our mind's eye. They enable us to hear it, to sense it, to recognize it.

All of us can enrich language with stories, references, and figures of speech; in fact, doing so is a natural way of communicating. One need only think of how children tell each other stories, how they love to have stories told to them. Or consider the days before television, when people loved to imagine scenes described by a radio announcer.

Metaphors are plentiful in our daily conversations. We talk of computers having memory and ships plowing the sea. We talk about time as money. We talk about knowledge as power. We talk about business as a game. Military metaphors are used in corporate strategy, while sports vernacular is heard daily in meetings. Metaphors and analogies are as common as numbers in organizations. Leaders make conscious use of metaphorical expressions to give vividness and tangibility to abstract ideas.

In this book, and in all our discussions of leadership, we use the journey metaphor to express our understanding of leadership. We talk about leaders as pioneers and trailblazers who take people on expeditions to places they've never been. We talk about vision as the magnetic north. We talk about climbing to the summit and about milestones and signposts. All of these metaphorical expressions are our way of communicating the active, pioneering nature of leadership.

Language is a powerful tool. We remember once listening to a bank officer rallying his managers to take on the competition. Here are some of the phrases he used:

- "You've got to watch out for the headhunters."
- "Keep your capital, and keep it dry."
- "We'll act like SWAT teams."
- "We're going to beat their brains out."
- "We won't tolerate the building of little fiefdoms."
- "There will be only a few survivors."

Contrast these with some of the phrases Jean-Louis Gassée used in a presentation to Apple managers when he was senior vice president of research and development for Apple Computer:

- "What we stand for is innovation . . . also hope, freedom, fun."
- "In our hearts, minds, guts, and muscle, . . . we stand for bringing computer power to the people so they can share in the fun."
- "We don't have to wear our suits in our heads."
- "Celebrate the human mind."
- "We share our love for Apple."

These two examples demonstrate how leaders can make use of the metaphorical power of language. In the first illustration, the bank officer portrayed a hostile environment and used military metaphors to rally the troops. In the second example, Gassée created an entirely different image—one of liberation and joy. Leaders learn to master the richness of figurative speech so that they can paint the word pictures that best portray the meaning of their visions.

Communication professor Roderick Hart of the University of Texas has identified four categories of words commonly used by leaders:

- "Realistic" words portray tangible and concrete objects, such as *automobile* and *highway*.
- "Optimistic" words express hope and possibilities.
- "Activity" words show motion.
- "Certainty" words express assuredness.

Hart says that Americans want language that's "highly certain, highly optimistic, highly realistic and highly active."[18] His research quantifies what successful leaders know intuitively, that leaders must

- Make the intangible image of the future tangible and concrete.
- Offer positive and optimistic predictions that the dream will be realized.
- Be resolute and confident that the goal will be reached.
- Propel the mission forward, infusing it with motion and energy.

POSITIVE COMMUNICATION STYLE

We want leaders with enthusiasm, with a bounce in their step, with a positive attitude. We want to believe that we'll be part of an invigorating journey. We want to feel alive, even at work. We follow people with a can-do attitude, not those who give 67,000 reasons why something can't be done or who don't make us feel good about ourselves or what we're doing.

There's energy in the leaders we most admire. They're electric, vigorous, active, full of life. We're reminded of Randi DuBois, discussed in Chapter Four, who gets people to stretch themselves by engaging in challenging physical tasks. Typically, her clients are nervous and often even a bit scared at first. But people of all ages, all sizes, and varying physical abilities have successfully completed her course. How does DuBois succeed in leading these people? Her secret is very simple: she's always positive that people can do the course, and she never says never. She conveys to all people she meets that they have the power within themselves to accomplish whatever they desire. (The authors know this from personal experience. We've been forty feet above the ground leaping for an iron ring while DuBois cheered us on.)

Less dramatic, perhaps, but every bit as effective, is the positive attitude and communication style that Joan Carter exhibited when she took over as general manager/executive chef of the Faculty Club at Santa Clara University. Before Carter's arrival, both membership and sales had been seriously declining for several years, remaining customers were unhappy, the restaurant's balance sheet was "scary," and the staff was divided into factions.

Carter took all this in, and what she saw was a dusty diamond. "I saw a beautiful and historic building full of mission-era flavor and character that should be, could be, would be *the* place on campus." In her mind's eye, she saw the club bustling. She saw professors and university staff chatting on the lovely enclosed patio and enjoying high-quality, appealing, yet inexpensive meals. She smiled as she envisioned the club assisting alumni in planning wonderful, personal, and professionally catered wedding receptions and anniversary celebrations. Carter could see a happy staff whose primary concern was customer satisfaction, a kitchen that produced a product far superior to "banquet food," and a catering staff that did whatever it took to make an event exceptional. She wasn't quite sure how the club had deteriorated to the extent it had, but that really didn't matter. She decided to ignore the quick fix and set out to teach everyone how unique and wonderful the club could be.

Over the next two years, as she talked with customers and worked with her staff, she instilled her vision of the club as a restaurant that gives 110 percent of itself, that values good food, and that wants to exceed the expectations of its customers—a restaurant that's a celebration of good food and good company. Not surprisingly, as food and service quality began to improve, smiles became more prevalent among customers and staff and sales began to rise: 20 percent the first year and 30 percent again the next. When a top financial manager of the university asked how she had managed to turn around the finances so quickly and dramatically, Carter responded, "You can't turn around numbers. The balance sheet is just a reflection of what's happening here, every day, in the restaurant. I just helped the staff realize what we're really all about. It was always here," she said, "only perhaps a little dusty, a little ignored, and a little unloved. I just helped them see it."

NONVERBAL EXPRESSIVENESS

In explaining why particular leaders have a magnetic effect, people often describe them as charismatic. But *charisma* has become such an overused and misused term that it's almost useless as a descriptor of leaders. Bernard Bass, professor emeritus of organizational behavior at the State University of New York, has done extensive research on charisma. He comments, "In the popular media, charisma has come to mean anything ranging from chutzpah to Pied Piperism, from celebrity to superman status. It has become an overworked cliché for strong, attractive, and inspiring personality."[19]

Social scientists have attempted to investigate this elusive quality in terms of observable behavior. Howard S. Friedman, professor of psychology at the University of California, Riverside, and his colleagues studied the communication of emotions from the perspective of nonverbal expressiveness.[20] They found that those who were perceived to be charismatic were simply more animated than others. They smiled more, spoke faster, pronounced words more clearly, and moved their heads and bodies more often. They were also more likely to touch others during greetings. What we call *charisma,* then, can better be understood as human expressiveness.

It's interesting to note that similar reactions to nonverbal behavior can be observed in the world of children. The French ethologist Hubert Montagner has been studying the gestural language of children for several decades. He has developed a system for classifying the way children relate to each other nonverbally into five categories of interpersonal behavior:[21]

- Attractive actions
- Threatening actions
- Aggressive actions
- Gestures of fear and retreat
- Actions that produce isolation

Montagner's findings reveal that the children who become the leaders in their groups use attractive actions, not aggressive actions. At least in the world of the very young, real leaders—those who are naturally followed—aren't the young Rambos. They're not the hitters, scratchers, pinchers, biters, and pullers. The natural leaders are those who offer toys to others, lightly touch or caress, clap hands, smile, extend a hand, lean sideways, and the like. Adults can learn much about leading from children: it's not aggression that attracts; rather, it's warmth and friendship.

Demonstrating Personal Conviction

Becoming more expressive in our daily lives isn't only about better technique—more examples, metaphors, word pictures, quotations, slogans, and the like. Neither is it simply learning to speak with more eloquence and style. While these elements do play an important role, they are not in themselves enough. The greatest inhibitor to enlisting others in a common vision is a lack of personal conviction. There's absolutely no way that you can convince others, over the long term, to share a dream if you're not convinced of it yourself. You must be sincere in your own belief.

Imagine recruiting people to give their all for a goal that you're not convinced should be pursued. You'd be unable to summon the energy to be animated. You'd find it difficult to be upbeat and positive. Even great communicators can't effectively present the same speech over and over again if they don't believe in the message.

We're all able to spot lack of sincerity in others. We detect it in their voices; we observe it in their eyes; we notice it in their posture. We each have a sixth sense for deceit and can usually tell the fraudulent from the real. So there's a very fundamental question that a leader must ask before attempting to enlist others: "What do I believe in?" The true force that attracts others is the force of the heart. Inspirational presentations are heart to heart, spirit to spirit, life to life. It's when you share what's in your soul that you can truly move others. (We'll say considerably more about authenticity in Chapters Nine and Ten, when we discuss modeling the way.)

We remember sitting across the lunch table from Phil Turner one afternoon. He had been promoted to plant manager of the Wire and Cable Division of Raychem a year before, and we were curious about how he was doing. Near the close of our interview, we asked, "Phil, why do you do what you do?" He didn't answer for a few seconds. His throat got that tightness we all get when a strong emotion wells up inside and chokes us. He paused, took a breath, and replied, "Kindness." Turner cares deeply for the people he leads. That single word, his tone of voice, and his facial expression spoke more volumes than the most eloquent sermon. For us, that was truly an inspiring moment.

Committing to the Challenge:
Leading with Shared Vision

Leaders breathe life into their visions. They communicate their hopes and dreams so that others clearly understand and accept them as their own. Leaders know what motivates their constituents. They show others how their values and interests will be served by a particular long-term vision of the future. Above all, they're convinced of the value of that vision and, like Turner, share that genuine belief with others.

Leaders use a variety of modes of expression to make their abstract visions concrete. Through skillful use of metaphors, symbols, positive language, and personal energy, they generate enthusiasm and excitement for the common vision. In this commitment, we provide some action-steps that you can take to enlist the support of others.

Commitment Number 4

Enlist Others in a Common Vision by Appealing to Their Values, Interests, Hopes, and Dreams

➤ Identify your constituents.

Make a list of all the individuals or groups of individuals you want to enlist in your vision of the future. Your organizational managers and direct reports are obvious groups. In all probability, you'll also want your peers, customers, and suppliers to buy into your dream. Perhaps you'll also want the support of the citizens of your local community. There are bound to be elements of your vision that will be of interest to the state and the nation in which you do business. You may even have a global vision. And don't limit your list to present constituents only. As your organization grows and develops, it will want to attract new people to it. You'll want future generations to take an active interest in what you want to accomplish. Their needs and values should also be considered. Today's students are tomorrow's employees, customers, and investors. They may be the ones who actually help you to realize what you only dream of today. The point is this: identify those who have a stake today and will have a stake tomorrow in the outcomes of what you envision.

➤ Find the common ground.

In order to attract people from diverse backgrounds and interests, you must discover what aspirations, goals, needs, and dreams they have in common. They're bound to differ in much of what they value; you must work through the differences to find what can bring them together. Your ability to enlist the people you want is dependent on how effective you are at detecting the tie that binds.

There are numerous ways you can find out what people want, from sophisticated market research techniques to simple surveys. Each has its usefulness. But no technique can substitute for face-to-face human interaction. The very best way to get to know what other people want is to sit down and talk with them on their turf. If you feel that you don't really understand people in the factory, move your desk onto the floor for the next few weeks. If you feel that you don't know much about the store owners who buy your packaged goods, ride the route trucks once a week for a year. Get out there and make contact. Ask one simple question: "What do you most want from this organization?"

Then, when you've gathered the data and have a true feel for your constituents, sit down and see what patterns and themes emerge. There are bound to be several. For example, Tom Melohn found out that customers of North American Tool and Die (NATD) wanted "quality, service, price"—in that order. At first, Melohn was surprised by this. He had spent twenty-five years in the packaged goods industry, where a fraction of a cent made a major difference. So he kept on asking, and the customers kept on telling him: first quality, then service, then price. Not surprisingly, the focus of NATD today is first and foremost on quality.

One other hint about finding the common ground: avoid being too specific. Vision statements aren't job descriptions. They're not product or service specifications. To have the broadest appeal, visions must be encompassing. They should transcend the day-to-day work (voluntary or paid) and find expression in higher-order human needs. Visions should uplift and ennoble.

➤ **Develop your interpersonal competence.**

If you feel your interpersonal abilities have room for improvement, sign up for the first available training opportunity. There is strong evidence that you can dramatically improve face-to-face communication skills through effective training. Every leader ought to know how to paraphrase, summarize, express feelings, disclose personal information, admit mistakes, respond nondefensively, ask for clarification, solicit different views, and so on.

Flexibility is an important demonstration of your interpersonal competence. The five fundamental practices of exemplary leadership that we've identified are demonstrated in every country in which we've done our research, yet there's no one best *style* of leadership. You should be able to use all the practices and behaviors we discuss in this book—and be versatile enough to adopt a style that's appropriate to each different situation you face.

Versatility also expands your capacity to function in a wide range of cultures and environments. If you get feedback that you're too one-dimensional in your approach to situations, look into a development program designed to expand your flexibility. And if you're planning a trip to another county, be sure to study the culture. Your international colleagues will feel more comfortable around you (and you around them).

The higher you advance in an organization, the more presentations you give to an ever-widening audience. A course in effective presentation skills will benefit you more than any other. Don't wait until your next promotion to improve your communication skills. If you haven't taken a public speaking course yet, sign up for the next available class.

Presentation workshops can help you learn effective techniques for getting your ideas across. They can also help you gain confidence in yourself. According to Bert Decker, founder and president of Decker Communications, a nationwide communication training and consulting firm, people are more afraid of having to give a speech than they are of dying.[22] Overcoming the anxiety of public speaking is a very important benefit of effective presentation programs.

➤ **Breathe life into your vision.**

Remember that vision statement you wrote at the end of the previous chapter? Critique it and look for places where you can add inspiration to it (breathe life into it) to make it come alive for your audience. Prepare yourself now to make the vision sing.

Use as many forms of expression as you can to transform the intangibles of your vision into tangibles. Enrich your language with stories, metaphors, analogies, and examples. Think of ways to use symbols, banners, posters, and other visual aids in your presentations. Use whatever will best help your audience hear, taste, smell, see, and touch the vision. Make any abstractions—such as freedom, service, respect, quality, or innovation—concrete so that others can recognize what you imagine. When it comes to visions, we're all from Missouri: we need to be shown.

Remember what Maureen Saltzer Brotherton told her staff at the *Valley Times?* The address quoted in the previous chapter wasn't Brotherton's first attempt at verbalizing her thoughts. She wrote her first draft at The Leadership Challenge Workshop™ and then revised, honed, edited, and revised again until she thought it expressed her ideas just right. Even Martin Luther King's famous "I Have a Dream" speech was tried out on several occasions for smaller gatherings and refined before its seemingly spontaneous presentation before the crowd at the Lincoln Memorial.

If you need some help in adding tangibility to your presentations, spend a little time studying advertising and the performing arts. Those in theater and advertising have to get their audiences to experience something vicariously. Both fields are rich sources of creative ideas on how to convey abstract concepts and how to appeal to human emotions.

➤ Speak positively.

When talking about mutual aspirations, don't say *try,* say *will* and *are.* There's no room for tentativeness or qualifiers in statements of vision. Sure, there are lots of contingencies and reasons why something might not happen. But citing eighty-three potential obstacles and thirty-three conditions that must be met will only discourage people from joining the cause. You need not be excessively Pollyannaish or unrealistic; go ahead and talk about the hardships and difficult conditions—just don't dwell on them.

Reasonable people know that great achievements require hard work. Let people know that you have the utmost confidence in their ability to succeed. Tell them that you're certain that they'll prevail. Tell them that you have faith in them. Remember, leaders are *possibility* thinkers, not *probability* thinkers.

Enthusiasm and emotions are catching, so let yours show. Smile. Use gestures and move your body. Speak clearly and quickly. Make eye contact. All of these signals are cues to others that you're personally excited about what you're saying.

If you don't perceive yourself as an expressive person, begin to practice expressiveness by talking to a favorite friend about what most excites you in life. As you do this, pay attention to your verbal and nonverbal behavior. If possible, turn on the video camera so that you can watch yourself later. We bet that you'll discover that when you talk about things that excite you, you do a lot of the things we've just described.

➤ Speak from the heart.

None of these suggestions will be of any value whatsoever if you don't believe in what you're saying. If the vision is someone else's, and you don't own it, it will be very difficult for you to enlist others in it. If you have trouble imagining yourself actually living the future described in the vision, you'll certainly not be able to convince others that they ought to enlist in making it a reality. If you're not excited about the possibilities, how can you expect others to be? The prerequisite to enlisting others in a shared vision is genuineness. The first place to look before making that speech is in your heart.

When asked how she was able to lead the development team for the PCnet family of Advanced Micro Devices, breaking all barriers and launching this extremely successful family of products, Laila Razouk, now director of engineering, replied simply, "I believed. Believing is a very important part of the action. You have to have faith. If you don't have that, then you're lost even before you get started." It's easy to understand why people are eager to follow her: "If I believe in something badly enough, and if I have the conviction, then I start picturing and envisioning how it will look if we did this or if we did that. Then by sharing these thoughts with other people, the excitement grows and people become part of that picture. Then without much effort—with energy, but not much effort—the *magic* starts to happen. People start to bounce ideas back and forth, they get involved, brainstorm, and share ideas. Then I know I don't have to worry about it."

How successful would the project have been if instead Razouk had thought, "This project will never work. The person who thought this up doesn't understand the details. I'm doing this because I'm forced to, but I really think this project is a stupid idea!" For Razouk, the net effect of speaking from the heart, as she explains, was that "by openly sharing what I saw, what I knew, and what I believed—not by dictating it, but by being willing to iterate and adjust things—I got other people involved."

➤ Make the intangible tangible.

Because visions exist in the future, leaders have to get others in the present to imagine what that future will look like, feel like, sound like, even smell like. In short, just as attributes such as quality, service, and responsiveness don't exist in nature but must be defined by reference to that which is concrete and identifiable, your vision—an intangible—must be made tangible.

Slogans, theme songs, poetry, quotations, and humor are powerful tools that you can use to express the vision and values of your organization. While underutilizing these forms of expression, some people overutilize numbers and acronyms, believing that these are more concrete or efficient ways of communicating an organization's strategy and practices. In fact, numbers and acronyms are more abstract and take more time to understand. They're not nearly as descriptive as images, metaphors, or analogies.

Symbols are another form of expression that can capture the imagination. The Statue of Liberty is a symbol of America as the land of freedom of opportunity. The eagle is a symbol of strength, the olive branch a symbol of peace, and the lion a symbol of courage. The bull is a hopeful symbol of rising prices in the stock market. Wells Fargo Bank uses the stagecoach to symbolize its pioneering spirit. Mary Kay Cosmetics uses the bumblebee as a symbol for doing what others say can't be done.

Robert Swiggett made apt use of metaphor in helping Kollmorgen Corporation employees get a sense of how the company saw itself. When he was chairperson and chief executive officer of the company, he would ask different groups of employees to try the following exercise, described here in his own words:

> Visualize a very bright white light. Visualize that light about three feet in front of your forehead toward the ceiling. It's bright, it's white, and

it's pure. Try to visualize the largest diamond you've ever seen coming in from the right. It's maybe three inches long. It's cut beautifully. The diamond moves over where the light is, and the light is absorbed into the heart of that brilliantly cut three-inch diamond.

Visualize the diamond slowly rotating, and every time one of the facets of the diamond lines up with your eyes, it scintillates . . . flashes . . . blue-white light coming out of the heart of that diamond. Think about the white light in a verbal sense. Think that it means number one. First. Absolutely first. Think about the diamond with the white light in the center that means first. I want to use that physical image to represent our vision of what we're trying to do in our company. . . . It all starts with the idea of being first. First with the best. And what we try to do in our business, in some way, is to measure everything we do against this big diamond in the sky, being the first with the best.

Using the metaphor of the "diamond in the sky" and the visualization exercise, Swiggett helped others to see the purpose of Kollmorgen and the concept of being number one technically and in every other way. He enlisted others in his vision of the company. He breathed life into the vision, made it scintillate, made it glitter. He communicated what he hoped others would come to accept and support as their own.

➤ Listen first—and often.

Listening is one of the key characteristics of exemplary leaders. In our discussion of challenging the process, we identified listening as part of a leader's repertoire for gaining outsight. To truly hear what your constituents want—what they desperately hope to make you understand, appreciate, and include within the vision—requires that you periodically suspend your regular activity and spend time listening to others. Note the ratio between the number of your ears and your mouth, and make certain that you listen twice as often as you talk.

Doug Podzilni, sales manager for Cargill, makes a point of finding off-line time with people, often spontaneously, as in the example he describes here:

As a sales manager traveling on the road with salespeople, I've found it's easy to fall into the trap of trying to fit more meetings into the day than the time allows. Recently, I surprised one salesperson by saying, "Let's stop and do something fun." We decided to go to a local ice cream parlor for a midafternoon snack. In that relaxed atmosphere, we talked about all sorts of things. As it turns out, this particular salesman had some serious personal issues on his mind. He took this opportunity to ask a few sensitive questions about his compensation, his future with the company, and the future of our division. He had been thinking about all of these questions for some time but had either not found the opportunity or had not felt comfortable in asking. I'm sure they were affecting his productivity and morale.

By taking the time to listen, Podzilni was able to find out information from this salesperson that would never have been revealed through formal communication channels. "Over chocolate sundaes," says Podzilni with a smile, "we addressed his concerns and strengthened the alignment between what he and the company were trying to achieve."

Even the most enthusiastic people can't get extraordinary things done unless they, as leaders and constituents, work together. In the next chapter, we'll explore how leaders foster collaboration and create unity of effort among group members.

Commitment Number 4

Enlist Others in a Common Vision by Appealing to Their Values, Interests, Hopes, and Dreams

➤ Identify your constituents.

➤ Find the common ground.

➤ Develop your interpersonal competence.

➤ Breathe life into your vision.

➤ Speak positively.

➤ Speak from the heart.

➤ Make the intangible tangible.

➤ Listen first—and often.

Source: The Leadership Challenge by James M. Kouzes and Barry Z. Posner. Copyright © 1995.

PART 4
Enabling Others to Act

➤ **Challenge the Process**

➤ **Inspire a Shared Vision**

➤ **Enable Others to Act**

➤ **Model the Way**

➤ **Encourage the Heart**

7

Foster Collaboration

Promoting Cooperative Goals
and Mutual Trust

We needed everyone to understand that it was our *business.*
We were the ones in control of our own destiny.
—ROBERT OWYANG
Program Manager
Hewlett-Packard

Early in our research, we asked Bill Flanagan, vice president of operations for Amdahl Corporation, to describe his personal best. After a few moments, Flanagan said that he couldn't do it. Startled, we asked him why. Flanagan replied, "Because it wasn't *my* personal best. It was *our* personal best. It wasn't *me*. It was *us.*"

In the more than 550 original cases that we studied, we didn't encounter a single example of extraordinary achievement that occurred without the active involvement and support of many people. And this hasn't changed with our subsequent research. In thousands of additional stories, from all professions and from around the globe, people continue to tell us, "You can't do it alone. It's a team effort."

151

In no one's personal-best narrative was creating competition between group members described as a way to achieve high performance. On the contrary, people passionately promoted teamwork as the interpersonal route to success, particularly when the conditions were extremely challenging and urgent. As our respondents recognized, getting extraordinary things done in organizations must be *everyone's* business. Our empirical analyses confirm the strong relationship between leadership effectiveness and enabling others to act.

Collaboration has at last assumed its rightful place among the processes for achieving and sustaining high performance. Bookstores bulge with new titles about cross-functional teams, task forces, networks, and groupware.[1] The increasing emphasis on reengineering, world-class quality, knowledge work, and electronic communication, along with the surging number of global alliances and local partnerships, is testimony to the fact that in a more complex, wired world, the winning strategies will be based upon the "*we* not *I*" philosophy.

Collaboration Improves Performance

If the goal is to improve performance, the winning bet will be on cooperation over competition every time. Competition almost never results in the best performance; pursuing excellence is a collaborator's game.

Author and university lecturer Alfie Kohn explains it this way: "The simplest way to understand why competition generally does not promote excellence is to realize that *trying to do well and trying to beat others are two different things.*"[2] One is about accomplishing the superior; the other, about making someone else inferior. One is about achievement; the other, about subordination. Rather than focusing on stomping the competition into the ground, true leaders focus on creating value for their customers, intelligence and skill in their students, wellness in their patients, and pride in their citizens.

Kohn's extensive review of the research on competition versus cooperation leads to this additional conclusion: "Competition also precludes the more efficient use of resources that cooperation allows."[3] Indeed, competition actually works at cross-purposes with success. It demands more resources than cooperation; thus, in a world that's trying to do more with less, competitive strategies naturally lose to strategies that promote collaboration. Maybe that's why we're seeing so many strategic alliances these days: cooperation and collaboration make good business sense.

Management professor Dean Tjosvold of Simon Fraser University in British Columbia describes the differences in behavior and results between people working in groups cooperatively and those working competitively:

> In cooperation, people realize that they are successful when others succeed and are oriented toward aiding each other to perform effectively. They encourage each other because they understand the other's priorities help them to be successful. Compatible goals promote trust. People expect help and assistance from others and are confident that they can rely on others; it is, after all, in others' self-interests to help. Expecting to get and give assistance, they accurately disclose their intentions and feelings, offer ideas and resources, and request aid. They are able to work out arrangements of exchange that leave all better off. These interactions result in friendliness, cohesion, and high morale.
>
> Competitors, by contrast, recognize that others' successes threaten and frustrate their own aspirations. They are closer to reaching their goals when others perform ineffectively and fail to reach theirs. They suspect that others will not help them, for to do so would only harm their own chances of goal attainment. Indeed, they may be tempted to try to mislead and interfere in order to better reach their own goals. They are reluctant to discuss their needs and feelings or to ask for or offer assistance. Closed to being influenced by the other for fear of being exploited, they doubt that they can influence others, except by coercion and threat. These interactions result in frustration, hostility, and low productivity, especially in joint tasks.[4]

Leaders also personally benefit from behaving collaboratively. In our research, we've found that a leader who fosters collaboration is much more likely to be seen as personally credible than one who promotes competition between members of the same organization. Indeed, as leaders foster collaboration and strengthen others, the constituents' assessments of the leaders' personal credibility, upward influence, and workgroup esprit de corps rise— as do constituents' own levels of job satisfaction and commitment. Dean and

Mary Tjosvold describe a study they conducted in a medical laboratory: "Leaders who had cooperative relationships, results suggested, inspired commitment and were considered competent. Competitive and independent leaders, on the other hand, were seen as obstructive and ineffective."[5]

Even more extensive research convincingly demonstrates that individuals and groups perform better when they cooperate. David W. Johnson and Roger T. Johnson, researchers from the University of Minnesota, reviewed 581 empirical studies that considered how cooperative, competitive, and/or individualistic goal situations affected achievement or performance.[6] Of the findings on the effects of cooperation versus competition on productivity and achievement, 60 percent favored cooperation, 8 percent favored competition, and 32 percent found no difference. In the studies examining the effects of cooperation versus individualism, 53 percent favored cooperation, 6 percent favored individualism, and 41 percent found no difference. The researchers concluded that "cooperation promoted greater productivity and achievement than did interpersonal competition or individualistic efforts. . . . [C]ooperation promoted higher achievement on all types of tasks."[7] Cooperation also promoted higher-quality reasoning, more frequent gains in process, and greater transfer of learning.

Other research findings offer no less dramatic data refuting the popular contention that competition enhances performance. Studies involving such diverse groups as business executives, research scientists, airline reservation agents, fifth- and sixth-graders, and college undergraduates show remarkable consistency.[8] Whether achievement is measured in terms of salary levels, academic citations, work performance, or grade-point averages, cooperation is much more likely to produce positive outcomes than is competition. For leaders the message is clear: *cooperate to succeed!*

As paradoxical as it might seem, leadership is *more* essential—not less—when collaboration is required. With multiple constituencies come diverse and frequently conflicting interests. World-class performances aren't possible unless there's a strong sense of shared creation and shared responsibility.[9] Central to the process is a leader who can skillfully

- Develop cooperative goals
- Seek integrative solutions
- Build trusting relationships

All leaders must master these three *essentials* of fostering collaboration.

Developing Cooperative Goals

Brian Coleman, manager of tool and dies, had a problem in his Dagenham, England, Ford Motor Company plant. Relationships between workers and management were antagonistic, quality was awful, productivity was low, and production scheduling was erratic. Coleman was asked by the operations manager and the manager of stamping and body construction to serve on a team of managers, engineers, and foremen to reduce costs and improve productivity.

As Coleman says, "They identified 11 existing systems that would supposedly solve the problem. At that point, I told the group, 'I don't buy it; you really believe these 11 procedures will make everything OK? They don't work!'"[10] After that initial meeting, the operations manager asked Coleman how things went. Coleman responded honestly—and was asked to head the quality program.

Coleman agreed, on the condition that he could pick his own team. His first choice was a union official, whom he invited to recruit anyone he wanted, as long as each person chosen was interested in quality. Subsequently, this team of management and labor collaboratively cut defects by over two-thirds, doubled productivity, and reduced warranty claims to one-sixth their previous rate. Not only that, the team won the award to develop the next Ford model for Europe. Team members achieved these results because they shared the common goal of quality.

Shared goals bind people together in collaborative pursuits. As individuals jointly work together and recognize that they need each other in order to be successful, they become convinced that everyone should contribute and that, by cooperating, they can accomplish the task successfully.

SUPPORTING RECIPROCITY

In any effective long-term relationship, there must be a sense of mutuality. If one partner always gives and the other always takes, the one who gives will feel taken advantage of and the one who takes will feel superior. In that climate, cooperation is virtually impossible. To develop cooperative goals, leaders must quickly establish a norm of reciprocity within teams and among partners.

Political scientist Robert Axelrod dramatically demonstrated the power of reciprocity in the best-known study of the situation known as "the prisoner's dilemma."[11] Axelrod invited scientists from around the world to submit their strategies for winning in a computer simulation of this test of win-win versus win-lose strategies. In the predicament, two parties (individuals or groups) are confronted with a series of situations in which they must decide whether or not to cooperate. They don't know in advance what the other party will do. There are two basic strategies—cooperate or compete—and four possible outcomes based on the choices players make—win-lose, lose-win, lose-lose, and win-win.

The maximum individual payoff comes when the first player selects a noncooperative strategy and the second player chooses to cooperate in good faith. In this "I win but you lose" approach, one party gains at the other's expense. Although this might seem to be the most successful strategy—at least for the first player—it rarely proves to be successful in the long run, largely because the second player won't continue to cooperate in the face of the first player's noncooperative strategy. Should both parties choose not to cooperate, each attempting to maximize individual payoffs, then both lose. This produces the poorest outcome. If both parties choose to cooperate, both win, though the individual payoff for a cooperative move is less than for a competitive one.

"Amazingly enough," says Axelrod, "the winner was the simplest of all strategies submitted: Cooperate on the first move and then do whatever the other player did on the previous move. This strategy succeeded by eliciting cooperation from others, not by defeating them."[12] Simply put, people who reciprocate are more likely to be successful than those who try to maximize individual advantage.

We should point out that the dilemmas that can be successfully solved by this strategy are by no means restricted to prisoners or theoretical research. We all face similar dilemmas in our everyday lives:

- Should I try to maximize my own personal gain?
- What price might I pay for this action?
- Should I give up a little for the sake of others?
- Will others take advantage of me if I'm cooperative?

Reciprocity turns out to be the most successful approach for such daily decisions, as well as for the prisoner's dilemma, because it demonstrates both a willingness to be cooperative and an unwillingness to be taken advantage of. As a long-term strategy, reciprocity minimizes the risk of escalation: if people know that you'll respond in kind, why would they start trouble? Clearly, the best way for people who know that you'll reciprocate to deal with you is to cooperate and become recipients of cooperation on your part.

Reciprocity also leads to predictability and stability in relationships, which can keep both relationships and negotiations from breaking down.[13] This is in part because the knowledge that we share goals and will reciprocate in their attainment makes working together less stressful.

In developing cooperative goals among individuals or groups, we don't have to rely on people's altruism. One of the methods that Antonio Zárate uses at Metalsa speaks to people's financial well-being instead. According to Zárate, Metalsa hasn't exceeded its expenses budget since it reduced complex departmental budgets into a simple plan that rewards cooperative cost-controlling efforts by individuals within each of its departments. At the beginning of each month, every department receives the total amount of its monthly operating budget as a lump-sum payment—in the form of play money. How the money is "spent" is entirely up to the department's discretion. (Training and maintenance budgets aren't affected by this exercise.) At the end of the year, Metalsa exchanges 50 percent of any play money a department has remaining for an equivalent amount of real currency, which is then distributed equally among all the members of the department. It's simple and it works: all personnel at Metalsa know that if they help their department keep its expenses below budget, they'll be rewarded at the end of the year in proportion to their cooperative success.

Whether the rewards of cooperation are monetary or not, when people understand that they have something to gain by cooperating, they're inclined to recognize the legitimacy of others' interests in an effort to promote their own welfare. The leader's job is to make sure that all parties understand each other's interests and how each can gain from collaboration.

SUSTAINING ONGOING INTERACTION

Axelrod says that the most essential strategy for eliciting cooperation is to "enlarge the shadow of the future."[14] This is because people who expect durable and frequent future interactions are likely to cooperate in the present.

The knowledge that we'll have to deal with someone in the future—that is, that our interactions are durable—ensures that we won't easily forget about how we've treated, and been treated by, others. And when durable interactions are frequent as well, the consequences of today's actions on tomorrow's dealings are that much more pronounced. In addition, frequent interactions between people promote positive feelings on the part of each for the other.[15] Empirical studies point out that as the complexity of the issues increases, greater face-to-face communication is required to integrate differences.[16] To interact, people must be close together. Leaders must therefore provide team members with frequent and lasting opportunities to associate and intermingle. Leaders must help to break down barriers between people by encouraging interactions across disciplines and between departments.

At Yhtyneet Kuvalehdet Oy, a large magazine publisher in Finland, there's a lounge on each floor where writers, editors, and other personnel can gather to watch CNN. There people quickly get into discussions of the late-breaking news stories. A central courtyard inside the building is open to all floors; it includes a stage for lunch-time announcements and afternoon concerts. Everyone must pass through that courtyard to get to the elevator and stairs. Balconies on each floor extend the courtyard by allowing people to lean out and observe the "street scenes." People working in this building couldn't avoid interaction if they wanted to.

Leaders can consciously use physical layout (as in the above example), shared resources, and a variety of other mechanisms to encourage frequent and durable interactions among employees. Even something as simple as a question is useful. One manufacturing manager told us that she frequently asked questions that required supervisors to gather input before they could respond. For example, she might ask a production supervisor, "What does the customer think of this new feature of our product?" The supervisor would then search out information from marketing or sales. The manufacturing manager's goal was to consciously create a communicating environment at all levels. She realized that the more frequent these types of interaction, the greater the cooperation—and the better the quality and service to the customer.

EMPHASIZING LONG-TERM PAYOFFS

Another strategy for promoting cooperation is to emphasize long-term payoffs—that is, to make certain that the long-term benefits of mutual cooperation are greater than the short-term benefits of taking advantage of the other party (or simply not cooperating). Leaders who align constituents with a common vision of the future are much more likely to gain their cooperation than those who focus on short-term victories. Here you can see the necessary relationship between the practices of inspiring a shared vision and enabling others to act.

City mayors understand that to successfully change the shape of their communities, they must pull together disparate local leaders—labor and trade councils, political activists, and business, education, and health care officials—to envision a future community that serves the best interests of everyone involved. Often each of these constituents must trade short-term gains for long-term payoffs.

Emphasizing the long term is also effective in helping people deal with short-term setbacks. Leaders reframe any such incidents as learning experiences that will help the team to meet more difficult challenges in the future. By emphasizing the ultimate goal, leaders strengthen team members' resolve.

Seeking Integrative Solutions

The conflict between Israel and the Palestinian Liberation Organization, stemming from a mutually fierce refusal to acknowledge the legitimate existence of the other (and the other's claim to the land they both call home), was ignited by the creation of the state of Israel following World War II. The growth of Israeli settlements in Israeli-occupied territories following the 1967 Middle East War further aggravated the tension. Thus, when Shimon Peres (Israel's foreign minister) and Mahmoud Abbas (the foreign policy aide for the PLO) began their historic negotiations in Madrid in 1990, it appeared that they had an intractable conflict before them. Indeed, as long as either/or thinking ruled, no agreement could be reached.

The stalemate was broken when an integrative solution, modeled after the 1978 Camp David accords, was proposed: since Israel was primarily concerned about protecting its citizens from terrorist activity and the PLO was primarily interested in securing self-determination for the Palestinian people (and gaining prestige), both sides agreed to an interim stage of Palestinian self-rule in Jericho and the Gaza Strip while permitting the 4,000-plus Jewish settlers who lived among the 900,000 Arabs in the area to retain Israeli Army protection and ownership of their land. They further agreed to work together on a five-year plan leading to Israel's return of the entire West Bank (except East Jerusalem) to Palestinian administration by 1998.

The Israeli-Palestinian accord, ceremoniously signed and sealed by a handshake between Israel's Prime Minister Yitzhak Rabin and PLO Chairman Yasser Arafat in September 1993, is a tribute to the leaders' success at finding an integrative solution to the deep-seated conflicts that divided their people, and it led to their being awarded the 1994 Nobel Peace Prize (together with Shimon Peres.)[17] Leaders who foster collaboration search for integrative solutions like these. With integrative solutions, people change their thinking from an either/or (or zero-sum) mentality to a positive perspective on working together.

FOCUSING ON GAINS RATHER THAN LOSSES

In order to find integrative solutions, leaders frame differences and problems so that participants focus on what's to be gained rather than what's to be lost. To hear Bob Phillips, managing partner at Phillips, Jack & Associates, a health care consulting partnership, tell it, there's no better way to create new ventures: "When I try to set up joint ventures—for example, a medical insurance product involving hospitals, physicians, and an insurer—the only way to make it work is to demonstrate to each party what they have to gain. And how what they have to gain can happen *only* if they work together. The emphasis today is on forming strategic alliances among former competitors."

Phillips's strategy finds support in research showing that people respond differently to problems framed in terms of losses than to those framed as gains.[18] Researchers have found that people are more willing to make concessions when negotiators focus on the profits to be achieved rather than on possible costs. The perspective that people bring with them to negotiations greatly influences the outcome as well. The importance of perspective—or the framing effect—suggests that when leaders are trying to get others to compromise, they should frame suggestions to show what both sides will gain from a settlement.[19]

SHARING INFORMATION AND RESOURCES

In our workshops, we put five people to work on a project that requires them to build five squares of equal size from a variety of puzzle pieces.[20] Each person is given a different set of pieces. Some can put a square together with their own pieces (and generally set about doing so immediately); others can't. But the only way the *group* can build five squares is by sharing resources. Group members who build squares with the pieces they receive must break up those squares and give pieces to other members, trusting that they'll get the pieces they need from someone else. As participants soon learn, they must each understand and be committed to their common goal—*and* be willing to share resources—in order to achieve success.

People realize that they can achieve cooperative goals when day-to-day organizational norms encourage them to share information, listen to each other's ideas, exchange resources, and respond to each other's requests through positive interdependence. As in the puzzle-assembly experience described above, people will collaborate when they can actively contribute to the goal of making a whole from their separate pieces.

By consulting with others and getting them to share information, leaders make certain that people feel involved in making decisions that affect them. This is no guarantee that a particular final decision will be accepted, but it's certain to decrease resistance. By seeking diverse inputs, leaders also help to get people's cards out on the table; they provide a more open forum for competing viewpoints to be aired and discussed. Knowing how other people feel about issues enables the leader to incorporate aspects of people's viewpoints into a project and demonstrate to others how their ideas have been heard and included.

Seeking out diverse opinions from a homogeneous group is one thing, but involving culturally diverse groups in problem solving and decision making can present significant challenges to a leader. Research indicates that it takes time to reach high levels of performance from culturally diverse groups. Homogeneous groups are likely to significantly outperform culturally diverse groups on measures of problem identification, quality of solutions, and overall performance in the initial weeks of a task.[21] Similarly, in the initial phase of a project, homogeneous groups are better at group processes than are mixed groups. These differences do, however, eventually disappear. Over time, both types of groups improve;

but the diverse groups improve more, and the performance converges. After thirteen weeks of working together, diverse teams close the performance gap with teams of like individuals and begin to take the lead in the range of perspectives they examine and in the generation of multiple alternatives. After seventeen weeks, differences in overall performance or group process disappear. Study coauthor Larry Michaelsen of the University of Oklahoma adds this observation: "The silver lining (of the study) is that diversity is not only a social imperative but makes good business sense; the dark cloud is that it takes a while to realize the gains."[22] As our workplaces and communities become more diverse, it's crucial that leaders take the time to realize those gains. They're clearly worth it.

GAINING SUPPORT THROUGH ALTERNATIVE CURRENCIES

It's easier and more effective to enlist people's support and backing for a concrete idea than to garner a general endorsement of anything you might want to do.[23] Supporting a specific proposal reduces others' level of risk taking. And while broad-based support seems enticing, it's actually easier to revoke than specific support: its very breadth creates ambiguity and accommodates ready excuses for torpedoing a range of specific proposals.

To gain specific support for a project or proposal, leaders must be able to satisfy the concerns and needs of various constituents. Leaders must generate alternative currencies, much as insurance agents offer specialized and even customized policies to match each prospective client's needs. Thus identifying what others want or need is crucial. Sometimes a constituent might want a specific benefit that the leader is unable to provide. If the leader is able to find an alternative benefit that the constituent values, however, agreement might be reached after all.

The search for alternative currencies that satisfy diverse needs requires that we see differences as creative opportunities.[24] If viewed creatively, differences can generate more alternatives than similarities do. And while we tend to think of currencies in hard-cash terms, in reality a currency can be intangible or tangible. Effective leaders are masters of finding appropriate alternative currencies by asking lots of questions and listening intently to the needs and problems thus exposed.[25]

In searching for integrative solutions, today's leaders must be sensitive to a broad range of political, cultural, organizational, and human issues. In today's global economy, as Rosabeth Moss Kanter emphasizes, "Intercompany relationships are a key business asset, and knowing how to nurture them is an essential managerial skill."[26] Leaders are the human connectors in a wired world, and unless they possess relationship-building skills, there's little hope for local, let alone global, alliances.

Building Trusting Relationships

Trust is at the heart of fostering collaboration. It's *the* central issue in human relationships within and outside the organization. Trust is also an essential element of organizational effectiveness. Individuals who are unable to trust other people fail to become leaders. Because they can't bear to be dependent on the words and work of others, they either end up doing all the work themselves or supervise work so closely that they become overcontrolling. Their demonstration of lack of trust in others results in others' lack of trust in them.

THE IMPORTANCE OF RESTORING TRUST

As we pointed out in Chapter Two, trust in our leaders and our major institutions has been steadily declining over the last few decades. We're now paying the price for that increased cynicism, and the evidence clearly indicates that only by restoring trusting relations can we hope to reinvent our companies and our communities.

Several major research efforts have identified the impact that various levels of interpersonal trust have on group effectiveness.[27] In one study, several groups of business executives in a role-playing exercise were given identical factual information about a difficult manufacturing-marketing policy decision and then asked to solve a problem related to that information as a group. Half of the groups were briefed to expect trusting behavior ("You have learned from your past experiences that you can trust the other members of top management and can openly express feelings and differences with them"); the other half, to expect untrusting behavior.

After thirty minutes of discussion, each team member completed a brief questionnaire. Other executives, who had been observing the team meetings, also completed the questionnaire. The responses of team members and observers were quite consistent: the group members who'd been told that their role-playing peers and manager could be trusted reported their discussion and decisions to be significantly more positive than did the members of the low-trust group on *every* factor measured. In the high-trust group,

- Members were more open about feelings.
- Members experienced greater clarity about the group's basic problems and goals.
- Members searched more for alternative courses of action.
- Members reported greater levels of mutual influence on outcomes, satisfaction with the meeting, motivation to implement decisions, and closeness as a management team as a result of the meeting.

In the group whose participants were told that their manager wasn't to be trusted, genuine attempts by the manager to be open and honest were ignored or distorted. Group members' distrust was so strong that the manager's candor was viewed as a clever attempt to deceive them, and they generally reacted by sabotaging the manager's efforts even further. Managers who experienced rejection of their attempts to be trusting and open responded in kind. Said one who played the manager role, "If I had my way I would have fired the entire group. What a bunch of turkeys. I was trying to be honest with them but they wouldn't cooperate. Everything I suggested they shot down; and they wouldn't give me any ideas on how to solve the problem."[28]

The responses of the other members were no less hostile. Said one, "Frankly, I was looking forward to your being fired. I was sick of working with you—and we had only been together for ten minutes."[29] Not surprisingly, more than two-thirds of the participants in the low-trust group said that they would give serious consideration to looking for another position. People don't want to stay very long in organizations devoid of trust.

What's crucial to keep in mind is that this was *just a simulation*; these people were executives from various organizations attending an executive development program. They behaved and responded as they did simply because they'd been told that they couldn't trust their role-playing manager. They wanted to be rid of each other after only about ten minutes! Trust or distrust can come with a mere suggestion, it seems, and in mere seconds. It's also highly contagious and can spread throughout the group.

After this simulation, participants were asked to think about what factors might have accounted for the differences between the outcomes and feelings reported by the various groups in the experiment. Not one person perceived that trust had been the overriding variable. One executive in the study reported this insight: "I never knew that a lack of trust was our problem (at work) until that exercise. I knew that things weren't going well, but I never really could quite understand why we couldn't work well together. After that experience, things fell into place."[30]

Remembering that trust is key, leaders who build trusting relationships within their team are willing to consider alternative viewpoints and to make use of other people's expertise and abilities. They feel comfortable with the group and are willing to let others exercise influence over group decisions. In contrast, managers in a distrustful environment often take a self-protective posture. They're directive and hold tight the reins of power. Those who work for such managers are likely to pass the distrust on by withholding and distorting information.[31] And as we have seen, when managers who aren't trusted try to be open and honest, their messages are perceived as fabrications.[32]

When people don't trust each other, they ignore and twist facts, ideas, conclusions, and feelings that they believe will increase their vulnerability. Not surprisingly, the likelihood of misunderstanding and misinterpretation increases under these conditions. When we don't trust someone, we resist letting that person influence us. We're suspicious of and unreceptive to his or her proposals and goals, suggestions for reaching those goals, and definitions of criteria and methods for evaluating progress. When we encounter low-trust behavior from others, we in turn are generally hesitant to reveal information to them and reject their attempts to influence us. This feedback only reinforces the originator's low trust. Unless there are changes in behavior, the relationship stabilizes at that low level of trust, increasing the probability that underlying problems will go undetected or be ignored, that inappropriate solutions will be difficult to identify, and that joint problem-solving efforts will deteriorate.

Trust has been shown to be the most significant predictor of individuals' satisfaction with their organization.[33] Regardless of a person's level of participation in decision making, and regardless of the fit between the levels of desired and actual participation, people who experience the most trust in organizational leaders—that is, those who trust their leaders and feel trusted in return—are the most satisfied with their level of participation. Trust makes work easier, because it forms the basis for greater openness between both individuals and departments.

THE TRUST RESPONSE

Psychologists have found that people who are trusting are more likely to be happy and psychologically adjusted than are those who view the world with suspicion and disrespect.[34] We like people who are trusting and seek them out as friends. We listen to people we trust and accept their influence. Thus the most effective leadership situations are those in which each member of the team trusts the others.

One of the clearest advantages of trusting others lies in the way people respond to individuals who are trusting: people who are trusting are regarded by others as trust*worthy*.[35] Conversely, those who don't appear to trust others—including leaders who fail to demonstrate that they trust their constituents—are themselves perceived as less deserving of trust. One especially powerful implication from our credibility research for those from the old command-and-control school of management is that *managers with the highest control scores have the lowest personal credibility.* Why? It's simple. Highly controlling behavior communicates a lack of trust. When individuals demonstrate that they don't trust us, we reciprocate—we don't trust them either. And since trustworthiness is *the* crucial ingredient in the credibility formula, controlling managers lose personal credibility every time they closely watch over others, check up on others, or don't let others make their own decisions.

People's perceptions of how trustworthy others are affect their relationships. For example, if you believe that an individual can't be trusted, you feel little moral pressure to be truthful with him or her. In fact, people often justify lying, cheating, and similar behaviors as self-protective in response to someone perceived as untrustworthy; they suspect that if they told the truth, they'd be fired or otherwise punished.

Because of that fear, the leader's behavior is more critical than that of any other person in determining the level of trust that develops in a group. A classic study conducted for the Life Insurance Agency Management Association revealed that the major difference between low- and high-performing groups of insurance salespeople was the degree to which they reported that they trusted their immediate supervisors.[36] In a recent study of sales managers, those direct reports who had high trust in their managers (in comparison to those with low trust) rated the organization's climate as higher in fairness, cohesiveness, recognition, innovation, and autonomy.[37] To trust the organization, individuals "must be confident that the organization, and especially its agents, will open communications and the opportunity to participate, that they will be dealt with fairly, and that they will be given support."[38] In our studies, we found statistically significant correlations between people's trust in their leader and their subsequent satisfaction with and evaluations of that person's overall leadership effectiveness.

THE NEED FOR VULNERABILITY

Trust is built when we make ourselves vulnerable to others whose subsequent behavior we can't control.[39] If neither person in a relationship takes the risk of trusting at least a little, the relationship is inhibited by caution and suspicion. If leaders want the higher levels of performance that come with trust and collaboration, they must demonstrate their trust *in* others before asking for trust *from* others. Leaders go *first,* as the word implies. That includes going first in the area of trust; it means a willingness to risk trusting others.

Going first to trust is akin to what psychologists refer to as "self-disclosure." Letting others know what we stand for, what we value, what we want, what we hope for, what we're willing (and not willing) to do means disclosing information about ourselves. That can be risky. We can't be certain that other people will want to enroll, will appreciate our candor, will agree with our aspirations, will buy into our plans, or will interpret our words and actions in the way we intend. But by demonstrating willingness to take such risks, leaders encourage others to reciprocate. Once the leader takes the risk of being open, others are more likely to take a similar risk—and thereby take the next step necessary to build interpersonal trust.

Leo Bontempo, president of Ciba-Geigy's U.S. Agricultural Group, knows how difficult self-disclosure can be. After conducting a survey to find out how employees felt about their management, Bontempo discovered that "employees perceived management as much more constrictive and dictatorial than managers perceived themselves. People felt they couldn't contribute." Bontempo and other members of his management team found the results painful and "tried to help each other change."[40]

Among the many actions that Bontempo took in response to survey results were the disclosure of his own scores on the survey and a request for feedback from his team on how he could improve. He also invited his colleagues to do the same with those who reported to them. Such demonstrations of vulnerability contribute to being seen by others as trustworthy and encourage others to take the trust risk.

Of course, it's one thing for Bontempo (or any other leader) to say he'll change as a result of feedback and another to do it. Bontempo did listen and act, however, and he reports that the changes made extraordinary differences to him personally. But for those differences to have happened, listening was critical.

LISTENING, LISTENING, LISTENING

Listening to what other people have to say, and appreciating their particular viewpoints, demonstrates respect for others and for their ideas. Sensitivity to people's needs and interests is an important ingredient in building trust.

We often ask groups why listening builds trust and credibility. The responses are always consistent and instant:

- "Because she's showing an interest in me."
- "Because he's communicating to me that I count, that I matter."
- "Because she's showing that she values my contributions."

People listen more attentively to those who listen to them. For instance, in one management simulation, whenever the person assuming the role of chief executive officer was informed that the financial vice president was a "friend," he or she accepted the latter's influence far more readily than when their relationship was merely professional—even though in all cases the "information" presented by the financial vice president was adequate to solve the company's problem.[41] Friends and family are the most important sources of believable information about everything from health care to restaurants, and leaders who listen are more likely to become accepted as members of the family than those who don't.

Harry Cleberg is one who certainly acts like one of the family, though you might not assume it from his title. Cleberg is CEO of Farmland Industries, the world's thirty-fourth-largest food company, number 145 in the Fortune 500. But you won't often find him on Wall Street or at the company's headquarters; he's most likely to be in his Ford pickup heading out to a farm cooperative.

Farmland is owned by 1,650 member cooperatives that represent 250,000 farm families in 22 states. About 200 days a year, Cleberg travels to meet with the cooperative members and Farmland employees. His purpose in these trips is getting to know the people and listening; in fact, he calls these small-group sessions his "listening posts." Don't complain to Cleberg about how difficult it is to communicate across long distances. He'll tell you quite directly that such an attitude is a cop-out.

And by the way, Cleberg generally isn't listening passively; he's likely to be helping as well. As he strode into the Farmland Feed Mill in Muncie recently, he hollered, "Anybody home? Got anything around here I can do?"[42] By attitude and action, Cleberg is earning the trust of his constituents.

Committing to the Challenge: Getting to Collaboration

Cooperation breeds teamwork as solutions integrating people's needs are sought. Focusing on what's to be gained fosters agreement in what might otherwise be divisive issues. Finally, when leaders bring people together to work on a project, they're concerned not only about the task or problem itself but also about how effectively the group members relate to each other. Relationships lacking in trust interfere with and distort team members' perceptions of the problem and divert energy and creativity from the search for comprehensive, realistic solutions. Leaders help to create a trusting climate by the example they set and through listening. To become trusted, leaders must first show trust in others.

Fostering collaboration begins with creating and sustaining cooperative goals. The best incentive for others to help you is knowing that you'll reciprocate, helping them in return. Help begets help just as trust begets trust. In the following commitment, we offer steps that you can take to foster collaboration and trust.

Commitment Number 5

Foster Collaboration by Promoting Cooperative Goals and Building Trust

➤ Always say *we*.

When considering what you plan to accomplish (or have already accomplished), it's essential that you think and talk in terms of *our* goals. Your task as a leader is to help other people reach *mutual* goals, not *your* goals. Because no one ever accomplishes anything significant alone, your attitude can't be "Here's what I plan to do" but rather "Here's what we plan to do." This inclusive language reinforces the belief that goals are truly collaborative, not exploitative.

Conduct an audit of your language. Take a piece of paper and divide it into two columns. Write *we* at the top of one column and *I* at the top of the other. Ask someone to observe one of your speeches or meetings and count the number of times you say *I* and the number of times you say *we*. On balance, there ought to be more references worded in first-person plural than first-person singular. You can also use this technique when interviewing candidates for positions in which leadership is required. Those who use *I* more than *we* will make poor leaders, and the organization will suffer from their attempts to claim credit for themselves.

➤ Increase interactions.

To make certain that people aren't working in isolation from one another, create physical and psychological opportunities for interaction. Find ways to intentionally create interaction, perhaps through one of the following means:

- By establishing a discussion group, in which people talk about their experiences and mutual needs and develop a sense of community.
- By using open office "landscaping" with low partitions that make access to others easy.
- By having common meeting spaces and bunched offices.

- By holding regular group meetings and having established times for consultation.
- By sharing resources (for example, printers, refrigerators, coffee pots, E-mail, and Internet).
- By limiting the size of any one department or plant to a recognizable number of people. (More than one leader we interviewed said that the size of a single site within the larger organization was limited to the number of people whose names he or she could remember.)
- By forcing people who must work together to get their issues out in the open and work them out within continuous improvement teams and other problem-solving groups.

Create a way for all people who must collaborate to meet at least once a month—more frequently, if possible. Periodic celebrations, office parties, Friday afternoon mixers, and exotic food-of-the-month luncheons are all healthy techniques for bringing people together. Barney Rosenzweig, executive producer of the Emmy Award–winning television program *Cagney & Lacey,* had a popcorn machine outside his office door. That popcorn machine was an important gathering place for members of the cast and crew, as well as for the union truck drivers; many a problem was solved there. Why not put a popcorn machine outside your office?

Some leaders may see these ideas as gimmicky and a waste of time and resources. But the reality is that we can't all be in this together unless we're face to face on both a personal and professional basis. We need opportunities to socialize, exchange information, and solve problems informally.

In addition to these general opportunities for interaction, meet one on one with people to let them know that you value and care about their input. While worthwhile in and of itself, such face-to-face communication also improves the likelihood that you will develop understanding with team members even when opposition or criticism is expected. Consulting on a one-to-one basis also decreases the chance that you'll be surprised by another's arguments or concerns.

The most genuine way to demonstrate that you care and are concerned about other people as human beings is to spend time with them, so schedule some time daily just to get acquainted with others. This time shouldn't be yet another business meeting; instead, plan on unstructured time to joke and kid and learn more about each other as parents, athletes, musicians, artists, or volunteers. Five or ten minutes at a time is sufficient, if done regularly. A few suggestions:

- Walk the halls at least thirty minutes each day, stopping to talk with people who aren't on your daily calendar.
- Forget the chain of command: strike up conversations with colleagues, customers, suppliers, shareholders, and the person next to you in the elevator.
- Don't eat alone at your desk; go out to lunch with people from other functional areas.
- Leave your office door open (if you have one).
- Move your desk onto the factory floor.
- Sip a cup of coffee in everyone's favorite gathering place.
- Put a popcorn machine outside your work area.

Whatever techniques you choose, make sure you take some kind of action *daily* that forces you to interact with people you know (and want to know better) and with people you don't know (and need to).

➤ Focus on gains, not losses.

Begin a problem-solving session by asking the involved parties to state their areas of agreement first, rather than their differences. Michael Doyle, a highly experienced consultant in collaborative problem solving, uses this simple, but extremely powerful, technique to keep people focused on gains, not losses. He also stops periodically and asks the parties to list the things upon which they've agreed. By doing this, Doyle gets people to see how many agreements they've reached rather than how many disagreements they have left to resolve.

In outside negotiations with customers and vendors and inside negotiations with colleagues, you can increase the number of win-win solutions by stating aloud how your goals and others' goals are aligned. This is one of the most effective techniques for creating a sense of mutuality.

Another simple technique for keeping interactions focused on gains rather than losses is to delete the word *but* from your vocabulary. At best, *but* stimulates disagreement; it's likely to be the beginning of an argument. *But* inspires an either-or mentality and is antithetical to integrative and possibility thinking. Eliminating *but* from your vocabulary will free you from focusing on constraints and force you to consider the alternatives about how to make things happen. It can be a difficult word to avoid—and doing so is well worth the effort.

➤ Make a list of alternative currencies.

Think about a current situation that requires negotiation between you and another party. Now divide a piece of paper into four sections. In the upper-left quadrant, write down your needs. In the lower-left quadrant, write down the other party's needs. In the upper-right quadrant, make a list of the alternative currencies—tangible and intangible resources—that the other party controls that might satisfy your needs. In the lower-right quadrant, record the alternative currencies that you control that might satisfy their needs. For an example of a chart in progress, see Exhibit 7.1.

Exhibit 7.1. Sample Alternative Currencies Chart.

My Needs	Other's Currencies
• To have colleagues take more ownership of the success of the business	• Spending time studying the business • Asking more questions about how the department is doing • Listening with understanding to discussion of margins • Submitting timely and accurate expense reports • Contributing cost-saving ideas • Learning other parts of the business—cross-training
Other's Needs	**My Currencies**
• To feel equitably rewarded for efforts to increase business success	• Instituting flextime • Converting to a four-day work week • Providing for employee participation in the bonus plan • Offering cafeteria benefits • Sharing financial information about the company • Showing more respect • Telecommuting

Review all four quadrants of your alternative currencies chart before you enter the negotiation. Then, in the course of the discussion, ask a lot of questions and listen hard for needs and currencies that you hadn't thought of. Instead of making demands and proposing offers, search for the best fit between needs and alternative currencies. You'll be pleasantly surprised at the creativity of the negotiation and the collaborative result.[43]

➤ Form planning and problem-solving partnerships.

Edward E. Lawler III, a University of Southern California professor, has said that high-involvement organizations have the "ultimate advantage." He finds that involvement takes many forms, including job enrichment, improvement groups, work teams, employee surveys, union-management quality-of-worklife programs, gainsharing, employee ownership, and certain pay systems and plant designs.[44] Any part of the organization can be made into an advantage through high involvement.

Take a good look at how you're now solving your problems or doing your planning, especially in those areas that involve the front lines, and consider the following questions:

- Who's currently involved in planning and problem solving?
- Have you delegated planning and problem solving to one of the managers who reports to you?
- Is that person trying to do those tasks alone?
- Have you delegated to staff professionals—the people with the professional and technical education/experience?
- Do you scrupulously avoid "secret" meetings and closed-door sessions?
- Do you keep others informed to prevent surprises and reduce the perceived threat that the unknown often entails?
- How many of the people who actually deliver the service or make the product are involved in solving the problems or planning innovative ways to do things in your organization?
- Have you involved customers, vendors, and other internal organizations on whom you're dependent or who are dependent on you?
- Have you involved other constituents, such as shareholders and citizens?

Your answers to these questions ought to indicate that you've involved the people closest to the work in planning or solving problems associated with it. Do you have 90 percent of the workforce involved in planning and problem solving? We believe that should be your goal—and ultimately, the norm in organizations.

If you're not involving people in planning and problem solving and in the execution of their responsibilities, you're underutilizing the skills and resources in your organization. By delegating authority, you involve others and signal your trust in them. If you don't have a system of delegation, establish one right now. If you're not personally experienced in high-involvement management, get some training yourself and start on a small scale. Begin with a pilot project, learn from that experience, and then broaden your efforts to include more of your colleagues and constituents.

Keep your constituents—including your own manager, your peers, and those who report to you—posted. Just as sharing information with your peers builds trust, so does sharing information with your managers. It increases their security so that they can provide any needed hierarchical blessing for your efforts. Only managers who understand what you're up to can truly support your actions. Make certain to provide people with the materials and coaching necessary to effectively support the project and sell it to those higher up in the company and/or to outside constituencies.

➤ Conduct a collaboration audit.

Just how collaborative is your organization? Conduct a collaboration audit, using the form shown in Exhibit 7.2, to find out. First make a list of the interested parties: for example, you, your peers from other units, anyone who reports directly to you, suppliers, and internal clients. Then, for each interested party, answer the questions included in the audit.

We can't stress enough the power of collaboration. The old American myth that competition is the path to business heaven has died a slow death. Now we need to bury it. We must all recognize that collaboration—whether in school, business, sports, health care, or government—produces more gains than trying to beat the stuffing out of someone or something.

Exhibit 7.2. Collaboration Audit.

Using a scale of 1 to 5, with 1 being low and 5 being high, rate the interested parties on the extent to which they do the following:

1. Talk more about what they will gain than what they will lose from working together _____

2. Involve in decision making those who will be affected by the outcome _____

3. Voluntarily offer help to other parties when they're having difficulty _____

4. Offer resources to other parties without being asked _____

5. Freely pass along information that might be useful to other parties _____

6. Pitch in to help when others are busy or running behind _____

7. Show respect and convey warmth to other people _____

8. Look for alternative currencies when seeking resolution of a dispute _____

9. Ask a lot of questions about the interests of others _____

10. Listen attentively to the needs of others _____

11. Intentionally distort information in order to confuse others _____

12. Intentionally withhold information they know would be valuable to others _____

If you rate any of items 1 through 10 below a 4, you need to take a look at what you can do to develop a more collaborative approach among your constituents. If you rate items 11 and 12 above a 2, take similar action.

➤ Go first.

There's no sure way to get others to trust you or anyone else. We do know, however, that building trust is a process that begins when one party is willing to risk being the first to open up. Demonstrating your trust in other people encourages them to trust in return. If you, the leader, show a willingness to trust others with information (both personal and professional), constituents will be likewise inclined to overcome any doubts they might have about sharing information. Distrust is equally contagious; if you exhibit distrust of others, those others will hesitate to place their trust in you or their colleagues.

To promote trust throughout the organization, be the first to do the following:

- Disclose information about who you are and what you believe.
- Listen attentively and eagerly to what others are saying.
- Seek others out for an informal cup of tea or coffee.
- Invite interested parties to important meetings.
- Ask questions and seek clarity when you don't understand something.
- Say, "I don't know."
- Admit mistakes.
- Acknowledge the need for personal improvement and ask others to help.
- Share information that's useful to others.
- Extend a helping hand.
- Show that you're willing to change your mind when someone else comes up with a good idea.
- Avoid talking negatively about other interested parties.
- Say, "We can trust them."

Trust can't be forced. If someone is bent on misunderstanding people and refuses to perceive them as either well intentioned or competent, there may be little you can do to change that perception. If you find yourself in a climate of fear and distrust created by someone else, recognize that it's quite natural for the people involved to be reluctant to trust others. Give them time, but don't give up.

People must feel safe and secure to develop trust. When contributors' thoughts and ideas are shot down or ridiculed, the climate isn't safe; neither is it conducive to vulnerability (the precursor to opening up and placing our trust in another person). Defensive communication strategies are an indication that we don't feel secure in some way, at some level.

You can moderate a defensive climate by taking these steps whenever possible:

- Providing descriptive rather than evaluative comments
- Paraphrasing others' ideas

- Asking questions for clarification
- Expressing genuine feelings of caring
- Avoiding game playing (such as mechanically patting people on the back) in favor of spontaneity

Being willing to actively seek out, listen to, understand, and utilize other people's perspectives in the projects and adventures you share builds trust. Ultimately, all you can do is demonstrate your trust in others and have faith that they'll respond in kind. But take some initiative: don't wait for others to make the first move. The opening gambit always involves risk—and leaders find that risk well worth taking.

With collaborative goals, integrative thinking, and trusting relationships, people are ready to work with one another to make extraordinary things happen. By strengthening others and giving power away, the leader turns this readiness into action. How this happens and what actions leaders take in the process are discussed in the next chapter.

Commitment Number 5

Foster Collaboration by Promoting Cooperative Goals and Building Trust

➤ Always say *we*.

➤ Increase interactions.

➤ Focus on gains, not losses.

➤ Make a list of alternative currencies.

➤ Form planning and problem-solving partnerships.

➤ Conduct a collaboration audit.

➤ Go first.

Source: The Leadership Challenge by James M. Kouzes and Barry Z. Posner.
Copyright © 1995.

8

Strengthen Others

Sharing Power and Information

Share information so your employees can see how to help—
and they'll improve the business.
—ANTONIO ZÁRATE
Coordinator of the Guiding Team
Metalsa

If citizens are to take responsibility for governing, says Sunne McPeak, they must first be empowered. As president and CEO of the Bay Area Economic Forum and a former member of the Contra Costa County (California) Board of Supervisors, McPeak takes great pride in the large number of her constituents who continue their participation in local government activities long after their direct involvement with her. McPeak knows that when coalitions of highly diverse interests (such as growers and environmentalists in the Coalition to Stop the Peripheral Canal, which she co-chaired) come together, it's impossible for them to reach consensus and forge commitment unless they're provided with the skills and knowledge needed to make good judgments. For McPeak, keeping people informed, developing personal relationships among the participants, involving people in important decisions, and acknowledging and giving credit for people's contributions are essential to any process for reinventing government.

We find that, like McPeak, exemplary leaders make other people feel strong. They enable others to take ownership of and responsibility for their group's success. Long before *empowerment* was written into the popular vocabulary, credible leaders knew that only when their constituents felt strong, capable, and efficacious could they ever hope to get extraordinary things done. Constituents who feel weak, incompetent, and insignificant consistently underperform, they want to flee the organization, and they're ripe for disenchantment, even revolution.

People who feel powerless, be they managers or individual contributors, tend to hoard whatever shreds of power they have. Powerless managers, for example, tend to adopt petty and dictatorial styles. Powerlessness creates organizational systems in which political skills are essential and "covering yourself" and "passing the buck" are the preferred modes of handling interdepartmental differences.[1]

When constituents have very little power, those in positions of authority can easily get people to follow orders. Under such circumstances, authority figures often attribute other people's behavior, no matter how good it is, to their own orders rather than to constituents' abilities and motivations. Stanford University researcher Jeffrey Pfeffer has found that "if behavior occurs in the presence of a great deal of external pressure—either positive in the form of monetary inducements or negative in the form of threats and sanctions—people are likely to conclude that the external forces both caused the behavior and were, in fact, necessary to produce it."[2]

The most insidious thing about external control is that it actually erodes the intrinsic motivation that a person might have for a task. In other words, even the constituents begin to assume that only outside forces will compel them to do anything. And yet intrinsic motivation is essential to getting extraordinary things done. When people do things because they're told to, not because they want to, they don't perform at their best. Thus reliance on external power and control—whether by the authorities or the members—over time diminishes the capacity of individuals and organizations to excel.

This phenomenon was cleverly documented in one experiment involving small workgroups. Employees in some workgroups were allowed to influence decisions about their work (were made powerful, in other words), while those in other workgroups were not (were made powerless). The managers of the powerless groups routinely complained that their employees weren't motivated to work hard. These managers saw their workers as unsuitable for promotion and downplayed their skills and talents, and they evaluated the work output of their employees less favorably than did the managers of powerful workgroups. In fact, the actual output of both groups was roughly equivalent; it was the lack of employee opportunity to exercise influence that caused the managers to see their groups as poor performers.[3]

The opportunity to create a climate where people are involved and important is at the heart of strengthening others. To create this climate, leaders use power in service of others, not in service of their own private interests.

Power in Service of Others

To get a better sense of how it feels to be powerless as well as enabled, try this exercise to clarify your own experiences: Take out a piece of paper and divide it into two columns. Label the left-hand column "Powerless Times" and the right-hand column "Powerful Times." Now think about work-related times when you felt powerless—weak, insignificant, like a pawn in someone else's chess game. Record the actions or situational conditions that contributed to your feelings of powerlessness. Once you've recorded a few examples of powerless times, turn your attention to those times you felt powerful—strong, efficacious, like the creator of your own experience.[4] Record the actions or conditions that contributed to your feelings of powerfulness.

Representative statements that we've received in response to this task in our workshops are shown in the list that follows. See how these compare to your own experiences:

Powerless Times

- I had no input into a hiring decision of someone who was to report directly to me. I didn't even get to speak to the candidate.
- People picked me apart while I was making a presentation, and the champion of the project didn't support me.
- I was told I couldn't ask questions because I lacked the appropriate educational level.
- They treated us like mushrooms. They fed us and kept us in the dark.
- I interviewed job candidates and then got no feedback on the results.
- I worked extremely hard—long hours and late nights—on an urgent project, and then my manager took full credit for it.
- My suggestions, whether good or bad, were either not solicited or—worse—ignored.
- The project was reassigned without my knowledge or input.
- I couldn't get answers to my questions.

Powerful Times

- I was able to make a large financial decision on my own. I got to write a check for $200,000 without being questioned.
- I was asked to take on a project for which I didn't have the experience. I was told, "I know you'll be successful."
- My president supported my idea without question.
- After having received a memo that said, "Cut travel," I made my case about why it was necessary to travel for business reasons; and I was told to go ahead.
- I was five years old, and my dad said, "You'll make a great mechanic one day." He planted the seed. Now I'm an engineer.
- I wanted to put a new program into effect, but we'd reached the funding limit so my project was rejected. I went to a meeting with the president and asked him to take another look at the project. He did, turned to the VP, and said, "Fund it."
- I got lots of helpful and useful suggestions without being criticized.
- All the financial data were shared with me.

As we examine powerless and powerful times, we're struck by one clear and consistent message: *feeling powerful—literally feeling "able"—comes from a deep sense of being in control of our own lives*. When we feel able to determine our own destiny, when we believe we're able to mobilize the resources and support necessary to complete a task, then we persist in our efforts to achieve. But when we feel we're controlled by others, when we believe that we lack support or resources, we show no commitment to excel (although we may comply).[5] Thus any leadership practice that increases another's sense of self-confidence, self-determination, and personal effectiveness makes that person more powerful and greatly enhances the possibility of success.[6]

Test this principle by thinking about a recent interaction with someone who attempted to influence you. Then, with that person and encounter clearly in mind, ask yourself this question: Did you feel more capable and therefore persist in your efforts to succeed? Or did you feel less capable and find your performance slumping? (See Figure 8.1.) Now apply the same test to your own attempts to lead others and consider the results.

Leaders' capacity to strengthen and empower others is naturally influenced by the power that they hold. Leaders' personal power can come from several sources:

Figure 8.1. Examining Interactions.

More capable

Performance and
desire increased

*As a result of the interaction
I've chosen, did I feel more
or less capable of getting
extraordinary things done?*

Less capable

Performance and
desire declined

- Interpersonal competence—the ability to communicate and persuade
- Technical knowledge, skill, and expertise
- Years of experience
- Connections to influential people or to needed resources
- Position and the capacity to dispense rewards and punishments[7]

And what makes constituents feel powerful? Not admiration of leaders' power, certainly. People don't feel strong just because someone else feels strong; they feel efficacious and capable only when they have power themselves. Thus leaders have a choice: they can use their power in service of others, or they can use it for purely selfish ends; they can give their own power away to others, or they can hold onto it for themselves.[8] Credible leaders choose to give it away in service of others and for a purpose larger than themselves. They take the power that flows to them and connect it to others, becoming power generators from which their constituents draw energy.

We've identified five leadership *essentials* for sharing power—what we consider imperative for strengthening others:

- Ensuring self-leadership
- Providing choice
- Developing competence
- Assigning critical tasks
- Offering visible support

By using these keys, leaders significantly increase constituents' belief in their own ability to make a difference.[9]

Ensuring Self-Leadership: Putting People in Control of Their Own Lives

Credible leaders accept and act on the paradox of power: *we become the most powerful when we give our own power away.* We were reminded of that paradox by retired Major General John Stanford, now the county administrator for Fulton County (outside Atlanta). When we first interviewed him at the U.S. Army's Military Traffic Management Command, he told us that "we don't get our power from our stars and our bars. We get our power from the people we lead." It's not exactly what you'd expect to hear from an Army general, yet Stanford's observation is precisely the attitude required of leaders who hope to strengthen others. But traditional thinking promotes the archaic idea that power is a fixed sum: if I have more, then you have less. Naturally, people with this view hold tightly to the power that they perceive is theirs and are extremely reluctant to share it with anyone. This notion is wrongheaded, however, and clearly inconsistent with all the evidence on high-performing organizations.

Among the most extensive and systematic programs of research on organizational power and influence was that of Arnold Tannenbaum and his colleagues at the University of Michigan's Institute for Social Research. Their research was carried out in a variety of public and private organizations in the United States and abroad and has included hospitals, banks, unions, factories, and insurance companies. A vital lesson that they've learned—and one that all leaders should take to heart—is this: the more people believe that they can influence and control the organization, the greater organizational effectiveness and member satisfaction will be.[10] Shared power results in higher job fulfillment and performance throughout the organization.

We discovered this ourselves in an investigation into why some branch offices of a nationwide insurance company were more effective than others.[11] Senior home-office management, familiar with the performance of the branches, identified ten branch offices as high performers and another ten as low performers. These designations were highly correlated with various financial variables (for example, profit, growth, and expense control) and with self-ratings by people within the branch offices. After careful consideration of financial factors, environmental factors (for example, location), and managerial factors, we found that employee power—the sense of being able to influence what was going on in their own offices—was the most significant factor in explaining differences between high- and low-performing branch offices.

All the people in that study recognized the authority that comes with position. Power in the various branch offices was still distributed across hierarchical levels in a typical fashion: people at every level of the organization had more total power than did the people at the level below them.

Despite the uniformity of this hierarchy, the total amount of perceived power in the high-performing branch offices was greater *at every level* than it was in the low-performing offices.

The leaders in the more successful branch offices understood, and acted on, the concept that "power is an expandable pie." They knew that power isn't a zero-sum commodity, requiring that for others to have more, the leader must have less. They knew that the more everyone in the organization felt a sense of power and influence, the greater the members' ownership of and investment in the success of the organization would be. Acceptance of this concept within an organization leads to greater reciprocity of influence: the leader and the constituent are willing to be mutually influenced by one another, and everyone's level of influence increases.

When leaders share power with others, they're demonstrating profound trust in and respect for others' abilities. Leaders create a covenant when they help others to grow and develop, and that help is reciprocated. People who feel capable of influencing their leaders are more strongly attached to those leaders and more committed to effectively carrying out their responsibilities. They *own* their jobs.

The leader who is most open to influence, who listens, and who helps others is the leader who is most respected and most effective—not, as traditional management myth has it, the highly controlling, tough-guy boss.[12] By showing respect, leaders build up credit that can be drawn upon later when they ask constituents to stretch for ever-higher levels of performance. Furthermore, when leaders know what other people want and are sensitive to their needs, they can make assignments that effectively match people's talents with job demands. Under these circumstances, others are less likely to resist direction and more likely to accept it.[13]

BELIEVING IN OTHERS

The importance and potential benefits of believing in others are well demonstrated in the success of Kim Greer's team in the face of an enormous challenge. Greer was vice president of property services at Household Credit Services (HCS) when the company announced its plan to launch a co-branded credit card with General Motors. The GM Card was to be launched within nine months and was expected to more than double the company's customer base of four million within the first year.

Every department at HCS would need to hit the ground running to meet the deadline, and *everyone* would need more staff. It was up to Greer and the property services staff to provide the space and workstations to accommodate the anticipated rapid and explosive growth in personnel in a facility that was already stretched at its seams.

Yet Greer knew the team was ready for the challenge: "We knew that we were going to have a problem long before senior management thought to tell us to do something about it. We have a better idea of what staffing it takes to do a certain volume of business. . . . We see it more globally. We knew what it was going to take to handle the business."

According to Greer, his team developed the only viable solution: "The key for me was getting everyone [on the property services staff] involved from the start, with input into developing and evaluating the alternatives. All I did was ask these questions: What problems will we have? And what can we do to best implement the best alternative? Everyone had to come up with what it would take from their areas to do each alternative and what the timeline and costs would be. By the time we finished, they all knew what the only viable alternative was. I didn't have to tell them."

After weighing a number of alternatives, the property services staff realized that downsizing the existing management workstations was the only way to provide the space needed and keep the departments together. It would be a complicated process, requiring the full buy-in and support of those involved. In fact, this solution was perhaps the most difficult to execute of the alternatives considered; however, the property services staff concluded that it would best serve the needs of the company.

Because Greer believed that a leader shouldn't need to tell talented people how to do their jobs, he simply made sure that staff members tackling the downsizing were all organized, on schedule, and headed in the same direction. In reviewing his role in the project, Greer emphasized the importance of trusting his staff: "After the alternatives were well defined, I knew what it meant and what we would have to do. There were no surprises. The team said that we would have to do this on weekends; it was their idea and decision. They dictated the schedule, the hours, the days. I also made it their responsibility to figure out how to get everyone else [in other departments] involved. . . . I stayed out and let them assume responsibility. It was the only way."

Trusting and respecting the talents of others are skills that appear to come naturally to Greer, as his philosophy regarding staff direction reveals: "I make sure to give the freedom to do it their own way, even if it's not the way I would do it."

Although Greer chose not to directly control the project, he felt that it was important that he control the process: "I insist on complete communication between team members and [insist] that timelines and deadlines are met. My role is to intervene, whether behind the scenes or by bringing people together to work it out, when teamwork isn't happening. It's important to recognize problems immediately and resolve them, or they will inevitably get worse. Little problems become huge personality conflicts. I cannot let that happen."

Greer stayed in close communication with key staff members, giving support and feedback—though without any formal meetings. According to Christin (Missy) Stockton, the facilities planner who worked on the project, Greer "gives us a lot of freedom in making decisions. There's a lot of trust. He says funny things like 'If you think it's OK, then it's probably right.' What's nice for us is that he gets very involved in the design—yet you never feel controlled; he's very hands off. It's essential that he knows and understands the details. He'd often come by at the end of the day to see what was happening and make suggestions. But then he'd always say, 'You should do what you want.' We knew what he meant and where we stood. It made it easier to work."

Stockton felt that Greer's unshakable faith in team members' abilities was one of the major reasons for the success of the project. According to Stockton, "The entire project was one gigantic risk. No one talked about what would happen if it didn't work; we all believed it was the only way." After describing the monumental tasks involved in nearly doubling the number of workstations and keeping productivity losses to a minimum during the transition, Stockton acknowledged that Greer's "biggest job was just getting us all to believe that it would really be fine. I figured that he knew better than we did, so I believed we could do it too."

And do it they did. Thanks in large part to the efforts of those in property services, the launch of the GM Card has been called the most successful introduction in the history of the credit card industry. It skyrocketed HCS from the tenth- to the fifth-largest credit card company in the nation.

Greer believed in others, and they in turn came to believe in themselves. A synergistic and circular process, such as that demonstrated in the

Greer case, is created as power and responsibility are extended to others and as people respond successfully. As constituents increase their competencies, even further amounts of power and responsibility can be extended. As more responsibility is assumed by constituents, leaders can expend more energy in other areas, enhancing their own sphere of influence and bringing additional resources back to their units to be distributed once again among the group members.

SHOWING SENSITIVITY TO OTHERS

Exercising the positive face of power and making others feel strong requires a great deal of sensitivity to others. Although it's impossible to imagine someone who doesn't intrinsically value being empowered, every employee's empowerment needs are different. Just listen to what Russ Barnett, proprietor of Russell Marketing in Western Australia, has to say: "Most leaders fail or succeed on their ability to know and understand the people they work with. You get the results of your efforts through other people, so you have to be very sensitive to each person and to their particular needs."

The positive regard for individuals that Kim Greer exhibits has won him the respect and loyalty of his staff. In discussing a recent project, Ron Hasse, one of Greer's direct reports, recalls, "It would have been easy to . . . not get input from the users. But Kim wouldn't go that way. He wanted to be sure that everyone felt they had some control over their destiny. It was important to me that he felt that way, that no one would feel diminished by the change."

Researchers from the Center for Creative Leadership have substantiated the importance of sensitivity. "Insensitivity to others" is cited in their studies as the primary reason why successful executives tumble off the track to the executive suite.[14] These researchers note that the ability to understand other people's perspectives is the most glaring difference between executives who make good and those who derail. Other "fatal flaws" include aloofness and arrogance, betrayal of trust, and overmanaging (or failing to delegate and build a team).

Studies of unsuccessful executives portray these people as loners—managers who prefer to work independently, who are highly critical of their staff, and who are unwilling to share control of projects and problem solutions. Unsuccessful executives generally view team participation and discussion as a waste of time and have poor interpersonal skills, according to these studies; they're ill at ease with others, frequently making insensitive and undiplomatic remarks, and they look on other people with a great deal of mistrust.[15]

Managers who focus on themselves and are insensitive to others fail, because there's a limit to what they can do by themselves. Those leaders who succeed realize that little can be accomplished if people don't feel strong and capable. In fact, by using their own power in service of others rather than in service of self, successful leaders transform their contituents into leaders themselves—and wind up with extraordinary results.

Providing Choice

Leaders actively seek out ways to increase choice and provide greater decision-making authority and responsibility for their constituents. Brian Baker, a family-practice physician and colonel in the U.S. Army, demonstrated these behaviors when he took over as hospital commander of Raymond Bliss Army Community Hospital located on Fort Huachuca near Tucson, Arizona. Upon his arrival at what he was told was the "most problematic hospital in the Army," Baker found a group of talented people in disarray and an organization with low morale, a set of rigidly followed institutional rules, and a high degree of conflict between doctors and nurses. He also found a stunningly unfavorable accreditation report by the Joint Commission for the Accreditation of Hospital Organizations (JCAHO). The JCAHO findings threatened to harm the military career of nearly everyone on staff. There was no vision, no camaraderie—only fear, hostility, and conflict. Yet within two years under Baker's leadership, the hospital reduced its more than twenty Category One deficiencies (the most serious) to just two (one was a physical/structural problem related to the age of the building; the other was due to staffing shortages caused by Desert Storm) and came "within inches" of receiving an exemplary rating, the JCAHO's highest score—*all without a single change in personnel.* Baker didn't fire anyone, nor did he reassign or significantly change anyone's job.

What Baker *did* do was listen, mentor, and fundamentally change the culture and the decision-making process at the hospital. Baker believed that in order to lay the foundation of the rebuilding process, he needed to restore his staff's sense of self-esteem as the first challenge. To that end, Baker held a series of meetings in rapid succession designed to allow him to meet and communicate openly with all of his constituents. No one's supervisor was allowed at these meetings: Baker wanted to ensure open and honest discussion. Baker promised that he would take no direct action as a result of the meetings, nor would he discuss what was said with anyone. He explained his philosophy of participatory and supportive (versus directive) management at these meetings and explained that he wanted to understand them and the hospital so that he could help them with any problems they felt existed. These meetings set a tone of openness, genuine concern, and trust that was key to ultimately restoring the organization's belief in its ability to succeed.

As for the JCAHO requirements, Baker always believed it was just a matter of educating an already very bright staff:

> All I had to do was point them toward the data and explain how important it was that we did what JCAHO required. That's why we're here. Not to tell these people *what* to do but to make sure they *understand* what needs to be done, understand *how* to do it, to support them as they do what they've told us needs to be done, and finally to coordinate the different groups so we get them working together on common goals. You can't just tell them to go out and do a monumental task if you aren't sure they really know what exactly needs to be done. So you ask lots of questions to guide their thinking—you ask, "How are you going to do this and such"—but you never assume control of the issue. They own it, not you. You coach and you mentor, but you make them decide and act. If it's their plan, they're more likely to make it happen. I helped add what I consider the most important ingredient: mutual respect and a feeling of togetherness. After that, everything just came together. That's what I'm the most proud of: we developed a culture of caring.

In organizations, we generally think of power as the control over valued resources.[16] The more control over important resources someone has, the more powerful. As Baker's case shows, however, the key to unleashing the organization's potential to excel is putting that power in the hands of the people who perform the work.

For proof of the importance of this shift, we look first to social psychologists who have studied the impact of giving people power. In one study, Connecticut residents in a state-run nursing home were given the responsibility for making seemingly trivial environmental choices, such as when to see a movie or how to arrange their rooms. General health and psychological well-being improved with that responsibility, and death rates were 50 percent lower than for a comparison group that had been informed that it was management's responsibility to keep them well.[17] This outcome suggests that the energy that can be unleashed as a result of giving people power is life-sustaining: *control over your destiny can save your life!* In the long run, it can also save the life of your organization. As we've seen time and again, a sure way to sink an organization in the turbulent seas of the changing economy is to centrally control the resources. The former Communist economies amply demonstrate the folly of hoarding power at the center.

In support of this principle, Harvard Business School professor Leonard Schlesinger and his colleagues have found that the supervisory behavior that most accounts for both job satisfaction and service capability is "latitude given to meet customer needs." The second-ranking variable is having "authority to serve the customer."[18] People will provide more responsive service and go the extra mile for the customer when they believe they have the discretion and authority to do so.

Providing choice and latitude are major contributors to enhancing people's sense of personal well-being and increasing their effectiveness.[19] In her studies of the relative power of particular jobs, professor Lisa Mainiero of Fairfield University found that frustration, panic, and a sense of helplessness—all demotivating experiences—result from being in work situations that create a dependence on others to get things done.[20] Not only does dependence on others create intense feelings of powerlessness; it also leads to acquiescence. Employees in powerless situations give in to authority and stop taking initiative. This, says Mainiero, can lead to "learned powerlessness" and continued acquiescence over time.[21] We come across learned powerlessness often, revealed in complaints from managers about people who don't want increased responsibility or would rather just be told what to do. But the fault lies in the jobs themselves rather than in the employees: certain jobs foster helplessness and dependence. Independent judgment and action can come only when tasks offer the opportunity for people to think and make choices for themselves.

If leaders want higher levels of performance and less dependence, they must be proactive in designing work that allows people discretion and choice. Having discretion and choice means being able to take nonroutine action, exercise independent judgment, and make decisions that affect how we do our work without having to check with someone else.[22] It means being creative and flexible—liberated from a standard set of rules, procedures, or schedules.

It means having more broadly defined jobs: while narrow job categories confine choices, broader ones permit increased flexibility. Those who hold broadly defined jobs have opportunities to use discretion, because they have more choice about *how* to accomplish the assigned objectives. The shift to fewer job classifications in large organizations is a clear sign that breadth is essential to rapid response. In fact, the old notion of work as a collection of "jobs" is being replaced by the more expansive concept of work as a series of "projects."[23] This restructuring allows people more space in which to maneuver in today's turbulent economy.

Having discretion and choice also means more freedom of movement and contact. The requirement that people go through multiple managerial layers and sign-offs to get a decision is disabling—and wasteful of time, money, talent, and motivation. That requirement also loses customers. Only increased contact among the people who make the product or provide the service and those whose resources or support they need will increase capacity and responsiveness.

In the dynamic environment of contemporary organizations, only adaptive individuals and organizations will thrive. To create increasingly adaptive systems, leaders must support more and more discretion to meet the changing demands of customers, clients, suppliers, and other stakeholders. With increased discretion comes an increased ability to use and expand our talents, training, and experience. The payoff is improved performance.

The Hampton Inn chain of hotels has seen the benefits of giving employees discretion. With their "100% Satisfaction Guarantee," they've removed the invisible wall of institutional regulations that often prevents employees from doing what they know is the right thing for the customer.

If any Hampton Inn customer isn't satisfied, it's understood that he or she won't pay. The effect on morale and motivation has been incredible, according to president and CEO Ray Schultz. Employees can provide the service they feel is necessary to satisfy the customer with no fear of reprimand—and they feel a part of the team.

Choice fuels our sense of power and control over our lives. Yet if we don't have the knowledge, skills, information, and resources to do our job expertly, if we don't feel competent to skillfully execute the choices that we make, we may feel overwhelmed and disabled. This result is just the opposite of what leaders are trying to achieve. Thus choice is necessary but insufficient.

Developing Competence

Springfield Remanufacturing Corporation (SRC) provides an example of the importance of competence. Read the following statements made by SRC employees and guess who made each:

- "Cash flow is projected to increase by $20,000 this month."
- "If we watch our material usage variance we could very well end the month making a profit large enough to qualify everyone for a bonus!"
- "Our labor figures are right on target."
- "Operating income for the month was $88,000, which represents a 3.4 percent return on sales."[24]

You may have guessed the controller, the production manager, the vice president of human resources, and the chief financial officer, respectively. These are sensible guesses, likely to be true in most businesses. But not at SRC. Each of these comments was made by a frontline employee.

Tradition suggests that only people with at least a master's degree in business administration or people in specialized roles can talk and think in these terms. But Jack Stack, president and CEO of SRC, felt he couldn't afford to make such an assumption. Back in 1983, when Stack was the manager of the plant, he was ordered by International Harvester to sell the factory or shut it down. He decided to see if the employees would buy it instead.

Stack succeeded, but after an extraordinary gamble. SRC managed to raise only $100,000 from employees against a loan of $8.9 million. That made it the highest leveraged buyout in corporate history: eighty-nine parts debt to one part equity. Stack believed that the only way to pull off the turnaround was to teach everyone what he calls "the Great Game of Business."[25]

At the heart of the Great Game, says Stack, is this proposition: "The best, most efficient, most profitable way to operate a business is to give everybody in the company a voice in saying how the company is run *and* a stake in the financial outcome, good or bad."[26] Critical to winning the Great Game is investing an extraordinary amount of time and energy in making *every* employee business-literate and then regularly sharing with employees information on the financial performance of the company.

"This experience," says Stack, "has convinced me that financial education of the workforce—we call it open-book management—is the key to extraordinary and sustained success. . . . Everyone at SRC, including the clean-up crew, knows how to read our balance sheet. Everyone understands how they personally affect the income and profitability of the company. They know where we are in terms of cash flow, how we generate it, and how we spend it."[27] At SRC, 86 percent of the training budget is spent on educating everyone to be a businessperson.

And what a success it has been. Since the buyout in 1983, SRC has experienced the following:

- An increase of over 23,000 percent in corporate stock values
- An absence of layoffs and a current workforce of over 750 people
- Sales growth exceeding 30 percent per year
- Employee education averaging an additional two years after hiring

And as if these numbers aren't impressive enough, sales for 1995 are expected to be $104 million (versus the first year sales of $16 million).

Stack and SRC are pioneers in open-book management. Their trailblazing efforts are attracting many others—from small and midsized businesses (such as Commercial Casework and Chesapeake Packaging Corp.) to large ones (such as Corning, Allstate Business Insurance, Manco, and Sprint)—to the method. The related practices of teaching everyone to become a businessperson and sharing business information regularly are the next stage in enabling people to act.

As we've learned from studying personal bests, leaders invest in developing people's skills and competencies. Leaders know that if people are to feel strong, they must develop their capacities. They also know that if people don't have important opportunities to put those talents to good use, they'll wind up frustrated. To strengthen others, leaders place their constituents, not themselves, at the center of solving critical problems and contributing to key goals.

Assigning Critical Tasks

People who are most central to solving the organization's crucial problems and ensuring the company's long-term viability have the most power. This is especially true when their particular resources are critical and in short supply.[28] In our case studies of personal bests, people talked of confronting critical organizational issues—whether improving quality, reducing manufacturing start-up times, changing customer perceptions, improving literacy rates, reengineering core agency processes, increasing access to acute care, creating a new food distribution system, or mobilizing legislative initiatives. Although it may seem obvious that we do our best when the work is critical to success, this principle is often lost in the day-to-day design of work.

It isn't lost, however, at Chaparral Steel Company, a minimill operation thirty miles outside of Dallas. Research and development is a critical task for any organization; at Chaparral Steel, R&D is brought out onto the factory floor. "We make the people who are producing the steel responsible for keeping their process on the leading edge of technology worldwide," explains Gordon Forward, president and CEO. "If they have to travel, they travel. If they have to figure out what the next step is, they go out and find the places where people are doing interesting things. They visit other companies. They work with universities."[29] This authority and power is bound to make people feel more involved and important.

What's critical to an organization is dynamic and ever-changing, of course. What's central this year may be peripheral the next. Who would have predicted ten years ago that frontline employees would be reading financial statements today? Not many of us, but Jack Stack did—and he acted on it. Now we take it for granted that frontline people should know statistical process control, be computer conversant, and be business-literate.

As these examples illustrate, changes in the economic, social, and polit-ical environment affect the relative importance of tasks and abilities. As we're faced with increasing global competition, international experience will become more highly prized. As alliances become more common, the ability to form and sustain partnerships will become more important. Forward-looking leaders will always scan the horizon for the next wave of critical tasks and educate themselves and their constituents accordingly.

In developing our own and our constituents' abilities to remain relevant and important in the future, we need to remember that one's ability to exe-cute important tasks depends upon three factors:

1. Being able to supply the resources that a unit needs, whether money, materials, staff, or time.
2. Having information, being "in the know."
3. Having the peer, managerial, and organizational support nec essary to work at full capacity.[30]

Given these factors, we then ought to ask the following questions:

- How can I give people more control over the resources they need to do their work?
- How can I make sure people are connected to the information they need, whether it's an electronic connection or a human connection?
- How can I make sure that I personally offer or acquire the support that people need to do the very best that they can?

Whatever answers we come up with to these questions, we must then act on those answers in order to make others feel more powerful and effective.

Offering Visible Support

Unfortunately, as many new organizational members soon discover, sim-ply doing a good job isn't enough to gain influence. Power doesn't flow to unknown people; becoming powerful requires getting noticed. Visibility is a precursor to access and recognition and is key to the formation of strategic alliances.[31]

Major General John Stanford demonstrated his dedication to increasing the visibility of his colleagues when he spoke at one of our workshops. From the back of the room, we noticed that Stanford had picked up someone else's nametag and put it on his uniform. At the end of his one-hour presentation, as he was about to step down from the podium, he pointed to the nametag and said, "My aide-de-camp Albert A. A. Cartenuto III couldn't be with me today. I hope I represented him well." We then realized that Stanford had intentionally picked up Cartenuto's nametag so that he could later give visibility to Cartenuto and acknowledge his contributions. His was a conscious leadership act, requiring caring and attention.

On another occasion, we had the opportunity to work with the people in Stanford's civilian and military command. During one training exercise, we sent some groups off to complete an assignment. Each group was to come back with a summary report written on newsprint (large chart paper). Stanford went off with one group, which included his aide, Cartenuto. When it came his group's turn to report, Stanford marched to the front of the room accompanied by Cartenuto, who was carrying a rolled-up sheet of newsprint under his arm. Instead of holding the newsprint, as his role might have dictated, Cartenuto unfurled the sheet and handed it to Stanford. The general stood like an easel while Cartenuto gave the group's report. Stanford often made gestures of support similar to these. It's no wonder that Cartenuto says of Stanford, "He's the greatest."

Leaders who want to strengthen their constituents ensure that they're highly visible and that individual and group efforts get noticed and recognized. Another way to show support is to connect individuals to other important people. There's a lot of wisdom in the saying, "It's not what you know but who you know that counts." Making connections and building strong relationships is empowering. It helps people to more easily get in contact with others who can help them accomplish their tasks. This networking is the grease that often smooths the way through interdepartmental boundaries and territorial disputes. Relationships that are durable and require frequent interactions also provide incentives for people to assist and support one another.

At furniture-maker Herman Miller, this empowering process is referred to as "theory fastball." As Max De Pree, chairperson, explains, "In the process of work many of us are outstanding pitchers, able to throw the telling fastball, but it is also true that those pitchers can only be effective if there are many of us who are outstanding catchers."[32]

Visibility is also enhanced when leaders keep their team members in contact with people outside of their department—for example, by placing people on task forces and committees whose members come from across the organization or by encouraging active participation in professional and community groups. By providing others with access to senior executives, fostering outside contacts, and developing and promoting people with promise, leaders help build those critical relational networks.

Committing to the Challenge: Acting on the Paradox of Power

Leaders are motivated to use their power in service of others because capable and confident people perform better. Strengthening others is essentially the process of turning constituents into leaders themselves—of making people capable of acting on their own initiative. Leaders strengthen others when they give their own power away, when they make it possible for constituents to exercise choice and discretion, when they develop competence to excel, when they assign critical tasks, and when they offer visible support. In the following commitment, we offer specific actions you can take to strengthen your constituents.

Commitment Number 6

Strengthen People by Giving Power Away, Providing Choice, Developing Competence, Assigning Critical Tasks, and Offering Visible Support

➤ **Increase the return on your square footage.**
You needn't show off or tell other people how powerful and influential you are. The thick carpet, the huge desk, and the price tag on the art are unnec-

essary displays of importance. Consider leaders such as Gandhi and Mother Teresa, and you can see that there's no connection between possessions and making a difference. In fact, in *Fortune* magazine's study of the "return on square feet" of CEO's offices, the winner was Andy Grove, whose office is a cubicle, just like everyone else's at Intel.[33]

Instead of decorating the office with symbols of power, decorate yours with personal mementos that say something about your interests, your family, your uniqueness. Besides the curiosity they generate, such mementos reflect your personality. Use your unique environment to tell a story about you. It really is you, after all, that people are following—not the title or the position. At Manco, Inc.—maker of Duck® Tape and other consumer products—the walls are lined with inspirational quotes. In fact, over every office door is a quotation reflecting the officeholder's philosophy. For chairman and CEO Jack Kahl, it's a quote from Socrates: "One thing only I know, and this is that I know nothing." For president and COO Tom Corbo, it's "The customer is king."

➤ Enlarge people's sphere of influence.

At the Ritz-Carlton Hotels, a winner of the Malcolm Baldrige National Quality Award, associates at the registration desk have the latitude and authority to correct an error of up to $2,000 without checking with a manager. We know many *managers* who don't have that kind of signature authority. If you really want people to feel more powerful (and personally responsible), try these steps:

- Substantially increase signature authority at all levels.
- Remove or reduce unnecessary approval steps.
- Eliminate as many rules as possible.
- Decrease the amount of routine work.
- Increase employee flexibility regarding processes.
- Assign nonroutine jobs.
- Support the exercise of independent judgment.
- Encourage creative solutions to problems.
- Define jobs more broadly—as projects, not tasks.
- Reduce the number of job classifications.
- Provide more freedom of access, vertically and horizontally, inside and outside.
- Open the doors and facilitate freedom of movement.

Remember that acquiescence increases with dependence on others and can result in learned powerlessness. For people to feel and act enabled, they have to have "space" in which to maneuver and the necessary resources to perform autonomously. That means materials, money, time, people, and information. And remember: there's nothing more disempowering than to have lots of authority to do something but nothing to do it with.

➤ Make sure delegated tasks are relevant.

People's increased sphere of influence ought to be over something relevant to the pressing concerns and core technology of the business. Choosing the color of the paint may be a place to start, but you'd better give people influence over more substantive issues as well:

- If quality is top priority, find ways to expand people's influence and discretion over issues of quality control.
- If innovation is a priority, increase people's influence over the development of new products, processes, or services.

Assess the critical tasks and issues in your organization and then make sure that your constituents are well represented on the task forces, committees, teams, and problem-solving groups dealing with them. If you're on one, make sure you take a key constituent or two with you to meetings.

➤ Educate, educate, educate.

When you increase the latitude and authority of your colleagues, you also have to increase expenditures on training and development. Successful quality programs, for example, all have in common the fact that the group members receive training in basic statistical measurement methods, group communication skills, and problem-solving techniques. "The Great Game of Business" at SRC works because people have been trained to read financial statements. Without education and coaching, people are reluctant to exercise their authority, in part because they don't know how to perform the critical tasks and in part out of fear of being punished for making mistakes.

You don't have to spend megabucks to have good training. In the early days at Solectron, the high-technology service manufacturer, we were on the road early to make a seven o'clock gathering of company managers. The first half-hour of the meeting was for reporting the quality numbers from the day before; the second, for learning something about management, finance, marketing, quality, communications, or other relevant topics. Founder and chairman Winston Chen was dedicated to education and information sharing—and years later, the efforts paid off for this winner of the Malcolm Baldrige National Quality Award.

➤ **Organize your own "great huddle."**
When Everett T. Suters of the Suters Group was CEO of a small but rapidly growing southwestern company, he learned just how important information sharing is. Everyone was putting in long hours and giving enormous effort, but Suters began to pick up on innuendos that seemed to say, "We're doing the work, but you're getting most of the credit and all of the money." He was irritated by these comments, because he didn't believe that what people were implying was true, so he called together the management team. He asked team members to write down what the company profits were and how much money they thought he was personally making. Suters was amazed: everyone had guessed much too high on both counts. So he passed out copies of the company's financial statement, went over it line by line, and indicated how much money was going to be needed to finance future growth. Everyone started asking questions and requesting more information. Suters could see people becoming "as interested in all facets of the company as I was." One manager told Suters some time later, "If I had to tell you in one sentence why I am motivated by my job, it is because when I know what is going on, and how I fit into the overall picture, it makes me feel important."[34]

Have regular "great huddles" and chalk talks to keep people informed about your organization's performance. The more that people know about what's going on in the organization, the better off you'll be. Without information, people won't extend themselves to take responsibility; armed with information, people's creative energies can be harnessed to achieve extraordinary results. Information empowers people, strengthening their resolve and providing them with the resources they need to be successful.

➤ Make connections.

Being connected to people who can open doors, offer support and backing, provide information, mentor and teach, and add to one's reputation increases power. You can increase your own power by forming strategic relationships, and you can strengthen others in the same way. Take the time to introduce the staff in your organization to the people they need to know. Get them access to influential others. Take members of your staff to important meetings, business lunches, and customer organizations. Find ways to connect them to sources of information.

Of all the tools within reach of leaders, the most valuable may be the Rolodex. It's the place we keep our network of connections. Whether you keep yours electronically or manually, it's as essential to your interpersonal influence as your watch is to punctuality. Tom Peters has this to say about it: "Security is proportional to (1) the thickness of your Rolodex, (2) the rate of Rolodex expansion, (3) the share of Rolodex entries beyond the corporate walls, and (4) the time devoted to Rolodex maintenance."[35] How would you rate your Rolodex on these dimensions?

While we strongly discourage use of position as a leadership tactic, it's important to keep in mind that people prefer to enlist in causes led by people who are upwardly and outwardly influential. Successful leaders know that it's necessary and important to let others know that they can and will use their power to help people get their jobs done. Ask the people who work for and with you what they need to do their jobs most effectively; then go get it for them. Watch how much more effective they can be when you make these kinds of connections. Notice, too, how much your esteem goes up in the eyes of others.

➤ Make heroes of other people.

The late Wilbert L. Gore, founder and chairperson of W. L. Gore & Associates, told us that one of his skills was "making heroes of other people." If there's one phrase that best expresses the philosophy of strengthening others, that would have to be it. Leaders find ways to shine the spotlight on the achievements of others rather than on their own accomplishments. They make other people the visible heroes and heroines of their organizations. As we've seen, Major General John Stanford did that by wearing the nametag of his aide.

There are hundreds of ways you can incorporate similar actions into your daily routine. Here are just a few:

- Tell people, both inside and outside the organization, about what team members are doing.
- Publicize the work of team members.
- Post pictures of exemplary members.
- Tell stories about people and their achievements in newsletters and advertisements.
- Make references to the team in private conversations and public speeches.
- Send letters of appreciation to key supporters and sponsors.
- Prominently display letters of appreciation from customers about key people.
- Build a trophy case.

We urge you to shine the spotlight on at least one person each day. Find someone doing what you wish everyone else were doing (or doing something that's moving in the right direction). Make that person visible doing critical tasks, and show others that you support him or her. Those steps will increase that person's power and build a stronger bond between you and your constituents.

In the next chapters, you'll see how many of these same approaches to strengthening and empowering others also serve to build people's commitment to action. You'll also read how, in order to build commitment, you must first demonstrate your own commitment through word and deed.

Commitment Number 6

Strengthen People by Giving Power Away, Providing Choice, Developing Competence, Assigning Critical Tasks, and Offering Visible Support

➤ Increase the return on your square footage.

➤ Enlarge people's sphere of influence.

➤ Make sure delegated tasks are relevant.

➤ Educate, educate, educate.

➤ Organize your own "great huddle."

➤ Make connections.

➤ Make heroes of other people.

Source: *The Leadership Challenge* by James M. Kouzes and Barry Z. Posner.
Copyright © 1995.

PART 5

Modeling the Way

> ➤ **Challenge the Process**
>
> ➤ **Inspire a Shared Vision**
>
> ➤ **Enable Others to Act**
>
> ➤ **Model the Way**
>
> ➤ **Encourage the Heart**

9

Set the Example

Doing What You Say You Will Do

You have to be a role model for others. You can't ask others to do anything you wouldn't be willing to do yourself.
—SYLVIA YEE
Senior Program Officer
Evelyn and Walter Haas, Jr., Fund

The first thing Les Cochran did after assuming his position as university president at Youngstown State University in July 1992 was to purchase an abandoned building on the edge of campus and spend his free weekends working with construction crews to transform it into a residence for his family. While it's not unusual for college presidents to live near their campuses, Cochran's determination to do so attracted a great deal of attention and set the tone for his presidency.

To many, Cochran was literally putting his life on the line, for the once-lovely neighborhoods surrounding YSU had surrendered to increasingly aggressive gangs and escalating drug-related crime following the collapse of Youngstown's steel mill–dependent economy in the early 1980s. Cochran believed that the only way to reclaim YSU from the fear, hopelessness, apathy, and mistrust that paralyzed both it and the surrounding community was to start the process by claiming as his one of these decaying neighborhoods. In doing so, he made it apparent that he was unquestionably dedicated to being an active participant "in making the world a better place to be." His message was clear: "We're responsible, both individually and collectively, for the fate of this community." Thus when he coined the slogan "Together we can make a difference"—his philosophy of individual contribution to community involvement—people knew he believed deeply in what he was saying. By buying and refurbishing a home in an area he was determined to reclaim for YSU, Cochran "walked the talk."

When leaders ask others to change, as Cochran did, it's not enough to simply deliver a rousing speech. While compelling words may be essential to lifting people's spirits, Cochran and other leaders know that constituents are more deeply moved by deeds. Constituents expect leaders to show up, to pay attention, and to participate directly in the process of getting extraordinary things done. Leaders take every opportunity to show others by their own example that they're deeply committed to the aspirations they espouse. Leading by example is how leaders make visions and values tangible. It's how they provide the *evidence* that they're personally committed. And that evidence is what people look for and admire in leaders—people whose direction they willingly follow.

In our extensive research on leader credibility, we learned without doubt that credibility is the foundation of leadership.[1] We asked people these questions:

- How do you know if someone is credible?
- How would you define credibility in behavioral terms?
- How would you recognize credible leaders?

Here are some of the phrases they used in reply:

- "They practice what they preach."
- "They walk the talk."
- "Their actions are consistent with their words."
- "They put their money where their mouth is."
- And the most frequent response: *"They do what they say they will do."*

These responses show just how essential example setting is to a leader's credibility. When it comes to deciding whether a leader is believable, people first listen to the words; then they watch the actions. They listen to the talk and watch the walk. Then they measure the congruence. A judgment of "credible" is handed down when the two are consonant. If people don't see consistency, they conclude that the leader is (at best) not really serious about the words or (at worst) an outright hypocrite.

Actions, then, are the evidence of a leader's commitment. This observation leads to a straightforward prescription for leader modeling:

DWYSYWD: Do What You Say You Will Do

DWYSYWD has two essential elements: *say* and *do*. To set an example, leaders must be clear about their values; they must know what they stand for. That's the "say" part. Then they must put what they say into practice: they must act on their beliefs and "do."

In the domain of leadership, however, DWYSYWD is necessary but insufficient. Doing what you say you will do may well make you credible—but not necessarily a credible *leader*. Leaders represent groups of people, and those constituents also have needs and interests, values and visions. To set an example—and to earn and strengthen *leadership* credibility—those of us who want to be leaders must base our actions on a *collective* set of aims and aspirations. We must DWWSWWD: Do What We Say We Will Do.

DWWSWWD reveals to us the *essentials* leaders have to master to set an example and sustain leader credibility. We call it the "say-we-do" process, and it means that leaders must be able to do the following:

- Clarify personal values and beliefs and those of others
- Unify constituents around shared values
- Pay attention constantly to how self and others are living the values

Let's now take a closer look at each of these essentials and at some tools leaders can use to set an example for all of their constituents.

Clarifying Values: Beliefs Guide Choices and Actions

Mike Leonard, while director of organization development for Alcoa Aluminum of Australia, had this to say about his personal best—an all-consuming process of designing a new plant: "We began with developing a shared understanding of our basic philosophy about how we ought to be doing business. These values served to guide us, not only with actual physical construction and sociotechnical designs but also with the various recruitment, promotion, and compensation strategies." In Leonard's case, values provided the common standard by which people could calibrate their decisions and actions. Like Leonard, the other leaders we studied reported that when they operated at their personal best, they and their teams were guided by a clear and agreed-upon set of values.

People expect their leaders to stand for something, and they expect them to have the courage of their convictions. Leaders who aren't clear about what they believe in are likely to change their position with every fad or opinion poll. Without core beliefs and with only shifting positions, would-be leaders are judged as inconsistent and derided for being "political" in their behavior. Therefore, the first milestone on the journey to leadership credibility is *clarity* of personal values.

What does it mean to have a value? The late Milton Rokeach, one of the leading researchers and scholars in the field of human values, referred to a value as an enduring belief. He noted that values are organized into two sets: means and ends.[2] In the context of our work on modeling, we use the term *values* to refer to here-and-now beliefs about how things should be accomplished—Rokeach's "means values." We use the term *vision* when we refer to the future and to the long-term "ends values" the organization aspires to attain. But however these concepts are defined, organizations must have both means values and ends values. When we're sailing through the turbulent seas of change, the crew needs a vision of what lies beyond the horizon and must understand the standards by which performance will be judged.

Values help us determine what to do and what not to do. They're the deep-seated, pervasive standards that influence every aspect of our lives: our moral judgments, our responses to others, our commitments to personal and organizational goals. Values set the parameters for the hundreds of decisions we make every day. Options that run counter to our value system are seldom acted upon; and if they are, it's done with a sense of compliance rather than commitment. Values constitute our personal "bottom line."[3]

Important as it is that leaders forthrightly articulate the principles for which they stand, what leaders say must be consistent with the aspirations of their constituents. Leaders who advocate values that aren't representative of the collective will won't be able to mobilize people to act as one. Leaders set an example for all constituents based upon a *shared* understanding of what's expected. Leaders must be able to gain consensus on a common cause and a common set of principles. They must be able to build a community of shared values.

Unifying Constituents: Shared Values Make a Difference

Unity is crucial to both leadership credibility and organizational credibility. A leader's promise is really an organization's promise—regardless of whether the organization is a team of 2, a plant of 200, a division of 2,000, a company of 20,000, or a community of 200,000. Unless there's agreement about what promises *we* can keep, leaders, constituents, and their organizations risk losing credibility.

In our own research, spanning a period of over fifteen years, we've carefully examined the relationship between personal and organizational values.[4] This research has involved thousands of managers from across the United States and around the globe, representing all types of public and private organizations and all organizational levels, from first-level supervisor to the highest executive. These findings clearly reveal that when there's congruence between individual values and organizational values, there's significant payoff for leaders and their organizations. Shared values make a significant difference in work attitudes and performance:

- They foster strong feelings of personal effectiveness.
- They promote high levels of company loyalty.
- They facilitate consensus about key organizational goals and stakeholders.
- They encourage ethical behavior.
- They promote strong norms about working hard and caring.
- They reduce levels of job stress and tension.
- They foster pride in the company.
- They facilitate understanding about job expectations.
- They foster teamwork and esprit de corps.

In our studies with the Australian Institute of Management and Hong Kong Management Association, we also found that when leaders seek consensus around shared values, constituents are more positive. People who report that their senior managers engage in dialogue around common values feel a significantly stronger sense of personal effectiveness than those individuals who feel that they're wasting energy trying to figure out what they're supposed to be doing.[5]

People tend to drift when they're unsure or confused about how they should be operating. The energy that goes into coping with, and possibly fighting about, incompatible values takes its toll on both personal effectiveness and organizational productivity. The effort of periodically taking the organization's pulse in regard to the clarity and consensus of its values is well worthwhile. It serves to renew commitment as well as to engage the institution in discussion of values (such as diversity) that are more inclusive of a changing constituency.

Once people are clear about the leader's values, about their own values, and about shared values, they know what's expected of them and can better handle the conflicting demands of work and personal affairs. In fact, research studies consistently demonstrate that in compatible work environments, people can manage higher levels of stress.[6]

Furthermore, studies of public-sector organizations support the importance of shared values to organizational effectiveness. Within successful agencies and departments, considerable agreement, as well as intense feeling, is found among employees and managers alike about the importance of their values and about how those values could best be implemented.[7]

Gustav Leven, chief of Source Perrier, gave voice to the values behind Perrier's 1990 recall of its product by saying simply, "We don't want the slightest doubt to weigh on Perrier." That force was behind the speed and efficiency with which Perrier suspended production at its plant in France and recalled 160 million bottles of Perrier from worldwide distribution when two to three times the U.S. Environmental Protection Agency's allowable level of the carcinogen benzene was discovered in its bottled water. Despite Food and Drug Administration assurances that the level of benzene posed a "negligible risk," Perrier pulled its product, at a cost of over $30 million, and announced a toll-free number to allow customers to address their concerns directly to the company.[8]

WHAT SHARED VALUES ARE IMPORTANT?

Research makes clear that shared values make a difference to organizational and personal vitality and that values form the bedrock of an organization's culture.[9] In a four-year study of nine to ten firms in each of twenty industries, management professors John Kotter and John Heskett found that firms with a strong corporate culture based on a foundation of shared values outperformed the other firms by a huge margin:[10]

- Their revenue grew more than four times faster.
- Their rate of job creation was seven times higher.
- Their stock price grew twelve times faster.
- Their profit performance was 750 percent higher.

Is there some particular value or set of values that's the springboard to organizational vitality? Consider these examples—three electronics companies, each of which has a strong set of values:[11] The first company prides itself on technical innovation and has a culture that's dominated by engineering values; it informally encourages and rewards activities such as experimentation and risk taking. The second company is much flashier; its important organizational values are associated with marketing, and the company gears itself toward providing outstanding customer service. The third company does things "by the numbers"; accounting standards dominate its key values, and energies are directed toward making the organization more efficient (by cutting costs, for example). Each of these companies is quite different and clearly communicates its own values. But all three companies compete in the same market, and all are successful, each with a different strategy. It's apparent, then, that successful companies may have very different values and that the specific set of values that serves one company may hurt another.

This view is supported by the research of Stanford University professors Jim Collins and Jerry Porras on "visionary companies." Collins and Porras found that high-performing organizations, compared to like companies in their industry, had a very strong "core ideology" but didn't share the *same* core ideology.[12]

The research of management professors David Caldwell and Charles O'Reilly demonstrates that while organizations may have different sets of values, there are three central themes in the values of highly successful, strong-culture organizations:[13]

- High performance standards
- A caring attitude toward people
- A sense of uniqueness and pride

High-performance values stress the commitment to excellence, *caring* values communicate how others are to be treated, and *uniqueness* values tell people inside and outside how the organization is different from all others. These three common threads seem to be central to weaving a values tapestry that leads to greatness.

RoseAnn Stevenson, organization and management development manager at Boeing, raises important issues about the true degree of consensus around organizational values statements, further extending our understanding of shared values. Stevenson performed a content analysis of values statements from seventy-seven different companies and found nineteen commonly identified values.[14] Although not a single value appeared on all statements, the most frequently mentioned values (representing 51 percent or more of the statements) were these: integrity, involvement, achievement, quality, creativity/innovation, respect, learning, fairness, and customer service. The extent of commonality ranged from 30 percent (for company growth) to 82 percent (for integrity).

Despite finding nineteen commonly identified values, Stevenson saw little agreement on the meaning of each of these values statements. She found, for example, that there were 185 different behavioral expectations around the value of integrity alone. Stevenson's findings that specific interpretations of values vary by organization point out how necessary it is for leaders to engage their constituents in a dialogue about values. A common understanding of values comes about through that dialogue; it emerges from a *process,* not a pronouncement. After all, if there's no agreement about values, then what exactly is the leader—and everyone else—going to model?

For values to be truly shared, they must be more than advertising slogans: they must be deeply supported and broadly endorsed beliefs about what's important to *us.* Constituents must be able to enumerate the values and must have common interpretations of how those values will be put into practice. They must know how the values influence their own jobs and how they directly contribute to organizational success.

AT&T's Mountain States Branch of the Mountain Plains Area began its quest to become a world-class sales organization with The Leadership Challenge Workshop™. In that workshop, the management team, with the leadership of general manager Jack Schiefer, began to explore personal goals and values. From that five-day experience, team members embarked on a four-year journey to develop vision and shared values statements for the branch. But they didn't do it alone: Schiefer and his team involved all organizational associates, and even customers, in discovering what they considered world class to be. It's this kind of interaction that's essential to forging consensus around shared values.

CAN VALUES BE IMPOSED?

Many senior executives have taken the shared values message to mean that they should set off on a week-long retreat to formulate a corporate credo, then return home and announce it to constituents. We confess to having once been advocates of this exercise. Experience has taught us, however, that no matter how extensive top management's support of shared values is, leaders can't impose their values on organizational members. Consensus about values is more difficult to achieve than clarity, and without consensus it's hard to get consistent implementation of values throughout an organization. Leaders must be proactive in involving people in the process of creating shared values.

Imagine how much more ownership of the vision and values there would be if leaders actively involved a wide range of people in their development. We now encourage leaders to invite everybody—or if that's not feasible, a representative group of constituents—to discuss the organization's vision and future and see what critical themes emerge.

Shared values don't result from laminated wallet cards, televised broadcasts, posters embellished with calligraphy, auditorium speeches, or executive roundtables. Shared values are instead the result of listening, appreciating, building consensus, and practicing conflict resolution. For people to understand the values and come to agree with them, they must participate in the process: *unity is forged, not forced.*

This explains why Honeywell recently updated its values statement with help from over 1,200 employees and managers worldwide. "Employees said values provide us with guideposts. They help us make decisions along the path to our vision and help us work together toward a common goal. Employees remind us," explains Michael Bonsignore, chairman and CEO, "that the values are more about deeds than about words." A company-wide feedback process has been designed to measure the company's progress in both pursuing its values and assessing their consistency with key actions and decisions. As part of that process, values congruence has been integrated into senior management's annual performance appraisals. "Our actions will speak very loudly about our values," says Bonsignore. Key to the process of forging unity at Honeywell is involving every employee in dialogue to make certain that the values are understood and acted upon in day-to-day activities.

When we took a deeper look at the question of shared values—or congruence between personal and organizational values—we discovered that people who had the greatest clarity about both personal and organizational values had the highest degree of commitment to the organization.[15] Consistent with previous research, we also confirmed that individuals who were unclear about their own and the organization's values had low commitment and were the most alienated from their work.

Somewhat to our surprise, we found that individuals who had a great degree of clarity about the organization's values but little clarity about their own values had no more commitment to the organization than those who had little understanding of their own *and* the organization's values. Even more astounding was the finding that the group with a great degree of clarity about personal values but less clarity about organizational values had almost as much commitment as the group that had high congruence between their own and the organization's values. See Figure 9.1 for a summary of our findings.

Having clarity about personal values may thus be more important, in relation to attitudes about work and ethical practices, than being clear about organizational values alone. Ultimately it's people and not organizations who bear the responsibility for decisions. Those individuals with the clearest personal values seem better prepared to make choices based on

Figure 9.1. Values Congruence and Individual Commitment.

	Low	High
High	4.87	6.26
Low	4.90	6.12

Clarity of
Organizational Values

Low   High

Clarity of Personal Values

Note: The cells represent the degree of clarity about personal and organizational values. The numbers in the cells represent the extent of individuals' commitment to their organizations on a scale of 1 to 7, with 1 being low and 7 being high.

Source: B. Z. Posner and W. H. Schmidt, "Values Congruence and Differences Between the Interplay of Personal and Organizational Value Systems," *Journal of Business Ethics* 12 (1993): 174.

principles—including deciding whether the principles of the organization fit with their own personal principles!

The implication for leaders is this: a unified voice on values results from discovery and dialogue. Leaders must provide a chance for individuals to engage in a discussion of what the values mean and how their personal beliefs and behaviors are influenced by what the organization stands for. Leaders must also be prepared to discuss values and expectations in the recruitment, selection, and orientation of new members. Better to explore early the fit between person and organization than to have members find out late some sleepless night that they're in violent disagreement over matters of principle.

One word of caution: values should never be used as an excuse for the suppression of dissent. The dominant silent value at play in all organizational settings is the preference for freedom over enslavement.

Paying Attention: Actions Speak Louder Than Words

"I try to lead by example, by being what I want privates to be. And I expect as much out of them." So says Sergeant Jill Henderson, the first woman to win the Army's Drill Sergeant of the Year award. She can do push-ups with the best of them—thirty-five per minute—and works seventeen-hour days. Even in the rain and mud, she insists on wearing a crisply pressed uniform and spit-shined boots. Her values are clear, and she lives them. "I lead from the heart. The more I take care of people the more they take care of me." She tells her trainees in boot camp, "A soldier does all the work. If somebody looks down at you, remember inside that you are the one who carries out the mission. If you stay in the Army, you *will* become a leader. Just never forget where you came from."[16] It's clear from her actions that Henderson hasn't forgotten this for a second. It's not just words that Henderson uses to convince and teach the privates she trains; it's her behavior—the match between what she demands of her people and what she demands of herself.

In our studies, we've found that leaders, when at their best, recognize (as Henderson does) that intentional modeling is essential to focusing people's attention, energy, and effort on the expected behaviors until such actions became standard operating procedures—part of the daily stream of activities. The third essential on the road to leader credibility, then, is *paying attention.* The intensity, vigor, and passion of our commitment to our espoused values finally determines whether people take us seriously. Constituents pay more attention to the values we *actually* use (the values-in-use) than to those we say we believe in (the espoused values).[17] No one actually sees the values themselves; they're intangible. What we see is the tangible evidence that people are true to their beliefs—their decisions, actions, allocations, attention, and use of time.

We can't stress enough the power of the leader's example. UCLA professor Donna McNeese-Smith, in her research on health care administrators, found that "the behavior most related to employee productivity was 'modeling the way.' If managers want productive employees they must set a good example, establish high standards, and then practice what they preach."[18] What's true in health care is also true in industry. According to research conducted by the Association of Quality and Participation, "Employees are proud when they can say their organization's leaders use actions to support their verbiage about quality. It's not just talk—they live their lives out in the same way."[19]

Leadership is a performing art.[20] Leaders don't "act" in the same sense as Broadway performers, of course. However, they *enact* the meaning of the organization in every decision they make and in every step they take toward the future they envision.[21] High-performing leaders understand the influence of their decisions and actions. Leaders understand that they can bring shared values to life in a variety of settings, from daily group meetings, one-on-one conferences, telephone calls, tours of facilities, and visits to clients, customers, suppliers, or community members.[22] Leaders also have a variety of "mundane tools" with which to support their guiding roles.[23] In the next sections, we'll look at some of the mundane tools that should be stocked in every leader's storehouse:[24]

- Calendars
- Critical incidents
- Stories
- Questions
- Language
- Symbols, artifacts, and rituals
- Measures
- Physical space

These tools are simple; it's their application that challenges aspiring leaders.

CALENDARS: SPENDING TIME AND PAYING ATTENTION

Among the busiest days in neighborhood convenience stores are Christmas Day and New Year's Day. Robert Gordon, president of Store 24, wants the employees in his stores to know that he cares about them, and he wants them to be able to spend time with their families. So he and other corporate office personnel work in the stores on these holidays. Gordon could easily delegate these shifts to others, but he believes that it's important to show them his concern, not just talk about it.

We don't have to wait to be CEO to show people we're serious about our beliefs. Take this example from 3DO's business development specialist, Greg Mills, who discusses his personal best at Menlo-Atherton High School: becoming captain of the water polo team.

> Even though I was probably the most motivated to work out and play, I kept reminding myself that it was a team sport, and I couldn't do it all myself. I could set my own high standards, but I couldn't force my standards on other players. I wanted the team to decide how much they wanted to practice. I decided to set an example for the team showing my dedication. . . . Everyone was expected to be at every workout and to practice seriously. I led by example by being at every workout and working out hard. . . . I was usually the last one out of practice, and I always helped our coach pick up after practice. . . . If I told people to go to all the workouts, and I kept missing a few workouts a week, they wouldn't listen to me, as their confidence in me would diminish. . . . I also helped the younger players who didn't know much about the game . . . and tried to build up their confidence. . . . Most importantly, I kept telling myself water polo is a game that one should also have fun in. When I noticed the team getting too tense—or myself—I joked around with the players to relieve the tension.

Setting an example means arriving early, staying late, working out, and being there to show you care. It's about being the first to do something that everyone else should value. Whether the value is family, teamwork, hard work, or fun, the truest measure of what leaders deeply believe is how they spend their time. Constituents look to see this measure and use it to judge whether a leader measures up to espoused standards. Visibly spending time on what's important shows that we're putting our time and money where our mouth is. For example, by attending operating meetings in the field, leaders provide visible evidence of their concerns and the direction they want to pursue.

The meeting agenda is another visible indicator of how we're investing our time. What issue is first on the agenda? Is it product quality, customer retention, profitability, new business development, collaboration with vendors? What is it, and what signal does it send about what people should consider to be important? The "primacy effect"—what comes first in a series of items—is a very powerful force in gaining attention. What goes last—the "recency effect"—is also crucial in getting people to retain what's important.[25] So in facilitating your meeting agenda, be sure to schedule what's first and last based on what you consider to be the most important messages you want people to understand.

The meeting roster is yet another simple leadership tool. Who attends, or doesn't attend, and who presents material sends signals about values and direction. Bear in mind that face-to-face communication is the preferred channel for information about the organization, and people want that communication from their direct supervisors.[26] The implication is clear: direct contact with one's immediate leader is critical to getting others to attend to important information, such as the values of the enterprise. Paying attention and spending time is every leader's business.

CRITICAL INCIDENTS:
SEIZING OPPORTUNITIES TO TEACH

Consciously choosing to spend time on what's important to us is critical to sending the signal that we're serious about an issue. Yet even the most disciplined leaders can't stop the intrusion of the unexpected and the serendipitous. There are constant interruptions, brief interactions, and extraordinary variety—all of which are likely to become more extreme in an era of downsizing, global competition, and increased diversity. Critical incidents—chance occurrences, particularly at a time of stress and challenge—offer significant moments of learning for leaders and constituents. Critical incidents present opportunities for leaders to teach important lessons about appropriate norms of behavior.

Retired U.S. Army General H. Norman Schwarzkopf was a master at creating moments of learning during critical incidents. One event during Schwarzkopf's first day as a new division commander illustrates how a leader can turn a chance encounter into a classroom:

> Although I'd delayed any sweeping changes, I *was* on the lookout for ways to establish myself as the leader from the moment I set foot on the base. The morning after we arrived I went out for a run. As I came up on the barracks area, a formation of troops raced by me, led by a guy who

looked as if he belonged in the Olympics. . . . [S]tretching back into the distance were the soldiers who hadn't been able to keep pace. The leaders stopped in front of their barracks and were catching their breath as I jogged up. . . . I stopped and asked the company commander what they were doing. "Sir, we've just completed our five-mile run."

"That's terrific. But what about all those people back there?" I asked.

"Sir, those are guys who couldn't keep up."

"But you've run off and left them." The captain gave me a puzzled look. "Think of it this way," I said. "Suppose you're a new recruit. You come to your new unit, you're just out of basic training, and you're feeling great about being a soldier. But then you find out that your new unit does a lot more running than you're used to. And the very first day you're out with them, you run and you run until your legs give out and your lungs give out—but your unit keeps going and leaves you. What kind of unit cohesion does that build?"

The light dawned on the captain's face. After suggesting ways he might reorganize the morning run so that nobody was ever left behind, I jogged off, satisfied that I'd just taught a young officer . . . that cohesion at every level be developed. I knew the episode would get talked about around the base.[27]

Notice that Schwarzkopf was consciously *on the lookout* for ways to establish himself as a leader. The morning run was mainly for exercise, but he know it could also become an opportunity if he stayed alert. While many leaders might have passed up this chance encounter, Schwarzkopf recognized it as an opportune moment for the captain and the soldiers to learn an important lesson about group cohesion. All that was required was the general's clarity of belief, perception that this was an opportunity, comfort in confronting someone about the behavior, and about five minutes of time.

Critical incidents are those events in leaders' lives that offer the chance to improvise while still staying true to the script. Although they can't be explicitly planned, we should keep in mind that how we handle these incidents says volumes about what's important.

STORIES: USING THE TIMELESS WAY
TO TEACH VIRTUES

Critical incidents are often the most dramatic sources of moral lessons about what we should and should not value, about how we should and should not behave. They become stories that are passed down, whether around the base (as Schwarzkopf predicted), across the country, or from generation to generation.[28]

Betsy Sanders told us a story demonstrating how powerful critical incidents are to organizational learning. Sanders, now on the board of several companies (including Wal-Mart and Carl Karcher Enterprises), is a former general manager and vice president of Nordstrom. To this day, she can clearly recall how Bruce Nordstrom brought home to her the seriousness with which the Nordstrom organization cared about the customer.[29]

She'd been with the company for two or three years and was a department manager. "I was in my department busily working one day when all five of the executive officers of the company started trooping through. And then, to my dismay, I saw Bruce Nordstrom get the most terrible frown on his face, shake his head in disgust, and walk over toward me. He came over and he said, 'Betsy, I just overheard a conversation that really has me upset. See those two ladies over there? They were just saying how disappointed they were. Would you go find out what we did to upset them and make it right?'"

Sanders told the women that Nordstrom had overheard them and had asked her to find out what was wrong. "They were delighted to know that he cared," she said. "Well, as it turned out, the two women had fallen in love with the dresses in the Gallery—the expensive dress department—but felt they couldn't afford the prices." Sanders just happened to manage the moderate-price dress department, and she was able to help them. The result was two more happy Nordstrom customers. Says Sanders, "I was impressed with Bruce Nordstrom. But more so when hours later he came out of a negotiating meeting that had certainly taken all of his time and attention and came back to check with me to find out what those customers had wanted and what I did about it."

For Sanders, this event left an indelible mark. She learned about the importance of customer service from her encounter with Bruce Nordstrom, and she learned how true to that value he really was. She's told that story again and again as an example of what Nordstrom stands for. We needn't work at Nordstrom to understand the lesson. Stories provide concrete advice and guidelines about how things are done and about what to expect in the organization.[30]

The power of stories in fostering beliefs is supported by research conducted by organizational sociologists Joanne Martin and Melanie Powers. They compared the persuasiveness of four different methods of convincing the MBA students in their study that a particular company practiced a policy of avoiding layoffs.[31] In one situation, Martin and Powers used only a story to persuade people. In the second, they presented statistical data that showed that the company had significantly less involuntary turnover than its competitors. In the third, they used the statistics and the story. And in the fourth, they used a straightforward policy statement written by an executive of the company. The students in the groups that were given the story believed the claim about the policy more than any of the other groups. Other research studies also demonstrate that information is more quickly and accurately remembered when it's first presented in the form of an example or story.[32]

QUESTIONS: FOCUSING THE VALUES

Used effectively, questions concentrate the mind. When leaders ask questions, they send constituents on mental journeys in search of answers. The questions that a leader asks send messages about the focus of the organization, and they're indicators of what's of most concern to the leader. They're one more measure of how serious we are about our espoused beliefs. Questions provide feedback about which values should be attended to and how much energy should be devoted to them. What questions should we be asking if we want people to focus on integrity? On trust? On customer/client satisfaction? On quality? On innovation? On growth? On personal responsibility?

Questions frame the issue and set the agenda.[33] In one of our workshops, we suggested that participants who wanted their constituents to stay focused on continuous improvement ask this simple question of every person attending their next group meeting: "What have you done in the last week to improve so that you're better this week than last?" We then recommended that they repeat this question for at least the next four weeks, predicting that it would take at least that many repetitions to sustain the focus.

About a month later, we heard from a participant in the workshop who had done what we recommended. The first time he asked the question, people looked at each other skeptically, apparently thinking, "Oh, this guy's just been to a seminar." The second time, some staff took him seriously and about 30 percent had a response. The third time, about 70 percent had something to report. And the fourth? Something very interesting happened: "They asked me what *I* had done in the last week to improve *myself* so *I* was better than I was last week." Questions can indeed be very effective tools for change!

Questions also demonstrate the sort of memory the leader has. Are questions asked about what was "assumed" last month? Last quarter? Are questions asked that follow up previous requests and/or dispositions of particular items? Do questions address the future or the past?

When we examine how leaders make people aware of key concerns or shifts in organizational focus, it's readily apparent that their questioning style has a pervasive effect on how organizational members direct their attention. Gayle Hamilton, division manager at Pacific Gas & Electric Company, describes how she shifted concerns from revenue to customer satisfaction: "I never let a day go by without spreading the word that our customers are what we're in business for. I ask each account representative about what our customers are telling them about our services." The first agenda items in her staff meetings—and therefore the first questions—are about customer satisfaction.

LANGUAGE: CHOOSING WORDS DELIBERATELY

Harvard professor Shoshana Zuboff has observed that we're "prisoners" of our organizational vocabulary.[34] Zuboff's choice of words is conscious and none too strong. If you disagree, try talking about an organization for even a day without using the words *employee, manager, boss, supervisor, subordinate,* or *hierarchy.* You may find this exercise nearly impossible. We've all come to accept the words we use as the reality of organizational life. Although we don't think about them, they can trap us into a particular way of thinking about our roles and relationships.

Leaders understand and are attentive to language. They know the power of words. The words we choose to use are metaphors for concepts that define attitudes and behaviors, structures and systems. Our words evoke images of what we hope to create and how we expect people to behave. To see how language influences thought and action, think about the language of mergers and acquisitions. What do you think of when you hear the words "shark repellent" and "war chest"? It's not exactly a friendly scene, is it? In contrast, the wonder of the Magic Kingdom at Disney World can be partially attributed to the deliberate use of language and metaphor. There are no employees at Disney World: everyone is a "performer," and the "personnel department" is called "Central Casting." There are no customers, only "Guests" (always capitalized). And in this family-oriented environment, everyone is on a first-name basis.

SYMBOLS, ARTIFACTS, AND RITUALS: EMPLOYING CEREMONIAL WAYS TO TEACH AND REINFORCE

Leaders pay heed to the informal channels by which organizational messages are conveyed. Foremost among these are the symbols and artifacts of workday life.

Sometimes symbols represent time-honored traditions. Much of the great power of Martin Luther King's "I Have a Dream" speech, as we noted earlier, arises from the ways in which he linked his civil rights message to familiar, time-honored traditions and concepts: the U.S. Constitution, freedom of opportunity, the human family, and the future of little children. The mission church adorns the letterhead of Santa Clara University, signaling the roots and credo of the institution.

In our offices at TPG/Learning Systems, we've hung a poster—one from the New York School of Visual Arts showing a zebra with rainbow-colored stripes. Above the rainbow zebra is a saying that reads, "Good is not enough when you dream of being great." We've adopted the zebra as our symbol of going above and beyond the call to produce greatness for our colleagues and clients. Anyone who does something extraordinary is likely to be awarded a zebra of some variety.

Posters, pictures on walls, objects on desks, and buttons or pins on lapels can be much more than decorative items. Each can serve as a visible reminder of some key organizational value. At Sequent Computer Systems, company president Casey Powell handed out buttons at one critical point. Most of the company wore green "How Can I Help?" buttons; people on the critical path wore red "Priority" buttons. People with green buttons were to do anything to remove obstacles for those with red buttons. Powell himself wore a green button. The buttons cost a total of $73.50; handing them out took fifteen minutes. But those hardware engineers with the red buttons got the message. As one engineer explained, "I think it was a way to make sure we understood how important what we were doing was."[35]

When organizations make major changes, they often proclaim new symbols and discard or destroy old symbols and artifacts in favor of the new. We need look no further than the toppling of the Berlin Wall and the statues of Lenin for dramatic evidence of this. On a smaller scale, when Antonio Zárate took over as general manager of Metalsa and wanted to emphasize a spirit of egalitarianism and teamwork, he had all the names on the parking spaces removed.

Leaders are also attentive to the use of ceremonies, both official and spontaneous, in the reinforcement of shared values. Recognizing that initiation rites are ancient rituals essential to the maintenance of any strong culture, organizations often use ceremonies to mark the entry of people into the group. As we'll discuss much more thoroughly in Chapter Twelve, ceremonies may indicate a transition, a new beginning, a loss, or a hallowed tradition.

The critical point is this: in the performing art of leadership, symbols and artifacts are a leader's props. They're necessary tools for making the message memorable and sustainable over time. Together with rituals, they're a means of keeping the vision and values present even when the leader is absent. When we glance around our office at TPG/Learning Systems and see a zebra, we're reminded that "good is not enough when you dream of being great."

MEASUREMENTS: RECOGNIZING THAT WHAT GETS MEASURED GETS DONE

In Chapter Seven, we mentioned the turnaround led by Brian Coleman, the manager of tool and dies, Ford Motor Company, Dagenham, England. One of the tools that he and his team of union employees developed was a simple device to measure car quality: "The workers would mark a tick on the outline of a car indicating the location of every defect that came down the line."

When they put the device to use, reported Coleman, "I was shocked by the result. After only five hours there were more than 1,400 ticks on our drawing! I asked the team where we should begin, and they pointed to the area with the densest mass of ticks. Why? 'Because that's where we'll have the greatest impact,' they said. That's the opposite of what a management team would have chosen at the time."[36]

For Coleman and his team, that simple measuring device was a major factor in reducing the number of defects by over 70 percent and nearly doubling productivity in three months. Score-keeping systems are essential to knowing how you're doing. In Coleman's case, the value of quality, the specific goal of reducing defects, and the scoring mechanism all converged to produce results. Research indicates clearly that measurement and feedback are essential to increased efforts to improve performance.[37]

Leaders can easily influence outcome by providing the tools for measuring progress. For example, if the organization's performance appraisal system fails to measure how well people perform against the standards of excellence set by corporate values, leaders can add clear performance measures that evaluate how well people are doing on quality, customer service, innovation, respect of others, contribution to profitability, fun, or whatever else is of critical value to the organization.

Rewards (discussed further in Chapter Eleven) are another tangible means of reinforcing values. While increasing member satisfaction is a notable goal of rewards, the most important role of rewards in modeling is to reinforce the key values important to sustaining an adaptive culture. All support systems—incentive, recruitment, training, information, and the like—must be aligned with this purpose.

PHYSICAL SPACE: BELIEVING THAT DESIGN ISN'T JUST FOR ARCHITECTS

In 1988, when Lars Kolind became president of Oticon Holding A/S, he took some rather radical and unorthodox steps to resuscitate the then-eighty-nine-year-old Danish hearing aid manufacturer.[38] Among them were the total elimination of private offices and assigned desks. No one at Oticon has a permanent desk. Instead, employees keep their personal belongings in a locker and their work materials in a rolling cart. They and the cart go wherever they're needed, based on the project at hand.

As if that change weren't enough, Kolind added several coffee bars and dialogue rooms, decorated with circular sofas and a small table, so that people would have places to talk. Elevators were locked, leaving stairwells the only way up and down. Kolind considers the staircase "a superb invention because while you're passing on the staircase you're often talking to each other."[39]

Architecture and the design of physical space send powerful signals about status, preferred ways of interacting, and the best ways to get work done. They reflect the leader's messages only if consciously managed, however; if not, they reflect community standards and the assumptions and preferences of architects and facilities planners.[40]

A current trend in workplace design is the "cave and commons" style, wherein workers who need acoustic solitude, such as software designers, have small private offices that open onto common areas to promote informal conversation. Stewart Brand—writer, inventor, and publisher of the *Whole Earth Catalog*—designed such a space for the Global Business Network, an organization he co-founded. Writes Brand, "The weekly staff meeting at Global Business Network takes place in the commons. Anyone having to miss the meeting because they're on deadline or taking an important phone call can nevertheless hear from their office what's going on. . . . The space has a certain buzz like a newspaper city room, but people can be quietly alone with their work when they need to be."[41]

Brand points out that most buildings adapt poorly to the changing needs of humans and organizations, and others don't adapt at all. We may have little control over the space we occupy, but to the extent that we can influence the design of the workplace, as Kolind and Brand have done, we can facilitate the commitment to shared values.

Committing to the Challenge: Making Actions Count

Leaders demonstrate their intense commitment to the values they espouse by setting an example: this is how they earn and sustain credibility over time. Setting an example is essentially *doing what we say we will do* in a three-stage process of say-we-do. It begins with the clarification of personal values and an appreciation of constituents' values.

Because a cohesive organization stands on common ground, leaders unify constituents around shared values. Shared values focus people's energies and commitments, and they result in more positive work attitudes and higher levels of performance.

The truest test of credible leadership is what leaders pay attention to and what they do. Leaders are measured by the consistency of deeds with words. In this sense, leadership is a performing art, and the repertoire of leaders includes how they spend their time, how they react to critical incidents, the stories they tell, the questions they ask, the language and symbols they choose, the measures they use, and their design of physical space.

Application of these tools of leadership isn't haphazard. While serendipity plays a role, leaders are constantly on the lookout for ways to establish themselves as leaders. They consciously manage the process of modeling. In the next commitment, we present several action-steps you can take to improve and practice setting an example for others.

Commitment Number 7

Set the Example by Behaving in Ways That Are Consistent with Shared Values

➤ Take a look in the mirror.

Clarification of personal values begins with becoming more self-aware. There are a variety of opportunities available, from sensitivity training groups to assessment centers to individual counseling. Whichever you choose, find some way to become better acquainted with who you are and how others see you.

Leadership scholar Warren Bennis has said, "'Know thyself' was the inscription over the Oracle at Delphi. And it is still the most difficult task any of us faces. But until you truly know yourself, strengths and weaknesses, know what you want to do and why you want to do it, you cannot succeed in any but the most superficial sense of the word."[42] Acquiring self-knowledge, says Bennis, demands reflection. There's absolutely no way we can get to know ourselves if we don't take some quiet time for meditation and contemplation.

You may wonder how you can possibly take time out of your schedule to reflect and meditate. Like everything else that's important, you simply make it a priority. There's probably no faster-paced industry than the one Ed McCracken, CEO of Silicon Graphics, is in. Yet McCracken has been meditating daily for over a decade. Says McCracken, "The most important trait of a good leader is knowing who you are. In our industry very often we don't have time to think. You have to do all your homework, but then you have to go with your intuition without letting your mind get in the way."[43]

The quiet time isn't of much value, though, if you aren't objective about yourself. Self-knowledge requires candor; thus, unless you get (and accept) honest, straightforward feedback, you have no objective measure of yourself. The option of 360-degree feedback—an option growing in popularity—suggests many possibilities for us to find out what our peers, bosses, spouses, friends, direct reports, customers, and other constituents think of us. Take advantage of these opportunities. And do it early in your career.

➤ Write your leadership credo.

Begin the critical task of clarifying the principles by which you'll guide others to places they've never been before by translating your personal values and beliefs into a one-page leadership credo. Think about your fundamental values by imagining that you'll be taking a six-month sabbatical to rejuvenate yourself for the challenges ahead. This sabbatical will take you to a remote place without modern communication tools—no phones, faxes, wireless devices, computers, E-mail, or even carrier pigeons. You won't be able to communicate with people back home by any means whatsoever.

Naturally, you'll want to say something before you leave about how you want others to operate in your absence. After all, you'll want to be able to fit back in on your return. Write a one-page memorandum to your constituents, recording the principles by which you want them to make their decisions and actions for the next six months. Since it's only one page, it can't be a detailed to-do list; it can be only a set of values and principles.

Participants who complete this exercise in our workshops find that it helps them clarify their beliefs. Whether you use this presabbatical method or another, do take the time to write your own one-page leadership credo. Then take that memo to your team members, colleagues, partners, customers or clients, and friends and ask them to react to it. Ask them first if they understand it. Then ask what needs to be clarified. Once you've edited your statement, prepare to use it as the basis for a dialogue with your constituents. Many leaders with whom we've worked have done just that—and with very satisfying results.

➤ Write a personal tribute and a tribute to your organization.

As we've noted, before you can stand up for your beliefs, you have to have beliefs for which to stand. You must make clear in your own mind the principles that will guide each of your steps along the way. The first leg of the journey is a process of self-discovery, an inner search for your personal values.

One way to begin the process of clarifying your values is to think first about your ideals—your conception of things as they should be or as you wish them to be. Start with your ideal image of yourself—how you would most like to be seen by others. Try this exercise: Imagine that tonight you'll be honored as Leader of the Year. Hundreds of people will gather to pay tribute to your contributions to your family, your colleagues, your organization, and your community. Several people will make speeches praising your performance and your character. What words or phrases would you most like to hear others say about you? How would you like to be remembered tonight? What descriptions would make you feel the proudest? If you could write these tributes yourself, what would you want them to say?

These descriptive adjectives and phrases may well be lofty and ideal. That's exactly the point: the greater the clarity of, belief in, and passion for our personal standards of excellence, the greater the probability we'll act in concert with them.

To help identify shared values, write a tribute to the organization, whether a small team, a department, a division, or a large institution. This should be similar to the personal tribute, except that it's written about a unit rather than a person. After all, it's not just what people say about you that's important; it's also what they say about the organizational unit you lead. Start with the phrase "Our organization always . . . " and keep completing the statement until you run out of things to say. Do this yourself, and ask your team to do it.

➤ Open a dialogue about personal and shared values.

We know that shared values make a difference and that leaders represent groups. Leaders do what *we* say *we* will do. So it's essential that you have a dialogue about your beliefs and those of your constituents.

Before you engage in dialogue, ask your constituents—whether your entire team or organization or a cross-section of members—to write their own credo statements. Then ask everyone to share aloud what's been written. Model the process by going first. Have every member of your team read his or her credo aloud and then compare notes. Ask yourself and team members these questions:

- How similar to or different from yours are constituents' credos?
- How similar to or different from each other are they?
- Is there a consistent focus?
- How much consensus is there within the team about the relative importance of the various standards?
- How consistent are the credos with the larger organization's values and standards?

Resolve any differences. If there are disagreements over importance, set priorities. Propose hypothetical situations and determine where there are congruent and incongruent points of view; then find the common ground. Ask people how they'll recognize the shared values. What can they do to practice what they preach? What should they avoid? Challenge people to come up with 101 ways that they'll know each shared value. This kind of list making, while often difficult and tedious, is essential to moving from what we *say* to what we *do*!

Take all the data you've generated on personal and organizational values and, perhaps with a facilitator to keep the group focused, develop a brief written credo for your unit. The end result should be a statement that records the shared values that will guide everyone in daily decision making and action taking.

We know many groups that have asked everyone to sign the credo that they jointly develop. After all, the framers of the Constitution signed their document. Shouldn't you have enough pride and conviction in your organization's credo to sign it?

Visibility is critical if you want to make shared values a prominent part of your group's day-to-day life:

- Post the document prominently in offices, branches, plants, and facilities.
- Make a videotape about the credo for people in other sites.
- Talk about the credo in your speeches.
- Put the credo on the back of business cards.
- Create symbols that will remind people of your organization's core values.
- Incorporate your values into personalized, monthly calendars.

Be creative about how you communicate and reinforce your shared values. Just make sure that colleagues, customers, vendors, and other stakeholders know the fundamental beliefs on which the organization is based.

➤ Audit your actions.

It's critical that others see you practicing what you preach. So begin to measure the consistency between your words and deeds by comparing your day-to-day practice against the published statement of shared values. Scrutinize your current routines—the things you do every day, the questions you always ask, the ways you react under pressure, and the ways you recognize and reward others. Are these routines, these habitual patterns of behavior, consistent with what you claim is most important to you and your organization? As management consultant Tom Peters says, "Attention is all there is. You are as good as, or as bad as, your calendar."[44]

Try this technique: Take a piece of paper and draw a vertical line down the middle. On the left side of the page, list the values you preach. Now take out your calendar, your meeting agendas, your interoffice memoranda, and your correspondence for the last two weeks. Using the information from these sources, in the right-hand column write down any actions you took that demonstrated your personal commitment to stated values. Assign an estimate of the amount of time you spent modeling each value. Consider the completed page and ask yourself these questions:

- What do you conclude from an examination of your daily behavior? What do how you spend your time and the issues you address tell you (and others) about what's really important to you?

- Are these the priorities you want to set?
- Are there consistencies between espoused values and values-in-use?
- Are there glaring discrepancies between what you preach and what you practice?
- On what are you spending most of your time?
- To what are you devoting little or no time?

You might also want to get some independent feedback on how others see you acting on your espoused values. One effective technique used by organization development consultants is "shadowing." Typically, a leader will ask a qualified consultant to follow him or her around for a week or two, taking detailed notes on every action, reading every memo, observing every meeting. The shadow consultant then offers feedback on the leader's behavior. This process can be extremely valuable in assessing what your behavior communicates about your values and priorities.

Your own analysis and the feedback from others will most likely suggest that you need to make some changes in how you spend your time. You may have to delegate certain tasks so that you free up time to devote to higher priorities. You may have to change your daily routines in order to send the right signals. Throw out those that are inconsistent and retain those that are well matched. In place of those that you discard, establish new ones that are more reinforcing of the appropriate values and norms. The purpose of the audit, after all, is to provide you with data so that you can make your walk more consistent with your talk. Start spending 30 to 40 percent of your time on your most important strategic priority. Book up your calendar for the next four months with activities that demonstrate your interest in and concern about this priority.

➤ Trade places.

Another way to get feedback about how you're doing and learn about someone else's job at the same time is to swap jobs for a day. That's what Aspect Telecommunications CEO Jim Carreker does once every year. One year he traded places with sales representative Debra Knotek. She got to do everything Carreker would have done that day, from attending meetings with executives to making presentations to major customers. She got to see the job from his point of view; and he, from hers.

Here's what Knotek had to say about her experience walking in Carreker's shoes: "That day, I learned there's a *consistent message* from our leaders to the field sales rep 2,000 miles away. That's indicative of how we communicate, and it's a message about Jim's leadership. . . . When I got back to my office, Jim had written a memo on everything he had done. He was a little nervous at first—if you make a mistake in sales, it directly relates to revenues. But he did a really nice job."[45]

Trading places is a marvelous way to get feedback about how others think you're doing (and to give feedback to someone else). It's a terrific mechanism for testing the consistency of the message and the behavior.

Instead of trading places every year, the management at Quad/Graphics simply leaves the multi-million-dollar printing equipment and all product decisions in the hands of the employees while they attend their annual off-site strategic planning sessions. "Management by walking away," as some people refer to this practice, is a public statement about the extent to which employees are trusted to act responsibly.

➤ Be dramatic.

Sometimes leaders have to consciously stage dramatic events to make a point about what they consider to be the fundamental values. This is particularly important at times of change and transition. We know an executive team that went mountain climbing to teach team members about taking risks with one another. Jack Kahl, CEO and chairman of Manco, chose a less risky—but still dramatic—way to get employees working together: he promised them that if they achieved a stretch goal of $60 million, he would swim across the duck pond at corporate headquarters near Cleveland, Ohio. They reached the goal, and Kahl followed through. He jumped in with the ducks and swam the width of the pond to the cheers of everyone. The event was such a hit that it's become a tradition, but now it's not just Kahl who swims it; others are challenged to join in. Kahl added some drama to the everyday life of the company and in doing so showed by example that he's good on his word.

These actions weren't drama for drama's sake. Instead, they were designed to draw attention to critical values and priorities. Sometimes you have to go out of your way to get a point across.

➤ Tell stories about teachable moments.

It would be exhausting and time-consuming to be at center stage each and every day. However, you can never really be completely offstage: the magic of the theater of leadership is that a story that illustrates an important virtue can be told over and over again.

Sister Dona Taylor, chief administrator of Providence Hospital, uses a parking lot story to illustrate her own (and the hospital's) value of equality:

> Parking spaces are always in short supply, and the only reserved spaces are for our hospital vans. One morning I pulled into the parking structure just about the same time as one of our clerical support staff was pulling into one of these reserved places. I stopped to tell her that these places were reserved, and she apologized for taking my space. I laughed and told her that I didn't have a reserved space, nor did anyone else in the hospital. We were all equal. This incident made the rounds that day throughout the hospital.

Sister Dona still relates this story when she wants to make a point with the staff about how they're all part of the same effort. She uses the story—and the teachable moment she found—to stress a critical value.

Be constantly on the lookout for teachable moments—those precious times when people's consciousness can be elevated. Often teachable moments occur at the peaks and valleys of organizational experience. At the summit, you may need to remind others of what they've accomplished, remind them why the journey was worth the effort, or provide perspective on how their achievement, a step in the right direction, proves the worth of their trials and tribulations. In times of despair, on the other hand, you may need to make the struggle noble and reframe any setbacks as learning experiences.

When you're clear about your values, you'll find it easier to identify these times, events, and activities of potentially momentous impact. Even so, you still have to be alert for them, just as General Schwarzkopf was alert for opportunity on his morning jog.

Never let a moment of learning pass you by—and use these teachable moments for stories after the fact. If you're intimidated by the idea of telling stories, rely on these tips from consultant Gail Wilson:[46]

- Use real-life examples.
- Collect stories and file them by category.
- Get in the habit of keeping a small notebook or diary.
- Attend a storytelling workshop or performance.
- Practice storytelling at home.
- Give stories interesting titles.
- When appropriate, start stories with, "Remember the time when you . . . ?"
- Use direct analogies.
- Start with stories about what you're fluent in.
- Remember who your audience is.

You'll find these tips for building your storytelling skills especially useful.

Many of the examples that we've given in this and other chapters have been about little things. The consistent purpose behind these examples is to encourage leaders to seek out brief moments of learning and seize small opportunities to make heroes of others. Most of leadership, like most of life, is about these little things, really. While the media may focus our attention on changes of a massive scale, most innovation is incremental, one step at a time.

Planning plays an important role, especially when combined with the power inherent in ensuring small wins with people. Both traditional and innovative strategies are involved in small wins. In the next chapter, we'll talk more about how leaders make effective use of a strategy of small wins—of persisting in putting one foot in front of the other.

Commitment Number 7

Set the Example by Behaving in Ways That Are Consistent with Shared Values

➤ Take a look in the mirror.

➤ Write your leadership credo.

➤ Write a personal tribute and a tribute to your organization.

➤ Open a dialogue about personal and shared values.

➤ Audit your actions.

➤ Trade places.

➤ Be dramatic.

➤ Tell stories about teachable moments.

Source: The Leadership Challenge by James M. Kouzes and Barry Z. Posner. Copyright © 1995.

10

Achieve Small Wins

Building Commitment to Action

You have to create a climate that suggests success is imminent.
—CHARLIE (CHARLENE) MAE KNIGHT
Superintendent
Ravenswood School District

Don Bennett is the first amputee to have reached the summit of Mount Rainier. That's 14,410 feet on one leg and two crutches. In fact, he actually had to make the climb twice. On his first attempt, a howling windstorm nearly blew Bennett and his climbing team off the mountain; they had to turn back 410 feet from the summit. But Bennett wasn't discouraged. For another full year, he worked out vigorously. On his second attempt, after five days of rigorous climbing, Bennett planted the flag signifying his triumph.

We asked Bennett how he did it. "One hop at a time," he replied. "I imagined myself on top of that mountain 1,000 times a day. But when I started to climb it, I just said to myself, 'Anybody can hop from here to there.' And I would. And when the going got roughest, and I was really exhausted, that's when I would look down at the path ahead and say to

242

myself, 'You just have to take one more step, and anybody can do that.' And I would."

Bennett faced a daunting challenge; climbing such a mountain is strenuous for any person. And the climb—regardless of the climber—would require a team. As Bennett told us, "You can't do it alone." Long before the team began preparing for the climb, Bennett clearly envisioned the future. Being the first amputee to climb Mount Rainier was part of it, but his vision was even grander than that: he wanted to show all physically challenged people that they could do more than they thought they could do. And Bennett had not only the vision but the method: once he started to climb, he knew he had to take it "one hop at a time."

Bennett's simple advice underscores social psychologists' observations about what's required to tackle "big" problems.[1] Problems that are conceived of too broadly overwhelm us, because they defeat our capacity to even think about what might be done, let alone begin doing something. Imagine right now solving the homelessness problem, or the health care problem, or the world hunger problem, or the global competitiveness problem. Where do we begin?

Leaders face a similar challenge in trying to accomplish the extraordinary: the mountain looks too steep and too high to even think about climbing. Getting ourselves and others to change old mindsets and habits and substitute new ones is a daunting process. Even with the best of intentions, people tend to revert to old and familiar patterns. Working out for a year to get in shape to climb a mountain requires discipline. Staying with it for five days in the freezing cold requires stamina and determination. And can you imagine then having to start all over again?

Getting commitment to new behaviors, like solving big problems, is often overwhelming. So how do leaders do it? How do they get people to *want* to change the way they're currently headed, to break out of existing behaviors, to tackle big problems, to attempt extraordinary performance? The answer: one hop at a time!

Major Change Is a Process of Small Wins

The most effective change processes are incremental; they break down big problems into small, doable steps and get a person to say yes numerous times, not just once. Bennett's example illustrates the psychology of change adopted by successful leaders and adventurers. They look at progress as incremental—one hop at a time. Leaders help others to see how progress can be made by breaking the journey down into measurable goals and milestones.

The scientific community has always understood that major breakthroughs are likely to be the result of the work of hundreds of researchers, as countless contributions finally begin to add up to a solution. Advances in medicine or physics, for example, often involve many experiments focused on various pieces of the problem. Likewise, the sum total of all the "little" improvements in technology, regardless of the industry, have likely contributed to a greater increase in organizational productivity than all the great inventors and their inventions.[2]

WHAT OF STRATEGIC PLANNING OR PARADIGM SHIFTS?

The traditional management approach to carrying out an objective is to start with strategic planning. Unfortunately, strategic planning doesn't even begin to convey the feelings and emotions that people experience when they reach milestones. Bennett said, "One hop at a time," not "One strategic plan at a time." Even more significant, strategic planning doesn't work—at least not as it's supposed to. Management scholar Henry Mintzberg's intensive study "found strategy making to be a complex, interactive, and evolutionary process, best described as one of adaptive learning. Strategic change was found to be uneven and unpredictable . . . especially when the organization faced unpredicted shifts in the environment."[3] More significant still is Mintzberg's finding that "a number of biased researchers set out to prove that planning paid, and collectively they proved no such thing."[4] Strategic planning, it turns out, is *not* a magic potion. It's a process that detaches strategy from operations, thinking from doing.

Bennett did have a plan, of course. He and his team had to choose the appropriate climbing season, purchase and pack the necessary food and gear, and select a safe route. But this was not a detached process. Like all successful leaders, Bennett had his head in the clouds (seeing himself on top of the mountain) *and* his feet on the ground (one hop at a time). Thinking wasn't separated from doing; Bennett was very much engaged in both.

Another recent school of thought portrays leaders as people who produce *paradigm shifts* in their constituents.[5] This phrase has captured a great deal of attention—in the training community, in particular—and is central to much discussion about change. While it's true that revolutionary breakthroughs in science and industry *do* result from new mental models, it would be misleading to suggest that a prerequisite for leadership is the ability to create a scientific or business revolution.

To be sure, leaders challenge standard operating procedures. They continually ask, "Why do we need to do it that way? Why not this way?" And occasionally they do invent entire new industries or technologies. But the leaders in our study didn't report many such revolutionary breakthroughs. These breakthroughs don't (and won't) happen very often. Indeed, if we had to wait for paradigm shifts before we could lead, we could be waiting decades.

The emphasis on paradigm shifts also contributes to the myth that only a few geniuses can lead. Yes, leaders must search for opportunities to grow and innovate; they must experiment and take risks. But progress *today* is more likely to be the result of a focus on incremental improvements in tools and processes than of tectonic shifts of minds. And a focus on one-hop-at-a-time leading will enable more of us ordinary mortals to take part in the joys of transforming our schools, congregations, communities, agencies, hospitals, corporations, governments, or small businesses into high-performing organizations.

HOW DO SMALL WINS WORK?

Another often-used term for the process Bennett employed is *small wins*. Leaders keep the dream in mind; then they act and adapt on the move. The small-wins process also enables leaders to build constituents' commitment to a course of action. Professional fund-raisers do much the same thing when they begin by asking for a small or indeterminate contribution from new donors. They know that it's easier to go back and request more (and they do) in the future from those who've made an initial contribution than to return to someone who's already said no.

When Charlie Mae Knight was appointed the new superintendent for the Ravenswood School District in East Palo Alto, she was the twelfth superintendent in ten years. She encountered a district in which 50 percent of the schools were closed and 98 percent of the children were performing in the lowest percentile for academic achievement in California. The district had the state's lowest revenue rate. There were buckets in classrooms to catch the rain leaking through decrepit roofs, the stench from the restrooms was overwhelming, homeless organizations were operating out of the school sites, and pilfering was rampant. Gophers and rats had begun to take over the facilities. As if this weren't challenging enough, Knight had to wrestle with a ten-year lawsuit, the intent of which was to dissolve the district for its poor educational quality and force the children to transfer to schools outside of their community.

Where would *you* start to improve a district such as this? Would you even take the job? Like other leaders who achieve extraordinary results, Knight used the small-wins process. She started with actions that were within her control, that were tangible, that were doable, and that would get the ball rolling. "It's hard to get anybody excited about just a vision. You must show something happening," she told us.

Knight immediately enlisted support from Bay Area companies and community foundations to get the badly needed resources. The first project she undertook was refurbishing the Garden Oaks School. Volunteer engineers from nearby Raychem Corporation repaired the electrical wiring and phone systems. The community helped paint the building inside and out, and hardware stores donated supplies. When pellet guns had eliminated the last of the rats and refurbishing was complete, 350 volunteers and community members stood together at the site of their new school singing, "We Shall Overcome."

"Winning at the beginning was so important," Knight said, "because winning provided some indication of movement. I had to show some visible signs that change was taking place in order to keep up the momentum and in order to restore confidence in the people that we *could* provide quality education."

And it worked. Before too long, local residents began calling to find out what color paint was used for the school so they could paint their houses in a matching shade. They went out and bought trees and planted sod in front of their homes. They stopped dumping old couches on school property. New leadership came forth from parents, who began to demand more of a say. In response, an "Effort Hours" program for parents was set up so that they could volunteer time at the school. Parents told Knight she didn't need to send the district gardeners out to the Garden Oaks School; they'd take care of it. Teachers began to notice that something was happening, and they wanted to be part of it too. Prior to these wins, new teachers had avoided the district like the plague; when the wins began to take effect, graduates from nearby Stanford University wanted to work in the district. More local companies joined in as well. The district was on a roll.

The momentum and visible signs of success have paid off: every school in the district is now open. In 1987, two years after Knight's arrival, all children were performing at least in the fifty-first percentile; one of the schools had climbed to the sixty-eighth percentile. Revenues went up from $1,900 per student to $3,500. It was one of the first schools in the state to use technology in every discipline, outdistancing almost every other school in California technologically. It was one of the first elementary schools in California to join the Internet. The lawsuit has been dropped. And for the first time ever, East Palo Alto received the state's Distinguished School Award based on improved test scores and innovative programs.

WHY DO SMALL WINS WORK?

Did Knight have a dream? Absolutely. A shifted paradigm or a strategic plan? Forget it. What worked in Ravenswood were "visible signs" and "momentum." Little victories over leaky roofs, rats, trash, and peeled paint propelled the change forward.

That small wins work isn't really news to scholars of technological innovation. An extensive study involving five Du Pont Chemicals plants documented that minor technical changes (for example, introduction of forklift trucks)—rather than major changes (for example, introduction of new chemical processing technologies)—accounted for over two-thirds of the reductions in production costs over a thirty-year period.[6] The minor technical changes were small improvements, made by people familiar with current operations. Less time, skill, effort, and expense were required to produce them than to implement the major changes. Much of the improvement was really part of the process of learning by doing.

The success of behavior-change programs such as Alcoholics Anonymous, Weight Watchers, and Smoke Enders is due in large part to their incremental change philosophies. None insists that participants become totally abstinent for the rest of their lives. Although this is the goal of the Alcoholics Anonymous program, alcoholics are told to stay sober one day at a time—or one hour at a time, if temptation is severe. The seeming impossibility of lifetime abstinence is scaled down to the more workable task of not taking a drink for twenty-four hours. This perspective drastically reduces the size of a win necessary to maintain sobriety.

A small win, points out organizational sociologist Karl Weick, is "a concrete, complete, implemented outcome of moderate importance."[7] Small wins form the basis for a consistent pattern of winning that attracts people who want to be allied with a successful venture. Small wins deter opposition for a simple reason: it's hard to argue against success, and thus small wins decrease resistance to subsequent proposals. In achieving a small win, leaders identify the place to get started. They make the project seem doable within existing skill and resource levels. This approach minimizes the cost of trying and reduces the risks of failing. What's exciting about this process is that once a small win has been accomplished, natural forces are set in motion that favor stepping out toward another small win.

Small wins build people's confidence and reinforce their natural desire to feel successful. Since additional resources tend to flow to winners, this means that slightly larger wins can be attempted next. A series of small wins therefore provides a foundation of stable building blocks. Each win preserves gains and makes it harder to return to preexisting conditions. Like miniature experiments or pilot studies, small wins also provide information that facilitates learning and adaptation.

When leaders deliberately cultivate a strategy of small wins, they make it easier for people to want to go along with their requests. If people can see that a leader is asking them to do something that they're quite capable of doing, they feel some assurance that they can be successful at the task. On the other hand, it's difficult to gain people's cooperation when they're unsure of their ability to meet the demands placed upon them or when the perceived costs of failure seem high. When the leader can reduce the size of the demand (for example, to paint a building or fix a phone or not take a drink for twenty-four hours), people don't get overwhelmed by the enormity of the task. Their energy goes into getting the job done, instead of wondering "how will we *ever* solve that problem?"

Leading the Small-Wins Process

Like Knight and Bennett, successful leaders actively use the small-wins process to make people feel like winners. In turn, people who feel like winners have heightened interest in continuing with the journey. This simple strategy of winning hop by hop succeeds while many massive overhauls and gigantic projects fail. Why? It's not just that it's easier. It's also because it builds personal and group commitment. Effective leaders use the essentials of

- Mobilizing for fast action and
- Sustaining commitment

to make it easy for people to change. They work hard at finding all the little ways that people can succeed at doing things differently. They also sustain commitment to difficult and distant dreams via the psychological process underlying the small-wins approach.

MOBILIZING FOR FAST ACTION

Leaders take certain steps to ensure that people can take fast, responsive action:

- They experiment continuously.
- They reduce items to their essence.
- They act with a sense of urgency.

These actions help keep momentum going and success at high levels.

Experimenting Continuously

The magic in small wins is the experimentation process—setting up little tests that continually help people learn something. Pilot studies, demonstration projects, laboratory tests, field experiments, market trials, and the like are all ways to generate lots of possibilities. One of those possibilities just might catch on.

Remember how important experimentation is to challenging the process? Well, it's equally important to goal attainment. As we've learned, "What have you changed lately?" is a wonderful question to ask to stimulate innovation. If you want to stimulate implementation, on the other hand, ask, "What have you initiated lately?"

When Dan McMullin was vice president of Mini Mart, Inc., he wanted to increase average sales per transaction in the stores. His team experimented with various merchandising and display programs, identified products for "plus selling," and organized recognition and awards contests. McMullin himself spent over five weeks behind sales counters, waiting on customers in different stores, suggesting that they "try our hot and tasty nachos." The results of this campaign added up to an overall 4 percent increase in average sales per transaction. A small win—and small wins add up.

Reducing Items to Their Essence

The pace of managerial work is fast and relentless. The average executive has nine minutes of uninterrupted time to spend on any one item.[8] Because of the brevity of their interactions, leaders are forced to act on their dreams in brief bursts. The beauty of a small win is that it's compact, it's simple, and it can catch the attention of people who have only nine minutes to listen to an idea or read a proposal. While the absolute amount of time spent on a task might be longer, the discipline of concentrating on short intervals of activity causes one to really focus on what's essential. And because small-win tasks are compact and simple, they make it easier to maintain an upbeat, noncontroversial atmosphere. Think about how much easier it was for Knight to get volunteers to paint a building than to get volunteers to attempt to raise their academic percentile ranking by fifty points (which they also did!).

Reducing a long-term, strategic change to its essence necessitates finding a core theme and, in many cases, a central person to carry the banner. As her first theme, Knight chose refurbishing the physical structure and environment of one school. She held the banner for all to see—and supporters picked up the cause.

A common method to reduce an item to its essence is the one-page memo. Because being restricted to a single page demands very sharp focus, leaders learn to boil issues down to the core. An added benefit is that concise, one-page notes are a lot more likely to be read than lengthy tomes.

Leaders also understand how critical it is to break problems down into small pieces so that they're more easily comprehended. In planning, leaders divide tasks into doable steps with milestones.[9] The benefit of breaking major changes down into smaller, incremental changes is well demonstrated by the experience of LuAnn Sullivan, a branch office manager for Wells Fargo Bank. Although core deposits in her office hadn't grown for several years, they doubled in two years under her leadership. How did she do it? Sullivan broke her overall goal down into smaller parts so that each person had individual monthly and weekly goals. Sullivan thus made the goal of doubling core deposits seem doable to her colleagues. Mary Delaney, a customer service representative, said that when Sullivan first told her of the broader goal, she thought that they would never be able to accomplish it. However, Delaney explains, "once I saw that I could achieve my weekly goals, the big goal didn't seem so crazy and it was easy to get motivated."[10]

Acting with a Sense of Urgency

Waiting for permission is *not* characteristic of people who get extraordinary things done, whether leaders or individual contributors. Acting with a sense of urgency *is*. Small wins allow for immediate action with near and clear success. Consultant Robert Schaffer describes the small-wins process as one with "zest," and that word certainly inspires the kind of images that personal bests represent.[11]

Consider, for instance, this story about Melissa Poe of St. Henry's School in Nashville, Tennessee. On August 4, 1989, as a fourth-grader fearful of the continued destruction of the earth's resources, Poe wrote a letter to President George Bush, asking for his assistance in her campaign to save the environment for the enjoyment of future generations.

After sending the letter, Poe worried that it would never be brought to the president's attention. After all, she was only a child. So, with the urgency of the issue pressing on her mind, she decided to get the president's attention by having her letter placed on a billboard. Through sheer diligence and hard work, the nine-year-old got her letter placed on one billboard free of charge in September 1989—and founded Kids for a Clean Environment (Kids F.A.C.E.), an organization whose goal is to develop programs to clean up the environment.

Almost immediately, Poe began receiving letters from kids who were as concerned as she about the environment. They wanted to help. By the time

Poe finally received a response from the president, the disappointing form letter wasn't enough to crush her dream. She no longer needed the help of someone famous to get her message across. Poe had found in herself the person she needed—that powerful someone who could inspire others to get involved and make her dream a reality.

By April 1990, more than 250 billboards across the country were displaying her letter free of charge, and Kids F.A.C.E. membership had swelled. As the organization grew, Poe's first Kids F.A.C.E. project, a recycling program at her school, led to a manual full of ideas on how to clean up the environment. Poe's impatience and zest motivated her to do something—and her work has paid off. Today there are more than 200,000 members and 2,000 chapters of Kids F.A.C.E.[12]

Poe is proof that small wins work—and for kids too. Leadership truly is everyone's business.

SUSTAINING COMMITMENT

Getting and keeping others committed is important to leaders, because commitment to one behavior has implications for a variety of other behaviors. Today's actions carry us into the future. To help ensure that the future matches the vision, leaders

- Give people choices.
- Make choices visible.
- Make choices hard to back out of.

Making a choice helps us to resolve our doubts and reconcile any inconsistencies between our attitudes and behavior. Announcing that choice and acting upon it make the decision more difficult to change.

When we decided to write this book (a conscious choice on our part), we told hundreds of people (that is, we went public with it). Before too long, the people we had told asked us, "How's the book coming?" At that point we had to get serious. Then we signed a contract with our publisher, making it harder still to back out. We were committed. Each one of these elements—choice, visibility, and irrevocability—is key to sustaining effort.

Once people have "signed up" for a project and put many hours into its success, they're unlikely to easily give up. To do so would imply an admission that they had made a mistake and that their previous efforts had been worthless. Being committed is a binding process. The small-wins approach contributes daily to sustaining commitment because it makes it easy to take the first step and each subsequent one.

Giving People Choices

Leaders wisely don't try to push people to change; instead, they invite people to join in the adventure, and they provide further choices along the way. The leader tries to tap people's natural drive for autonomy: if you and I are sitting at a table predicting the probability of pulling my number out of a hat, I'll predict that I have a much better chance of winning if I know that it's *my* hand that will do the picking rather than yours (even though the odds are the same). People tend to believe that, given the chance, they can make a difference.[13]

What does it mean to have choice? Essentially, it means feeling personally responsible for a decision or action. Internally, the dialogue goes something like this: "It was *my* choice. I wasn't forced. I had alternatives. I had a realistic picture of what one alternative would entail over another, and I chose this one. In the end, there's no person or factor other than myself to take responsibility for the success or failure of this decision or action."

Choice is the cement that binds actions to the person, motivating individuals to accept responsibility for their acts. A good example of the power of choice in creating commitment comes from an internal study done by Texas Instruments. That organization found that the best predictor of a project's failure or success was whether people had volunteered or had been assigned to the project.[14] In choosing, people are indicating their belief that they can do what's required. People who expect to succeed are considerably more likely to be successful than those who don't expect to do well. Choice unleashes the power of expectations.

What's important in the "choice" process is making certain that people really have alternatives. A forced decision between working on a particular project and looking for a new job in another company fails the test of choice—so don't expect it to build commitment. On the other hand, if the focus is on growth rather than downsizing and reengineering, commitment could be built by involving people in seeing how a new combination of their talents could create business opportunities.

Accentuating the intrinsic rewards of tasks rather than emphasizing an external rationale creates higher levels of commitment. Employees who work hard primarily for the big bucks are unlikely to be able to sustain energy and effort over the long haul. It's too easy for them to say, "Well, I never really liked the work or believed we could make the project happen successfully. I was just doing it for the money." If organizations hope for commitment, their members need some other reason for signing up, whether it's what they'll learn from the path-breaking work, or the thrill of inventing a pioneering new product, or the chance to save a school system. These intrinsic opportunities are often the only "real" choices that leaders have to offer.

Giving people a realistic picture of the journey before asking them to sign up is another aspect of choice. Researchers find that those who have "realistic job previews" are significantly more likely to stay longer with that organization and are likely to report higher levels of productivity and job satisfaction.[15] The New York investment banking house of Morgan Stanley encourages job candidates to discuss the demands of the job with their spouses, because new recruits sometimes work 100 hours a week. The firm's managing directors and their spouses take promising candidates, along with their significant others, out to dinner to bring home to them what they'll face. They want to make certain that a candidate whose family won't be comfortable with these job demands won't consider taking a position with Morgan Stanley.[16]

Making Choices Visible to Others
Commitment is also more likely if choices are made visible. By announcing our choices to the public and by making the subsequent actions visible, we offer tangible, undeniable evidence of our commitment to the cause. We also become subject to other people's review and observation.

Testimonials in behavior-change programs such as Alcoholics Anonymous and Weight Watchers make an individual's level of commitment quite visible to others. Stating one's days or years of sobriety or stepping on the scale with others watching is more binding than the promise to do better next week.

Visibility makes it nearly impossible for people to deny their choice or to claim that they forgot about it. When Shiseido in Japan decided to reform the company in order to "bring joy to customers," the dress code became a very visible signal. Ryuzaburo Kaku, chairman and representative director of Canon, Inc., reported that "we proposed dressing more casually in order to make the working atmosphere liberal so as to encourage liberal thinking. . . . [We] considered that this was a part of the entire reform process. Besides the reforms which would take some time to put in place, we wanted all the employees to feel that 'the company is being reborn' by introducing specific reforms that could be implemented immediately."[17]

Levi Strauss & Co. has some unique and innovative mechanisms for making choices more visible. Because "ethical management practices" is one of that organization's stated business aspirations, part of the LS&CO Core Curriculum is a three-day program dedicated to teaching processes for thinking and acting ethically. Participants are asked to write down some of the ethical dilemmas they face in the workplace and to post them on a "Deliberation Wall." Issues that participants then problem-solve together, using ethical decision-making processes, are selected directly from the Deliberation Wall. This method of emphasizing ethics enables people to be more public about their ethical issues not only in the workshop but also back at work. The emphasis on going public with issues has enabled LS&CO to apply its "ethical reasoning approach" to numerous business decisions, including the selection of business partners.

In addition, because LS&CO often struggles with some rather difficult issues, such as whether or not to close a plant in China due to human rights issues, the senior management of LS&CO decided to go public with deliberations on these questions in Town Meetings—meetings at which managers openly discuss the issues before company employees and get feedback from them. It's easy to deny a decision made in secret; but when your deliberations are visible, you can't escape.

The Deliberation Wall and the Town Meeting illustrate another potent effect of visibility: it calls on leaders to serve as role models. By demonstrating their own commitment openly, they're setting the stage for other members of the organization to visibly demonstrate their levels of commitment. When we see that everyone around us is contributing, not doing our part is difficult to excuse.

Leaders foster visibility when they spread news of the activities of their group members. As Sunne McPeak, president and CEO of the Bay Area Economic Forum, points out, building stable political coalitions is often based on making certain that participants' involvement is publicized. "Good press," she notes, "is an essential political currency." Getting good press for constituents is extremely sage advice. Not only do people want to be associated with those who get and give good press; they also become more committed to decisions and actions that air on the evening news or in the company newsletter.

Creating Choices That Are Hard to Revoke

For people to become committed to a choice, making the decision public is necessary but insufficient. In addition, the choice must be one that can't be easily changed. The harder a choice is to change, the greater a person's investment in it. Choices that are easy to reverse are taken lightly; ones that are difficult to undo are treated very seriously.

Think about this example for a moment. Let's suppose that you've considered for a long time a move to the country. You've been telling your friends and family for years that you're so sick of the smog, the traffic, and the congestion of the city that you're heading out. You even periodically rent a vacation home out in the country or up in the mountains. But you never make the move. Then one day you decide to do it. You put your house up for sale and *buy* that home in the country. Which is harder to back out of: renting the house in the country or buying it? In view of the obvious answer, leaders find ways to get people to *own*, not just rent, their decisions.

One method of communicating the importance of a hiring decision, as well as making that decision both more free and more binding, is the process of multiple interviews. Both large and small organizations use this process to test candidates' fit with them (and their fit with candidates; the method is effective in both directions). Some companies engage in lengthy discussions with their applicants, telling them the bad side as well as the good to make sure they're not overselling the position. The process may include as many as six different days of interviews, as well as a day in the field with key sales or field engineering personnel. Although this process weeds out many applicants, the ratio of acceptances to job offers is fairly high. After all, once applicants have invested so much energy trying to get hired, they're more likely to believe they really want to join the organization.

Strong social and interpersonal ties within an organization make staying with that organization much more attractive for people, and the multiple interview process is one approach to strengthening such bonds. After all, how committed would you feel to a company that would hire just anyone off the street? And because people are less committed to their actions when they're less committed to the people, strong interpersonal bonds can also serve to reinforce productive work norms. If our peers are dedicated, we'll more likely be dedicated.

Once we've taken an action that can't be easily reversed, we're required to find and accept salient arguments that support and justify our actions. This process results in a strong, *internalized* rationale that deepens personal responsibility and confirms our belief in the correctness of our actions. In other words, we convince ourselves that the course of action we took was the proper one, thus minimizing any misgivings about alternatives not selected.

Because leaders understand the intensity of this process, when they find it necessary to change a previous course of action—perhaps one set by a predecessor—they provide people with *external* justifications for the change. Just as we bind people to a decision by creating *internal* justification, we unbind them so that they can commit to a new course by offering external explanations. Leaders may also need to either separate people who used to work together or bring in new people in order to loosen the social glue that ties people to old habits. External rationales—the circumstances demand a change, the market has changed dramatically, the customers' needs have changed—make people feel that they're not solely responsible for their behavior. This reduces some of the pain associated with a change, makes it easier for people to distance themselves from previous positions, and readies people to commit to a new course. It's a way for all of us to save face when times do in fact change and we have to abandon something we've previously fervently supported.

Committing to the Challenge: Small Wins Strengthen Commitment and People

Leading by example, which we discussed in the previous chapter, is a perfect illustration of the process of becoming committed. Leaders make choices and are perceived, especially by constituents, to have considerable latitude in what they say and do. Leaders' behavior is quite public and conspicuously visible to others: leaders always have an audience. Leaders' actions tend to be binding because they're irrevocable: leaders take a position and stake their reputation on the prescribed course of action. Committing ourselves as leaders is often a struggle. That struggle is a little bit easier when we can claim a few tiny victories every day.

We need those victories. Without them, the quest for the summit—for peak performance in ourselves and our organizations—can seem dauntingly difficult. Making a dent, let alone a difference, in the major problems we face seems to require such overwhelming force that many people are too discouraged to set out on the journey. An ancient philosopher remarked that "the journey of a thousand miles begins with the first step." Leaders know this—and that they must get us started. They convince us that the impossible is possible. They show us the way.

Achieving small wins is the leadership strategy of choice. Small wins breed success and propel us down the path. Experiments, pilot projects, and market trials all facilitate the process of getting started. Breaking problems into manageable pieces keeps us from being overwhelmed. When our work and community lives are fast-paced and full of interruptions, to get extraordinary things done we must stay focused on what's essential. Above all, *leaders just do it.* Small victories attract constituents, so leaders get out there and make something happen.

Achieving small wins is all about creating momentum and getting people to remain on the path. Indeed, the process of building and sustaining commitment is intriguingly similar to the process of strengthening others. People feel strong—and more committed to their tasks—when they take part in setting goals and when their jobs offer discretion and self-determination. People are more committed when they feel in control of decisions, and they're stronger when not closely supervised or monitored. Choice strengthens both us and our bonds to the group.

Visibility also has this dual effect. By publicizing others' contributions, leaders open the door to potential new relationships. Success is an attractive magnet, pulling people together and increasing their attachment to the project. Publicity also calls attention to the significance of people's actions, creating both internal and external expectations that an action is worthy of time and energy. Commitment—staying the course—is thus facilitated when people feel that they have a choice, when their decisions and actions are visible, and when they can't easily deny or back out of actions.

In this commitment, we present action-steps that you can use to increase your own and others' dedication and resolve.

Commitment Number 8

Achieve Small Wins That Promote Consistent Progress and Build Commitment

➤ Take it personally.

Bob Galvin, chairman of the executive committee of Motorola—a Malcolm Baldrige National Quality Award–winning company known for its quality and innovation—has said, "Quality is a very personal obligation. If you can't talk about quality in the first person . . . then you have not moved to the level of involvement of quality that is absolutely essential."[18]

Whether you lead a small or a large group, the first small win "unit" is you. Substitute any critical issue—education, health care, innovation, profitability, community—in Galvin's statement, and the message is the same: our particular challenge starts with each one of us personally. So the place to start is with your own work, in your own cubicle, in your own home. What have you done today to take a hop toward improvement? What about in the last five minutes? What have you done to take your issue personally? What have you initiated lately?

Remember that progress is made incrementally, one hop at a time. Lists serve as our memories for all those hopping ideas. Make a list of all the simple things that you can do to move your constituents toward the summit—things you can do yourself, without anyone's approval. Alternatively, you can make this list as a small group or team, brainstorming a number of possible actions and then choosing a handful to implement.

If you're having trouble coming up with your own list, read one of the many published books of things to do in a variety of arenas. For pure joy and inspiring stimulation, try these for starters:

- EarthWorks Group, *50 Simple Things You Can Do to Save the Earth* (Berkeley: EarthWorks Press, 1989).
- EarthWorks Group, *50 Simple Things Your Business Can Do to Save the Earth* (Berkeley: EarthWorks Press, 1991).
- Faculty of the UCLA School of Public Health, *50 Simple Things You Can Do to Save Your Life* (Berkeley: EarthWorks Press, 1992).
- Sara P. Noble, ed., *301 Great Management Ideas from America's Most Innovative Small Companies* (Boston: *Inc.* magazine, 1991).

260 THE LEADERSHIP CHALLENGE

- Sara P. Noble, ed., *Managing People: 101 Proven Ideas for Making You and Your People More Productive* (Boston: *Inc.* magazine, 1992).

Whatever you choose, *do it!* Actions speak louder than words. They're what earns us credibility, after all. So take a lesson from Melissa Poe: *do something.*

➤ Make a plan.

We've devoted this book to discussing the behavioral side of leadership. That's been intentional, since most of what people have told us involves the human dimension. It would, however, be misleading to say that people will commit themselves to a course of action that's unconscious and unarticulated. High-performance projects are carefully planned. No mountain climber would ever think of setting out to scale a summit without extensive groundwork. Indeed, every personal best we examined was characterized by attention to the details of planning and preparation.

There are a few things to keep in mind when planning:

- Drive your planning by your values and vision, not by technique. There are many useful planning tools, but none should determine what you want to do.
- Involve as many of the people who'll have to implement the plan as possible in the planning process. Both empowerment and commitment are increased through choice, and involvement in planning increases people's discretion over what they do.
- Break the project into manageable pieces. One of the greatest benefits of planning is that needed events and milestones are made explicit.
- Use the planning process as a means of getting people to mentally walk through the entire journey. This act of visualizing the events, milestones, tasks, and goals enables people to anticipate the future and imagine their success.

➤ Create a model.

One very effective way to get started on the road to success is to select one site or program with which to experiment. Use it as a model of what you'd like to do in other programs or locations. That's what Charlie Mae Knight did with the Garden Oaks School. She recruited some volunteers, and they proceeded to fix the leaks, paint the building, exterminate the rats, and repair the phone system. Soon they had an example to show people what could be done. This success uplifted people's spirits, and they wanted to join in—at the school and at home. Thus the school became a showcase for a dream.

When you make a model, don't require that every subsequent project or facility track the showcase exactly. People's commitment is increased if they sense that what they're doing has its own distinctive image and is unique. If people are forced to copy the model, they won't develop a feeling of ownership of their project. Instead, use the model as a visual aid in teaching people about the principles of achieving excellence and then challenge them to improve on it and adapt it to their environment.

Models are experiments, really. As such, they can serve as laboratories for trying, failing, and learning. Challenge one of your teams to go off and experiment with something. If your organization is a small-town store whose sales per square foot need improving, team members might change the floor layout, widen the aisles, reorganize the shelves, or visit a successful competitor in the area for good ideas. Whatever team members do, your job is to encourage them to test and learn.

➤ Break it up and break it down.

Try this exercise. Take a hundred cards and count them one at a time. Now count again, this time stacking the cards in ten piles of ten. Which was easier and faster? We bet it was the ten piles of ten. Why? Because—as with most of life's tasks—you were probably interrupted (even if only by a thought), losing your place and having to start all over again. This illustrates why breaking things into smaller tasks is such a smart tactic.

Once you've set your sights, move forward incrementally. Don't attempt to accomplish too much at once, especially in the beginning. Break large groups and goals into small cohesive teams and doable tasks. Provide orientation and training at the start of every new project, even if members of the team are experienced. Every new project has a shakedown period: group members may not have worked together before, and the project is likely to be unique.

The key to getting started is *do*ability. Identify something that people feel they can do with existing skills and resources; this makes it easier for people to say yes. Make sure you include a few early successes in your plan. There's nothing more discouraging than being confronted initially with tasks that you don't know how to do and at which you know you'll fail. Assigning tasks that team members are unequipped to handle is like sending a novice to the expert ski slope. Instead, let people start on the beginners' slope and work their way up to the advanced.

Keep people focused on the meaning and significance of the vision, and remind them to take it one day at a time (or one hour at a time, if necessary). Implement things in small, planned increments. If your task is to improve the productivity of your plant, for example, painting the walls and refurbishing the bathrooms are little tasks that move in that direction. Phil Turner had the machines that spool wire in Raychem's wire and cable plant torn down, repaired, and reassembled one by one instead of trying to fix them all at once. As most college students who've pulled an all-nighter before a final exam come to realize, it's a lot more productive to make a little progress daily than to attempt to do the whole task all at once.

➤ Ask for volunteers.

Instead of mandating improvements at the Garden Oaks School or starting a ballot initiative to raise taxes, Superintendent Knight asked for volunteers from local businesses to help out. When you give people a *choice* about being part of what's happening, they're much more likely to be committed. Choice builds commitment and creates ownership, and making people feel like owners is key. (When was the last time you washed a rental car?) Unless people feel like owners, unless they have choices to make, they can't truly exercise personal responsibility.

Choice can be as simple as talking over a change with your team. What needs to be done? Who's going to do what? What decisions will people have to make along the way? If you already have an established, clear vision, team consensus, and shared strong feelings about the right way to do things in your organization, you have an opportunity for "guided autonomy." Your team can autonomously determine how to reach the summit, with team members guided by the agreed-upon direction. Although choice is always bounded, people have varying amounts of space within which they have to operate. The larger the space, the greater the maneuvering room. The art of leadership lies in knowing how to create a sense of spaciousness while staying focused on the horizon.

➤ Use a bulletin board.

Be certain to make decisions visible. Remember, it's a lot more difficult to reverse a decision that's been made public than one still unexpressed. By making visible the choices that people have made, you create binding forces that increase the energy and the drive those people direct at accomplishing and succeeding with the task. When the team is assembled, let the group know what choices team members have made. Better yet, let them tell their peers what they've decided to do, and why. Publicize their decisions in newsletters, memos, and posters. Remember how effective Melissa Poe's billboards were in getting attention and in keeping Poe and her colleagues committed? Pick a theme and plaster it on T-shirts, mugs, caps, plaques. How about a town crier? And if you want to create dialogue about a decision, why not try your own version of Levi Strauss & Co.'s Deliberation Wall?

As important as it is to make choices visible, it's equally critical to make progress visible. Many manufacturing plants now use electronic signs controlled by a computer to visibly display hourly or daily progress, but even a cardboard sign will do. The point is to let people know how they're doing in a timely manner. We can't imagine any sports team that would wait until the end of the game for some official to tell them the score. In addition, schedule regular opportunities for people to meet to discuss progress and problems.

➤ Sell the benefits.

There are two ways to bring about change: you can force it, or you can let it happen naturally. The former is faster, but it increases resistance and can be extremely expensive. The latter is slower but tends to receive greater acceptance. Wherever possible, make use of the natural dynamics of change. That doesn't mean you must sit idly by while people slowly learn to accept new ideas, however. Rather, you should understand how change works and put that knowledge to productive use.

An innovation that offers the promise of solving a persistent and difficult problem and that promises a clear advantage over existing solutions for a critical mass of people will have a higher degree of acceptance than one that appeals only to a select group or doesn't appear to address a felt need. In other words, you stand a better chance of gaining acceptance of and commitment to an innovation if you show people how they'll benefit from it. Salespeople call this "benefit selling." So when you begin a change effort in your organization, clearly communicate the benefits of the change; don't assume that the benefits are obvious to others just because they're obvious to you.

Innovations are more easily adopted if they seem to be compatible with accepted values and norms. Rather than positioning changes as something revolutionary, show how they fit into the accepted beliefs and expectations of the company and the individuals. Changes that are easy to understand and to implement—changes that are "user-friendly," to borrow a term from technology—will be accepted far more quickly than those that aren't and are thus more likely to succeed. So keep things simple, design them for use at the skill level of the largest number of potential users, and provide training where necessary.

Successful innovations are always strongly advocated by influential people. Find highly respected individuals or groups in the organization who agree with you, and ask those people to introduce the change with their peers.

➤ Take people to dinner (or breakfast).

When Dan Davey arrived as the new manager for one of the Northern California offices of Pacific Gas & Electric Company, he found very poor morale, minimal efficiency, and serious interdepartmental conflict. He was the seventh manager for this group within a two-year period. People weren't particularly glad to see him arrive, and they wondered how soon he, too, would be gone from the scene. What to do was not immediately obvious to Davey. He decided to start with a small win.

He invited all the department supervisors and their spouses to his house for dinner. This was the first time in more than five years that this group of people had gotten together socially. It seemed that there had been an unwritten rule that managers weren't supposed to socialize with their direct reports or peers. As Davey said, "This just didn't make any sense to me if I really expected people to be helping one another out."

He followed this dinner with weekly breakfasts. "At first these breakfasts were just that—breakfast; but within a few weeks, people began to
voluntarily start bringing up and talking about work-related issues. Within
a few months, people came to breakfast prepared to tell the other departments about problems they were having. Soon thereafter, people started
offering help and suggesting ways that they could assist other departments. I convinced these people that we could achieve excellence only
through a team effort!"

If you want people to hang in there over the long term, if you want people to stay committed to the task, they have to stay committed to each
other. Whether it's a dinner, a breakfast, an afternoon reception, or even
just a meeting, gather people together to help cement social bonds.

Once we've headed down a path and have convinced others to join us on
the journey, we've accepted an extraordinary responsibility. People will
need encouragement all along the way to continue the quest, especially
when we encounter obstacles, detours, unexpected disasters, and uncharted forks in the road. We'll look at how leaders "encourage the heart" in the
next two chapters.

Commitment Number 8

Achieve Small Wins That Promote Consistent Progress and Build Commitment

➤ Take it personally.

➤ Make a plan.

➤ Create a model.

➤ Break it up and break it down.

➤ Ask for volunteers.

➤ Use a bulletin board.

➤ Sell the benefits.

➤ Take people to dinner (or breakfast).

Source: The Leadership Challenge by James M. Kouzes and Barry Z. Posner. Copyright © 1995.

PART 6

Encouraging the Heart

➤ **Challenge the Process**

➤ **Inspire a Shared Vision**

➤ **Enable Others to Act**

➤ **Model the Way**

➤ **Encourage the Heart**

11

Recognize Contributions

Linking Rewards with Performance

People value being appreciated for their contributions.
Recognition does not have to be elaborate, just genuine.
—ALFONSO RIVERA
Engineering Consultant

"I was teaching math to sixth-graders. We were working with students who had been 'low performers' and felt like they were already failures in math. Their attention spans seemed to be about two minutes long! The challenge was to increase their speed and accuracy in solving math problems." So begins Cheryl Breetwor's "personal best"—her story about a time when she accomplished something extraordinary as a leader. Breetwor, who went on to direct investor relations for Rolm Corporation before starting her own company (ShareData), chose this experience as a sixth-grade teacher as one of her personal bests. Why?

"Because it's all about how you make work fun and rewarding. We wanted to show these kids they could win. If you can do that, you can get the best out of anybody," explains Breetwor. "And what's more, I knew we could do it!" Every day, Breetwor handed out awards—awards primarily for "speed, skill, and accuracy," but also for persistence. Breetwor used these opportunities to recognize the small wins and milestones reached by the kids on their path toward mastering math fundamentals.

It's not unusual for people to work very intensely and for extraordinarily long hours during personal bests. To persist for months at such a pace, people need encouragement; they need the heart to continue with the journey. One important way that leaders give heart to others and keep them from giving up is by recognizing individual contributions. When participants in our workshops and seminars summarize the key leadership practices that make a difference in getting extraordinary things accomplished, recognizing people's contributions is on just about every list.

Likewise, when nonmanagers are polled regarding the skills their managers need in order to be more effective, at the top of the list is the ability to recognize and acknowledge the contributions of others.[1] Executives, too, need recognition, as indicated in a recent survey about why they leave their jobs: the number one reason given was limited praise and recognition.[2] To some people, praise and recognition may seem unimportant or inappropriate, even trivial. But *assuming* that constituents will know when their manager thinks they've done a good job doesn't work.

This assumption helped to account for the gap Paul Moran discovered between his perception of encouraging the heart and the views of his constituents (as measured by the Leadership Practices Inventory): "In the past, I usually neglected to celebrate my team's accomplishments (and my own accomplishments), because I never personally placed much importance on this aspect of the job for myself and I tended to forget about recognizing the accomplishments of others. Rather, I treated their accomplishments as part of their normal job, which required no unique recognition." To rectify this situation, when Moran was at Pacific Bell, he developed a specific outline of various recognition techniques to remind him of the importance of recognition and to make available a few simple techniques to recognize various types of accomplishments. When his team reached a key milestone in reengineering corporate accounting processes, he shook the hand of each member of the project team, took several key team members out to lunch, made telephone calls to all members thanking them personally for their efforts in the project, and invited them all to a small office party for cake and coffee. Upon further reflection, Moran felt that he should have done even more. The reason is found in an insight from Leonard (Swamp) Marsh, COO and executive vice president of Medical Coaches Inc.: recognition "would have made folks more excited to get started on our next project," he noted, faulting his own personal-best leadership experience for inadequate recognition.

But there's much more at stake here than simply recognizing individuals for their contributions. Breetwor and the other leaders in our study practiced these *essentials* in their recognition of individuals:

- Building self-confidence through high expectations
- Connecting performance and rewards
- Using a variety of rewards
- Being positive and hopeful

By putting these four essentials into practice and recognizing contributions, leaders can stimulate and motivate the internal drives within each individual.

Building Self-Confidence Through High Expectations

Successful leaders have high expectations, both of themselves and of their constituents. These expectations are powerful, because they're the frames into which people fit reality: we often wind up seeing what we expect rather than what's actually occurring. Social psychologists have referred to this as the self-fulfilling prophecy or the Pygmalion effect. In Greek mythology, the sculptor Pygmalion carved a statue of a beautiful woman, fell in love with the statue, and brought it to life by the strength of his perceptions. Leaders play Pygmalion-like roles in developing people. Research on the phenomenon of self-fulfilling prophecies provides ample evidence that other people act in ways that are consistent with our expectations of them.[3] If we expect others to fail, they probably will.

The self-fulfilling prophecy can be applied in a variety of situations. For example, Dov Eden, director of Israel's Institute of Business Research, Tel Aviv University, and his colleagues have shown that the rate of volunteering for special-forces military service can be increased by raising candidates' expectations about their ability to succeed. In a study he directed, the only difference between the experimental and control groups was that the recruiters stressed their own personal similarity to the experimental candidates (for example, "I've been where you are, and look where I am now").[4] In another study, the self-fulfilling prophecy was able to raise the productivity of an entire group, not just individuals (illustrating the fact that producing higher expectations for some doesn't require *not* raising expectations for others).[5]

Indeed, when we ask people to describe exemplary leaders, they consistently talk about people who have been able to bring out the best in them. This is one of the defining characteristics of a leader, one of the things that make constituents willing to be led: that person has our best interests at heart and wants us to be as successful as possible. Leading others requires that leaders have high expectations about what people can accomplish. Consequently, leaders treat people in ways that bolster their self-confidence, thereby making it possible for those people to achieve more than they may have initially believed possible. Leaders' belief in others creates a self-fulfilling prophecy: we do as we're expected to do. Leaders understand that feeling appreciated increases a person's sense of self-worth, which in turn precipitates success at school, home, and work.

It's also evident that the self-fulfilling prophecy is a reciprocal process; not only can leaders influence the expectations of others, but the expectations of constituents can influence the behaviors of their leaders. If constituents communicate high expectations of how good an individual could be as a leader, that potential leader may adjust his or her self-concept and self-expectation to be congruent with that of others. With this motivation for exemplary leadership behaviors, the constituents' prophecy is fulfilled.[6]

Nathaniel Branden, one of the pioneers in the field of self-esteem, has noted that "of all the judgements we pass in life, none is more important than the judgement we pass on ourselves. That judgement impacts every moment and every aspect of our existence. Our self-evaluation is the basic context in which we act and react, choose our values, set our goals, meet the challenges that confront us. Our responses to events are shaped in part by whom and what we think we are."[7] Research and everyday experience confirm that men and women with high self-esteem—regardless of their age, level of education, and socioeconomic background—"feel unique, competent, secure, empowered, and connected to the people around them."[8]

To illustrate this point, social psychologists Robert Wood and Albert Bandura had working professionals manage a simulated organization. Participants had to match employee attributes to job requirements and master a complex set of decision rules in how best to guide and motivate their employees. Half the subjects were told that decision-making skills are developed through practice (and hence are acquired skills); the others were informed that decision-making skills reflect the basic cognitive capabilities that people possess (and hence are stable skills).

Throughout the simulation, the subjects rated the strength of their perceived self-efficacy in getting the group they were managing to perform at various productivity levels. Initially, subjects in both groups expressed a moderately strong sense of managerial effectiveness. However, as they tried to fulfill the difficult production standard, those in the stable-skill condition displayed a progressive decline in perceived self-efficacy, while those in the acquired-skill condition maintained their sense of managerial efficacy. Those in the stable-skill group were quite uncharitable in their views of their employees, regarding them as incapable of being motivated, unworthy of supervision, and deserving of termination. In contrast, those in the acquired-skill condition set more challenging goals in subsequent trials and made more efficient use of analytical strategies, because from their perspective errors didn't imply a basic cognitive deficiency.[9]

Nancy Tivol, executive director of Sunnyvale Community Services (SCS), believes strongly in her own ability and in the capacity of every staff member and volunteer at SCS to contribute something valuable. When Tivol first arrived, in 1991, volunteers were working at SCS in a very limited capacity. Certain staff members insisted, for example, that volunteers couldn't run the front office because they wouldn't be able to handle client and corporate contact adequately. Tivol refused to share that view, however; and today SCS has volunteers doing things that only staff members did previously. Indeed, every department at SCS is run by a volunteer over seventy years of age. And SCS is the county's only emergency assistance agency that doesn't turn people away, having increased its funding for preventing evictions, utility disconnections, and hunger by 421 percent and having increased the number of families served by its monthly food program by 365 percent—even while funding for operations was cut back significantly.

By recognizing the valuable contributions that others make, we can help bring about the achievement of extraordinary things. Tivol demonstrated this not only through her belief in the volunteer staff but through her faith in another unexpected group of volunteers. Tivol recognized how desperately the agency needed to become computerized. With some donated computers but no money for computer training, Tivol entrusted her fifteen-year-old son with that responsibility. For his Eagle Scout project, he wrote a forty-one-page manual and trained ten Boy Scouts to teach agency staff and volunteers. Each Scout then "adopted" a staff member or volunteer and tutored that person in computer and software skills. Now everyone at SCS is computer-literate, and all office operations are computerized.

As Tivol demonstrated, leaders have a high degree of confidence in others and in themselves. To be sure, some people we surveyed were nervous or anxious on the eve of their personal bests, but each was also ready for the plunge. All were excited by and willing to accept the challenges they faced (either by circumstance or by choice). Without exception or hesitation, these people expressed confidence that they could work well with others and assemble a team to address whatever problems might lie ahead. The high expectations that leaders have of others are based in large part on their expectations of themselves. This is one reason why leaders model the way. What gives their expectations for others credibility is their own record of achievement and dedication, along with their daily demonstrations of what and how things need to be done.

Leaders' expectations have their strongest and most powerful influence in times of uncertainty and turbulence. When accepted ways of doing things aren't working well enough, leaders' strong expectations about the destination, the processes to follow, and the capabilities of the team serve to make dreams come true.

What's more, leaders tend not to give up on people, because doing so means giving up on themselves, their judgment, and their ability to get the best out of other people. Breetwor was convinced that she was a capable enough teacher to improve that group of sixth-graders' math skills. She never gave up on them; she never gave up on herself. Likewise, when Antonio Zárate turned Metalsa from a company with a 10 percent rejection rate and only a domestic market into an award-winning, world-class automotive metal stamping company with 40 percent exports, he did so using the same local Mexican workforce that had always staffed Metalsa.

The difference was in what Zárate believed those workers could do. He believed that there are no poor-quality workers, only underled companies. He never gave up on his workers; he never gave up on himself.

Connecting Performance and Rewards

The outcomes of our present actions play a major role in determining our future actions. People repeat behavior that's rewarded, avoid behavior that's punished, and drop or forget behavior that produces neither result.[10] If especially hard work and long hours on a project go unnoticed and unrewarded, people will soon minimize their efforts. That's why manufacturing support manager Russ Douglass used what he called "spot strokes" on his personal-best project—"instant payoffs like 'Have this lunch on me' or 'Take the afternoon off.'" As he said, "Sometimes we'd put on a party in the parking lot on a half-hour notice."

One of the oldest, most important, and strongest prescriptions for influencing motivation is to tie job-related outcomes (such as rewards and recognition) to job effort and/or performance.[11] If a concern for quality is desired, rewards should be given to those who consistently meet quality standards, and low-quality performers shouldn't be rewarded until they conform to this norm. Today we see performance-reward linkages everywhere.[12]

AT&T, General Mills, Continental Bank, and Nucor Steel, for example, have all instituted pay-for-performance systems or variable pay systems. Saloman Brothers, the New York investment firm, has found that linking performance and rewards works for brokers and traders with profit responsibility—and for staff and support groups as well. Under a system the organization calls Teamshare, as training and technology push costs down, back-office staffers (over 500 people in all) get to keep 10 percent of the savings.[13]

Another example of how specific performance-reward linkages affect behavior comes from U.S. Healthcare, a Pennsylvania-based health maintenance organization. U.S. Healthcare's quality-oriented compensation plan rewards primary-care providers for attaining certain quality-of-care standards as well as for controlling costs. Like most HMOs, U.S. Healthcare pays its physicians a monthly fee for each patient. However, unlike most HMOs, it also pays up to a 28 percent premium to physicians based upon a number of quality and customer service goals. Scheduling office hours at night, linking up with the HMO by computer, and attaining high immunization rates for children and mammography rates for women over age forty are all rewarded, for example, as are accepting and retaining new U.S. Healthcare patients. And while doctors whose patients spend fewer days in the hospital or see fewer specialists are rewarded, those whose referral rate seems *too* low can be penalized. In evaluating physician performance, U.S. Healthcare audits medical records and surveys its members, whose views and satisfaction ratings further influence each physician's compensation. U.S. Healthcare physicians receive monthly reports on their quality and customer service performance.

The success of the program is evident. As a result of the organization's quality emphasis, all six U.S. Healthcare HMOs received full three-year accreditation, the best performance of any U.S. managed-care company. In addition, despite the bonus system (which can result in primary-care physicians' receiving greater compensation for their U.S. Healthcare patients than for traditional fee-for-service patients), U.S. Healthcare has been able to keep its premiums competitive with other HMOs and well below traditional health insurance premiums, while providing a healthy return to investors. Since 1988, U.S. Healthcare's stock has risen twelve-fold.[14]

When integrating performance with rewards, leaders must

- Make certain that people know what's expected of them.
- Provide feedback about contributors' performance.
- Reward only those who meet the standards.[15]

It's not always easy to meet these criteria, yet their significance shouldn't be underestimated. They've been shown across a wide variety of organizational settings to improve the job performance of such diverse workgroups as clerks in a small grocery store, mountain beaver trappers, engineers, telephone service crews, truck drivers, and salespeople.[16]

Consider how Nolan Dishongh (profiled in Chapter Five) linked performance and rewards—and achieved extraordinary results. During his first day as construction trades instructor and education coordinator for at-risk students at Alice Johnson Junior High School, he saw no order, no plan. When he asked students what they were supposed to be working on, they said it didn't matter: the instructor who had just quit had let them do anything they wanted, including doing nothing. Not surprisingly, most of them were failing not just construction trades but their other classes also.

Dishongh began planning projects and events to increase interest. To participate, however, his students had to do more than merely show up. Taking his role as education coordinator seriously, Dishongh required all construction trades students to give him a report from each of their academic instructors regarding their academic performance (class attendance and homework completion) before they could participate in class activities each week. And Dishongh graded each of these reports. Reports revealing unexcused absences or incomplete homework received a 0 and the student was "benched"; reports showing completed homework and perfect attendance were given a mark of 100. Each Monday morning, the reports were reviewed openly during a group discussion, with Dishongh giving praise and encouragement and eliciting group involvement when a member wasn't keeping up his commitments. Dishongh made it clear that each student's weekly average of what he called the "zero-zeros" reports counted for a full third of the grade in construction trades—and that no one with a class average below 70 would be allowed to attend the end-of-the-year field trip he was organizing to a wildly interesting and otherwise inaccessible location: the local heavy-metal radio station.

As the year progressed, the group's grades began to improve—in all academic classes as well as construction trades. Dishongh is still amazed by the dramatic change in Weldon Creech: he went from a depressing academic record of 47 F's to an astounding record of all A's and B's within one year. And Creech wasn't alone: Dishongh made it possible for all of his students to accomplish something significant and was rewarded by seeing the growth of their self-respect. Kenton Miles reflected the deep feelings of many of his classmates when he handed Dishongh a plaque inscribed, "Thanks for being my friend and showing me even I can make a difference in the world."[17]

Like Dishongh, successful leaders strive skillfully and diligently to see that the system works. Two additional notes about the significance of *linking* performance and rewards. First, feedback is the loop that provides learning, both to the individuals involved and to the organizational system. Experience without feedback is unlikely to build or enhance competence. Put another way, learning results when people can see the relationship between what they're doing and how their needs are (or aren't) being met, as was certainly the case with Dishongh's students. This assessment is possible only when people are able to measure their performance, of course, whether through satisfaction surveys or units sold or words typed per minute. The most powerful measurements are those that offer timely feedback and can be monitored by the individuals doing the work. No one could imagine designing a measurement system for driving in which only the police could determine one's speed. Instead, each automobile is equipped with a speedometer, always visible to the driver. Why, then, do many organizations design feedback systems in which only the inspectors and managers (the police) have the tools to monitor performance?

Second, although compensation plans include rewards as a critical element, these are just one part of a total strategy—along with communication, employee involvement, feedback, and financial justifications. As a result, the size of rewards is important but not critical.[18]

Using a Variety of Rewards

Leaders use many types of rewards to recognize the efforts and contributions of their constituents. Indeed, the creative use of rewards is another defining characteristic of leaders. Leaders tend not to be dependent upon the organization's formal reward system (typically financial), which offers only a limited range of options. Breetwor, for example, relied on much more than grades to motivate students. In the business world, promotions and raises are scarce resources and can't be applied frequently. On the other hand, verbal or written praise, "spot strokes," buttons, and other informal and more personal rewards are almost unlimited resources.

Furthermore, relying upon an organization's formal reward system typically requires considerable effort and time. In one study, we found that the time lapse between performance and promotion is seldom less than six months. Similarly, most organizations' performance appraisal systems allow for raises or any other merit awards to be handed out only once per year.[19] Naturally enough, this delay limits people's ability to see the connection between their efforts, performance, and rewards and thereby diminishes motivation.

INTRINSIC REWARDS

Instead of relying only (or even primarily) on formal rewards, leaders make tremendous use of *intrinsic* rewards—rewards that are built into the work itself. As Chapter Three emphasized, challenge is a powerful motivator. If work lacks challenge, no incentive system in the world can sustain long-term success. Other intrinsic rewards include a sense of accomplishment and the thrill of creation—rewards that are immediate outcomes of an individual's effort. Intrinsic rewards can also be as subtle as the leader's lending a helping hand and listening without interrupting. Other, more personal currencies include lunch with the a key executive, a night out on the company, tickets for a ballgame or the theater, and the afternoon off.

Some people make the mistake of assuming that individuals respond only to money. Although salary increases and bonuses are certainly appreciated, individual needs for and appreciation of rewards extend much further. Verbal recognition of performance in front of one's peers and visible awards (such as certificates, plaques, and other tangible gifts), for example, are powerful rewards. Spontaneous and unexpected rewards are often more meaningful than the expected formal rewards. The motivational impact of Christmas bonuses, for example, is limited, because they're expected; the only unknown is what their amount will be. Many people consider these "entitlements" to be part of their annual salary expectations, not something extra for their efforts during a particular year. Thus annual bonuses are generally linked in workers' minds only to job level or even longevity, not performance.

Praise is a significant and underutilized form of recognition. Not enough people make adequate use of a very powerful and inexpensive two-word reward—"Thank you." Personal congratulations rank at the top of the most powerful nonfinancial motivators identified by employees.[20] There are few, if any, more basic needs than to be noticed, recognized, and appreciated for our efforts. That's as true for volunteers, teachers, doctors, priests, and politicians as it is for the maintenance staff and those in the executive suite. There's little wonder, then, that a greater volume of thank-yous is reported in highly innovative companies than in low-innovation firms.[21] Extraordinary achievements don't come easily and seldom bloom in barren and unappreciative settings.

Joan Carter, whose work was discussed in Chapter Six, discovered the powerful effect of publicly giving thanks when she was general manager and executive chef of the Faculty Club at Santa Clara University. Following her extremely successful (but difficult) first year at the club, in which revenues increased by 20 percent and costs decreased by 5 percent (ending a period of deficits that had threatened the club's continued existence), she sent a letter to all club members, club staff members, and university departments. In this "Open Letter of Thanks," she not only described in glowing detail the party the club had thrown to celebrate its dramatic turnaround but took the opportunity to describe the contributions of individuals, both on her staff and within the university community, who had made that night, and the past year, so successful. As she recalls,

> So many people had come up to me during that party to thank *me* for the changes that had occurred at the club, and all I could think about was that it was my *staff* whose efforts and willingness to make changes had made us successful; *they* were the ones who needed to be thanked. So I wrote the letter. But as I wrote it, I realized that the list of people who needed to be thanked was endless, and I began feeling very humble. I needed to thank each staff member by name and contribution. I also needed to thank so many others on campus who helped every day—and our customers. I wanted them all to know that I knew we couldn't have done it without them.

The response, she recalls, was totally unexpected: "I received dozens of phone calls and personal notes echoing the mutual admiration that had grown between the club and the university during that year. Those notes were posted on the bulletin board in the kitchen for the staff and further reinforced the staff's commitment to their customers. It was incredible. I never dreamed saying thank you would make *me* feel so good or be so good for our business."

Certainly, you can't buy people's commitment—to get them to care, to stay late, or come in early—with just thank-you notes, stickers, or plaques. What makes these effective is the leader's genuine concern and respect for those who are doing the work. Being at our personal best as leaders requires acknowledgment that we can't do it alone and recognition that unless constituents feel appreciated by their leaders, they're not likely to put forth great effort. Social scientist Daniel Yankelovich points out that overall organizational effectiveness and efficiency depend on employees' personal dedication and sense of responsibility. You get these intangibles, he says, "only when people are moti-vated to work hard, to give of themselves."[22] With this kind of motivation, leaders are able to help others get extraordinary things accomplished.

Consider the case of Albert "Smitty" Smith, room service captain for Marriott's Marquis in Atlanta. National Football League (NFL) teams play-ing in Atlanta had been staying with the Marriott for several years when a local competitor substantially reduced its rates. In response to that reduc-tion, some of the teams began staying at that hotel instead. Smith was deeply disappointed. He loved football, and he wanted the NFL teams back at Marriott. Whenever a team was staying at the competing hotel, Smith would take the day off, contacting the coaches and team manage-ment to let them know that he was available to meet all of their special needs and reminding them that he understood those needs well after working with the teams for so many years. The teams were so impressed by Smith's one-person marketing effort that they all returned to the Atlanta Marriott the following year. At Marriott's International Marketing Meeting, Smith was featured as the guest speaker on salesmanship and received a special leadership trophy from J. Willard Marriott, Jr. Following his remarks, the group gave Smith the first standing ovation to be received at any of the organization's marketing meetings.[23]

Leaders are constantly on the lookout for ways to spread the psycholog-ical benefits of making people feel like winners, because winners con-tribute in important ways to the success of their projects. Leaders often serve as a mirror for the team, reflecting back to others what a job well done looks like and making certain not only that the members of the team know that they've done well but that others in the organization are aware of the group's effort and contributions.

Think about the impact of the "fabulous bragging sessions" held once per quarter at the corporate headquarters of Milliken & Company in Spartanburg, South Carolina. While attendance is voluntary, as many as 200 people participate in each Corporate Sharing Rally, as the sessions are called. Dozens of teams of workers from all areas of the company give crisp, five-minute reports in rapid-fire succession about improving product quali-ty, describing their own programs and quantifying their impact. Everyone who attends receives an award signed by the president and framed on the spot. And everyone who attends is likely to go back to one of the compa-ny's sixty plants with a host of ideas—not demands that have been forced on them by top management but suggestions from their peers—about how all of them can be doing their jobs better and making the company more competitive and successful. These rallies are a wonderful example of providing recognition and celebrating people's accomplishments.

THE BLEND OF INTRINSIC AND EXTRINSIC REWARDS

What happens if people are given both intrinsic and extrinsic rewards? Unfortunately, while the idea of an additive effect is intuitively appealing, it doesn't always occur. There's some evidence that intrinsic and extrinsic rewards are negatively related and may actually work against one another. For example, in a situation that's already intrinsically rewarding, the addition of extrinsic rewards may reduce the effectiveness of the intrinsic rewards.[24] On the other hand, some studies show that while achievement-oriented people do find success rewarding in and of itself, money and fame are also important rewards, serving as symbols of that success.[25] One executive referred to this combination as the "fun being in playing the game down on the field, while the results are posted on the scoreboard." What we found among leaders wasn't so much an either/or mentality as a both/and type of thinking. Leaders are remarkably skillful in using these two types of rewards in complementary ways.

The Hampton Inn hotel group offers an example of creatively incorporating a variety of rewards. Winning the quarterly President's Award as an employee of the hotel group is a big deal, and everyone knows it. It starts with a personal phone call of thanks and congratulations from Ray Schultz, president and CEO. The phone call is followed by two plaques (one for the employee to take home and one for the hotel to display); a check for $500; publication of the winner's photo and profile in the company's quarterly magazine—a profile that features the winner's "extra mile" example and his or her personal guest service philosophy, as well as both a guest comment and a co-worker comment about the recipient; and a trip to the company's annual conference for the Hampton Inn System Conference Awards Ceremony, where the current year's President's Award recipients take a prominent place in the ceremony's program.

Who wins these awards? Any employee—head housekeepers, guest service representatives, sales directors, maintenance workers, room attendants, and breakfast hostesses. The winners are the stars who "shine brightly in the Hampton Inn system" and who make its "100 % Satisfaction Guarantee" a reality.

Being Positive and Hopeful

By recognizing individual achievement, leaders give courage to their constituents. This courage enables people to maintain composure during anxiety-producing situations and to endure hardships. Courage to continue the quest and hope in a positive future were central elements of Don Quixote's legacy: "to dream the impossible dream."

Don Bennett's teenage daughter stayed by his side for over four hours during one particularly difficult stretch of his seemingly impossible dream of scaling Mount Rainier. With each new hop across the ice field, she told him, "You can do it, Dad. You're the best dad in the world. *You can do it, Dad.*" This spontaneous verbal encouragement kept Bennett going, strengthening his commitment to make it to the top. Bennett told us that there was no way he could have quit with his daughter voicing such words of love and encouragement.

Research points to the impact that positive feedback has on motivation and physical stamina. One study involved soldiers who had just finished several weeks of intensive training and were undergoing a forced march in competition for places in special units.[26] Motivation was extremely high among the recruits; failure to maintain the pace during the forced march meant losing the chance to join the special units. The soldiers were divided into four groups, which were unable to communicate with one another. All the men marched twenty kilometers (about twelve and one-half miles) over the same terrain on the same day. The first group was told how far the soldiers were expected to go and was kept informed of its progress along the way. The second group was told only that "this is the long march you hear about." These soldiers received no information about the total distance they were expected to travel or how far they had marched. The third group was told to march fifteen kilometers, but when the soldiers had gone fourteen kilometers, they were told that they had to go six kilometers farther. Members of the fourth group were told that they had to march twenty-five kilometers, but when they reached the fourteen-kilometer mark, they were told that they had only six more kilometers to go.

The groups were assessed as to which had the best performance and which endured the most stress. The results indicated that the soldiers in the first group—those who knew exactly how far they had to go and where they were during the march—were much better off than the soldiers who didn't get this information. The next-best group was the soldiers who thought that they were marching only fifteen kilometers. Third-best was the group told to march a longer distance and then given the good news at the fourteen-kilometer mark. Those who performed worst were the soldiers who received neither information about the goal (total distance) nor feedback about the distance they had already traveled. Blood tests taken during the march and again twenty-four hours later showed similar patterns: blood levels of cortisol and prolactin (chemical substances whose levels rise as stress increases) were, as expected, highest for the group that knew the least about the march and lowest for those soldiers who knew exactly where they were and how much farther they were expected to go.

Even with highly motivated, achievement-oriented people, the type of leadership provided makes a definite difference in performance, in the levels of stress experienced, and in long-term health. Leaders provide people with a positive sense of direction that encourages them to reach inside and do their best. By having a positive outlook and being hopeful, leaders make the impossible a possibility and then motivate people in their drive to transform the possible into reality.

Committing to the Challenge: Building Confidence and Courage

Leaders have high expectations of themselves and of their constituents. They create self-fulfilling prophecies about how ordinary people can produce extraordinary actions and results. They provide people with clear directions, substantial encouragement, personal appreciation, and a positive outlook. Along the way, they offer feedback in response to small wins, stimulating, rekindling, and focusing people's energies and drive.

Leaders make people winners, and winning people like to up the ante, raise the standards, and conquer the next mountain. They want to serve more people, raise more money, enlarge market share, lower costs, increase production, reduce reject rates, experiment with technologies and processes, and explore uncharted territory. Leaders recognize and reward what individuals do to contribute to vision and values. And leaders express their appreciation far beyond the limits of the organization's formal performance appraisal system. Leaders enjoy being spontaneous and creative in saying thank you, whether they send personal notes, hand out stickers and buttons, listen without interrupting, or try one of the myriad other forms of recognition.

In this commitment, we provide a variety of strategies that you can adapt to your situation for help in using recognition as a leadership process.

Commitment Number 9

Recognize Individual Contributions to the Success of Every Project

➤ Be creative about rewards and recognition and give them personally.

People respond to all kinds of rewards other than promotions and raises. One of our university colleagues takes his highest-performing students each term out for lunch and bowling to show his appreciation for their hard work. A shop foreman we know presents employees who achieve their production objectives with a new chair for the workplace. The chairs are a good reward themselves, but a major part of the reward—the part that's even more pleasurable than comfortable seating to the employees—comes with the presentation. The employee being rewarded is called into the foreman's office, presented with the new chair, and then wheeled in the chair back to the work station by the foreman—amid the cheers of co-workers.

Make rewards and recognition tangible. By themselves, a meal, chair, check, or plaque won't significantly contribute to sustaining the value of the action rewarded. But tangibility does help sustain the memory and importance of the act and contributes positively to repetition of the behavior.

There's no limit—except your creativity—to creative rewards. Consider the following:

- "Super person of the month" awards
- Employee photographs with the president
- Verbal encouragement
- Spot strokes

- Pictures in annual reports and company newsletters
- Published thank-yous
- Contributions to employees' favorite charities
- Gift certificates and merchandise credits
- Embossed business cards
- Gifts for spouses and families
- Banners displayed in the cafeteria
- Symbolic stuffed animals
- Flextime

Place your emphasis on noticing and recognizing small wins—and do so personally. A sincere word of thanks from the right person at the right time can mean more to the recipient than fame, fortune, or a whole wall of certificates and plaques. It's well worth the effort.[27] Even movements in the right direction warrant your personal seal of appreciation and encouragement to continue the effort.

➤ Make recognition public.

You may be reluctant to recognize people in public, fearing that to do so might cause jealousy or resentment. But private rewards do little to set an example; and often the recipient, not wanting to brag or appear conceited, has no opportunity to share the story with others. So tell your workers and colleagues that they've done well as soon as you find out about it, and let other people know about the accomplishment too. When recognition is public, the individual's self-esteem is bolstered, the behavior being recognized serves as a model to others, and employees see that doing the right things will be noticed and rewarded. While all recognition encourages others to continue their good work, public recognition portrays the recipient as a role model, conveying to all employees the message, "Here's someone just like you. You too can do this."

Recognition also helps to empower recipients by increasing their visibility. Military organizations, for example, make tremendous use of medals and insignias, which are almost always handed out at ceremonies. Awards serve the same purpose. Nolan Dishongh planned well in advance for a ceremony to reward and recognize his students. During the year, he entered his students' work in every contest he could find, collecting in a classroom display case the winning ribbons and trophies that would be awarded formally to their owners during the year-end banquet attended by parents and students.

Public recognition also builds commitment, because it makes people's actions visible to their peers and therefore difficult to deny or revoke.

At Household Credit Services, extra effort by members of the young clerical staff is often rewarded with "casual dress" passes. For many staff members right out of high school, being able to wear their nice casual clothes (while their friends and co-workers have to wear business attire) provides public recognition. The passes are immediate (supervisors don't need higher-level approval to award them), inexpensive, and fun, and they're a very visible way to show appreciation for a job well done.

➤ Design the reward and recognition system participatively.

People are most excited about activities and events that they've had a hand in designing. In addition, when you involve others, you're more likely to design a system in which rewards are closely linked to performance norms. Because it's *their* system, people will feel more strongly that they can influence it directly through their efforts. For example, when the CEO of Alta Bates Hospital, in Berkeley, California, raved to food service staffers about the great job they were doing, expressing his pride in the creativity and conscientiousness of their attempt to make hospital food imaginative and tasty, they were pleased. But what they really wanted was to demonstrate just how good they were, to show that working in a hospital didn't mean that they were second-class restaurateurs and chefs.

After some discussion, food service personnel were given the chance to offer a Sunday buffet in the hospital cafeteria, open to the public and complemented by ice sculptures and a string quartet. During the buffet, crew members walked the line talking with customers (many of whom were on the hospital staff). The crew's pride in their food preparation and presentation created an atmosphere of sheer delight, increased their motivation, and generated more efficient operations overall.

➤ Provide feedback en route.

People produce best when they're given feedback about how they're progressing. Production may continue without feedback, but it will be less efficient and will exact a significant toll in the form of increased levels of stress and anxiety. Recognition signals successful accomplishment, reinforcing both the employee's "I can do it" attitude and the leader's expectations: "I knew you could do it."

A study of the winningest high school and college athletic coaches revealed that they pay great attention to providing real-time feedback on their players' performance and will, as appropriate, recognize and reward outstanding contributions. Players—regardless of fame or fortune—need to hear when they do well and when they don't. As the coaches explained, ongoing feedback "is a highly effective way to shape the behavior of the athletes so as to increase the team's ability to continue winning. Without immediate and precise feedback, the learning process ends and mediocrity is sure to emerge. Ongoing evaluation of the players' ability to play your game, to your expectations, is critical given the constant need to restock the team with younger athletes."[28] What's true of athletes also applies to those on the factory floor, behind the counter, in city hall, and in the corner office.

By giving feedback, leaders enable people to persevere in moments of hardship and times of uncertainty and turbulence. In fact, studies show that learning is severely hampered without feedback and that people's motivation (and subsequent performance) diminishes over time unless they know how they're doing.[29] Leaders use feedback to make sure that people acquire the competence that should come with experience.

➤ Create Pygmalions.

Be more conscious about realizing that your behavior toward people is based upon your expectations about them. Treating people in a friendly, pleasant, and positive fashion and being attentive to their needs—behavior that reflects your high expectations of them—produces increased performance, because that behavior has a favorable effect on their motivation. Likewise, when you have high expectations of others, you tend to give them more input—suggestions, helpful hints, and responsive answers to their questions—and more feedback about the results of their efforts. Both of these factors enhance people's learning and increase the likelihood that they'll achieve competence and mastery rather than repeat mistakes or let ineffective habits become ingrained.

Finally, the standards of performance (or "output levels") that you set communicate what your expectations of others are, and these in turn affect others' levels of aspiration. Therefore, make sure that these standards are high and that they're linked directly to what's important to the success of your organization. Make sure, too, that your performance standards include what's important to constituents as well as what's important to management, stockholders, or the larger organization.

Creating Pygmalions entails developing a winner's attitude, since only those who envision themselves as winners are likely to work hard, try new actions, and become leaders in their own right. This means paying considerable attention to your constituents' successes and, should those people stumble or fall, discussing this result with them as only a temporary lack of success. If criticism is necessary, comments should be restricted to behavior rather than character. Similarly, feedback—preferably extensive—should stress continuous progress in terms of past performance rather than comparisons with other people.[30] Leaders also make certain that constituents understand that (and how) goal achievement is the result of their own efforts.

➤ Find people who are doing things right.

Rewards are most effective when they're highly specific and in close proximity to the appropriate behavior. In order to provide such timely and specific feedback, you have to go out and find the behavior you want to foster. One of the most important results of being out and about as a leader is that you can personally observe people doing things right and then reward them either on the spot or at the next public meeting.

Consider initiating a system for collecting information from constituents and customers about people who are observed doing things right. Weekly breakfast meetings are perfect opportunities to ask for such incidents. Add to your agenda the question, "Who have you seen doing something special this week that's really helped our organization?"

Once you've selected people for recognition, be sure to tell them—and everyone else—*why* they've been chosen. Make the recognition effective. Tell the story of why the person is being recognized, and make it specific. Stories that describe valued actions are very powerful ways to communicate what behaviors are expected and will be rewarded. Walk employees through the specific actions that contributed to goal attainment and explain why they were consistent with the shared values.

You might say something along these lines: "Sue was selected as the employee of the month because she called five different stores to locate an item that a customer requested but that we didn't have in stock. And because the store couldn't deliver the item until the next week, she picked it up on her way home from work so that the customer could have it in time for an important event. That's the kind of behavior that makes us so highly valued by our customers. Thank you, Sue. We make this award to you in appreciation of your contribution to our organization's goal of delighting every customer."

This kind of positive example can be particularly useful to leaders trying to get people to understand the right things to do to achieve a high standard. It provides a behavioral map that people can store in their minds and rely on when a similar situation arises in the future.

To broaden the net for recognition, set up systems that make it possible for people to be recognized by their constituents—be they peers, customers, or suppliers—not just managers. This encourages everyone in the organization to be on the lookout for good behaviors—and to be mindful that others are observing their actions as well. The nursing home at Saint Francis Hospital in Memphis, Tennessee, recognizes its staff with a simple pin that says, "Caught Caring." In an environment where the patients often can't say thank you, the pins mean a great deal to staff members: they announce that someone recognizes how much they give.[31]

➤ Coach.

Athletic coaches don't wait until the season is over to let their players know how they're doing, and neither should you. Coaching involves spending time with people on the job day by day, talking with them about game strategies, and providing them with feedback about their efforts and performance. Then, when the game is over, you need to get together with the players and analyze the results of your efforts. Where did we do well? Where do we need to improve our efforts? What will we have to do differently, better, or more of the next time? And then it's time for practice again and getting ready for the next game.

The best teams, whether in athletics, business, education, health care, government, or religion, always emphasize the fundamentals of their game. This means being clear about your vision and values, to which recognition and celebration should always be linked.

The next chapter adds to our discussion of individual recognition by focusing on how leaders encourage people to continue the journey by working as a team.

Commitment Number 9

Recognize Individual Contributions to the Success of Every Project

➤ Be creative about rewards and recognition and give them personally.

➤ Make recognition public.

➤ Design the reward and recognition system participatively.

➤ Provide feedback en route.

➤ Create Pygmalions.

➤ Find people who are doing things right.

➤ Coach.

Source: The Leadership Challenge by James M. Kouzes and Barry Z. Posner. Copyright © 1995.

12

Celebrate Accomplishments

Valuing the Victories

*We kept morale up by consistently acknowledging group and
individual contributions.*
—ANN MARIE DOCKSTADER
Sorority Vice President
Drake University

Everyone at Advanced Decision Systems was in a dither the day we were
there doing a seminar; the participants were anticipating the announcement of a major government contract. It was difficult at times to keep
everyone's attention, because at each break several participants would
gleefully run around shouting such things as, "Has anyone heard?" "Is the
party on?" The enthusiasm was infectious, and even we got caught up in
it. At two o'clock, the director of human resources asked that we take a
break at three so that everyone could hear the expected announcement
together in the conference room. At ten minutes before three, we joined
sixty to seventy people packed into the conference room and overflowing
into the hallway in both directions.

The general manager began speaking in a quiet and somber voice about all
the hard work, time, and sweat that had gone into drafting the proposal. He

292

told a funny story about one employee who thought she'd lost some critical papers left in her car when it was towed away—towed because she'd stayed so long at the office. He told about having received a speeding ticket on the way to work because he was daydreaming about the proposal. He thanked several people personally for their efforts and spoke about the challenges and opportunities that receiving this contract would bring, adding that everyone in the company would have to "make more sacrifices doing more of the work they love doing." Then he gave a wink and a sheepish grin, reached into his ancient leather satchel—and popped the cork, spraying champagne on everyone nearby while shouting, "We got it! We got it! We got it!" We finished the seminar in the warm afterglow of this celebration, with people talking about how they loved working for this leader and this company. He was demanding and caring, challenging and supportive, intense and playful.

Cheerleading—you won't find the word *cheermanaging* in the dictionary—is a crucial dimension of personal-best leadership experiences. "I was a cheerleader," is how Ted Avery, general manager for the Houghton Winery in Western Australia, began describing his personal best: "I would see the great things that were going on in marketing, for example, and I'd tell them, 'Way to go!' I'd hear about a new development in operations and I'd go into the plant and tell them, 'Fantastic!' If they figured out a more efficient process in the fields, I'd go out and find those responsible and let them know how much we appreciated their hard work."

Encouraging the heart isn't the practice of recognizing individual achievements only; it includes celebrating the efforts of the entire group. Breetwor's math awards weren't already on the students' desks when they arrived in the morning; they were given out in a class celebration. Likewise, the awards at North American Tool and Die weren't presented in the corner office; the line was shut down and all personnel gathered to learn about another "super person" in their midst and to celebrate with one another. What often distinguishes one team or volunteer group from others in an organization is the wide variety and frequency of celebratory and expressive events.[1]

David Campbell, senior fellow with the Center for Creative Leadership, poetically summarizes the importance of ceremonies:

> They act as a cohesive glue, giving expression to common beliefs; they provide a source of stability by marking calendar events; they provide mileposts in our lives by setting aside noteworthy occasions and

enlightening special accomplishments. A leader who ignores or impedes organizational ceremonies and considers them as "frivolous" or "not cost-effective" is ignoring the rhythms of history and our collective conditioning. [They] are the punctuation marks that make sense of the passage of time; without them, there are no beginnings and endings. Life becomes an endless series of Wednesdays.[2]

Celebration Essentials

Cheerleading and celebrating are the processes of honoring people and sharing with them the sweet taste of success. Masters of celebrations master these four *essentials:*

- Cheering about key values
- Making ceremonies public
- Being personally involved
- Creating social support rituals

In this way, leaders reinforce the team spirit necessary for extraordinary achievements.

Cheering About Key Values

Determining what's to be celebrated is the starting point for cheerleaders. People in the stands lose interest and fail to get really involved in the game if a rally cry goes up *every* time the team gets the ball. The hoopla and celebration aren't simply for the sake of fun alone. Celebrations should also call attention to and reinforce key organizational values. Celebrations that do so let others know what's valued and encourage people to try for their opportunity in the spotlight.

If an important agency objective is to obtain new grants, for example, leaders ensure that people celebrate when grants are signed. If an organization values loyalty, leaders celebrate that loyalty with years-of-service dinners and recognition pins. And if developing new products is a goal, leaders hand out awards with every patent granted. The point is that everything about a celebration must be matched to its purposes.[3] Without expressive events to recognize an achievement, important organizational values have little impact upon people's behavior. Celebrations are to the culture of an organization "what the movie is to the script or the concert is to the score—they provide expression of values that are difficult to express in any other way."[4]

In any celebration, the need for consistency with key values is an essential part of maintaining a leader's credibility. What leaders say and what's being celebrated should be one and the same; otherwise, the celebration will come off as inconsistent, insincere, and phony. Authenticity is what makes most conscious celebrations work.[5] The celebration must be an honest expression of commitment to certain key values and to the hard work and dedication of those people who have lived the values.

Here's an example of how Tom Melohn, former president and CEO of North American Tool and Die (NATD) celebrated and emphasized values:

> "We got a new award today," Tom Melohn announces to the assembled group. "It's called the North American Tool and Die Freezer Award. Now who knows what that's for and who won it? Anybody got an idea?"
>
> Somebody shouts out, "Kelly."
>
> "There's something in the freezer," says Melohn. "Kelly—go on, Kelly—look in the freezer. Come on, hurry up!"
>
> Kelly opens the freezer door. In it he finds a metal part. Stuck to it is an envelope.
>
> "Come on up here." Melohn laughs. Everyone laughs. Kelly walks up and Melohn shakes his hand. Melohn laughs some more, obviously delighted with the fun the group is having at this ceremony. He shakes Kelly's hand, hands him the envelope, and takes the part. "Oh, that's cold," he exclaims.
>
> Kelly opens the envelope and pulls out a check. It's for $50. "Okay?" Melohn asks Kelly. Smiling broadly, Kelly shyly replies, "Yeah."
>
> "Remember this job?" Melohn asks of the NATD associates. Then he tells this story: "I went through the shop one day and I saw Kelly going in the freezer. I thought, 'What is going on? Is he goofing off or making margaritas, or what? You know what he did? He couldn't get this

[Melohn points to a metal rod] into here [a metal cylinder], so he said, 'Hey, I'm going to put this in the freezer. It'll shrink and then I'll put the part together.' And it worked. And I said, 'Where did you get that idea?' He said 'What? It's just part of the job, right?'" Melohn looks at Kelly.

Kelly responds, "Yep."

Melohn turns to the group, holds the part in the air, and says, "And remember: no rejects, no rejects, no rejects. That's why we're here."[6]

Leaders understand the crucial significance of getting people together to celebrate accomplishments. Even while Kelly's is an individual achievement, the entire group acknowledges, applauds, and applies the lessons from his behavior to themselves. Indeed, what Kelly and the NATD employees remember most was *not* the check for $50 but the round of applause from their peers when the award was presented.

Making Ceremonies Public

We've seen how the *public* nature of events makes people's actions more visible to others and therefore has a strong bonding effect. Because celebrations and cheerleading are public events, they reinforce commitment to key values and demonstrate visibly to others that the leader is serious about the importance of adhering to these values. Fifteen or more times a year, some new and promising project at the 3M Company reaches $1 million in profitable sales. You might not expect this level of achievement to get much attention in a $14 billion company, but it does. Lights flash, bells ring, and video cameras are called out to recognize the entrepreneurial team responsible for the achievement.

Public ceremonies and rituals are the ingredients that crystallize personal commitment. They help to bind people together and let them know that they're not alone. Where's the joy in celebrating alone, whether it's a birthday, an anniversary, or New Year's Eve? Because they're generally lighthearted, celebrations tend to reduce conflicts and minimize differences. Celebrations can also inform and thereby empower those who attend; they provide a meaningful reminder about which key values are celebrated in the organization.

Every quarter, staff members at Big Brothers/Big Sisters of Santa Clara County get together to review individual and team objectives. Each person talks about what he or she has been doing and identifies how those accomplishments have helped to achieve the agency's aspirations. Then a staff member puts a checkmark next to each of the goals and priorities (posted on the wall) that each person has helped the agency come closer to realizing. This process is followed by rounds of applause, whoops, and hollers. At the end of the session, says executive director Sheila Kriefels, "We have a visual statement about what we have all been able to accomplish as an agency. This also gives us the chance to notice any gaps between what each of one of us is doing and what we all had said we wanted the agency to achieve, and then where we might need to focus more of our energies in the future to achieve our common vision."

Jerry Lukach is the plant manager for a small factory making patio doors for Norco Windows in Marenisco, a small town on Michigan's upper peninsula. He explains quite clearly the impact that ceremonies have on his facility:

> They break down barriers, particularly between departments. The events remove people from their cast roles at the plant and cause them to relate to each other in new manners. Celebrations do not solve problems, but a celebrative atmosphere washes away some of the stress and bitterness that surrounds those problems. The positive atmosphere at the plant makes people more positive about managing day-to-day challenges of working in a manufacturing facility.[7]

Some of the most significant and memorable public celebrations are those that occur spontaneously. From the pat-on-the-back and let-me-take-you-all-out-to-lunch variety to the party-in-thirty-minutes-in-the-parking-lot variety, relatively unplanned celebrations create a favorable impression on the recipients. Such celebrations create a real sense of importance because of their timeliness: they occur when the thrill of victory is still a thrill. Because there are no rehearsals, the feeling of celebration is on a more personal level. Messages such as "We're in this together" and "I really care about all of you" are most sincerely communicated in small-group settings and on relatively unplanned occasions.

Being Personally Involved

Think about your impressions of your own manager, teacher, volunteer coordinator, pastor, or agency executive. When we've asked people to talk about leaders such as these, what they most often relate are the interpersonal details—such as whether or not they feel treated with dignity, respect, importance—and how these emotional connections affect their relationship. Leadership is clearly a relationship predicated on personal involvement.

When we organized a conference for the National Association of Convenience Stores, we asked the chief executives to prepare for it by writing descriptions of true-life critical customer service incidents that detailed how they, by their own example, had demonstrated excellence in customer service. One company president wrote this:

> When a store celebrated its Grand Opening, I was there greeting customers and carrying groceries. By personally participating, I was showing the customers that we're happy to be in and a part of their community. It also shows everyone with the company the importance I give to customer service. I didn't realize the importance that people in the company placed in my being there. I used your assignment as a tool to interview several people in the company and learned that my absence at the past several Grand Openings was noted. I was missed! I've learned not to miss any more.

Leaders play a very special role in the art of celebration, because they're enormously visible to others in the organization and serve as role models. Because organizations, like any living system, go through a multitude of changes, leaders have many opportunities to provide celebration and, in so doing, to focus attention on key organizational values and to interpret key organizational events.

Joe Costello once volunteered to be fired if he couldn't, within three months, turn around the sales situation of the company for which he was director of operations. Costello had no previous sales experience, yet in this—his personal-best leadership experience—he turned around the psychology of the company by increasing sales quickly and significantly. A large thermometer-type chart was put in the main lobby to track the daily progress of sales activity. The overall push was to get everyone in the company focused on these sales goals: zero in the first month, $250,000 in the second month, and $1 million in the final month!

To capture people's attention and get everyone involved, Costello used what he called the "closing coat" ceremony. The coat was a bright yellow polyester jacket—one that carried a huckster-salesperson image to the extreme. Whenever a sale was made, the salesforce would select someone from the company to wear the "closing coat." That person would then walk around the company with Costello and tell colleagues the details of that particular sale. When people saw someone wearing the "closing coat," they knew they were one step closer to their goal. Costello's idea was "to make sure everyone had fun." The final monthly goal of $1 million in sales was exceeded by $400,000, and an $800,000 backlog was carried into the next quarter!

The importance of celebrations like that of the "closing coat"—and the leader's role in them—comes as a surprise to some people. "I was unprepared for the scrutiny of being placed under a microscope by the people around me," explains Leigh Belden, president of Verilink. "But I soon learned that I was on stage. And while I'm not always comfortable with the role required, I look for real-time opportunities to celebrate with others our accomplishments and hard efforts." Leaders are always on the lookout for people who are doing the right things in the right way so that they can celebrate those victories.

In October 1993, with the first product set to launch in December, Shelli Meneghetti, 3DO's human resource manager, could understand why the atmosphere at the small software company was fairly intense. As one of the managers in the finance and administration (F&A) department—a service department that included finance, accounting, information systems, and human resources—she was aware of the toll the company's prelaunch stress was taking on her department's morale. Feeling underappreciated, the F&A staff complained about not getting credit for the thousands of things they did right every day yet being hammered by impatient people in other departments for the few things that went wrong. Although Meneghetti couldn't fully disagree with them, she also knew that maligning other departments wouldn't help. Instead, she suggested that perhaps they weren't the only department feeling less than appreciated and asked what their department could do to make 3DO a more enjoyable place to work.

Meneghetti started the fun by staying late one night to decorate her department for Halloween—and to place 150 "F&A SAYS THANK YOU" cards on each desk in the department, with instructions to send at least two cards to people in other departments who had done something worth saying thank you for. The latter effort spurred some staff members to come to Meneghetti requesting more cards. It inspired another F&A staff member to organize the first volleyball match against another department, held later in the week. Two of the accounting staff stayed late one night making 250 photocopied "masks" out of a picture of the company's CEO, which they placed on desks throughout the organization with instructions for employees to wear them at the company meeting planned for the next day (Halloween). Many did just that, which surprised and delighted the CEO and boosted morale throughout the company. Not so surprisingly, the F&A department no longer felt underappreciated; department staffers were having fun and enjoying the positive reactions of other departments. Meneghetti had made effective use of LBFA—leadership by fooling around!

While special celebrations such as kick-off meetings, annual award dinners, jubilees, and rallies serve an important purpose, they're insufficient unless the day-to-day behavior of senior managers reflects concern about key values. When Synergistic Systems, Inc., reached a major financial milestone, it was CEO Jean Campbell herself who rolled a big cart loaded with blue canvas totebags emblazoned with the company name to the front door. She personally handed one to each of the company's 200 employees as she thanked them for their contribution. Likewise, after engaging in a serious safety campaign, it was Bob Buuck, CEO at American Medican Systems, who handed out a $1 bill and a personal note of thanks to every employee wearing a seat belt when he or she entered the company's parking lot. The personal touch of leaders has enormous importance, especially in a high-tech world. On these personal occasions, leaders also find further opportunities to let others know what they value and to share stories about corporate heroes and heroines.

Bob Greene, a syndicated columnist for the *Chicago Tribune*, describes talking with a group of people about a particular manager. Some of them liked the person; some didn't. But everyone agreed about one thing: he never said thank you. As Greene pondered this behavior, he concluded that perhaps for some managers the reluctance to say thank you is a device used to maintain a symbolic distance between themselves and the troops.[8] Saying thank you establishes a personal and very human connection between people.

And that's exactly what leaders need to do. Once a human connection has been established, it's much easier to create a commonness, to share visions, values, and experiences, and to establish deeper empathy with other people. Personal involvement, created through public and mutual celebration, brings about the sort of togetherness and commitment that the preacher showed each morning by praying, "Lord, nothing's going to happen to me today that You and I can't handle together."

Creating Social Support Networks

Researchers have long recognized that supportive relationships at work are critically important to maintaining personal and organizational vitality.[9] Through the process of celebrating accomplishments, leaders create social support networks; they bring together people who share the same goals. And as organizational members interact on more than just a professional level, they're likely to come to care about one another. Celebrating achievements reinforces the common stake that people have in reaching the destination. Making people feel included is a major function of celebrations. Believing that we're not just part of the team but part of something significant and larger than the moment creates a compelling motivation to achieve and succeed. Being included and close to others increases our sense of belonging and esprit de corps. Celebrations bring people together so that information can be exchanged, relationships can be nourished, and a sense of shared fate can be sustained.

One of the significant lessons learned from an extensive ten-year study of service quality is that social support networks are essential for sustaining servers' motivation to serve: "Coworkers who support each other and achieve together can be an antidote to service burnout." This research demonstrates convincingly that service-performance shortfalls are highly correlated with the absence of social support and teamwork. As the researchers point out, "Working with others should be rejuvenating, inspirational, and fun."[10]

This is just what Bob Branchi, managing director of western Australia's largest network of automobile dealerships, told one of the parts delivery drivers. When Branchi attended a celebration at the large parts supply facility and mingled with those attending, he came across a fellow who held himself in low esteem. The man said that he was just a delivery driver and didn't feel that he had made any real contribution. Branchi said that if this was the criterion, then he (Branchi) shouldn't have been there himself, but "each of us makes an important contribution, and in doing our best makes this company a success. We're in this together. It's important that you get involved in these celebrations so people know that you can be counted as part of this team." Branchi made it a point to introduce the delivery driver to others at the celebration "as an important contributor to our team and to our success."

Investigations from a wide variety of disciplines consistently demonstrate that social support—the quality of interpersonal relationships—serves to enhance productivity, psychological well-being, and physical health. The California Department of Mental Health states strongly that "friends can be good medicine."[11] That department reports that social support not only enhances wellness but also buffers against disease, particularly during times of high stress. This latter finding was true irrespective of an individual's age, gender, or ethnic group. Even after adjusting for such factors as smoking and histories of major illness, people with few close contacts were dying two to three times faster than those who regularly had friends to turn to.[12]

Traditional managerial wisdom has long asserted, "Don't get too close to people, or you won't be able to make those tough decisions." But it cuts both ways. Extraordinary accomplishments aren't achieved without everyone—leader and constituent alike—getting personally involved with the task and with one another. Some leaders liken the emotional attachment to being in a chorus. Others say it's like being family. Most agree, however, that leaders have to be partners with their constituents. Our personal-best cases are filled with the importance of building genuine personal relationships between the members of the team and the leader.

The conference and catering department at UCLA was preparing for its summer season—its busiest time—when it became aware that members of other departments on campus (such as physical plant, central receiving, and scheduling and facilities) were upset that they'd have to put out a great deal of effort to help conference and catering be successful but would receive very little in the way of rewards themselves. Because Mary Pat Hanker, director of conference services, realized that the department's success was dependent on the helpfulness of these other units, she decided to figure out a way to gain their support, commitment, and involvement. She realized that the intervention had to be pleasant, playful, and humorous in order for people to want to participate (and to feel good about participating wholeheartedly rather than feeling threatened—and hence reluctant to participate).

So the conference and catering department staged a celebration: department employees held a barbecue for the people they were calling upon for help. Unlike most office parties, however, at this event the managers—the people responsible for generating the heavy summer business traffic— were the ones who cooked and served the food. This symbolic reversal of roles did indeed foster a spirit of cooperation.

Hanker separated these celebrations from everyday work roles and work relationships. People across departments had the opportunity to interact with one another outside of the more formal and structured work context. Peter Tommerup, an ethnographer studying these events at UCLA, analyzed how they gave people permission to interact with one another in a friendly and intimate manner, increasing their feelings of camaraderie, cooperation, and appreciation of the reasons behind the hectic summer season. This social support network enhanced collaborative efforts and facilitated amiable interpersonal relationships throughout a stressful and highly productive period.[13]

The expression "misery loves company" is often misunderstood as having negative connotations. Leaders understand that what makes us most miserable is being alone. The morbidity rate for widows, for instance, is three to thirteen times as high as the rate for married women for every known major cause of death. The warm family support given to artificial heart recipient Barney Clark was considered by his doctor to have been crucial to his remarkable endurance after receiving the heart. Even studies of former Vietnam prisoners of war have revealed that communication with fellow captives, sometimes involving complex tapping codes, was a vital factor in their survival.[14] Celebrations create positive interactions among people, providing concrete evidence that people generally care about each other. Knowing that we aren't alone in our efforts and that we can count on others if necessary provides us the courage to continue in times of turmoil and stress.

The case for social support is based, too, on the exchange of information facilitated by both official and informal interactions.[15] When celebrations cut across functional and hierarchical boundaries, as they frequently do, people get a chance to exchange ideas with and be stimulated by people outside their own specialties. The monthly TGIF get-togethers at our university, for example, mix faculty and administrators outside of their formal responsibilities and committees and give them an opportunity to get a sense of others' agendas. While we might not make an appointment to let the academic vice president know our concerns about some particular campus issue (for example, changing from a semester to a quarter system), we're likely to say, "Let's catch Steve's attention at the TGIF and ask him about the calendar." Likewise, it's at these events that we've been asked informally about serving on a university task force, invited to nominate people for awards, and given the chance to brag about our research and discuss how it might be useful to someone else in the organization (or could be expanded with further funding).

Our experience is echoed by others in their own contexts. Without group celebrations, we might all come to believe that the organization revolves around our individual work and that we're independent and not responsible to others. Social interaction and support work both ways, as we've noted: as people give, they get; and thus they become interconnected and caught up in one another's lives. It always takes a group of people working together with a common purpose in an atmosphere of trust and collaboration to get extraordinary things done.

The Secret of Success Is Love

We once asked then–U.S. Army Major General John H. Stanford to tell us how he would go about developing leaders, whether at Santa Clara

University, in the military, in government, in the nonprofit sector, or in private business. He replied,

> When anyone asks me that question, I tell them I have the secret to
> success in life. The secret to success is to stay in love. Staying in love
> gives you the fire to really ignite other people, to see inside other peo-
> ple, to have a greater desire to get things done than other people. A per-
> son who is not in love doesn't really feel the kind of excitement that
> helps them to get ahead and to lead others and to achieve. I don't know
> any other fire, any other thing in life that is more exhilarating and is
> more positive a feeling than love is.

"Staying in love" isn't the answer we expected to get, at least not when we *began* our study of leadership bests. But after numerous interviews and case analyses, we noted that many leaders used the word *love* freely when talking about their own motivations to lead. The word *encouragement* has its root in the Latin word *cor,* meaning "heart." When leaders encourage others, through recognition and celebration, they inspire them with courage—with heart. When we encourage others, we give them heart. And when we give heart to others, we give love.

Vince Lombardi, the unforgettable coach of the Green Bay Packers, believed in love. In a speech before the American Management Association, he made these remarks: "Mental toughness is humility, simplicity, Spartanism. And one other, love. I don't necessarily have to like my associates, but as a person I must love them. Love is loyalty. Love is teamwork. Love respects the dignity of the individual. Heartpower is the strength of your corporation."[16] Retired General H. Norman Schwarzkopf emphasizes love as well. When Barbara Walters asked him, during a TV interview, how he would like to be remembered, he replied, "That he loved his family. That he loved his troops. And that they loved him."[17]

Of all the things that sustain a leader over time, love is the most lasting. It's hard to imagine leaders getting up day after day, putting in the long hours and hard work it takes to get extraordinary things done, without having their hearts in it.

We suspect that the best-kept secret of successful leaders is love: being in love with leading, with the people who do the work, with what their organizations produce, and with those who honor the organization by using its work. Leadership is an affair of the heart, not of the head.

Committing to the Challenge: Leading and Loving the Team

Celebrating team accomplishments recognizes that extraordinary performance is the result of many people's efforts and reinforces the binding-in feeling that "we're all in this together." By celebrating people's accomplishments visibly and in group settings, leaders create and sustain team spirit; by basing celebrations on the accomplishment of key values and milestones, they sustain people's focus. Public ceremonies provide opportunities not only to reiterate key values but to make heroes (and therefore role models) of individuals with whom everyone can identify. Social interaction increases people's commitments to the standards of the group and results in both strong peer pressure for individuals to do their fair share and consensus about required actions. When people are asked to go beyond their comfort zones, the support and encouragement of their colleagues enhance their resistance to the possible debilitating effects of stress. Leaders' personal involvement (and cheerleading) reduces any we-they demarcations between themselves and constituents. Finally, making hard work fun and exciting is what encouraging the heart is all about.

In this next commitment section, there are several action-steps you can take to celebrate accomplishments with the team.

Commitment Number 10

Celebrate Team Accomplishments Regularly

➤ Schedule celebrations.

Labor Day, Victoria Day, Bastille Day, and ANZAC Day are national celebrations in which people are reminded of struggles, sacrifices, legacies, and continuing responsibilities to one another. Have certain of your organizational celebrations fall at the same time and have the same meaning each year, as these do. Select a few celebrations that you want people to put on their calendars.

In setting up your celebrations, your first task is to decide which organizational values or events of historical significance to the company are of such importance that they warrant an annual ritual, ceremony, or festivity. Perhaps you want to commemorate founder's day, recognize the top 5 percent of the salesforce, honor the group or team of people who created the year's important innovations, praise those who gave extraordinary customer service, or thank the families of your constituents for their support. Whatever you wish to celebrate, formalize it, announce it, and tell people how they become eligible to participate. At a minimum, you ought to have at least one celebration each year that involves everyone, though not necessarily at the same site, and one that draws attention to each of the key values of your organization.

In addition to these annual affairs, bring celebration into as many other critical events as you can. Many celebrations are, and should be, spontaneous. The following list of reasons for celebration that Cathy DeForest, an expert on this subject, developed may help prime your spontaneity:

- *Stages of organizational change:* expansions, reorganizations, closings, mergers, the end of an old technology and the introduction of a new one, moves to new locations
- *Success:* financial success, promotions, awards, expansions to new markets
- *Loss:* of old procedures, financial opportunities, contracts, a job, status; death of a colleague; an experiment that failed
- *People:* teamwork, team successes, founders, winners of sales contests, employee awards, individual birthdays, marriages, reunions
- *Events:* a company's anniversary, opening day, holidays, articulation of an organization's vision
- *The unknown:* paradox, ambiguity in the marketplace[18]

Add to this list all the ways you can think of to bring more ceremony, ritual, commemoration, observance, and convivial good times into your organization.

A word of caution: as we mentioned earlier, don't make *everything* that people accomplish a reason for celebrating. You don't want to replace people's intrinsic motivation with external motivators or justifications, nor do you want to trivialize recognition so that it's taken for granted. However, in our studies, *overdoing* recognition and celebration was not a problem; more typically, the concern was about how to increase encouragement and recognition.

➤ **Be a cheerleader *your* way.**

You can cheerlead for your group better than anyone else: this is another instance of modeling the way. Yet if you have limited views of what it means to cheerlead, based upon traditional views of school cheerleaders, you may find this task difficult. There's much more to cheerleading than standard cheers and flashy shows, however. Foremost is being clear on your personal values and what it is that you want to celebrate. Celebrations must be organized around evident performance-reward linkages. For example, in the Chemicals Division of Milliken & Company, everyone receives free doughnuts and coffee when quality milestones are achieved. A sign is prominently displayed giving the responsible group credit for achieving the milestone—and for the free doughnuts!

As with individual recognition, all kinds of rewards can be used for celebrating. Use your imagination. But most important, be authentic. You may be comfortable giving out plaques, flowers, T-shirts, and the like, and you may not. So celebrate—but do it your way. When leaders give gifts of the heart, it's the thought that counts the most. If you can't think of anything to celebrate, try a thank-goodness-it's-Monday party or a we-blew-the-roof-off-this-week get-together. These work in tough times and good times. Try celebrating with champagne or sparkling cider every milestone achieved, as one design group did at Apple Computer. They had lots of milestones *and* lots of milestones *achieved*. Celebrations such as this are excellent ways to acknowledge progress and small wins.

➤ **Be part of the cheering squad.**

If others in the organization are better at celebrating than you are, give them your support and encouragement. Join in the fun. You don't always have to lead celebrations as long as you're a part of them, letting others around you know that it's okay to laugh, to have fun, and to enjoy each other's company. In this way, you let people know that you're human, creating an important commonality that minimizes we-they (for example, management-labor or principal-teachers) differences. If you want others to join in the party, give it your personal support and your visible presence.

At the Global Fund for Women, several celebrations are held each year. At the winter solstice, for example, participants pass a flame from one person's candle to the next, and the room fills with the symbolic light that the organization is spreading throughout the world. For their fifth anniversary, the Global Fund also empowered its grantees through celebration. The Fund gave $10,000 to ten groups, each of which kept $5,000 and then chose five groups to pass $1,000 grants on to.

➤ Have fun.

Fun isn't a luxury, even at work. Most personal-best leadership experiences people have described to us were a combination of hard work and fun. In fact, most people we spoke with agreed that without the fun and the pleasure that they experienced with one another on the team, they wouldn't have been able to sustain the level of intensity and hard work required.

Empirical research has found a significant relationship between fun and productivity.[19] Doug Podzilni, sales manager with Cargill, decided to buy a box of candy suckers and place them out in a common area of the office. Very quickly "everyone had a sucker sticking out of their mouth and a smile on their face," he said. Later that afternoon, during the break in a particularly tedious and combative meeting, he put a bunch of suckers in the middle of the table. Before he knew it, Podzilni said, people were reaching for their favorite flavors, and the tone of the meeting got noticeably friendlier: "It's hard to be too combative or in a bad mood when you have a sucker in your mouth!"

Having fun sustains productivity, but don't take Podzilni's word for it. Consider Nancy Tivol's experience as well. Tivol, executive director of Sunnyvale Community Services (SCS), makes it a habit to catch people doing things right. She explains, "If you talk to each other only when there's a problem, it doesn't work. We have to stress looking for the good; not just knowing it's there, but *doing* something—celebrating!" And celebrate she does. As one way, Tivol creates personalized songs to celebrate members of the SCS team and their contributions. Whether the song is a revised version of "La Cucaracha" to honor the Chinese seniors for stuffing newsletters, a tribute to Charlie for faithfully organizing the food program, or an Irish jig on St. Patrick's Day honoring volunteers for their efforts, Tivol finds ways to let people know that they matter.

➤ Determine your social network—and bolster it.

Take out a piece of paper. Draw a circle in the middle about the size of a half-dollar. Write your name in it. Now begin drawing smaller circles around the big circle. These circles represent members of your support group. Think about the people with whom you have the strongest and closest bonds and begin filling in the various circles with their names. Draw the circles and jot down names quickly, just as they come to mind. Include the people who've given you strong social support all through your life as well as those who give you support now.[20]

What does your support network look like? Does it include people from all aspects of your life? Where does your manager or team leader fall? Where would you put your co-workers? Examine where you placed your friends, close colleagues, mentors, and sponsors. Are there people whom you haven't seen for a long time and with whom you're out of touch? Think about clubs, associations, even religious or political groups you belong to now or have belonged to in the past. Determine which relationships need to be strengthened or renewed and get in touch with those people.

Take another few minutes to answer the six questions included in Exhibit 12.1. The California Department of Mental Health considers your response to them a measure of the strength of your social support network. Once you've completed the assessment, consider whether your score reflects the degree of support you feel. If your score is low, take steps now so that you don't find yourself in the unfortunate position of really needing support that no longer exists—or that never did. Don't neglect relationships or take them for granted; if you do, support from those people may no longer be available at a critical time. Bear in mind that you need to maintain and sustain personal relationships, especially in times of change and crisis. When you want extraordinary accomplishments, you'll need these relationships in order to assist you in coping with excessive stress levels that cause mental and physical illness.

Exhibit 12.1. Assessing Your Social Support Network.

Circle one response for each item below.

1. At work, how many persons do you talk to about a job hassle?

      none (or not employed) (0)   one or two (3)

      two or three (4)   four or more (5)

2. How many neighbors do you trade favors with (loan tools or household items, share rides, babysit, and so on)?

      none (0)   one (1)

      two or three (2)   four or more (3)

3. Do you have a spouse or partner?

      no (0)   several different partners (2)

      one steady partner (6)   married or living with someone (10)

4. How often do friends and close family members visit you at home?

      rarely (0)   about once a month (1)

      several times a month (4)   once a week or more (8)

5. How many friends or family members do you talk to about personal matters?

      none (0)   one or two (6)

      three to five (8)   six or more (10)

6. How often do you participate in a social, community, or sports group?

      rarely (0)   about once a month (1)

      several times a month (2)   once a week or more (4)

Add the numbers in parentheses next to each item you circled. According to the California Department of Mental Health, if your score is

- Less than 15, your social support network has low strength and probably doesn't provide much support. You need to consider making more social contacts.
- From 15 to 29, your support network has moderate strength, and it's likely to provide enough support except during periods of high stress.
- 30 or more, your support network has high strength, and it's likely to support your well-being even during periods of high stress.

Source: Adapted from California Department of Mental Health, *Friends Can Be Good Medicine* (San Francisco: Pacificon Productions, 1981).

➤ Stay in love.

Are you in your job to do something, or are you in your job for something to do? If your answer is the former, what is it that you want to do? We know, of course, that this is a much too rational question, because so much of leadership is a "fire in the belly" kind of experience. You must put your heart in the business and the business in your heart. So many extraordinary leaders have told us, "I really love what we're doing." Ask yourself what it is that you love to do. Your passion for leadership will emanate from there, so find ways to put that into your business. If you find that you can't, then change the business you're in.

We know of a medical doctor who, given a few years to live, decided her heart was in establishing a girls' camp. She did so and ran it for fifty years, putting medicine in second position in her much-expanded life. Who's to say whether the diagnosis was wrong or whether practicing her love accounted for her longevity? Ann Tompkins Gibson certainly exuded love and strength all along—and strengthened the spirit of generations of girls in the process.

➤ Plan a celebration right now.

We conclude every one of our workshops by asking participants in small groups to plan and perform a celebration for the rest of their colleagues. They've performed rap songs and poems, led us in sing-alongs, roasted the trainers, played Leadership Jeopardy, taken us on walks on the beach, and sent us on scavenger hunts. You name it; we've done it.

The Sacred Heart Community Service team contributed to one of our leadership workshops by presenting the following poem, which they sang to the tune of "Joyful, Joyful, We Adore Thee."

> *We are leaders one and all,*
> *   We invite you to the call.*
> *We ask you to dream our vision*
> *   As we share our joyful mission.*
> *Feed the hungry, clothe the needy,*
> *   Welcome strangers, one and all.*
> *Homeless, immigrant, children, poor*
> *   All find refuge at our door.*

Serving others needs five keys,
   Leaders practice all of these,
Listen closely and you'll learn
   Leadership is always earned.
Challenge the process, inspire shared vision,
   Enable others, model the way.
The last one is to encourage the heart,
   Barry says it's the leadership art.

We'll return to SHCS
   Ready to deal with all duress:
Cuts in funding, rising prices,
   Volunteer fallout, pantry mices,
Board dilemmas, United Way deadlines,
   Clients lined up, computer down.
Our results will be extraordinary,
   Aptly taught and blessed by Barry!

We realize that encouraging the heart doesn't necessarily come at the end of the seminar, belong just at the conclusion of a project, or follow sequentially the other leadership practices we've been describing. It's not the end of the process but a continual part of the leadership journey. It's vital that leaders give courage, spread joy, and care about people, product, and process all along the way.

In the next and final chapter, we describe how you can develop yourself as a leader to take on all of these tasks with grace and love.

Commitment Number 10

Celebrate Team Accomplishments Regularly

➤ Schedule celebrations.

➤ Be a cheerleader *your* way.

➤ Be part of the cheering squad.

➤ Have fun.

➤ Determine your social network—and bolster it.

➤ Stay in love.

➤ Plan a celebration right now.

Source: The Leadership Challenge by James M. Kouzes and Barry Z. Posner.
Copyright © 1995.

PART 7

Beginning the Journey

➤ **Challenge the Process**

➤ **Inspire a Shared Vision**

➤ **Enable Others to Act**

➤ **Model the Way**

➤ **Encourage the Heart**

13

Become a Positive Force

The Leader Who Makes a Difference

Each of us has within us the capacity to lead.
—David Aronovici
Director of Human Resources
Trident Microsystems Inc.

Beyond the horizon of time is a changed world, very different from today's world. Some people see beyond that horizon and into the future. They believe that dreams can become reality. They open our eyes and lift our spirits. They build trust and strengthen our relationships. They stand firm against the winds of resistance and give us the courage to continue the quest. We call these people *leaders.*

In our study, we set out to discover what it took to become one of these leaders. We wanted to know the common practices of ordinary men and women when they were at their leadership best—when they were able to take people to places they'd never been before. As we've noted, our analysis of thousands of cases and surveys revealed five fundamental practices of exemplary leadership, each embodied in two commitments:

317

➤ **Leaders challenge the process.**

They *search for opportunities* to change the status quo. They look for innovative ways to improve the organization. They *experiment and take risks*. And since risk taking involves mistakes and failure, leaders accept the inevitable disappointments as learning opportunities.

➤ **Leaders inspire a shared vision.**

They passionately believe that they can make a difference. They *envision the future*, creating an ideal and unique image of what the community, agency, or organization can become. Through their strong appeal and quiet persuasion, leaders *enlist others* in the dream. They breathe life into the shared vision and get people to see the exciting future possibilities.

➤ **Leaders enable others to act.**

They *foster collaboration* and build spirited teams. They actively involve others. Leaders understand that mutual respect is what sustains extraordinary efforts; they strive to create an atmosphere of trust and human dignity. They *strengthen others* by sharing information and providing choice. They give their own power away, making each person feel capable and powerful.

➤ **Leaders model the way.**

They create standards of excellence and then *set an example* for others to follow. They establish values about how constituents, colleagues, and customers should be treated. Because complex change can overwhelm and stifle action, leaders *achieve small wins*. They unravel bureaucracy, put up signposts, and create opportunities for victory.

➤ **Leaders encourage the heart.**

Getting extraordinary things done in organizations is hard work. To keep hope and determination alive, leaders *recognize contributions* that individuals make in the climb to the top. And because every winning team needs to share in the rewards of team efforts, leaders *celebrate accomplishments*. They make everyone feel like a hero.

How do leaders learn these practices? More specifically, how can *you* become a better leader? In this closing chapter, we offer insights you can use in developing your capacity to lead, regardless of your position in the company, community, or congregation. But developing yourself as a leader requires effort—and the heart to care enough to make a difference.

Leaders Make a Difference

In our classes and workshops, we regularly ask people to share a story about a leader they admire and whose direction they would willingly follow. From this exercise, we hope they'll discover for themselves what it takes to have an influence on others. We have another objective as well: we want them to discover the power that lies within each one of us to make a difference.

Virtually everyone we've asked has been able to name at least one leader whose compelling impact they've felt. Sometimes it's a well-known figure—perhaps someone out of the past who changed the course of history. Sometimes it's a contemporary role model who serves as an example of success. And sometimes it's a person who's personally helped them learn—a parent, friend, member of the clergy, coach, teacher, manager.

Verónica Guerrero made us realize just how extraordinary those around us can be. Guerrero selected her father, José Luis Guerrero, as the leader she admired. She told the story of her father's leadership in the Unión Nacional Sinarquista (UNS) back in the early 1940s. (UNS is now part of another political party—Partido Democrata Mexicano (PDM), or Mexican Democratic Party.) She related in detail what her father did and then summed up his influence with this remembered observation from José Luis: "I think the work that I did back then helped me extend myself and others to levels that I didn't know I could reach. . . . If you feel strongly about anything, and it's something that will ultimately benefit your community and your country, don't hold back. Fear of failing or fear of what might happen doesn't help anyone. . . . Don't let anyone or anything push you back."

Verónica Guerrero closed her description of her father (who was then dying of pancreatic cancer) with this observation: "As I heard his story and I saw a sick, tired, and weak man, I couldn't help thinking that our strength as humans and as leaders has nothing to do with what we look like. Rather, it has everything to do with what we feel, what we think of ourselves. . . . Leadership is applicable to all facets of life." That's precisely the point. If *we* are to become leaders, we must believe that we, too, can be a positive force in the world. Leadership *does* have everything to do with what we think of ourselves.

"Now the very concept of leadership implies the proposition that individuals make a difference to history," observed historian Arthur M. Schlesinger, Jr.[1] Yet there has never been universal acceptance of this proposition. Determinism and fatalism govern the minds of many. Some management scholars claim, in fact, that leaders have little impact on organizations, that other forces—internal or external to the organization—are the determinants of success. Others claim the role of the leader is largely symbolic, even romantic, but not very substantive.[2] Our evidence suggests quite the contrary. Managers, nonmanagers, volunteers, pastors, government administrators, teachers, school principals, and other leaders who begin to use the five fundamental practices of exemplary leadership more frequently are seen by others as better leaders:

- They're more effective in meeting job-related demands.
- They're more successful in representing their units to upper management.
- They create higher-performing teams.
- They foster renewed loyalty and commitment.
- They increase motivational levels and willingness to work hard.
- They promote higher levels of parental involvement.
- They enlarge the size of their congregations.
- They raise more money and expand gift-giving levels.
- They extend the range of their agency's services.
- They reduce absenteeism, turnover, and dropout rates.
- They possess high degrees of personal credibility.[3]

Additionally, people working with leaders striving to abide by these fundamental practices are significantly more satisfied with the actions and strategies of their leaders, and they feel more committed, excited, energized, influential, and powerful. In other words, the more you engage in the practices of exemplary leaders, the more likely it is that you'll have a positive influence on others in the organization.

Other researchers have also found that leaders can have a significant impact on their organizations. Bernard M. Bass, noted leadership scholar and professor emeritus at the State University of New York at Binghamton, has investigated the nature and effects of two types of leaders: *transformational* and *transactional*. Transformational leaders closely resemble the leaders we describe in this book, inspiring others to excel, giving individual consideration to others, and stimulating people to think in new ways. Transactional leaders, on the other hand, tend to maintain a steady-state situation and generally get performance from others by offering rewards. (The transactional leader closely resembles the traditional definition of the manager.) In measuring the influence of both types of leaders, Bass and his colleagues found that, while both were positively associated with effectiveness, "transformational leadership factors . . . were more highly related than transactional leadership factors to satisfaction and effectiveness."[4]

Other studies reveal that leadership can account for improved performance as measured by a variety of factors: net income; sales, profits, and net assets; employee commitment, job satisfaction, and role clarity; and employee turnover, achievement of company goals, and teamwork.[5] In a longitudinal study of ministers, researchers found that those who exhibited outstanding leadership practices had a significant positive effect on organizational performance: "Churches that superior performers led repeatedly experienced greater giving, membership growth, and property development than did other churches."[6]

Leaders *can* make a difference. If you want to have a significant impact on people, on communities, and on organizations, you'd be wise to invest in learning to become the very best leader you can. But first you must believe that a leader lives within each of us.

Believing That You Can Lead

We're often asked, "Are leaders born or made?" The answer we give, with a smile, is this: "Yes, all leaders are born. We have no empirical evidence to the contrary. Furthermore, we've never come across a person who can't tell us about at least one personal-best leadership experience."

Consider what we learned from working with Mary Beth Cahill-Phillips and her study of twelve "ordinary" women.[7] These women were mostly

young or middle-aged, many were single parents, less than half had graduated from college, many worked at home, and all lacked substantial years
of work experience, unique professional talents, and prestigious organizational positions. They hadn't had any formal (or perhaps even informal)
training or special preparation to be leaders. Based upon a priori criteria,
they wouldn't have been singled out from the population for their leadership potential. Yet each suffered through the death or serious injury of her
child and determined that this situation would (must) not happen again
for another parent or another child. So they became leaders, creating organizations (for example, Vanished Children's Alliance and the Head Trauma
Clinic at Children's Hospital in San Diego) and galvanizing people and
special interests. Their efforts resulted in new product standards and
recalls (for example, new safety requirements for pool covers by the
national Products Safety Commission), social movements (for example,
Mothers Against Drunk Driving—MADD), and government legislation
(for example, California's TRUSTLINE, which allows parents to obtain
background checks on individuals offering to provide unlicensed child
care). These women got extraordinary things done because they cared.
There's no denying the leadership within them—or within each of us.

Like these women, many of the leaders we studied didn't initiate the
personal-best leadership projects that they wrote and talked about, yet
they rose to the occasion. Some got angry and caught fire. Others accepted
an assignment and then found something within themselves that they
hadn't known they had. Perhaps none of us knows our true strength until
challenged to bring it forth.

We find it interesting that no one has asked us, "Can *management* be
taught? Are *managers* born or made?" These questions are always raised about
leadership and leaders, never about management and managers. It's a curious
phenomenon. Why is management viewed as a set of skills and abilities, while
leadership is typically seen as a set of innate personality characteristics?

Because people assume that management can be taught, hundreds of
business schools have been established and thousands of management
courses taught. Schools and companies have educated hundreds of thousands of managers and spent billions of dollars. By assuming that people
can learn the attitudes, skills, and knowledge associated with good management practices, these organizations have generally raised the caliber of
managers (although certainly some are still better than others).

Leadership training can accomplish the same kind of improvement. By viewing leadership as a nonlearnable set of character traits, we've created a self-fulfilling prophecy that dooms society to having only a few good leaders. It's far healthier and more productive for us to start with the assumption that it's possible for *everyone* to lead. If we assume that leadership is learnable, we can discover how many good leaders there really are, and new leadership can be exhibited on behalf of the school, the church, the community, the agency, the company, the union, or the family. Somewhere, sometime, the leader within each of us may get the call to step forward.

We wouldn't have written this book if we didn't believe that it's possible for ordinary people to learn to get extraordinary things done. We wouldn't have written this book if we didn't believe that ordinary people can become extraordinary leaders. We cast our votes on the side of optimism and hope. Chances are that you also believe that leadership can be learned, or you wouldn't have read this far.

Leadership is, after all, a set of skills. And any skill can be strengthened, honed, and enhanced if we have the proper motivation and desire, along with practice and feedback, role models and coaching. We believe in the self-fulfilling prophecy. Adults in the workplace and children in school tend to perform to the level of the authority figure's expectations.[8] For example, leaders' high expectations of team members are likely to produce higher levels of performance (provided that constituents perceive the high expectations as achievable and realistic); similarly, their low expectations of others are likely to lead to lower performance. If we, as parents, teachers, managers, and friends, begin with the assumption that some people "have" leadership and some people don't, then we're likely to find it only in those from whom we expect it—and in exactly the form we expect.

Certainly, we shouldn't mislead people into believing that they can attain unrealistic goals. However, neither should we assume that only a few will ever attain excellence in leadership (or in any other human endeavor). Those who are most successful at bringing out the best in others are those who set achievable "stretch" goals and believe that they have the ability to develop the talents of others.[9]

We do know for certain that effective leaders are constantly learning. They see *all* experiences as *learning* experiences, not just those in a formal classroom or workshop. They're constantly looking for ways to improve themselves and their organizations. By reading this book and engaging in other personal development activities, you're demonstrating a predisposition to lead. So even if some people think that they're not able to learn to lead, you believe that you can. And that's where it all starts—with your own belief in yourself.

Jim Whittaker, president of Whittaker/O'Malley, Inc., of Seattle and the first American to climb Mount Everest, once observed, "You never conquer the mountain. You conquer yourself—your doubts and your fears." We would say the same for leadership. You don't conquer your organization. You don't conquer leadership. You conquer your own doubts and fears about leading.

Learning to Lead

So how do you become the best leader possible? To find the answer to that question, we asked the people in our study to tell us how they learned to lead. Typical responses included these:

- I'm not sure I've yet "learned to lead." I've observed methods and skills of my bosses that I respected. I've had some experience (trial and error) since this project was initiated, and I previously had some courses relating to people skills, communications, etc.
  Tom Kellett
  Harshaw/Filtrol Partnership

- By purposefully engaging with others to get things done, by taking risks, trying, and learning from my mistakes.
  Gretchen Imlay
  Levi Strauss & Co.

- I learned to lead from experience and from trying to adapt techniques used by others that I thought were successful. I also enjoy reading autobiographies of leaders I admire to try to understand how they think.
  Don Danielson
  KLA Instruments

- Watching people that I admire and modeling myself after them.
  Cindy Haverland
  Pacific Bell

- From working with and listening to leaders and from my own management experience—lots of practice.

  Lennart Grafstrom
  Swedish Employers' Organization

- Most of my leadership traits are based on my basic value system of dealing with people, as ingrained in me in my youth and fine-tuned through experience.

  Dan Wible
  Unisys

- By reading, by watching others who are leaders versus those who aren't, and by making mistakes myself and trying a different approach.

  Ruth Klopp
  Du Pont

- Observing examples of an excellent leader and poor manager and the impact their behavior had on others. Also learned by doing, through successes and mistakes; as well as learned about other leaders and leadership theories through my academic research.

  Mary Eckenrod
  Johnson Controls

- By being put in positions of responsibility that other people counted on, and by observing other leaders.

  Suzi Mendoza
  Adopt-A-School Coordinator
  Santa Clara University

From our analysis of thousands of such responses, we've identified three major opportunities for learning to lead, listed here in order of importance:

- Trial and error
- Observation of others
- Education

Other studies support these conclusions. The Center for Creative Leadership interviewed successful executives to find out what career events they considered to be important to their development and clustered the results into these categories:[10]

- Job assignments that the executives had had
- Other people with whom they had come into contact
- Hardships that they had endured
- Miscellaneous, including formal training

At the Honeywell Corporation, senior executives wanted to improve the ways they developed their managers. As part of this project, Honeywell undertook a six-year research program to determine how managers learn to manage. The Honeywell study resulted in these categories:[11]

- Job experiences and assignments
- Relationships
- Formal training and education

While neither of these studies asked exclusively about leadership, as we did, their results and ours are so similar that we can conclude that experience is by far the most important opportunity for learning, whether you're talking about managing or leading. Other people rank a close second in importance. Formal education and training are also significant contributors. (All these opportunities for learning to lead are depicted in Figure 13.1, under the broad learning-opportunity categories that emerged from our own study.)

TRIAL AND ERROR: LEARNING ON THE MOVE

There's no suitable substitute for learning by doing. Whether it's facilitating your team's meetings, leading a special task force, heading your favorite charity's fund-raising drive, or chairing your professional association's annual conference, the more chances you have to serve in leadership roles, the more likely it is that you'll develop the skills to lead—and the more likely that you'll learn those important leadership lessons that come only from the failures and successes of live action.

Just any experience, however, doesn't by itself support individual development. In Chapter Three, we talked about how important challenge is to doing our best as leaders. Seeing change as a challenge is important to psychological hardiness, and challenge is the key ingredient in people's enjoying what they do. Challenge is also crucial to learning and career enhancement.[12] Boring, routine jobs don't help you improve your skills and abilities, and

Figure 13.1. Opportunities for Learning to Lead.

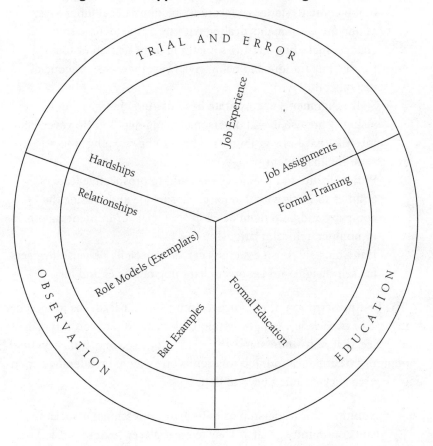

they don't help you move forward in your career. You must stretch. You must take opportunities to test yourself against new and difficult tasks. So experience can indeed be the best teacher—if it contains the element of personal challenge.

There are other ingredients in the recipe of job assignments that advance careers and learning. In her review of developmental experiences in managerial work, Cynthia D. McCauley and her colleagues from the Center for Creative Leadership have reached the following conclusions:[13]

- Managers must be given increasingly broad responsibility if they're to blossom into senior executives—for example,

switching from line to staff and vice versa; experiencing changes
in job content, status, or location; making radical job moves;
taking on assignments dealing with the implementation of
change, including starting something from scratch or fixing a
troubled operation; and being given vast increases in scope of
responsibility.

- Staff assignments at corporate headquarters that give high
  visibility are useful—and personally empowering. However, staff
  jobs that have low visibility tend not to be stepping stones to
  senior management.
- Project teams and task forces can add to prospective leaders'
  abilities to work with diverse groups inside and outside the
  company and help them develop strategies for influencing others
  in nonhierarchical relationships.
- Hardships and business crises can be especially powerful triggers
  for self-insight and lessons in handling obstacles and loss.

The first prescription, then, for becoming a better leader is to broaden
your base of experience. People are more likely to follow you if they have
confidence that you understand their situation, setting, industry, field,
community, or organization. Job rotation is one way of broadening experience, but we suggest going beyond that:

- Volunteer for leadership roles in your professional association
  and community groups. They're great places to develop skills in
  getting people to want to do things, and such organizations are
  always in need of good people.
- Seek leadership opportunities and new project assignments early
  in your career. Don't hesitate to ask for a new assignment within
  two years. If you're in the same job for longer than that, you're
  out of the learning curve.
- Volunteer for the tougher assignments. They have higher risk and
  greater payoff: they're typically the most beneficial to your
  development.

Even the most venturesome jobs won't help you grow if you don't take
the time to reflect upon what you've learned from life's trials and errors.

When we do recall, in vivid detail, the people, the places, the events, the struggles, the victories—the very smell and texture of the action—we discover lasting lessons about how to more effectively lead others. We find embedded in experience the grains of truth about ourselves, others, our organizations, and life itself.

But unexamined experiences don't produce the rich insights that come with reflection and analysis. Proceeding from observations based on experience to principles and applications—that is, inductive learning—is a far better process for learning leadership than beginning with an a priori "truth." Learning from experience is much like watching the game films after an athletic event: we see how we executed our plan, what we did well, and where we need to improve. Athletic teams make extensive use of postgame review. Why not leaders?

The personal-best case methodology is one approach to reaping the educational benefits of experience. As we've noted, we used this technique to gather data on exemplary leadership practices. Those we studied benefited by learning lessons about their own strengths, weaknesses, assumptions, strategies, and tactics. You may wish to write a personal best for yourself. Exhibit 13.1 shows how you can get started right now. As we mentioned in Chapter Four, we also recommend that you consider a personal-worst experience. Failures can be as instructive as successes, if we take the time to reflect upon them.

OBSERVING PEOPLE: LEARNING FROM OTHERS

Other people are essential sources of guidance. We all remember the parent(s) we looked to for advice and support; the special teacher who filled us with curiosity for our favorite subject; the neighbor who always let us watch, and sometimes even take part in, the tinkering in the garage; the coach who believed that we had promise and inspired us to give our best; the counselor who gave us valuable feedback about our behavior and its impact; the master artisan who instructed us in the fundamentals and nuances of a craft; or the first manager who taught us the ropes to skip and the hoops to jump. McCauley found that of all the potential relationships at work, the three most important are mentors, immediate supervisors/managers, and peers.[14]

Exhibit 13.1. Writing a Personal-Best Case.

Think back over your own leadership experiences and choose one that you consider to be a "personal best"—a time when you believe you performed at your peak as a leader. In reviewing the experience, ask yourself these questions:

1. What characterized the situation? Who was involved? Where and when did it take place? Who initiated it?

2. What motivated you to engage in this project? How did you challenge yourself and others?

3. What did you aspire to achieve? How did you build enthusiasm and excitement?

4. How did you involve others? How did you foster collaboration? How did you build trust and respect? How did you build the capacity to excel?

5. What principles and values guided you and others? How did you set an example? What structures and systems did you apply? How did you progress from one milestone to another?

6. How did you recognize individuals? How did you celebrate successes?

7. What lessons did you learn about leadership from this experience?

Mentors are particularly valuable as informal sponsors and coaches.[15] They help us learn how to navigate the system, they make important introductions, and they point us in the right direction.

Managers are obviously important to our careers. They can help us to advance or slow our progress. Managers serve as extremely important sources of performance feedback and modeling. The best ones are those who challenge us, trust us, are willing to spend time with us, and are consistent in their behavior. Managers, like all other leaders, must be credible to us if we're to learn and develop. Chances are that most of us have had good and bad managers in our careers. Good ones are obviously preferred, but bad ones aren't necessarily roadblocks to development. They can, however, create unwanted stress in our lives. If you ever find yourself stuck with a bad boss—whether a tyrant or a weakling, uninvolved or meddlesome—your best bet is to learn to manage amid that behavior. Because it's unlikely that you'll change such people, your best growth strategy is to treat them as you wish to be treated, remain positive about yourself, and deal with them in an assertive but nonconfrontational manner.[16] Bad managers may not be pleasant to work with, but they can be great examples of what not to do.

All leaders are in a network of relationships. Not only must they influence their managers and colleagues; they must also influence others and important constituents, both internal and external, even when they lack formal authority. Harvard Business School professor John Kotter found in his study of general managers that developing effective lateral relationships is one of the critical job challenges and a key predictor of job success.[17] Peers are valuable sources of information; they can tell us what's happening in other parts of the organization. Trusted peers can also serve as advisers and counselors, giving us feedback on our personal style and helping us to test out alternative ways of dealing with problems.

Finally, we can learn from people without having a relationship with them. As often as people mention learning from managers, peers, or mentors, they mention outside role models. Many of us look to historical figures or to well-known contemporary leaders for inspiration and learning. In fact, we're just as apt to look to great men and women of the past for guidance as we are to look to those with whom we work today.

Too little has been said of the influence of historical role models. Biographies have always been a rich source of information on the great military, governmental, religious, community, and business leaders of the past. The popularity of biographies of modern business executives—and of their books about management—is evidence of a keen interest in discovering the secrets of others' success. Advancements in video technology and CD-ROM make contemporary leaders even more accessible as exemplars of the art of leadership.[18] To gain access to the wealth of knowledge others have about leadership, we recommend that you interview, observe, read about, or study leaders you admire. Make the next book you buy or check out of the library a biography of a leader you admire. Then make a practice of reading one biography a month for the next year.

Because mentors are difficult to find—in fact, usually they find you—many of us will never have the experience of being the protégé of an influential leader. However, you can still learn firsthand from those you think are masters of the craft. Ask to interview a leader whom you admire. Usually the person will be flattered and agree to meet. (After all, that's how we got the material for this book.) It's tougher to get busy executives to allow you to follow them through a typical day, but if you ever have the opportunity, take it.

EDUCATION AND TRAINING:
LEARNING THROUGH LIFE

Formal leadership education and training represent a third way you can learn to lead. The "1994 Industry Report" by *Training* magazine found that corporations spend over $50 billion dollars each year for employee education.[19] Employee orientation, offered by 75 percent of companies, is the most common type of training; next comes leadership training.[20] Unfortunately, formal training still doesn't reach the majority of U.S. employees, especially those in the public and nonprofit sector, and thus doesn't play as significant a role in leadership development as it could. While the majority of large organizations provide formal training, only 16 percent of the workers in the labor force receive formal training from their companies.[21]

Although less important as a source of learning than either experience or other people, formal training and education can be of greater importance in developing your skills as an executive and leader than you might assume. Training is a high-leverage way of improving your chances of success. "Research shows," reports the American Society for Training and Development, "that learning on the job accounted for more than half of the productivity increases in the United States between 1929 and 1989. . . . Additional research shows that people who are trained formally in the workplace have a 30 percent higher productivity rate after one year than people who are not formally trained."[22]

You should be spending, at a minimum, 50 hours (six days) annually on your personal and professional development. At Malcolm Baldrige National Quality Award–winning companies such as Motorola and Solectron, it's 100 hours per year! If you want to be an award-winning leader, take a clue from these companies. Baldrige Award–winning companies spend about twice as much on training as the U.S. average of 1.4 percent of payroll.[23] The return on investment in your own training—and the training of your constituents—will be worth it.

There's an even more compelling reason to invest in building your knowledge and skills. Management scholar Peter Drucker observes that "the basic economic resource—'the means of production' to use the economist's term— is no longer capital, nor natural resources (the economist's 'land'), nor 'labor.' *It is and will be knowledge.* "[24] Today 75 to 95 percent of a manufacturer's payroll is allocated to service or knowledge work.[25] Of the total economy, 70 percent of us are employed in services and 15 percent in information—a total of 85 percent.[26] And we would maintain that, because accountability for quality and service is shifting to the front lines, the number of us employed in knowledge work is actually 100 percent. You can't expect people to take responsibility for continuous improvement and then not enable them to use their minds. We've become a knowledge economy, and only by investing in knowledge can we expect economic improvement.

Nonprofit organizations that have no budget for training or whose donors are unwilling to fund non-client-serving activities must be creative in drawing upon the educational resources of their board members and local organizational contacts. For example, the Center for Excellence in Nonprofits coordinates with local companies to offer a "corporate-best" training program, at no cost, to executives from the center's membership of nonprofit, community-based volunteer organizations.

Training doesn't need to be in a classroom for several days in a row. You might make it one day every other month or one morning each month. Or a group of you might teach yourselves: have everyone read a magazine article or book (chapter by chapter); then hold a brown-bag discussion at lunch time of how the ideas might be used or adapted or modified in your department, workgroup, or function. For a relatively small investment of your time, you get two to four times the educational value from the hours you spend in training than you do from the hours you spend "on the job." That's a pretty efficient and effective use of resources.

And you get an even greater payoff if you increase the time that you spend consciously trying to improve yourself through organized programs. Training and education are vastly underdeveloped and underutilized opportunities for creating a personal edge in learning to lead. Here are some suggestions to help you hone that personal edge.

Determine Your Needs

Don't wait to "get fixed." Don't wait for others to tell you what you need to do to improve. Make your own list of developmental needs. If you're not clear about your strengths and weaknesses, sit down right now and begin your assessment. Ask for feedback from people you know, and ask personnel professionals or colleagues if they can recommend any useful diagnostic questionnaires. If, for example, you'd like to assess how you use the practices we describe in this book, take our Leadership Practices Inventory (discussed in the Appendix).

Initiate your own learning agenda, and find the opportunities to build on your strengths and overcome your weaknesses. Charting career success in the next century, predicts Walter Kiechel, executive editor of *Fortune* magazine, will require the following:[27]

- *Being self-reliant.* You must think about yourself as a business of one.
- *Being connected.* You must be a team player.
- *Being specialized.* You must have a deep understanding of something.
- *Being a generalist.* You must know enough of different disciplines and functions to be able to mediate among them.

Important as it is to stay up-to-date in your field, bear in mind that the most effective leaders are generalists. Measure your breadth and add to it as early as possible—and continuously.

Continue Learning

We can all be better leaders by strengthening our interpersonal skills and our strategic thinking capabilities. Take courses in functional areas about which you know little. Take advantage of programs offered by your organization. Even if your own organization has great programs, remember that we often need to get away from our day-to-day work to get some perspective—and we all need stimulation from other sources. Think about taking classes from your customers and vendors. Volunteer to participate in outside training and development programs. There's great value in the connections you can make at such programs.

Knowledge and skill, like other assets, depreciate in value if left untended.[28] The key to success (and perhaps even survival) in the next century—for all of us, but for leaders especially—is the familiar expression "lifelong learning." Continuous process improvement, another expression familiar from the total quality management movement, has to apply to each of us individually as well as to organizational products and services.

Our education must continue. Kindergarten through high school (K–12) or even college just doesn't cut it anymore. Instead, think about K–80, K–90, K–100! Yesteryear's career path is just that: a thing of the past. According to career counselors, today's college graduates will have twelve or more jobs and at least five careers over their lifetime. We have to be prepared for a future in which we'll have to use every opportunity to learn new skills, change work (not just jobs) often, and know how to market our talents. Learning—including knowing how to and realizing the importance of—is the sine qua non for both personal and organizational vitality.

Look Within

Facing uncertain and ambiguous career paths and little job security, we'll find in the years to come that the most critical knowledge for all of us—and for leaders especially—will turn out to be self-knowledge. "Leaders have to heed the voice within," urges a recent *Fortune* magazine article, exclaiming that "in the fast-moving New Economy, you need a new skill: reflection."[29] As *Fortune* editor Stratford Sherman says, "To the degree that individuals are successful at plumbing their depths, those people should be better off, and the companies that employ them may gain competitive advantage. In fast-shifting markets, the unexamined life becomes a liability."[30]

This liability is evident from studies by Southern Methodist University psychology professor James W. Pennebaker. He and his colleagues have reported that people who are able to be introspective or are afforded the opportunity to be reflective—people who've lost their jobs, for example, and are asked to put their stress into words by writing down their deepest thoughts and feelings, including anger and hostility at being laid off—are able to stay healthier and more productive and get on with their lives (and find new jobs) more quickly than people who don't face their feelings or are unable or unwilling to give personal meaning to what's happening in their lives.[31]

Do you know anyone who's heard this deathbed confession: "I wish I'd spent more time at the office"? The National Study of the Changing Workforce, conducted by the Families and Work Institute, shows strong sentiment among all workers (and especially younger ones) in favor of more balanced lives.[32] What's striking about the institute's findings is that those people with more autonomy in their jobs and more social support from their colleagues and leaders are the most successful in balancing their lives; they report less work-family conflict and fewer negative job-to-home spillovers. In developing your leadership abilities, don't neglect the places, activities, and people that bring you joy outside of the workplace. Remember that there are lots of opportunities to develop, practice, and sharpen your leadership skills and talents. You might find just the spot in voluntary organizations, civic activities, churches, synagogues, temples, clubs, professional associations, or parent-teacher associations.

Leadership Development as Self-Development

Wanting to lead and believing that you can lead are the departure points on the path to leadership. Leadership is an art—a performing art—and the instrument is the self. The mastery of the art of leadership comes with the mastery of the self. Ultimately, leadership development is a process of self-development.

We often ask participants in our workshops to think about a leader from history whom they wish they could have over for dinner and a conversation. We ask, "If you really had this chance, what questions would you ask this person?" Invariably, the questions are variations of these themes: What made you believe that you could do this? What kept you from giving up? How did you get the courage to continue? What did you do when you were discouraged or afraid? These questions are at the heart of leadership for any one of us who aspires to lead others, and they're in the minds of those who would be led.

The quest for leadership is first an inner quest to discover who you are. Through self-development comes the confidence needed to lead. Self-confidence is really awareness of and faith in your own powers. These powers become clear and strong only as you work to identify and develop them.

As you begin this quest, you must wrestle with some difficult questions:

- How much do I understand about what's going on in the organization and the world in which it operates?

- How prepared am I to handle the complex problems that now confront my organization?
- Where do I think the organization ought to be headed over the next ten years?
- What are my beliefs about how people ought to conduct the affairs of my organization?
- How strong is my own conviction for my stated vision and values?
- What are my strengths and weaknesses?
- What do I need to do to improve my abilities to move the organization forward?
- How solid is my relationship with my constituents?
- Am I the right one to be leading at this moment?

Honest answers to these questions (and to those that arise from them) tell you that you must open yourself to a more global view. The leader, being in the forefront, is usually the first to encounter the world outside the boundaries of the organization; and the more you know about the world, the easier it is to approach it with assurance. Thus you should seek to learn as much as possible about the forces that affect the organization, be they political, economic, social, moral, or artistic.

Honest answers to the above questions also tell you that if you're to become as effective as possible, you must strive to improve your own understanding of others and build your skills to mobilize people's energies toward higher purposes. While scholars may disagree on the origins of leadership, there's a strong consensus that leaders must be interpersonally competent. You must be able to listen, take advice, lose arguments, and follow, and you must be able to develop the trust and respect of others; otherwise, you can't lead.

Struggling with these questions reveals fundamental contradictions in the concept of leadership. Any leadership practice *can* become destructive. Challenging the status quo to promote innovation and progressive change, for example, can create needless turmoil, confusion, and paranoia if taken to extremes. Likewise, a singular focus on one vision of the future can blind us to other possibilities as well as to the realities of the present. Exploiting our powers of inspiration can cause others to surrender their will. An overreliance on collaboration and trust may reflect an avoidance of critical decisions or cause errors in judgment. An obsession with being seen as a role model can push us into isolation for fear of losing privacy or being "found out"; it can also cause us to be more concerned with style than substance. Constantly worrying about who should be recognized and when we should celebrate can turn us into gregarious minstrels.

Far more insidious than all of these potential problems, however, is the treachery of hubris. It's fun to be a leader, gratifying to have influence, and exhilarating to have scores of people cheering our every word. It's empowering to set direction and have people fired up to march. In more subtle ways than many of us would like to admit, we can be seduced by our own power and importance. All evil leaders have been infected with the disease of hubris, becoming bloated with an exaggerated sense of self. They've used the gifts of leadership to pursue their own sinister ends. Leadership practices per se are amoral. But leaders—the men and women who use the practices—are moral or immoral. There's an ethical dimension to this discussion of leadership that neither leaders nor constituents should take lightly.

John Gardner, Stanford professor, former secretary of Health, Education, and Welfare and founding chairperson of Common Cause, has written that there are four moral goals of leadership:[33]

- Releasing human potential
- Balancing the needs of the individual and the community
- Defending the fundamental values of the community
- Instilling in individuals a sense of initiative and responsibility

Attending to these goals will always direct your eyes to higher purposes. As you work to become all you can be, you can start to let go of your petty self-interests. As you give back some of what you've been given, you can reconstruct your communities. As you serve the values of freedom, justice, equality, caring, and dignity, you can constantly renew the foundations of democracy. As each of us takes individual responsibility for creating the world of our dreams, we can all participate in leading.

You can resolve the conflicts and contradictions of leadership only if you establish for yourself an ethical set of standards on which to base all your actions. You can avoid excessive pride only if you recognize that you're human and need the help of others. All of your individual complexities are held together by a fundamental set of values and beliefs. Developing yourself as a leader begins with those key convictions; it begins with your value system. Clarifying your own values and vision is a highly personal matter. No one else can do it for you. To exhibit harmonious leadership—leadership in which your words and deeds are consonant—you must be in tune internally.

All great leaders have wrestled with their souls. For instance, while attending Crozer Seminary, Martin Luther King, Jr., read extensively in history. The more he read, the more he questioned whether Christian love could be a potent force in the world. He doubted his own capacity to be a pacifist. His faith in love was deeply shaken by Nietzsche's writings glorifying war and power and proclaiming the coming of a master race to control the masses. It wasn't until he was introduced to the teachings of Gandhi that King was inspired to live by the discipline of nonviolent resistance. And it was through reading Gandhi's biography that King also learned that the Indian lawyer himself had struggled to overcome his own tendencies to hatred, anger, and violence. Only after resolving his internal conflicts was King able to enthusiastically embrace the philosophy of nonviolence.[34]

Such personal searching is essential in the development of leaders. You can't elevate others to higher purposes until you've first elevated yourself. Like King, you must resolve those dissonant internal chords. Extensive knowledge of history and the outside world increases your awareness of competing value systems, of the many principles by which individuals, organizations, and states can choose to function. You can't lead others until you've first led yourself through a struggle with opposing values.

When you clarify the principles that will govern your life and the ends that you will seek, you give purpose to your daily decisions. A personal creed gives you a point of reference for navigating the sometimes-stormy seas of organizational life. Without a set of such beliefs, your life has no rudder, and you're easily blown about by the winds of fashion. A credo to guide you prevents confusion on the journey. The internal resolution of competing beliefs also leads to personal integrity, which is essential to believability. A leader with integrity has one self, at home and at work, with family and with colleagues. Such a leader has a unifying set of values that guide choices of action regardless of the situation.

This doesn't mean that leaders are one-dimensional people who focus narrowly on their work. Leaders may have numerous pursuits and interests—arts, literature, science, technology, entertainment, sports, politics, law, religion, and family. Nor does it mean that leaders are flawless, perfect human beings. Leaders are human and make mistakes. We're not suggesting that the ideal leader is a saint; however, we are suggesting that leaders who can't personally adhere to a firm set of values can't convince others of the worth of those values. Leaders without integrity are putting on an act. The believability and credibility so essential for leadership are earned when your behavior is consistent with your beliefs. Thus the first step in summoning the courage of your convictions is clarifying for yourself the beliefs that will guide your actions.

We've said that leaders take us to places we've never been before. But there are no freeways to the future, no paved highways to unknown, unexplored destinations. There's only wilderness. To step out into the unknown, begin with the exploration of the inner territory. With that as a base, we can then discover and unleash the leader within us all.

APPENDIX

Theory and Evidence Behind the Practice

The Leadership Practices Inventory (LPI)

The purpose of the Appendix is to provide empirical support for the Kouzes Posner leadership framework by tracing an overview of the development and validation of the Leadership Practices Inventory (LPI). Comparisons of LPI scores along a number of critical dimensions are also provided, as well as some brief insights into findings by other researchers utilizing the LPI. Readers and scholars interested in a more academic discussion of the LPI are directed to several more technical reports.[1]

Summary
The Leadership Practices Inventory was developed through a triangulation of qualitative and quantitative research methods and studies. In-depth interviews and written case studies from people's personal-best leadership experiences generated the conceptual framework, which consists of five key leadership practices:

- Challenging the process
- Inspiring a shared vision

- Enabling others to act
- Modeling the way
- Encouraging the heart

The actions that make up these practices were translated into behavioral statements. Following several iterative psychometric processes, the resulting instrument has been administered to managers and nonmanagers across a variety of organizations, disciplines, and demographic backgrounds. The LPI has also been adapted for use with college students.[2] Validation studies that we, as well as other researchers, have conducted over a ten-year period consistently confirm the reliability and validity of the Leadership Practices Inventory (and the Kouzes Posner leadership framework).

Instrument Development

The LPI is based upon responses to the Personal-Best Leadership Experience Questionnaire. This survey is twelve pages long and consists of thirty-eight open-ended questions such as these: Who initiated the project? What made you believe you could accomplish the results you sought? What special, if any, techniques or strategies did you use to get other people involved in the project? Did you do anything to mark the completion of the project, at the end or along the way? What did you learn most from this experience? What key lessons would you share with another person about leadership from this experience?

Completing the personal-best questionnaire generally requires about one to two hours of reflection and expression on the part of the respondent. More than 2,500 of these surveys have been collected, and more than 5,000 additional respondents have completed a short form of this survey (containing just four or five items).

In addition to the case studies, in-depth interviews have been conducted, primarily with managers in middle- to senior-level organizational positions in a wide variety of both public- and private-sector companies around the world. These interviews have generally taken forty-five to sixty minutes; in some cases, they have lasted four to five hours. Building from an initial base of forty-two, the total number of interviews over the past decade now numbers well over 300 respondents.

We and other experts familiar with the model wrote statements describing each of the various leadership actions and behaviors. Each statement is cast on a five-point Likert scale. A higher value represents greater use of a leadership behavior, as noted below:

1. Seldom or rarely do what is described in the statement
2. Once in a while do what is described
3. Sometimes do what is described
4. Fairly often do what is described
5. Very frequently, if not always, do what is described

The statements were then modified, discarded, or included following (1) lengthy discussions and repeated feedback sessions with respondents and assorted subject-matter experts and (2) empirical analyses of various sets of behaviorally based statements. Ongoing analysis and refinements in the instrument continue, with a database involving nearly 60,000 respondents.

LPI Instrument and Procedure

The LPI currently contains thirty statements—six statements for measuring each of the five leadership practices. Both a Self and an Observer (previously labeled "Other") form of the LPI have been developed.[3] Participating individuals first complete the LPI-Self and then ask five or six people who are familiar with their behavior to complete the LPI-Observer. The LPI-Observer is voluntary, however, and generally anonymous. Typically, the instruments are returned directly to the researchers or seminar facilitator. The LPI takes approximately eight to ten minutes to complete, and it is capable of being either self- or computer-scored.

Means, Standard Deviations, and Reliability

Means and standard deviations for each LPI scale are presented in Table A.1, as are reliability scores.[4] Based upon mean scores, enabling others to act is perceived by respondents and their constituents as the leadership practice most frequently used. This is followed by challenging the process, modeling the way, and encouraging the heart. Inspiring a shared vision is perceived by both respondents and their constituents as the leadership practice least frequently engaged in.

Internal reliabilities (Chronbach alphas) on the LPI range between .81 and .91. Reliabilities for the LPI-Self (ranging between .71 and .85) are somewhat lower than those for the LPI-Observer (ranging between .82 and .92). Other studies have found similar levels of internal reliability. For example, reliabilities ranged from .80 to .92 in a study of engineering managers and their constituents[5] and between .71 and .82 in a study of women in executive positions in banking and higher education.[6] With college presidents, internal reliabilities for the LPI-Self ranged between .71 and .84, while reliabilities for the LPI-Observer ranged between .85 and .93; combining Self and Observer responses produced reliabilities ranging between .84 and .92.[7] Reliabilities ranged between .61 and .80 for correctional institution leaders,[8] between .79 and .90 for agricultural education department executive officers,[9] between .80 and .90 for frontline supervisors in a large telecommunications firm,[10] between .78 and .90 for a cross-section of midlevel managers,[11] and between .70 and .88 for home health care agency directors.[12] With Australian bank managers, reliabilities on the LPI-Self ranged from .70 to .82, while for the LPI-Observer they ranged from .81 to .94.[13] Internal reliabilities for a Spanish-language version of the LPI, with Mexican respondents,[14] ranged

Table A.1. Means, Standard Deviations, and Reliability Indexes for the Leadership Practices Inventory.

Leadership Practice	Mean	Standard Deviation	LPI (N = 43,899)	LPI-Self (N = 6,651)	LPI-Observer (N = 37,248)
Challenging the Process	22.38	4.17	.81	.71	.82
Inspiring a Shared Vision	20.48	4.90	.87	.81	.88
Enabling Others to Act	23.89	4.37	.85	.75	.86
Modeling the Way	22.18	4.16	.81	.72	.82
Encouraging the Heart	21.89	5.22	.91	.85	.92

between .81 and .89, and reliabilities for a French-language version, involving Canadian high-technology managers, ranged between .70 and .86. Reliabilities for non-Caucasians ranged between .68 and .80, while for their white counterparts the range was between .60 and .78. Test-retest reliability for the five practices in our studies has been at the .93 level and above; others have reported test-retest reliabilities in the .80 level and above.[15]

Scores on the LPI have been relatively stable over time. Comparing the LPI scores of participants in The Leadership Challenge Workshop™ every two years since 1987, for example, reveals considerable consistency across the five leadership practices for each time-period comparison.

Furthermore, LPI scores have been found, in general, not to be related with various demographic factors (for example, age, marital status, years of experience, educational level) or with organizational characteristics (for example, size, functional area, line versus staff position). This finding extends across a wide variety of nonbusiness settings as well, as suggested by research with school superintendents, principals, and administrators,[16] with health care administrators,[17] with female executives in banking and higher education,[18] with church pastors of large congregations,[19] and with family support center directors.[20]

Factor Structure of the LPI

Responses to the thirty leadership behavior items were subjected to a principle factoring method with iteration and varimax rotation. Five factors were extracted with eigenvalues greater than 1.0 and accounting for 60.5 percent of the variance. Five interpretable factors were obtained—consistent with the five subscales of the LPI—although a few item-factor loadings share some common variance across more than one factor. The stability of the five factors was tested by factor-analyzing the data from different subsamples. In each case, the factor structure was essentially similar to the one shown in Table A.2 (which involves the entire sample). Other researchers have reported achieving comparable factor structures.[21]

Georgia Tech professor David Herold and his colleagues, with their own LPI data, performed a confirmatory factor analysis using LISREL VII, analyzing a covariance matrix prepared from the raw data by PRELIS. Their conclusion:

> Estimating a correlated factors model corresponding to the oblique factor rotation, modified to reflect the intercorrelations among the error items for the LPI items that had correlations with other items exceeding .50, resulted in a confirmatory model with acceptable fit (Chi-Square = 399.9, d.f. = 363, $p < .09$). In addition, all of the hypothesized structural coefficients linking the observed variables to the five factors were highly significant with all t values exceeding 7.0, suggesting that when modeled appropriately, the LISREL estimates confirm the LPI factor model.[22]

Comparisons Between Self and Observer Perspectives

Table A.3 compares mean scores from the LPI-Self with those from the LPI-Observer. Average frequency scores have a tendency to be somewhat higher on the LPI-Self than on the LPI-Observer. These differences, however, reach statistical significance for only

Table A.2. Factor Structure (Factor Loadings) for the Leadership Practices Inventory (N = 43,899).

Item Number	Challenging the Process	Inspiring a Shared Vision	Enabling Others to Act	Modeling the Way	Encouraging the Heart
26	**.664**	.235	.173	.046	.185
16	**.641**	.285	.188	.223	.153
1	**.577**	.250	.147	.157	.156
11	**.557**	.220	.023	.234	.094
21	**.406**	.276	.311	.276	.199
6	**.388**	.152	.246	.259	.158
7	.239	**.697**	.164	.109	.236
2	.262	**.662**	.162	.128	.183
17	.281	**.594**	.187	.232	.235
22	.375	**.505**	.267	.254	.117
27	.421	**.480**	.220	.037	.288
12	.300	**.439**	.317	.141	.223
8	.032	.074	**.717**	.096	.238
23	.188	.194	**.701**	.246	.231
18	.115	.153	**.689**	.189	.234
13	.118	.124	**.577**	.018	.144
28	.224	.252	**.506**	.215	.239
3	.119	.251	**.469**	.248	.233
29	.221	.221	.220	**.588**	.195
9	.156	.076	.327	**.527**	.190
14	.220	.309	.186	**.468**	.200
24	.220	.128	.365	**.404**	.163
19	.238	.342	.110	**.378**	.138
4	.230	.311	.251	**.369**	.173
25	.183	.209	.153	.109	**.755**
5	.121	.225	.140	.119	**.726**
15	.119	.141	.370	.128	**.711**
20	.146	.181	.391	.168	**.708**
10	.164	.109	.327	.198	**.695**
30	.233	.231	.203	.201	**.577**

Table A.3. *T*-Tests of Differences Between Scores on the LPI-Self
and LPI-Observer.

Leadership Practice	LPI-Self		LPI-Observer	
	Mean	Standard Deviation	Mean	Standard Deviation
Challenging the Process*	22.74	3.26	22.31	4.32
Inspiring a Shared Vision	20.62	3.96	20.46	5.05
Enabling Others to Act*	24.81	2.91	23.72	4.56
Modeling the Way	22.26	3.24	22.17	4.30
Encouraging the Heart	21.90	3.99	21.89	5.41

*There were statistically significant differences ($p < .001$) between LPI-Self and LPI-Observer responses on this leadership practice.

two practices (challenging the process and enabling others to act).[23] It has not been unusual to find Self scores higher than Observer scores in specific workshop or research settings,[24] although the rank order of the practices has been generally consistent across sample populations. Some researchers have reported no significant differences between Self and Observer responses.[25]

Comparisons Between Male and Female Respondents

The possible impact of gender on LPI scores was analyzed by looking at differences between male and female respondents. The samples, compared in Table A.4, include men and women across a wide variety of organizations and professions. Women total about 22 percent of this sample ($N = 1,267$ versus $N = 4,571$ for men). Generally, the leadership practices were not significantly different for males and females on the LPI-Self. Both groups reported engaging in challenging the process, inspiring a shared vision, enabling others to act, and modeling the way with the same approximate frequency. Female managers reported engaging in the leadership practice of encouraging the heart significantly more often than did their male colleagues, however.

Other researchers have reported similar results with regard to gender and leadership practices within specific sample populations. For instance, no gender differences were reported for studies involving public health agency directors,[26] fraternity and sorority chapter presidents,[27] school superintendents,[28] and college presidents.[29] Likewise, gender made no difference in the leadership practices of Mexican managers.[30] The LPI scores of female elementary school principals were reported as higher than their male counterparts, although gender made no difference in the outcome variables.[31] Female university professors reported engaging in encouraging the heart more than their male counterparts, but the two groups did not differ on the remaining four leadership practices.[32]

Looking further into possible gender differences, we examined the extent to which the constituents' gender interacted with a leader's gender. This study took place within a nationwide retail organization. No differences were found for inspiring a shared

**Table A.4. Comparisons Between Male and Female Managers
on the LPI-Self.**

Leadership Practice	Males (N = 4,571)		Females (N = 1,267)	
	Mean	Standard Deviation	Mean	Standard Deviation
Challenging the Process	22.76	3.22	22.71	3.37
Inspiring a Shared Vision	20.70	3.95	20.51	4.13
Enabling Others to Act	24.81	2.91	24.88	2.88
Modeling the Way	22.21	3.25	22.39	3.18
Encouraging the Heart*	21.60	3.97	23.08	3.90

*There were statistically significant differences ($p < .001$) between male and female respondents on this leadership practice.

vision, enabling others to act, or encouraging the heart; there were statistically significant interactions, however, for challenging the process and modeling the way. Female constituents were more likely than male constituents to report that their leaders, whether male or female, engaged in challenging the process and modeling the way. Female constituents were also more likely to report that their male leaders engaged in challenging the process and modeling the way than were male constituents of female leaders. When same-gender dyads were compared with mixed-gender dyads, statistically significant differences were found for only one leadership practice: constituents of the same gender as their managers reported more inspiring a shared vision behavior than did constituents from mixed-gender dyads.

Comparisons Between Government and Business Respondents

Scores on the LPI for government managers were matched with a comparable group of business managers. Overall, there were no statistically significant differences between the two groups of managers. LPI-Self scores did not differ between these two groups of managers, nor did the scores reported by their constituents (LPI-Observer). A study involving leaders employed in public- or private-sector health positions also found no differences.[33]

Comparisons Across Functional Disciplines

LPI scores across functional areas (customer service, finance, information systems, manufacturing, and marketing) were also compared (see Table A.5). Functional field or discipline made no statistically significant difference for three leadership practices: challenging the process, enabling others to act, and modeling the way. Post hoc comparison tests revealed that the differences for inspiring a shared vision and encouraging the heart were due primarily to respondents in the finance area being substantially different (lower) in these two practices than their counterparts in other fields.[34] Overall, though, there were few significant differences based upon the respondent's functional area.

Table A.5. Comparisons Between Managers by Functional Field on the LPI-Self.

Functional Field	Challenging the Process		Inspiring a Shared Vision*		Enabling Others to Act		Modeling the Way		Encouraging the Heart*	
	Standard	Mean	Standard	Mean	Standard	Mean	Standard	Mean	Standard	Mean
Customer Service	22.31	2.82	20.17	3.55	24.89	2.86	21.34	2.91	21.15	3.47
Finance	22.14	3.28	18.33	3.78	24.09	2.97	20.98	2.88	19.86	4.03
Information Systems	22.24	3.24	20.09	3.94	24.77	3.04	21.61	3.12	21.43	3.93
Manufacturing/Development	22.49	3.24	20.47	3.69	24.58	3.08	21.62	3.52	21.57	3.88
Marketing	22.32	3.09	19.79	3.56	24.74	2.93	21.44	3.05	21.84	3.59

*There were statistically significant differences ($p < .001$) by functional field between respondents on this leadership practice.

Comparisons Across Ethnic Background

Possible LPI differences due to ethnic background were investigated in a study involving executive directors of community development organizations. LPI scores for Caucasian directors were compared with those for directors of color (African-Americans, Hispanics, and Asians). The two groups did not differ on challenging the process, enabling others to act, or encouraging the heart, but directors of color reported significantly higher scores than their Caucasian counterparts for inspiring a shared vision and modeling the way. However, assessments provided by their constituents revealed no systematic differences between the leadership practices of managers based upon their ethnic background. Reexamination of the data by respondent gender also made no difference in the pattern of results. In a study involving Native American and non–Native American secondary school administrators, LPI scores were not found to be statistically different.[35]

Cross-Cultural Comparisons

Several cross-cultural comparisons of LPI scores have been made between, for example, U.S. and European managers from various countries, U.S. and Pacific Rim managers, U.S. and Australian managers, and U.S. and Mexican managers.

Few differences were found between U.S. and United Kingdom managers working for the same multinational chemical company. Enabling others to act was rated most frequently by managers as well as their constituents from both countries. The same consistent pattern was observed for challenging the process (rated second-most frequently by all parties) and inspiring a shared vision (rated least frequently by all parties).

Within a large high-technology firm, no significant differences were found between U.S. managers and their counterparts in either England, the Netherlands, or Germany. This was true for both LPI-Self and LPI-Observer scores.

Managers from small factories in four Pacific Rim countries (Korea, the Philippines, Taiwan, and Malaysia) completed the LPI as part of a multinational semiconductor company's management development program. LPI-Self scores were significantly higher than those reported by their constituents for all leadership practices, with the exception of encouraging the heart. The rank order for the LPI-Self scores was the same for the Pacific Rim managers as it was for their U.S. counterparts. This pattern was true for LPI-Observer scores as well.

When midlevel Australian managers were matched with comparable U.S. managers, no statistically significant differences between the two groups were found for any of the five leadership practices. While the LPI scores of Mexican managers were, on average, lower than their U.S. counterparts, there were no differences between the two groups in the rank order of the leadership practices.[36]

Validation of the LPI

Utilizing only the responses from the LPI-Observer, we examined the relationship between leaders' effectiveness and their leadership practices (as measured by the LPI).[37] By including only the responses from constituents about their managers, we were using relatively independent assessments, thereby minimizing potential self-report bias. Regression analysis was performed, with leader effectiveness as the dependent variable and the five leadership practices as the independent variables. The regression equation was highly significant ($F = 318.88$, $p < .0001$). The leadership practices explained over

55 percent (adjusted R^2 = .756) of the variance around constituents' assessments of their managers' effectiveness.

We examined another aspect of the validity of the LPI by determining how well LPI scores differentiated between high- and low-performing managers. For this, we used discriminant analysis as a classification technique. We wanted to determine how well LPI scores could group managers into various performance-based categories.

The lowest third and highest third of the managers on the LPI-Observer leader effectiveness scale formed the low- and high-performing categories. Approximately 85 percent of the sample of LPI-Observer respondents was used to create the canonical discriminant function, with the remaining 15 percent used to create a holdout sample for classification purposes. One discriminant function was derived; and, as shown in Table A.6, it correctly classified 92.6 percent of the known cases and 77.8 percent of the cases in the holdout sample. Including the middle third of the sample in this analysis resulted in correct classification of 71.1 percent of the known cases and 67.9 percent of the holdout sample. All four of these results are beyond the .001 level of chance probability.

Further Validation of the LPI

A variety of other researchers have utilized the Leadership Practices Inventory in their investigation of various leadership issues. It has been successfully used in studies looking at the following:

- Effectiveness and professional credibility of high school principals[38]
- Principals in effective and ineffective schools in Canada[39]
- The ethical philosophy of middle school administrators[40]
- Principals of high-performing schools versus their counterparts from less effective schools[41]
- Elementary school principals and levels of parental involvement[42]
- Heads of postsecondary vocational schools and community colleges[43]

Table A.6. Classification Results from Discriminant Analysis on Effectiveness by LPI Scores.

Group	Known Sample		Holdout Sample	
	Actual Members	Predicted Members	Actual Members	Predicted Members
Low Group	169	154	23	16
High Group	156	147	31	26
Correctly Classified*	92.6 percent		77.8 percent	
Low Group	169	123	18	13
Moderate Group	108	64	28	15
High Group	156	121	35	27
Correctly Classified*	71.1 percent		67.9 percent	

*These percentages are significantly beyond probabilities due to chance ($p < .001$).

- The relationship between scores on the Myers-Briggs Type Indicator and LPI scores[44]
- The differences between effective and ineffective bank managers and between effective and ineffective work teams[45]
- The leadership behaviors of managers within two midsized hospitals and organizational commitment, job satisfaction, and productivity[46]
- LPI behaviors of hospital administrators and the extent of change experienced in the organization[47]
- Contemporary public health leaders[48]
- College presidents and organizational effectiveness, from the perspective of their vice presidents[49]
- Presidential assistants in higher education[50]
- The thinking styles or brain dominance among community college presidents[51]
- Community Development Corporation executive directors and their modes of dealing with conflict[52]
- The effectiveness of college presidents[53]
- Perceptions of organizational unit performance[54]
- The leader's impact on constituent motivation and commitment in a cross-sectional study of midlevel managers[55]
- The similarities between leaders in churches and those in business enterprises[56]
- Pastors involved in the start-up of new churches[57]
- Christian school principals[58]

Such independent efforts substantiate the utility and robustness of the LPI. Correlations with other sociological and psychological instruments in these studies further enhance confidence that the LPI measures what it is purported to measure and not some other phenomenon.

Conclusions

The Leadership Practices Inventory has sound psychometric properties. Internal reliabilities for the five leadership practices (as assessed by both Self and Observer versions) are very good and are consistent over time. The underlying factor structure has been sustained across a variety of studies and settings, and support continues to be generated for the instrument's predictive and concurrent validity. For the most part, findings are relatively consistent across people, genders, and ethnic and cultural backgrounds, as well as across various organizational characteristics (such as the functions the organization employs, its size, and its public- or private-sector status). The LPI, when used as a management/leadership *development* instrument, has also proven quite powerful in assessing individuals' leadership behaviors and in providing useful feedback for enhancing one's leadership capabilities. Overall, the Kouzes Posner leadership framework contributes richly to our understanding of the leadership process and in the development and unleashing of leadership capabilities.

NOTES

CHAPTER 1

1. Unless otherwise noted, all quotations from leaders are taken from personal interviews or from personal-best cases written for this study by the leaders and analyzed by the authors and case writers. (Please see Acknowledgments for a list of case writers for this edition.) The titles and affiliations of the leaders in this study may be different today than they were at the time of publication. We expect many to move into other leadership responsibilities.
2. W. Bennis, *On Becoming a Leader* (Reading, Mass.: Addison-Wesley, 1988), 146.

CHAPTER 2

1. For more information about these findings, see W. H. Schmidt and B. Z. Posner, *Managerial Values and Expectations: The Silent Power in Personal and Organizational Life* (New York: American Management Association, 1982); B. Z. Posner and W. H. Schmidt, "Values and the American Manager: An Update," *California Management Review* 26 (3) (1984): 202–216; and B. Z. Posner and W. H. Schmidt, "Values and Expectations of Federal Service Executives," *Public Administration Review* 46 (5) (1986): 447–454.
2. J. M. Kouzes and B. Z. Posner, *Credibility: How Leaders Gain and Lose It, Why People Demand It* (San Francisco: Jossey-Bass, 1993).
3. J. M. Kouzes, B. Z. Posner, and M. Krause, "Summary of the Executive Challenges Survey" (Executive Development Center, Leavey School of Business and Administration, Santa Clara University, 1986).
4. Korn/Ferry International and Columbia University Graduate School of Business, *Reinventing the CEO* (New York: Korn/Ferry International and Columbia University Graduate School of Business, 1989), 90.

5. S. Terkel, *Working* (New York: Pantheon Books, 1974), xxiv.
6. This phase of our research built upon earlier work by C. A. O'Reilly, "Charisma as Communication: The Impact of Top Management Credibility and Philosophy on Employee Involvement," paper presented at the annual meeting of the Academy of Management, Boston, Aug. 1984.
7. For a study of the believability of politicians and journalists, and the difference in their roles, see Times Mirror Company, *The People and the Press* (Los Angeles: Times Mirror, 1986). For a recent analysis of trust in major political institutions and prospective presidential candidates, see Times Mirror Center for the People and the Press, *The New Political Landscape* (Washington, D.C.: Times Mirror, 1994).
8. S. M. Lipset and W. Schneider, *The Confidence Gap: Business, Labor, and Government in the Public Mind* (New York: Free Press, 1984), 399.
9. P. H. Mirvis, personal correspondence, Jan. 1992. See also D. L. Kanter and P. H. Mirvis, *The Cynical Americans: Living and Working in an Age of Discontent and Disillusion* (San Francisco: Jossey-Bass, 1989).
10. For an analysis of the relationship between constituent and leader, see G. Wills, *Certain Trumpets: The Call of Leaders* (New York: Simon & Schuster, 1994), 18–19. See also R. A. Heifetz, *Leadership Without Easy Answers* (Cambridge, Mass.: Belknap Press, 1994).
11. We acknowledge Vance Packard's insight that leadership involves mobilizing others "to want to." See V. Packard, *The Pyramid Climbers* (New York: McGraw-Hill, 1962), 170.

CHAPTER 3

1. E. Partridge, *Origins: A Short Etymological Dictionary of Modern English* (New York: Macmillan, 1966, 4th ed.), 342.
2. Partridge, *Origins*, 378.
3. P. M. Carrigan, "Up from the Ashes," *OD Practitioner 18* (1) (1986): 2–3.
4. Carrigan, "Up from the Ashes," 2.
5. P. M. Carrigan, introduction as keynote speaker to the OD Network National Conference, San Francisco, 16 Oct. 1985.
6. P. M. Carrigan, telephone conversation, 16 Oct. 1986.
7. See, for example, A. J. Mento, R. P. Steel, and R. J. Karsen, "A Meta-Analytic Study of the Effects of Goal Setting on Task Performance: 1966–1984, *Organizational Behavior and Human Decision Processes 39* (1987): 52–83.
8. M. Fox, *Reinvention of Work: A New Vision of Livelihood for Our Time* (San Francisco: HarperSanFrancisco, 1994), 49.
9. A. Kohn, *Punished by Rewards* (New York: Houghton Mifflin, 1993).
10. M. Csikszentmihalyi, *Beyond Boredom and Anxiety: The Experience of Play in Work and Games* (San Francisco: Jossey-Bass, 1975); and M. Csikszentmihalyi and I. S. Csikszentmihalyi, *Optimal Experience: Psychological Studies of Flow in Consciousness* (Cambridge, England: Cambridge University Press, 1988).
11. Csikszentmihalyi, *Beyond Boredom and Anxiety,* 30.
12. Csikszentmihalyi, *Beyond Boredom and Anxiety,* 33.
13. W. Bennis, *Why Leaders Can't Lead: The Unconscious Conspiracy Continues* (San Francisco: Jossey-Bass, 1989), 14. Italics in original.
14. Bennis, *Why Leaders Can't Lead,* 15.

15. R. Ackoff, *Management in Small Doses* (New York: Wiley, 1986), 110.
16. J. M. Utterback, "Innovation in Industry and the Diffusion of Technology," in M. L. Tushman and W. L. Moore (eds.), *Readings in the Management of Innovation* (New York: Pitman, 1982), 29–42, p. 30.
17. M. Maidique, "Why Products Succeed and Why Products Fail," presentation to the Executive Seminar in Corporate Excellence, Santa Clara University, 29 May 1985.
18. Another review of over 567 innovations puts the percentage at 75: see D. G. Marquis, "The Anatomy of Successful Innovations," in M. L. Tushman and W. L. Moore (eds.), *Readings in the Management of Innovation* (New York: Pitman, 1982), 79–87, p. 84.
19. R. Katz, "The Influence of Group Longevity: High-Performance Research Teams," *Wharton Magazine 6* (3) (1982): 28–34; R. Katz and T. J. Allen, "Investigating the Not Invented Here (NIH) Syndrome: A Look at the Performance, Tenure, and Communication Patterns of 50 R&D Project Groups," in M. L. Tushman and W. L. Moore (eds.), *Readings in the Management of Innovation*, 2nd ed. (New York: Ballinger, 1988), 293–309. See also T. J. Allen, D. Lee, and M. Tushman, "R&D Performance as a Function of Internal Communication, Project Management, and the Nature of Work," *IEEE Transactions on Engineering Management 27* (1980): 2–12; and R. Katz and M. L. Tushman, "Communication Patterns, Project Performance, and Task Characteristics: An Empirical Evaluation and Integration in an R&D Setting," *Organizational Behavior and Human Performance 23* (1979): 139–162.
20. Katz, "The Influence of Group Longevity," 31.
21. Katz, "The Influence of Group Longevity," 32.
22. R. Henderson, "Managing Innovation in the Information Age," *Harvard Business Review*, Jan.-Feb. (1994): 100–105.
23. I. Federman, "A Personal View of Leadership," presentation to the Executive Seminar in Corporate Excellence, Santa Clara University, 16 Oct. 1983.
24. Operation Raleigh USA recruitment poster, Raleigh, N.C., n.d.
25. R. M. Kanter, *The Change Masters: Innovation for Productivity in the American Corporation* (New York: Simon & Schuster, 1983), 125.
26. J. M. Burns, *Leadership* (New York: HarperCollins, 1978), 461.
27. D. W. Bray and A. Howard, "The AT&T Longitudinal Studies of Managers," in K. W. Shaie (ed.), *Longitudinal Studies of Adult Psychological Development* (New York: Guilford Press, 1983), 281–282. See also P. L. Wright, "Teller Job Satisfaction and Organization Commitment as They Relate to Career Orientations," *Human Relations 43* (4) (1990): 369–381; and D.M.S. Lee, "Job Challenge, Work Effort, and Job Performance of Young Engineers: A Causal Analysis," *IEEE Transactions on Engineering Management 39* (3) (1992): 214–226.
28. S. Greco, "Letting Workers Play Customers," *Inc.*, Oct. 1994, 119.
29. "Why Kodak Is Starting to Click Again," *Business Week*, 23 Feb. 1987, 134.
30. P. F. Drucker, "Drucker on Management: The Five Deadly Business Sins," *Wall Street Journal*, 21 Oct. 1993, A25.
31. J. Eckhouse, "HP Plant Licks Labor Problem," *San Francisco Chronicle*, 9 Nov. 1987, C1, C7.
32. For information on renewing your teams, see D. T. Jaffe, C. D. Scott, and G. R. Tobe, *Rekindling Commitment: How to Revitalize Yourself, Your Work, and Your Organization* (San Francisco: Jossey-Bass, 1994).
33. For more information on workplace humor, see W. J. Duncan, L. R. Smeltzer, and T. L. Leap, "Humor and Work: Applications of Joking Behavior to Management," *Journal of Management 16* (2) (1990): 255–278; and W. J. Duncan and J. P. Feisal, "No Laughing Matter: Patterns of Humor in the Workplace," *Organizational Dynamics 17* (4) (1989): 18–30.

34. Interesting information about Southwest Airlines and CEO Herb Kelleher is provided in J. C. Quick, "Crafting an Organizational Culture: Herb's Hand at Southwest Airlines," *Organizational Dynamics* 21 (2) (1992): 45–56; and K. Labich, "Is Herb Kelleher America's Best CEO?" *Fortune*, 2 May 1994, 44–50.

35. Partridge, *Origins*, 598.

CHAPTER 4

1. B. Biro, "Beyond Success: The Fifteen Secrets of a Winning Life" (unpublished manuscript, Hamilton, Mont., 1994).

2. G. Day, "New Directions for Corporations: Conditions for Successful Renewal," *European Management Journal* 11 (2) (1993): 229–237; S. D. Saleh and C. K. Wang, "The Management of Innovation: Strategy, Structure, and Organizational Climate," *IEEE Transactions on Engineering Management* 40 (1) (1993): 14–21; D. W. Ingwerson, "Participation . . . Beyond the Catchword Phase," *Journal for Quality and Participation* 16 (1) (1993): 44–47; B. Schneider, S. K. Gunnarson, and K. Niles-Jolly, "Creating the Climate and Culture of Success," *Organizational Dynamics* 23 (1) (1994): 17–29; and A. Abbey and J. W. Dickson, "R&D Work Climate and Innovation in Semiconductors," *Academy of Management Journal* 26 (2) (1983): 362–368.

3. M. Maidique, "Why Products Succeed and Why Products Fail," presentation to the Executive Seminar in Corporate Excellence, Santa Clara University, 29 May 1985; see also M. Maidique and B. J. Zinger, "The New Product Learning Cycle," *Research Policy* 14 (1985): 299–313.

4. For discussions of hardiness and health, see S. C. Kobasa, S. R. Maddi, and S. Courington, "Personality and Constitution as Mediators in the Stress-Illness Relationship," *Journal of Health and Social Behavior* 22 (1981): 368–378; S. C. Kobasa, S. R. Maddi, and S. Kahn, "Hardiness and Health: A Prospective Study," *Journal of Personality and Social Psychology* 42 (1) (1982): 168–177; S. C. Kobasa and M. C. Puccetti, "Personality and Social Resources in Stress Resistance," *Journal of Personality and Social Psychology* 45 (4) (1983): 839–850. See also M. Csikszentmihalyi and I. S. Csikszentmihalyi, *Optimal Experience: Psychological Studies of Flow in Consciousness* (Cambridge, England: Cambridge University Press, 1988); and R. Karasek and T. Theorell, *Healthy Work: Stress, Productivity, and the Reconstruction of Working Life* (New York: Basic Books, 1992).

5. See, for example, T. L. Tang and M. L. Hammontree, "The Effects of Hardiness, Police Stress, and Life Stress on Police Officers' Illness and Absenteeism," *Public Personnel Management* 21 (4) (1992): 493–510; S. R. Maddi and M. J. Hess, "Personality Hardiness and Success in Basketball," *International Journal of Sport Psychology* 23 (4) (1992): 360–368; F. Rhodewalt and J. B. Zone, "Appraisal of Life Change, Depression, and Illness in Hardy and Nonhardy Women," *Journal of Personality and Social Psychology* 56 (1) (1989): 81–88; M. Westman, "The Relationship Between Stress and Performance: The Moderating Effect of Hardiness," *Human Performance* 3 (1990): 141–155; and P. T. Bartone, "Predictors of Stress-Related Illness in City Bus Drivers," *Journal of Occupational Medicine* 31 (1989): 857–863.

6. S. R. Maddi and S. C. Kobasa, *The Hardy Executive: Health Under Stress* (Chicago: Dorsey Professional Books/Dow Jones–Irwin, 1984), 31–32.

7. L. A. Isabella and T. Forbes, "Managerial Mindsets Research Project: Executive Summary" (Charlottesville, Va.: Darden Graduate School of Business Administration, University of Virginia, Apr. 1994); and interview with the authors, 13 June 1994.

8. Isabella and Forbes, "Managerial Mindsets Research Project," 7.
9. Maddi and Kobasa, *The Hardy Executive*, 59.
10. J. Huey, "Managing in the Midst of Chaos," *Fortune*, Apr. 5, 1993, 38.
11. M. Wheatley, *Leadership and the New Science* (San Francisco: Berrett-Koehler, 1992).
12. For another discussion of leadership and uncertainty, see J. D. Thompson and A. Tuden, "Strategies, Structures, and Processes of Organizational Decision," in J. D. Thompson and others (eds.), *Comparative Studies in Administration* (Pittsburgh, Pa.: University of Pittsburgh Press, 1959).
13. M. Korda, "The King of the Deal," *New Yorker*, 29 Mar. 1993, 43.
14. W. Bridges, "Ten Rules for Living in the Age of Joblessness," *Transitions* (newsletter of William Bridges & Associates) 6 (1) (Winter 1993): 6. See also W. Bridges, *JobShift: How to Prosper in a Workplace Without Jobs* (Reading, Mass.: Addison-Wesley, 1994).
15. G. Calvert, *Highwire Management: Risk-Taking Tactics for Leaders, Innovators, and Trailblazers* (San Francisco: Jossey-Bass, 1993).
16. S. Barlay, "On a Wing and a Prayer," *Images*, 19 May 1991, 15. Excerpted from S. Barlay, *The Final Call* (New York: Pantheon, 1990).
17. R. J. Kriegel and L. Patler, *If It Ain't Broke . . . Break It!* (New York: Warner Books, 1991).
18. T. J. Peters, *Thriving on Chaos* (New York: Knopf, 1987).
19. For more information about these and other examples, see F. R. Gulliver, "Post-Project Appraisals Pay," *Harvard Business Review*, Mar.-Apr. (1987): 128–130, 132; D. A. Garvin, "Building a Learning Organization," *Harvard Business Review*, July-Aug. (1993): 78–91; and P. Senge, *The Fifth Discipline: The Art and Practice of the Learning Organization* (New York: Doubleday/Currency, 1990).
20. See, for example, J. E. McGrath, *Groups: Interaction and Performance* (Englewood Cliffs, N.J.: Prentice-Hall, 1984); C. M. Moore, *Group Techniques for Idea Building* (Newbury Park, Calif.: Sage, 1987); and W. M. Fox, *Effective Group Problem Solving: How to Broaden Participation, Improve Decision Making, and Increase Commitment to Action* (San Francisco: Jossey-Bass, 1987).
21. A. Van de Ven, A. L. Delbecq, and R. J. Koenig, "Determinants of Coordination Modes Within Organizations," *American Sociological Review 41* (2) (1976): 322–338.

CHAPTER 5

1. A. Blum, *Annapurna: A Woman's Place* (San Francisco: Sierra Club Books, 1980), 9.
2. Blum, *Annapurna*, 12.
3. Blum, *Annapurna*, 12.
4. A. Taylor III, "GM's $11,000,000,000 Turnaround," *Fortune*, 17 Oct. 1994, 54–56.
5. See, for example, J. Collins and J. Porras, *Built to Last: Successful Habits of Visionary Companies* (New York: HarperBusiness, 1994); and G. Hamel and C. K. Prahalad, *Competing for the Future: Breakthrough Strategies for Seizing Control of Your Industry and Creating the Markets of Tomorrow* (Boston: Harvard Business School Press, 1994), 4.
6. W. B. Bennis and B. Nanus, *Leaders: The Strategies for Taking Charge* (New York: HarperCollins, 1985), 89.
7. L. Eisenberg, "Taking the Long, Sharp View," *Esquire 100* (6) (1983): 305.
8. For other discussions of the role of vision and purpose in leadership, see J. M. Burns, *Leadership* (New York: HarperCollins, 1978); C. I. Barnard, *The Functions of the Executive* (Cambridge, Mass.: Harvard University Press, 1968); P. Block, *The Empowered Manager:*

Positive Political Skills at Work (San Francisco: Jossey-Bass, 1987); S. R. Covey, *The Seven Habits of Highly Effective People* (New York: Simon & Schuster, 1989); B. Nanus, *Visionary Leadership: Creating a Compelling Sense of Direction for Your Organization* (San Francisco: Jossey-Bass, 1992); J. V. Quigley, *Vision: How Leaders Develop It, Share It, and Sustain It* (New York: McGraw-Hill, 1993); and T. J. Peters and N. Austin, *A Passion for Excellence: The Leadership Difference* (New York: Random House, 1985).

9. B. S. Moskal, "A Shadow Between Values and Reality," *Industry Week,* 16 May 1994, 24.

10. Korn/Ferry International and Columbia University Graduate School of Business, *Reinventing the CEO* (New York: Korn/Ferry International and Columbia University Graduate School of Business, 1989), 90.

11. *Wall Street Journal,* 22 Sept. 1994, A1.

12. E. Partridge, *Origins: A Short Etymological Dictionary of the English Language* (New York: Macmillan, 1966, 4th ed.), 778.

13. *2003 Annual Report* (San Diego: TRW Avionics & Surveillance Group [One Rancho Carmel, 92128], 1993).

14. Hamel and Prahalad, *Competing for the Future,* 4.

15. Partridge, *Origins,* 359, 742.

16. Reprinted by permission of the *Harvard Business Review.* Excerpts from "Planning on the Left Side and Managing on the Right" by Henry Mintzberg (July/Aug. 1976, p. 57). Copyright © 1976 by the President and Fellows of Harvard College; all rights reserved.

17. Mintzberg, "Planning on the Left Side," 53.

18. See, for example, R. Rowan, *The Intuitive Manager* (Boston: Little, Brown, 1986), 11.; W. H. Agor, *Intuition in Organizations* (Newbury Park, Calif.: Sage, 1989); S. Wally and J. R. Baum, "Personal and Structural Determinants of the Pace of Strategic Decision Making," *Academy of Management Journal* 37 (4) (1994): 932–956; H. Beh, "Don't Knock Intuition," *Asian Business* 29 (6) (1993): 65; T. C. Seebo II, "The Value of Experience and Intuition," *Financial Management* 22 (1) (1993): 27; E. Schmall, "Managing by Intuition as Well as Reason," *Network World* 10 (10) (1993): 41, 43; and R. G. Lord and K. J. Maher, *Leadership and Information Processing: Linking Perceptions and Performance* (Boston: Unwin-Hyman, 1991).

19. J. M. Kouzes, B. Z. Posner, and M. Krause, "Summary of the Executive Challenges Survey" (Executive Development Center, Leavey School of Business and Administration, Santa Clara University, 1986).

20. O. A. El Sawy, "Temporal Perspective and Managerial Attention: A Study of Chief Executive Strategic Behavior" (Ph.D. diss., Stanford University, 1983). See also O. A. El Sawy, "Temporal Biases in Strategic Attention" (research paper, Department of Decision Systems, School of Business Administration, University of Southern California, Nov. 1988).

21. El Sawy, "Temporal Perspective and Managerial Attention," 7:35.

22. El Sawy, "Temporal Perspective and Managerial Attention," 7:43. We should note that El Sawy's research doesn't rigorously ascertain whether looking into the past first or the future first yields a better estimate of the "true" future. He didn't follow executives over time to see which group was more accurate in its predictions. But his point that one way to improve upon our abilities to see farther into the future is to look into our past remains valid.

23. For a useful discussion of the role of assumptions in vision creation, see T. Sowell, *A Conflict of Visions* (New York: Morrow, 1987).

24. H. A. Shepard and J. A. Hawley, *Life Planning: Personal and Organizational* (Washington, D.C.: National Training and Development Service Press, 1974).

25. Professors G. Hamel and C. K. Prahalad offer a scale for rating your company's attention to the future in *Competing for the Future*, 2–3.

CHAPTER 6

1. The group participated in a workshop entitled "Leadership Is Everyone's Business™," offered through The Tom Peters Group/Learning Systems (Palo Alto, Calif.).
2. M. L. King, Jr., "I Have a Dream," in C. S. King (ed.), *The Words of Martin Luther King, Jr.* (New York: Newmarket Press, 1983), 95–98. Reprinted by permission of Joan Daves, copyright © 1963 by Martin Luther King, Jr.
3. H. Cleveland, *The Knowledge Executive: Leadership in an Information Society* (New York: Truman Talley Books/Dutton, 1985), 40. Copyright © 1985, reprinted by permission of E. P. Dutton, Inc.
4. Cleveland, *The Knowledge Executive*, 41–42.
5. Cleveland, *The Knowledge Executive*, 42.
6. Telephone interview by the authors with D. E. Berlew, 14 Nov. 1994.; see also D. E. Berlew, "Leadership and Organizational Excitement," *California Management Review 17* (2) (1974): 21–30.
7. C. Caggiano, "What Do Workers Want?" *Inc.*, Nov. 1992, 101–102.
8. Caggiano, "What Do Workers Want?"
9. S. Caudron, "Motivation?" *Industry Week*, 15 Nov. 1993, 33.
10. E. Galinsky, J. T. Bond, and D. E. Friedman, *The National Study of the Changing Workforce* (New York: Families and Work Institute, 1993), 14.
11. Work has been referred to by some as "the new neighborhood." See, for example, J. Autrey, *Love and Profit* (New York: Morrow, 1991). See also J. Conger, *Spirit at Work* (San Francisco: Jossey-Bass, 1994); and M. Fox, *Reinvention of Work: A New Vision of Livelihood for Our Time* (San Francisco: HarperSanFrancisco, 1994), 49.
12. M. S. Peck, *The Road Less Traveled* (New York: Simon & Schuster, 1978).
13. P. Senge, *The Fifth Discipline: The Art and Practice of the Learning Organization* (New York: Doubleday/Currency, 1990), 206.
14. H. Mintzberg, "The Rise and Fall of Strategic Planning," *Harvard Business Review*, Jan.-Feb. (1994): 107. For extensive treatment, see also H. Mintzberg, *The Rise and Fall of Strategic Planning* (New York: Free Press, 1994).
15. Mintzberg, "The Rise and Fall of Strategic Planning," 109.
16. J. M. Burns, *Leadership* (New York: HarperCollins, 1978), 20.
17. King, "I Have a Dream," 95–98.
18. R. P. Hart, *Verbal Style and the Presidency* (San Diego: Academic Press, 1984); for a related look at the relationship of charisma to the effectiveness of U.S. presidents, see R. J. House, W. D. Sprangler, and J. Woycke, "Personality and Charisma in the U.S. Presidency: A Psychological Theory of Leader Effectiveness," *Administrative Science Quarterly 36* (3) (1991): 364–395.
19. B. M. Bass, *Leadership and Performance Beyond Expectations* (New York: Free Press, 1985), 35.
20. H. S. Friedman, L. M. Prince, R. E. Riggio, and M. R. DiMatteo, "Understanding and Assessing Nonverbal Expressiveness: The Affective Communication Test," *Journal of Personality and Social Psychology 39* (2) (1980): 333–351.

21. M. Pines, "Children's Winning Ways," *Psychology Today 18* (12) (1984): 58–65.
22. B. Decker, *You've Got to Be Believed to Be Heard* (New York: St. Martin's Press, 1993), 155.

CHAPTER 7

1. See, for example, B. Gray, *Collaborating: Finding Common Ground for Multiparty Problems* (San Francisco: Jossey-Bass), 1989; R. S. Wellins, W. C. Byham, and J. M. Wilson, *Empowered Teams: Creating Self-Directed Work Groups That Improve Quality, Productivity, and Participation* (San Francisco: Jossey-Bass, 1991); W. E. Baker, *Networking Smart: How to Build Relationships for Personal and Organizational Success* (New York: McGraw-Hill, 1994); P. R. Scholtes, *The Team Handbook* (Madison, Wis.: Joiner Associates, 1988); S. Baxler and D. Lisburn, *Reengineering Information Technology: Success Through Empowerment* (Englewood Cliffs, N.J.: Prentice-Hall, 1994); V. D. Hunt, *Reengineering: Leveraging the Power of Integrated Product Development* (Essex Junction, Vt.: Wight, Oliver, 1993); J. Champy, *Reengineering Management* (New York: HarperBusiness, 1994); M. Hammer and J. Champy, *Reengineering the Corporation: A Manifesto for Business Revolution* (New York: HarperBusiness, 1993); J. N. Lowenthal, *Reengineering the Organization: A Step by Step Approach to Quality Revitalization* (Milwaukee, Wis.: ASQC Quality Press, 1994); B. Brocka and M. S. Brocka, *Quality Management: Implementing the Best Ideas of the Masters* (Homewood, Ill.: Business One Irwin, 1992); and U. D. Black, *Computer Networks* (Englewood Cliffs, N.J.: Prentice-Hall, 1993).
2. A. Kohn, *No Contest: The Case Against Competition* (Boston: Houghton Mifflin, 1986), 55. See also A. Kohn, *Punished by Rewards: The Trouble with Gold Stars, Incentive Plans, A's, Praise, and Other Bribes* (Boston: Houghton Mifflin, 1993).
3. Kohn, *No Contest,* 61.
4. D. Tjosvold, *Working Together to Get Things Done* (Lexington, Mass.: Heath, 1986), 25.
5. D. W. Tjosvold and M. M. Tjosvold, *Leading the Team Organization: How to Create an Enduring Competitive Advantage* (New York: Lexington Books, 1991), 34.
6. D. W. Johnson and R. T. Johnson, *Cooperation and Competition: Theory and Research* (Edina, Minn.: Interaction, 1989). See also D. W. Johnson and others, "Effects of Cooperative, Competitive, and Individualistic Goal Structures on Achievement: A Meta-Analysis," *Psychological Bulletin 89* (1981): 47–62.
7. Johnson and Johnson, *Cooperation and Competition,* 54. See also D. W. Johnson and R. T. Johnson, "The Socialization and Achievement Crises: Are Cooperative Learning Experiences the Solution?" in L. Bickman (ed.), *Applied Social Psychology Annual*, vol. 4 (Newbury Park, Calif.: Sage, 1983), 146.
8. For a review of recent research on cooperation in education, see M. Deutsch, "Educating for a Peaceful World," *American Psychologist 48* (5) (1993): 510–517. For other research results, see R. L. Helmreich, W. G. Beane, W. Lucker, and J. T. Spence, "Achievement Motivation and Scientific Attainment," *Personality and Social Psychology Bulletin 4* (1978): 222–226; R. L. Helmreich, L. L. Saurin, and A. L. Carsrud, "The Honeymoon Effect in Job Performance: Temporal Increases in the Productive Power of Achievement Motivation," *Journal of Applied Psychology 71* (1986): 185–188; R. L. Helmreich and others, "Making It in Academic Psychology: Demographic and Personality Correlates of Attainment," *Journal of Personality and Social Psychology 39* (1980): 896–908; R. L. Helmreich, "Pilot Selection and Training," paper presented at the annual meeting of the American Psychological Association,

Washington, D.C., Aug. 1982; and J. T. Spence and R. L. Helmreich, "Achievement-Related Motives and Behavior," in T. Spence (ed.), *Achievement and Achievement Motives: Psychological and Sociological Approaches* (New York: W. H. Freeman, 1983).

9. For an extensive discussion of true collaboration and its role in the creative process and technology, see M. Schrage, *Shared Minds: The New Technologies of Collaboration* (New York: Random House, 1990).

10. "Brian Coleman, Manager, Tool and Dies, Ford Motor Co., Dagenham, England," *On Achieving Excellence 8* (8) (1993): 2–3, p. 3 (newsletter from TPG/Communications, Palo Alto, Calif.).

11. R. Axelrod, *The Evolution of Cooperation* (New York: Basic Books, 1984). See also W. Poundstone, *Prisoner's Dilemma: John Von Neumann, Game Theory, and the Puzzle of the Bomb* (New York: Doubleday, 1992).

12. Axelrod, *The Evolution of Cooperation,* 20, 190.

13. R. B. Cialdini, *Influence: How and Why People Agree to Things* (New York: Morrow, 1984); P. Blau, "Cooperation and Competition in a Bureaucracy," *American Journal of Sociology 59* (1954): 530–535.

14. Axelrod, *The Evolution of Cooperation,* 126.

15. G. Homans, *The Human Group* (Orlando, Fla.: Harcourt Brace Jovanovich, 1950).

16. A. Van de Ven, A. L. Delbecq, and R. J. Koenig, "Determinants of Coordination Modes Within Organizations," *American Sociological Review 41* (2) (1976): 322–338.

17. T. Friedman, "Rabin and Arafat Seal Their Accord as Clinton Applauds 'Brave Gamble,'" *New York Times,* 14 Sept. 1993, A1, A13.

18. D. Kahneman and A. Tversky, "Prospect Theory: An Analysis of Decision Under Risk," *Econometrica 47* (1979): 263–291; A. Tversky and D. Kahneman, "The Framing of Decisions and the Psychology of Choice," *Science 211* (1981): 453–458; M. H. Bazerman and M. A. Neale, "Heuristics in Negotiation: Limitations to Dispute Resolution Effectiveness," in M. H. Bazerman and R. J. Lewicki (eds.), *Negotiating in Organizations* (Newbury Park, Calif.: Sage, 1983), 51–67; and M. A. Neale and M. H. Bazerman, "Systematic Deviations from Rationality in Negotiator Behavior: The Framing of Conflict and Negotiator Overconfidence," *Academy of Management Journal 28* (1) (1985): 34–49.

19. M. H. Bazerman, "Why Negotiations Go Wrong," *Psychology Today 20* (6) (1986): 54–58, p. 58; and M. H. Bazerman and M. A. Neale, *Negotiating Rationally* (New York: Free Press, 1993).

20. This exercise is drawn from "Broken Squares: Nonverbal Problem-Solving," in *A Handbook of Structured Experiences for Human Relations Training,* vol. 1 (San Diego: Pfeiffer, 1970), 25–30.

21. W. E. Watson, K. Kumar, and L. K. Michaelsen, "Cultural Diversity's Impact on Interaction Process and Performance: Comparing Homogeneous and Diverse Task Groups," *Academy of Management Journal 36* (3) (1993): 590–602.

22. Quoted in "In Practice," *Training and Development Journal,* Oct. 1993, 9.

23. R. M. Kanter, "The Change Masters," presentation to the Executive Seminar on Corporate Excellence, Santa Clara University, 26 Mar. 1984.

24. Bazerman and Neale, *Negotiating Rationally,* 94. See also R. Fisher and W. Ury, *Getting to Yes* (Boston: Houghton Mifflin, 1981).

25. Bazerman and Neale, *Negotiating Rationally,* 90–93.

26. R. M. Kanter, "Collaborative Advantage: The Art of Alliances," *Harvard Business Review,* July-Aug. (1994): 96–108, p. 108.

27. See, for example, D. E. Zand, "Trust and Managerial Problem Solving," *Administrative Science Quarterly 17* (2) (1972): 229–239; W. R. Boss, "Trust and Managerial Problem Solving Revisited," *Group and Organization Studies 3* (3) (1978): 331–342; "Trust Traps," *Training & Development Journal 48* (7) (1994): 11–12; and V. Brunard and B. H. Kleiner, "Developing Trustful and Cooperative Relationships," *Leadership & Organizational Development Journal 15* (2) (1994): 3–5.

28. Boss, "Trust and Managerial Problem Solving Revisited," 338.

29. Boss, "Trust and Managerial Problem Solving Revisited," 338.

30. Boss, "Trust and Managerial Problem Solving Revisited," 341.

31. C. A. O'Reilly and K. H. Roberts, "Information Filtration in Organizations: Three Experiments," *Organizational Behavior and Human Performance 11* (1974): 253–265.

32. Boss, "Trust and Managerial Problem Solving Revisited."

33. J. W. Driscoll, "Trust and Participation in Organizational Decision Making as Predictors of Satisfaction," *Academy of Management Journal 21* (1) (1978): 44–56.

34. See M. B. Gurtman, "Trust, Distrust, and Interpersonal Problems: A Circumplex Analysis," *Journal of Personality and Social Psychology 62* (1992): 989–1002. See also G. D. Grace and T. Schill, "Social Support and Coping Style Differences in Subjects High and Low in Interpersonal Trust," *Psychological Reports 59* (1986): 584–586.

35. J. B. Rotter, "Trust and Gullibility," *Psychology Today 14* (5) (1980): 35–38; Boss, "Trust and Managerial Problem Solving Revisited."

36. R. Likert and J. M. Willits, *Morale and Agency Management* (Hartford, Conn.: Life Insurance Agency Management Association, 1940).

37. D. Strutton, A. Toma, and L. E. Pelton, "Relationship Between Psychological Climate and Trust Between Salespersons and Their Managers in Sales Organizations," *Psychological Reports 72* (1993): 931–939.

38. D. G. Carnevale and B. Wechsler, "Trust in the Public Sector: Individual and Organizational Determinants," *Administration and Society 23* (4) (1992): 471–494, pp. 488–489.

39. M. Deutsch, "Cooperation and Trust: Some Theoretical Notes," in R. Jones (ed.), *Nebraska Symposium on Motivation* (Lincoln: University of Nebraska Press, 1962), 275–319; Zand, "Trust and Managerial Problem Solving."

40. "Leo Bontempo, President, Ciba-Geigy's U.S. Agricultural Group, Ardsley, New York," *On Achieving Excellence 8* (8) (1993): 7 (newsletter from TPG/Communications, Palo Alto, Calif.).

41. Zand, "Trust and Managerial Problem Solving"; J. W. Driscoll, "Trust and Participation in Organizational Decision Making as Predictors of Satisfaction," *Academy of Management Journal 21* (1) (1978): 44–56.

42. A. Wolfe, "Can't Take the Farm out of the Boy," *Ingram's*, Aug. 1993, 31; and personal conversation, 13 July 1994.

43. This activity is found in *Positive Negotiation Skills Workshop* (Plymouth, Mass.: Situation Management Systems, 1980).

44. E. E. Lawler III, *High-Involvement Management: Participative Strategies for Improving Organizational Performance* (San Francisco: Jossey-Bass, 1986). See also E. E. Lawler III, *The Ultimate Advantage: Creating the High-Involvement Organization* (San Francisco: Jossey-Bass, 1992).

CHAPTER 8

1. See R. M. Kanter, *The Change Masters: Innovation for Productivity in the American Corporation* (New York: Simon & Schuster, 1983). For more recent studies by Kanter on power see R. M. Kanter, *When Giants Learn to Dance: Mastering the Challenges of Strategy, Management, and Careers in the 1990s* (New York: Simon & Schuster, 1989); and R. M. Kanter, B. A. Stein, and T. D. Jick, *The Challenge of Organizational Change: How Companies Experience It and Leaders Guide It* (New York: Free Press, 1992).

2. J. Pfeffer, *Competitive Advantage Through People: Unleashing the Power of the Work Force* (Boston: Harvard Business School Press, 1994), 104.

3. D. Kipnis, S. Schmidt, K. Price, and C. Stitt, "Why Do I Like Thee: Is It Your Performance or My Orders?" *Journal of Applied Psychology* 66 (3) (1981): 324–328.

4. As discussed in a telephone interview by the authors with D. E. Berlew, former president of McBer and Company, on 14 Nov. 1994, this exercise is adapted from a training program on power developed by McBer.

5. For a summary of the research on self-efficacy—the belief in one's ability to get things done—see A. Bandura, "Conclusion: Reflections on Nonability Determinants of Competence," in R. Sternberg and J. Kolligian, Jr. (eds.), *Competence Considered* (New Haven, Conn.: Yale University Press, 1990), 315–362. See also A. Bandura, *Social Foundations of Thought and Action: A Social Cognitive Theory* (Englewood Cliffs, N.J.: Prentice-Hall, 1986).

6. See, for example, J. Conger, "Leadership: The Art of Empowering Others," *The Academy of Management Executive* 3 (1) (1989): 17–24; T. L. Tang and D. B. Reynolds, "Effects of Self-Esteem and Perceived Goal Difficulty on Goal Setting, Certainty, Task Performance, and Attributions," *Human Resource Development Quarterly* 4 (2) (1992): 153–170; and K. A. Karl, A. M. Leary-Kelly, and J. J. Martocchio, "The Impact of Feedback and Self-Efficacy on Performance in Training," *Journal of Organizational Behavior* 14 (4) (1993): 379–394.

7. The classic assessment of sources of power can be found in J.R.P. French, Jr., and B. H. Raven, "The Bases of Social Power," in D. Cartwright and A. Zander (eds.), *Group Dynamics: Research and Theory*, 2nd ed. (New York: HarperCollins, 1960), 607–623.

8. For an extensive discussion of the positive and negative faces of power, see D. C. McClelland, *Power: The Inner Experience* (New York: Irvington, 1975); D. G. Winter, *The Power Motive* (New York: Free Press, 1973).

9. In the first edition of this book, we used a similar framework based upon work by Rosabeth Moss Kanter, which we've subsequently revised. For a more extensive treatment by Kanter of this topic see, *The Change Masters*, 156–179. Another important resource is J. Pfeffer, *Managing with Power: Politics and Influence in Organizations* (Boston: Harvard Business School Press, 1992); see also Pfeffer's earlier works: J. Pfeffer, *Power in Organizations* (Marshfield, Mass.: Pitman, 1981); and J. Pfeffer and G. Salancik, *The External Control of Organizations: A Resource Dependence Perspective* (New York: HarperCollins, 1978).

10. See, for example, A. Tannenbaum, *Control in Organizations* (New York: McGraw-Hill, 1968); A. Tannenbaum and others, *Hierarchy in Organizations: An International Comparison* (San Francisco: Jossey-Bass, 1974); and A. Tannenbaum and R. A. Cooke, "Organizational Control: A Review of Studies Employing the Control Graph Method," in D. J. Hickson and C. J. Lammers (eds.), *Organizations Alike and Unlike* (London: Routledge & Kegan Paul, 1979).

11. D. A. Butterfield and B. Z. Posner, "Task-Relevant Control in Organizations," *Personnel Psychology* 32 (1979): 725–740.

12. Indeed, highly controlling people are less trusted than highly enabling ones; as a consequence, the capacity of highly controlling people to get extraordinary things done is greatly diminished. It's ironic that those who control the most are also most at risk of losing their ability to lead when leadership may be most needed: during volatile and dynamic times of change. See D. Tjosvold, I. R. Andrews, and J. T. Struthers, "Power and Interdependence in Work Groups: Views of Managers and Employees," *Group and Organizational Studies 16* (3) (1991): 285–299.

13. D. L. Bradford and A. R. Cohen, *Managing for Excellence* (New York: Wiley), 1984.

14. M. W. McCall, Jr., and M. M. Lombardo, *Off the Track: Why and How Successful Executives Get Derailed,* Technical Report no. 21 (Greensboro, N.C.: Center for Creative Leadership, 1983).

15. See, for example, R. A. Hagberg, Jr., I. Conti, and R. J. Mirabile, *Profile of the Terminated Executive* (Menlo Park, Calif.: Ward, Hagberg, 1985); and J. Ramos, "Why Executives Derail," *Across the Board 31* (10) (1994): 16–20.

16. See, for example, Pfeffer, *Managing with Power.*

17. E. J. Langer and J. Rodin, "The Effects of Choice and Enhanced Personal Responsibility for the Aged: A Field Experiment in an Institutional Setting," *Journal of Personality and Social Psychology 34* (2) (1976): 191–198; and J. Rodin and E. J. Langer, "Long-Term Efforts of a Control-Relevant Intervention with the Institutionalized Aged," *Journal of Personality and Social Psychology 35* (12) (1977): 897–902. For more examples of how personal control influences personal well-being, see E. J. Langer, *Mindfulness* (Reading, Mass.: Addison-Wesley, 1989).

18. L. A. Schlesinger and J. Zornitsky, "Job Satisfaction, Service Capability, and Customer Satisfaction: An Examination of Their Linkages and Management Implications," *Human Resource Planning* (Spring 1991). See also L. A. Schlesinger and K. L. Heskett, "Enfranchisement of Service Workers," *California Management Review* (Summer 1991): 83–100; J. L. Heskett and others, "Putting the Service-Profit Chain to Work," *Harvard Business Review,* Mar.-Apr. (1994): 164–174.

19. R. Karasek and T. Theorell, *Healthy Work: Stress, Productivity, and the Reconstruction of Working Life* (New York: Basic Books, 1990), 9.

20. L. A. Mainiero, "Coping with Powerlessness: The Relationship of Gender and Job Dependency to Empowerment-Strategy Usage," *Administrative Science Quarterly 31* (4) (1986): 633–653.

21. Mainiero, "Coping with Powerlessness," 648.

22. See R. M. Kanter, "Power Failures in Management Circuits," *Harvard Business Review,* July-Aug. (1979): 67.

23. See, for example, W. Bridges, *JobShift* (Reading, Mass.: Addison-Wesley, 1994). See also "Special Report: Rethinking Work," *Business Week,* 17 Oct. 1994, 74–117.

24. J. Stack, "The Great Game of Business," presentation for the Consortium on Executive Education, Santa Clara University, 11 Nov. 1994.

25. For a detailed account of this story, see J. Stack, *The Great Game of Business: The Only Sensible Way to Run a Company* (New York: Doubleday/Currency, 1992).

26. Stack, *The Great Game of Business,* 3.

27. Stack, "The Great Game of Business," presentation.

28. See, for example, Pfeffer, *Managing with Power.*

29. Reprinted by permission of the *Harvard Business Review.* Excerpts from "Wide-Open Management" by Alan M. Kantrow (May/June 1986, p. 99). Copyright © 1986 by the President and Fellows of Harvard College; all rights reserved.

30. This view is consistent with frameworks generated by scholars working from different perspectives. See, for example, Kanter, *The Change Masters,* and Pfeffer, *Managing with Power.*
31. G. Yukl, *Leadership in Organizations,* 3rd ed. (Englewood Cliffs, N.J.: Prentice-Hall, 1994).
32. M. DePree, "Theory Fastball," *New Management 1* (4) (1983): 29–36; see also M. DePree, *Leadership Is an Art* (New York: Doubleday, 1989), 27–44.
33. See A. Deutschman, "The Managing Wisdom of High-Tech Superstars," *Fortune,* 17 Oct. 1994, 197.
34. E. T. Suters, "Show and Tell," *Inc.,* 1987, 111–112.
35. T. J. Peters, *The Tom Peters Seminar: Crazy Times Call for Crazy Organizations* (New York: Vintage Books, 1994), 109.

CHAPTER 9

1. J. M. Kouzes and B. Z. Posner, *Credibility: How Leaders Gain and Lose It, Why People Demand It* (San Francisco: Jossey-Bass, 1993).
2. M. Rokeach, *The Nature of Human Values* (New York: Free Press, 1973), 5.
3. W. H. Schmidt and B. Z. Posner, *Managerial Values and Expectations: The Silent Power in Personal and Organizational Life* (New York: American Management Association, 1982).
4. See, for example, B. Z. Posner and R. I. Westwood, "A Cross-Cultural Investigation of the Shared Values Relationship," *International Journal of Value-Based Management 8* (2) (1995): 1–10; B. Z. Posner and W. H. Schmidt, "Values Congruence and Differences Between the Interplay of Personal and Organizational Value Systems," *Journal of Business Ethics 12* (1993): 171–177; and B. Z. Posner, J. M. Kouzes, and W. H. Schmidt, "Shared Values Make a Difference: An Empirical Test of Corporate Culture," *Human Resource Management 24* (3) (1985): 293–310. For a related study, see also J. W. Haas, B. D. Sypher, and H. E. Sypher, "Do Shared Goals Really Make a Difference?" *Management Communication Quarterly 6* (2) (1992): 166–179.
5. B. Z. Posner and R. I. Westwood, "An International Perspective on Shared Values," paper presented at the Western Academy of Management International Conference, Brisbane, Australia, July 1994.
6. See, for example, J. Chapman, "Collegial Support Linked to Reduction of Job Stress," *Nursing Management 24* (5) (1993): 52–56; S. M. Jex and D. M. Gudanowski, "Efficacy Beliefs and Work Stress," *Journal of Organizational Behavior 13* (5) (1992): 509–517; M. T. Matteson, "Individual-Organizational Relationship: Implications for Preventing Job Stress and Burnout," in J. C. Quick, R. S. Bhagat, J. E. Dalton, and J. D. Quick (eds.), *Work Stress: Health Care Systems in the Workplace* (New York: Praeger, 1987), 156–170; M. T. Matteson and J. M. Ivancevich, *Controlling Work Stress: Effective Human Resource and Management Strategies* (San Francisco: Jossey-Bass, 1987); W. B. Schaufeli, C. Maslach, and T. Marek (eds.), *Professional Burnout* (Washington, D.C.: Taylor & Francis, 1993); and J. E. Newman and T. A. Beehr, "Personal and Organizational Strategies for Handling Job Stress: A Review of Research and Opinion," *Personnel Psychology 32* (1979): 1–43.
7. K. A. Gold, *A Comparative Analysis of Successful Organizations* (Washington, D.C.: Workforce Effectiveness and Development Group, U.S. Office of Personnel Management, 1981).
8. B. Laurence, "A Case Study in Crisis Management: The Perrier Recall," *Industrial Management and Data Systems 91* (7) (1991): 6–8; and S. Toy and L. Driscoll, "Can Perrier Purify Its Reputation?" *Business Week,* 26 Feb. 1990, 45.

9. T. E. Deal and A. A. Kennedy, *Corporate Cultures* (Reading, Mass.: Addison-Wesley, 1982).

10. J. P. Kotter and J. L. Heskett, *Corporate Culture and Performance* (New York: Free Press, 1992).

11. Described in D. F. Caldwell, "The Face of Corporate Culture," *Santa Clara Today*, Nov. 1984, 12.

12. J. Collins and J. Porras, *Built to Last: Successful Habits of Visionary Companies* (New York: HarperBusiness, 1994), 103.

13. C. O'Reilly and D. F. Caldwell, "The Power of Strong Corporate Cultures in Silicon Valley Firms," presentation to the Executive Seminar in Corporate Excellence, Santa Clara University, 13 Feb. 1985; see also C. O'Reilly, "Corporations, Culture, and Commitment: Motivation and Social Control in Organizations," *California Management Review* 23 (1989): 9–17.

14. R. A. Stevenson, "Clarifying Behavioral Expectations Associated with Espoused Organizational Values" (Ph.D. diss., Fielding Institute, 1995), 54–57.

15. B. Z. Posner and W. H. Schmidt, "Values Congruence and Differences Between the Interplay of Personal and Organizational Value Systems," *Journal of Business Ethics* 12 (1993): 171–177.

16. "Lead by Example: Use High Personal Standards, Not Words, to Motivate Performance," *On Achieving Excellence* 8 (8) (1993): 2 (newsletter from TPG/Communications, Palo Alto, Calif.).

17. C. Argyris, *Knowledge for Action: A Guide to Overcoming Barriers to Organizational Change* (San Francisco: Jossey-Bass, 1993). See also C. Argyris, "Double Loop Learning in Organizations," *Harvard Business Review* 55 (5) (1977): 115–125.

18. D. K. McNeese-Smith, "The Impact of Leadership Behaviors Upon Job Satisfaction, Productivity, and Organizational Commitment of Followers" (Ph.D. diss., Seattle University, 1991).

19. "Continuous Journey," *Quality*, Association of Productivity and Quality Control, Aug./Sept. 1993, 78–92.

20. For an inspiring series of examples of the art of leadership, see M. DePree, *Leadership Is an Art* (New York: Doubleday, 1989); and M. DePree, *Leadership Jazz* (New York: Doubleday, 1992).

21. For a discussion of enactment as an organizing principle, see K. E. Weick, *The Social Psychology of Organizing*, 2nd ed. (Reading, Mass.: Addison-Wesley, 1979).

22. For a discussion of the adaptive role of leaders, see R. A. Heifetz, *Leadership Without Easy Answers* (Cambridge, Mass.: Belknap Press, 1994).

23. T. J. Peters, "Symbols, Patterns, and Settings: An Optimistic Case for Getting Things Done," *Organizational Dynamics* 7 (2) (1978): 2–23; T. J. Peters, "Management Systems: The Language of Organizational Character and Competence," *Organizational Dynamics* 8 (1) (1980): 2–26.

24. This discussion draws upon Peters, "Management Systems"; and E. H. Schein, *Organizational Culture and Leadership*, 2nd ed. (San Francisco: Jossey-Bass, 1992), 228–253.

25. E. Aronson, *The Social Animal*, 3rd ed. (New York: W. H. Freeman, 1980), 79–82.

26. B. Whitworth, "Proof at Last," *Communication World*, Dec. 1990, 28–31; and "Varian Employees Speak Out," *Varian Magazine* 38 (1) (1993), 4. For an extensive discussion of this principle, see T. J. Larkin and S. Larkin, *Communicating Change: Winning Employee Support for New Business Goals* (New York: McGraw-Hill, 1994).

27. H. N. Schwarzkopf with P. Pietre, *It Doesn't Take a Hero* (New York: Bantam Books, 1992), 240–241.

28. While many collections of stories line the bookshelves, in 1993 and 1994 *The Book of Virtues* climbed to the best-seller list and remained there for weeks, giving testimony to a renewed search in America for moral lessons. W. J. Bennett, *The Book of Virtues: A Treasury of Great Moral Stories* (New York: Simon & Schuster, 1993). For excellent advice on how to use stories in organizations, see P. C. Neuhauser, *Corporate Legends and Lore: The Power of Storytelling as a Management Tool* (New York: McGraw-Hill, 1993).

29. B. Sanders, "There's No Secret to Serving the Customer," presentation to the Executive Seminar in Corporate Excellence, Santa Clara University, 28 Oct. 1986; see also her recent book, *Fabled Service* (San Diego: Pfeiffer, 1995).

30. See, for example, A. L. Wilkens, "The Creation of Company Culture: The Role of Stories and Human Resource Systems," *Human Resource Management* 23 (1) (1984): 41–60; Y. Gabriel "Turning Facts into Stories and Stories into Facts," *Human Relations* 44 (1991): 857–875; and M. L. McConkie and R. W. Boss, "Using Stories as an Aid to Consultation," *Public Administration Quarterly* 17 (4) (1994): 377–395.

31. J. Martin and M. Powers, "Organizational Stories: More Vivid and Persuasive Than Quantitative Data," in B. M. Staw (ed.), *Psychological Foundations of Organizational Behavior,* 2nd ed. (Glenview, Ill.: Scott, Foresman, 1983), 161–168.

32. A. L. Wilkens, "Organizational Stories as Symbols Which Control the Organization," in L. R. Pondy, P. J. Frost, G. Morgan, and T. C Dandridge (eds.), *Organizational Symbolism* (Greenwich, Conn.: JAI Press, 1983), 81–92. See also D. Armstrong, *Managing by Storying Around: A New Method of Leadership* (New York: Doubleday/Currency, 1992).

33. For more on the framing of issues, see Heifetz, *Leadership Without Easy Answers,* 115–116.

34. S. Zuboff, *In the Age of the Smart Machine: The Future of Work and Power* (New York: Basic Books, 1988), 394.

35. S. Benner, "Culture Shock," *Inc.,* Aug. 1985, 73–82, p. 80.

36. "Brian Coleman, Manager, Tool and Dies, Ford Motor Co., Dagenham, England," *On Achieving Excellence 8* (8) (1993): 3 (newsletter from TPG/Communications, Palo Alto, Calif.).

37. A. Bandura and D. Cervone, "Self-Evaluation and Self-Efficacy Mechanisms Governing Motivation Effects of Goal Systems," *Journal of Personality and Social Psychology* 45 (1983): 1017–1028.

38. P. LaBarre, "The Dis-Organization of Oticon," *Industry Week,* 19 July 1994, 23–28.

39. LaBarre, "The Dis-Organization of Oticon," 28.

40. For a discussion of research concerning the importance of physical settings, see S. Ornstein, "Organizational Symbols: A Study of Their Meanings and Influences on Perceived Psychological Climate," *Organizational Behavior and Human Decision Processes* 38 (2) (1986): 207–229; and F. Steele and S. Jenks, *The Feel of the Work Place* (Reading, Mass.: Addison-Wesley, 1977).

41. S. Brand, *How Buildings Learn: What Happens After They're Built* (New York: Viking, 1994), 174.

42. W. Bennis, *On Becoming a Leader* (Reading, Mass.: Addison-Wesley, 1989), 40.

43. S. Sherman, "Leaders Learn to Heed the Voice Within," *Fortune,* 22 Aug. 1994, 93.

44. T. J. Peters, "Changing Habits Is the First Step to Changing Priorities," *San Jose Mercury News,* 5 Feb. 1987, 8C.

45. "Trading Places: A Tool for Credibility," *On Achieving Excellence, 8* (8) (1993): 8.

46. "Ten Tips for Building Your Storytelling Skills," *On Achieving Excellence,"* Nov. 1990, 9.

CHAPTER 10

1. Much of the discussion of the "small-win" process draws upon the theoretical basis originally set out in K. E. Weick, "Small Wins: Redefining the Scale of Social Problems," *American Psychologist 39* (1) (1984): 40–49. For a related treatment of this topic, see R. H. Schaffer, *The Breakthrough Strategy: Using Short-Term Successes to Build the High-Performance Organization* (New York: Ballinger, 1989).
2. Similar assertions have been made by others. See, for example, F. Machlup, *The Production and Distribution of Knowledge in the United States* (Princeton, N.J.: Princeton University Press, 1962). See also B. Bunch, *The Henry Holt Handbook of Current Science and Technology: A Source of Facts and Analysis Covering the Most Important Events in Science and Technology* (New York: Holt, 1992).
3. H. Mintzberg, *The Rise and Fall of Strategic Planning* (New York: Free Press, 1994), 110.
4. Mintzberg, *The Rise and Fall of Strategic Planning*, 134.
5. The reference to paradigm shifts as the source of scientific revolutions was first discussed by Thomas Kuhn. See T. S. Kuhn, *The Structure of Scientific Revolutions*, 2nd ed. (Chicago: University of Chicago Press, 1970). See also J. Barker, *Paradigms: The Business of Discovering the Future* (New York: HarperBusiness, 1993).
6. S. Hollander, *The Success of Increased Efficiency: A Study of Du Pont Rayon Plants* (Cambridge, Mass.: MIT Press, 1965).
7. Weick, "Small Wins," 43.
8. H. Mintzberg, *The Nature of Managerial Work* (New York: HarperCollins, 1973).
9. For more information, see W. A. Randolph and B. Z. Posner, *Getting the Job Done: Managing Teams and Task Forces with Success* (Englewood Cliffs, N.J.: Prentice-Hall, 1992).
10. *The Leading Edge*, video (Santa Cruz, Calif.: Langsford Communications, 1986).
11. R. H. Schaffer, *The Breakthrough Strategy: Using Short-Term Successes to Build the High-Performance Organization* (New York: Ballinger, 1989), 52–60.
12. "Melissa Poe," *Caring People* (6) (1993), 66, supplemented by an interview with Trish Poe on 3 Nov. 1994.
13. M. H. Bazerman and M. A. Neale, *Negotiating Rationally* (New York: Free Press, 1992).
14. As discussed in T. J. Peters and R. H. Waterman, *In Search of Excellence* (New York: HarperCollins, 1982), 203.
15. S. R. Duncan, "A Key to Selection: Providing Realistic Job Previews," *Managers Magazine 67* (12) (1992): 6–7; M. W. Mercer, "Turnover: Reducing the Costs," *Personnel 65* (12) (1988): 36–42; B. M. Meglino and A. S. DeNisi, "Realistic Job Previews: Some Thoughts on Their More Effective Use in Managing the Flow of Human Resources," *Human Resource Planning 10* (3) (1987): 157–167; and M. K. Suszko and J. A. Breaugh, "The Effects of Realistic Job Previews on Applicant Self-Selection and Employee Turnover, Satisfaction, and Coping Ability," *Journal of Management 12* (4) (1986): 513–523.
16. R. Pascale, "Fitting New Employees into the Company Culture," *Fortune*, 28 May 1984: 28–40, p. 30.
17. R. Kaku, speech to the Second Global Conference on Management Innovation, London, England, 2–4 Dec. 1991.
18. Quoted in H. V. Roberts and B. F. Sergesketter, *Quality Is Personal: A Foundation for Total Quality Management* (New York: Free Press, 1993), xiii.

CHAPTER 11

1. T. E. Deal and W. A. Jenkins, *Managing the Hidden Organization: Strategies for Empowering Your Behind-the-Scenes Employees* (New York: Warner Books, 1994).
2. Survey by Robert Half International, Inc. (Menlo Park, Calif.), 31 Aug. 1994.
3. See, for example, E. C. Jones, "Interpreting Interpersonal Behavior: The Effects of Expectancies," *Science 234* (1986): 41–46; R.H.G. Field and D. A. Van Seters, "Management by Expectations (MBE): The Power of Positive Prophecy," *Journal of General Management 14* (2) (1988): 1–33; D. Eden, *Pygmalion in Management: Productivity as a Self-Fulfilling Prophecy* (New York: Lexington Books, 1990); and D. Eden, "Leadership and Expectations: Pygmalion Effects and Other Self-Fulfilling Prophecies in Organizations," *The Leadership Quarterly 3* (4) (1992): 271–305.
4. D. Eden and J. Kinnar, "Modeling Galatea: Boosting Self-Efficacy to Increase Volunteering," *Journal of Applied Psychology 76* (6) (1991): 770–780.
5. D. Eden, "Pygmalion Without Interpersonal Contrast Effects: Whole Groups Gain From Raising Manager Expectations," *Journal of Applied Psychology 75* (4) (1990): 394–398.
6. D. Eden, "Pygmalion, Goal Setting, and Expectancy: Compatible Ways to Boost Productivity," *Academy of Management Executive 13* (4) (1988): 639–652.
7. N. Branden, *The Six Pillars of Self-Esteem* (New York: Bantam Books, 1994).
8. R. J. Blitzer, C. Petersen, and L. Rogers, "How to Build Self-Esteem," *Training and Development Journal*, Feb. 1993, 59.
9. R. Wood and A. Bandura, "Impact of Conceptions of Ability on Self-Regulatory Mechanisms and Complex Decision Making," *Journal of Personality and Social Psychology 56* (3) (1989): 407–415.
10. A. R. Cohen, S. L. Fink, H. Gadon, and R. D. Willits, *Effective Behavior in Organizations*, 6th ed. (Homewood, Ill.: Irwin, 1994).
11. Cohen, Fink, Gadon, and Willits, *Effective Behavior in Organizations*.
12. J. L. McAdams and E. J. Hawk, *Executive Summary: Organizational Performance & Rewards* (Scottsdale, Ariz.: American Compensation Association, 1993), 35; see also C. Braddick, M. Pfefferle, and R. Gandossy, "How Malcolm Baldrige Winners Reward Employee Performance," *Journal of Compensation and Benefits 9* (3) (1993): 47–52.
13. S. Tully, "Your Paycheck Gets Exciting," *Fortune*, 1 Nov. 1993, 98.
14. R. Winslow, "U.S. Healthcare Cuts Costs, Grows Rapidly, and Irks Some Doctors," *Wall Street Journal*, 6 Sept. 1994, A1.
15. C. C. Pinder, *Work Motivation: Theory, Issues, and Applications* (Glenview, Ill.: Scott, Foresman, 1984), 286–298; see also V. H. Vroom, *Work and Motivation* (San Francisco: Jossey-Bass, 1994).
16. Pinder, *Work Motivation*, 226.
17. K. Huber, "A Growing Desire to Learn," *Houston Chronicle*, 14 July 1994, C1; and discussion with Nolan Dishongh, Aug. 1994.
18. McAdams and Hawk, *Executive Summary*, 12.
19. J. L. Hall, B. Z. Posner, and J. W. Harder, "Performance Appraisal Systems: Matching Theory with Practice," *Group and Management Studies 14* (1) (1989): 51–69.
20. G. Graham, "Going the Extra Mile: Motivating Your Workers Doesn't Always Involve Money," *San Jose Mercury News*, 7 Jan. 1987, 4C.
21. R. M. Kanter, "The Change Masters," presentation to the Executive Seminar in Corporate Excellence, Santa Clara University, 13 Mar. 1984.

22. M. VerMeulen, "When Employees Give Something Extra," *Parade,* 6 Nov. 1983, 11.

23. R. J. Dow, "Keeping Employees Focused on Customer Service," presentation to the Executive Seminar in Corporate Excellence, Santa Clara University, 28 Oct. 1986.

24. E. L. Deci, *Intrinsic Motivation* (New York: Plenum, 1975); E. L. Deci and R. M. Ryan, *Intrinsic Motivation and Self-Determinism in Human Behavior* (New York: Plenum, 1985). For an intelligent critique of incentive systems and the potentially detrimental effect of reliance on rewards on long-term performance, see A. Kohn, *Punished by Rewards* (Boston: Houghton Mifflin, 1993).

25. D. C. McClelland, *The Achieving Society* (New York: Van Nostrand Reinhold, 1961).

26. S. Squires, "Clinging to Hope," *San Jose Mercury News,* 25 Feb. 1984, 12C. See also S. Breznitz, "The Effect of Hope on Coping with Stress," in M. H. Appley and R. Trumbell (eds.), *Dynamics of Stress: Physiological, Psychological, and Social Perspectives* (New York: Plenum, 1986), 295–306; M.E.P. Seligman, *Learned Optimism* (New York: Knopf, 1990); and C. Peterson and L. M. Bossio, *Health and Optimism: New Research on the Relationship Between Positive Thinking and Physical Well-Being* (New York: Free Press, 1991).

27. For more ideas, see B. Nelson, *1001 Ways to Reward Employees* (New York: Workman, 1994); and B. Basso and J. Klosek, *This Job Should be Fun!* (Holbrook, Mass.: Bob Adams, Inc., 1991).

28. A. E. Schnur and C. Butz, "The Best Finish First: Top Coaches Talk About Winning," Towers Perrin (San Francisco), 1994.

29. A. Bandura and D. Cevone, "Self-Evaluative and Self-Efficacy Mechanisms Governing the Motivational Effects of Goal Systems," *Journal of Personality and Social Psychology* 45 (1983): 1017–1028.

30. Field and Van Seters, "Management by Expectations (MBE)."

31. S. Shepard, "Quality Buy: St. Francis Avoids Reinventing Wheel," *Memphis Business Journal* 15 (14) (1993): 3; and phone conversation on 12 Sept. 1994 with the vice president of quality management, St. Francis Hospital.

CHAPTER 12

1. M. O. Jones and others, "Performing Well: The Impact of Rituals, Celebrations, and Networks of Support," paper presented at the Western Academy of Management conference, Hollywood, Calif., 10 Apr. 1987.

2. D. P. Campbell, *If I'm in Charge Here, Why Is Everybody Laughing?* (Greensboro, N.C.: Center for Creative Leadership, 1980), 62–64.

3. See, for example, W. Kiechel III, "Celebrating a Corporate Triumph," *Fortune,* 20 Aug. 1984, 262; T. Gable, "Going Beyond Ordinary Anniversary Celebrations," *Public Relations Journal* 47 (12) (1991): 25–27; and R. Nelson, "Let the Good Times Roll," *Incentive 168* (6) (1994): 51–54.

4. T. F. Deal and A. K. Kennedy, *Corporate Cultures* (Reading, Mass.: Addison-Wesley, 1982), 63.

5. C. DeForest, "The Art of Conscious Celebration: A New Concept for Today's Leaders," in J. D. Adams (ed.), *Transforming Leadership: From Vision to Results* (Alexandria, Va.: Miles River Press, 1986).

6. This scene is from *In Search of Excellence: The Film* (Waltham, Mass.: Nathan/Tyler Productions, 1985), distributed by Video Arts. For more on Tom Melohn and his leadership adventures with NATD, see his book, *The New Partnership: Profit by Bringing Out the Best in*

Your People, Customers, and Yourself (Essex Junction, Vt.: Oliver Wright Publications, 1994).

7. T. E. Deal and W. A. Jenkins, *Managing the Hidden Organization: Strategies for Empowering Your Behind-the-Scenes Employees* (New York: Warner Books, 1994), 204.

8. B. Greene, "Why Working for Some Bosses Is a Thankless Job," *San Jose Mercury News*, 27 Jan. 1986, 14B.

9. See, for example, S. L. Kirmeyer and T. Lin, "Social Support: Its Relationship to Observed Communication with Peers and Superiors," *Academy of Management Journal 30* (1) (1987): 138–151; K. J. Fenlason and T. A. Beehr, "Social Support and Occupational Stress: Effects of Talking to Others," *Journal of Organizational Behavior 15* (2) (1994): 157–175; G. F. Koeske and R. D. Koeske, "Underestimation of Social Support Buffering," *Journal of Applied Behavioral Science 27* (4) (1991): 475–489; D. L. Nelson and J. C. Quick, "Social Support and Newcomer Adjustment in Organizations," *Journal of Organizational Behavior 12* (6) (1991): 543–554; and J. S. Mulbert, "Social Networks, Social Circles, and Job Satisfaction," *Work and Occupations 18* (4) (1991): 415–430.

10. L. L. Berry, A. Parasuraman, and V. A. Zeithaml, "Improving Service Quality in America: Lessons Learned," *Academy of Management Executive 8* (2) (1994): 32–45, p. 41.

11. California Department of Mental Health, *Friends Can Be Good Medicine* (San Francisco: Pacificon Productions, 1981).

12. L. F. Berkman and S. L. Syme, "Social Networks, Host Resistance, and Mortality: A Nine-Year Follow-Up Study of Alameda County Residents," *American Journal of Epidemiology 109* (2) (1979): 186–204.

13. P. Tommerup, "Inspiring Self-Management: On Symbols, Synergism, and Excellence," paper presented at the Western Academy of Management conference, Hollywood, Calif., 10 Apr. 1987.

14. C. Wallis and others, "Stress: Can We Cope?" *Time*, 6 June 1983, 50.

15. See, for example, Kirmeyer and Lin, "Social Support"; Fenlason and Beehr, "Social Support and Occupational Stress"; S. Cohen and T. A. Wills, "Stress, Social Support, and the Buffering Hypothesis," *Psychological Bulletin 98* (1985): 310–357; and I. P. Erera, "Social Support Under Conditions of Organizational Ambiguity," *Human Relations 45* (3) (1992): 247–264.

16. T. J. Peters and N. Austin, *A Passion for Excellence: The Leadership Difference* (New York: Random House, 1985), 290.

17. *20/20*, ABC television, Mar. 1991.

18. DeForest, "The Art of Conscious Celebration," 223.

19. J. Towler, "Laughter Is Profitable," *Canadian Banker 97* (3) (1990): 32–33.

20. This exercise is adapted from California Department of Mental Health, *Friends Can Be Good Medicine*.

CHAPTER 13

1. A. M. Schlesinger, Jr. *The Cycles of American History* (Boston: Houghton Mifflin, 1986), 419–420.

2. See, for example, J. R. Meindl, S. B. Ehrlich, and J. M. Dukerich, "The Romance of Leadership," *Administrative Science Quarterly 30* (1985): 78–102; and J. Pfeffer, "The Ambiguity of Leadership," *Academy of Management Review 2* (1977): 104–112.

3. See the Appendix for more information about these and other studies.

4. B. M. Bass, *Leadership and Performance Beyond Expectations* (New York: Free Press, 1985),

219. See also B. M. Bass and B. J. Avolio, "Transformational Leadership and Organizational Culture," *Public Administration Quarterly* 17 (1) 1993: 112–121; D. A. Waldman, B. M. Bass, and W. D. Einstein, "Leadership and Outcomes of Performance Appraisal Processes," *Journal of Occupational Psychology* 60 (3) (1987): 177–186; J. J. Hater and B. M. Bass, "Superiors' Evaluations and Subordinates' Perceptions of Transformational and Transactional Leadership," *Journal of Applied Psychology* 73 (4) (1988): 695–702; and F. J. Yammarino, W. D. Spangler, and B. M. Bass, "Transformational Leadership and Performance: A Longitudinal Investigation," *The Leadership Quarterly* 4 (1) (1993): 81–102.

5. M. R. Barrick, D. V. Day, and R. G. Lord, "Assessing the Utility of Executive Leadership," *Leadership Quarterly* 2 (1) (1991): 9–22; A. B. Thomas, "Does Leadership Make a Difference to Organizational Performance?" *Administrative Science Quarterly* 33 (1988): 388–400; B. P. Niehoff, C. A. Enz, and R. A. Grover, "The Impact of Top-Management Actions on Employee Attitudes and Perceptions," *Group and Management Studies* 15 (3) (1990): 337–352; and J. C. Sarros, *Leadership Report 1993: Australian Trends in Corporate Leadership* (Victoria, Australia: Leadership Research Unit, Monash University, 1993).

6. J. E. Smith, K. P. Carson, and R. A. Alexander, "Leadership: It Can Make a Difference," *Academy of Management Journal* 27 (4) (1984): 765–776, p. 774. See also L. H. Weems, Jr., *Church Leadership: Vision, Team, Culture, and Integrity* (Nashville: Abingdon Press, 1993); and J. P. Murphy, *Vision and Values in Catholic Higher Education* (Kansas City: Sheed & Ward, 1991).

7. M. B. Cahill-Phillips, "The Demeter Effect: Trauma and Reparation in Mothers of Victimized Children" (Ph.D. diss., California School of Professional Psychology, 1992).

8. See, for example, K. A. Karl, "Effects of Optimistic and Realistic Previews of Training Programs on Self-Reported Transfer of Training," *Human Resource Development Quarterly* 3 (4) (1992): 373–380; D. Eden, "Pygmalion, Goal Setting, and Expectancy: Compatible Ways to Boost Productivity," *Academy of Management Review* 13 (4) (1988): 639–652; L. A. Learman, J. Avorn, and D. E. Everitt, "Pygmalion in the Nursing Home: The Effects of Caregiver Expectations on Patient Outcomes," *Journal of the American Geriatrics Society* 38 (7) (1990): 797–803; and J. S. Livingston, "Pygmalion in Management," *Harvard Business Review*, July–Aug. (1969): 81–89.

9. Livingston, "Pygmalion in Management"; see also D. Eden, *Pygmalion in Management: Productivity as a Self-Fulfilling Prophecy* (New York: Lexington Books, 1990).

10. M. W. McCall, M. M. Lombardo, and A. M. Morrison, *The Lessons of Experience: How Successful Executives Develop on the Job* (New York: Lexington Books, 1988).

11. R. Zemke, "The Honeywell Studies: How Managers Learn to Manage," *Training*, Aug. 1985, 46–51.

12. For a discussion of the role of challenge in executive development, see C. Magierson and A. Kakabadse, *How American Chief Executives Succeed* (New York: American Management Association, 1984); D. W. Bray and A. Howard, "The AT&T Longitudinal Studies of Managers," in K. W. Shaie (ed.), *Longitudinal Studies of Adult Psychological Development* (New York: Guilford Press, 1983); R. F. Morrison and T. M. Brantner, "What Enhances or Inhibits Learning a New Job? A Basic Career Issue," *Journal of Applied Psychology* 77 (1992): 926–940; C. W. Wick, "How People Develop: An In-Depth Look," *HR Report* 6 (7) (1989): 1–3; and D. E. Berlew and D. T. Hall, "The Socialization of Managers: Effect of Expectations on Performance," *Administrative Science Quarterly* 11 (1966): 207–223.

13. See, for example, C. D. McCauley, *Developmental Experiences in Managerial Work: A Literature Review*, Technical Report no. 26 (Greensboro, N.C.: Center for Creative Leadership, 1986);

C. D. McCauley, M. N. Ruderman, P. J. Ohlott, and J. E. Morrow, "Assessing the Developmental Components of Managerial Jobs," *Journal of Applied Psychology* 79 (4) (1994): 544–560; M. N. Ruderman, P. J. Ohlott, and C. D. McCauley, "Assessing Opportunities for Leadership Development," in K. E. Clark and M. B. Clark (eds.), *Measures of Leadership* (West Orange, N.J.: Leadership Library of America, 1990), 547–562; and P. J. Ohlott, M. N. Ruderman, and C. D. McCauley, "Gender Differences in Managers' Developmental Job Experiences," *Academy of Management Journal* 37 (1) (1994): 46–67.

14. McCauley, *Developmental Experiences*, 9–14.
15. See especially R. M. Kanter, *Men and Women of the Corporation* (New York: Basic Books, 1977); K. E. Kram, *Mentoring at Work: Developmental Relationships in Organizational Life* (Glenview, Ill.: Scott, Foresman, 1985); D. J. Levinson, *The Season's of a Man's Life* (New York: Knopf, 1978); T. C. Gibbons, "Revisiting the Question of Born vs. Made: Toward a Theory of Development of Transformational Leaders" (Ph.D. diss., Fielding Institute, 1986); and J. G. Clawson, "Mentoring in Managerial Careers," in C. B. Derr (ed.), *Work, Family and the Career* (New York: Praeger, 1980), 144–165.
16. See, for example, D. Goleman, "When the Boss Is Unbearable," *New York Times,* 28 Dec. 1986, C-1, C-29; and J. J. Gabarro and J. B. Kotter, "Managing Your Boss," *Harvard Business Review,* May-June (1993): 150–157.
17. J. P. Kotter, *The General Managers* (New York: Free Press, 1982).
18. See, for example, *The Entrepreneurs: An American Adventure,* video, part 1 (Waltham, Mass.: Martin Sandler Productions, 1992); *Gandhi,* movie (Culver City, Calif: Columbia–Tri Star Home Video, 1982); *Leaders and Legends* series, particularly programs on General Douglas MacArthur, Harry S Truman, and Winston Churchill (Bethesda, Md.: Discovery Channel, 1991).
19. "1994 Industry Report," *Training,* Oct. 1994, 30.
20. "1994 Industry Report," 49.
21. "Training Jumps 45 percent Since 1983 as Companies Restructure," *People Trends,* June 1994, 11.
22. A. P. Carnevale, "Put Quality to Work: Train America's Workforce" (Alexandria, Va.: American Society for Training and Development, 1990), 11. See also E. Denison, *Accounting for United States Economic Growth 1929–1969* (Washington, D.C.: Brookings Institution, 1974, 1976, 1980, 1985, 1988).
23. Carnevale, "Put Quality to Work," 11.
24. P. F. Drucker, *Post-Capitalist Society* (New York: HarperBusiness, 1993), 8.
25. T. J. Peters, *Liberation Management: Necessary Disorganization for the Nanosecond Nineties* (New York: Knopf, 1992), 11.
26. "The Real Truth About the Economy," *Business Week,* 7 Nov. 1994, 116.
27. W. Kiechel III, "A Manager's Career in the New Economy," *Fortune,* 4 Apr. 1994, 68–72.
28. D. H. Maister, *How's Your Asset?* (Boston: Maister Associates, 1991).
29. S. Sherman, "Leaders Learn to Heed the Voice Within," *Fortune,* 22 Aug. 1994, 92.
30. Sherman, "Leaders Learn to Heed the Voice Within," 93.
31. See, for example, J. W. Pennebaker, *Opening Up: The Healing Power of Confiding in Others* (New York: Avon, 1990); M. E. Francis and J. W. Pennebaker, "Putting Stress into Words: The Impact of Writing on Physiological, Absentee, and Self-Reported Emotional Well-Being Measures," *American Journal of Health Promotion* 6 (4) (1992): 280–287; J. W. Pennebaker, "Putting Stress into Words: Health, Linguistic, and Therapeutic Implications," *Behavior Research and Therapy* 31 (1993): 539–548; and S. P. Spera, E. D. Buhrfeind, and J. W.

Pennebaker, "Expressive Writing and Coping with Job Loss," *Academy of Management Journal* 37 (3) (1994): 722–733.

32. Families and Work Institute, *The National Study of the Changing Workforce* (New York: Families and Work Institute, 1993).

33. J. W. Gardner, *The Moral Aspect of Leadership,* Leadership Papers no. 5 (Washington, D.C.: Independent Sector, 1987), 10–18; see also R. W. Terry, *Authentic Leadership* (San Francisco: Jossey-Bass, 1993).

34. S. B. Oates, *Let the Trumpet Sound: The Life of Martin Luther King, Jr.* (New York: Mentor/New American Library, 1985).

APPENDIX

1. See, for example, B. Z. Posner and J. M. Kouzes, "Development and Validation of the Leadership Practices Inventory," *Educational and Psychological Measurement* 48 (2) (1988): 483–496; B. Z. Posner and J. M. Kouzes, "Leadership Practices: An Alternative to the Psychological Perspective," in K. Clark and M. Clark (eds.), *Measures of Leadership* (West Orange, N.J.: Leadership Library of America, 1990); B. Z. Posner and J. M. Kouzes, "Psychometric Properties of the Leadership Practices Inventory—Updated," *Educational and Psychological Measurement* 53 (1) (1993): 191–199; and B. Z. Posner and J. M. Kouzes, "An Extension of the Leadership Practices Inventory to Individual Contributors," *Educational and Psychological Measurement* 54 (4) (1994): 959–966.

2. See, for example, B. Z. Posner and B. A. Brodsky, "Leadership Development Instrument for College Students," *Journal of College Student Development* 33 (1992): 231–237; "The Leadership Practices of Effective RAs," *Journal of College Student Development* 34 (4) (1993): 300–304; and "Leadership Practices of Effective Student Leaders: Gender Makes No Difference," *NASPA Journal* 31 (2) (1994): 113–120.

3. Additional forms of the Leadership Practices Inventory have been developed for use with various populations. For example, there's a version for use with individual contributors or non-managers (LPI–Individual Contributor), another for use with a group of people (LPI-TEAM), and another for use with college students (LPI-Student). Still another version, the LPI-Delta, assesses the extent to which respondents have changed their leadership practices over some specified time period (typically since participating in a leadership development workshop or seminar). These instruments have both a Self and Observer (or Constituent) version, and all have been subject to the same psychometric analyses that were applied originally to the LPI.

4. Unless otherwise noted, all analyses reported have been conducted by the authors on all or appropriate portions of the normative database.

5. D. M. Herold, D. L. Fields, and C. W. Hyatt, "Using Leadership Instruments in a Management Development Context: What Are We Measuring?" paper presented at the annual meeting of the Academy of Management, Atlanta, Aug. 1993.

6. D. C. Ottinger, "Differences in Leadership Practices and Selected Demographic Characteristics of Women Executives in the Top Three Positions of Higher Education and Banking" (Ph.D. diss., Bowling Green State University, 1990).

7. M. Bauer, "Are the Leadership Practices of College Presidents in the Northeast Distinct from Those of Leaders of Business and Industry?" (Ph.D. diss., University of New Haven, 1993).

8. M. Mactavish, "Toward a Leadership Model in Corrections" (Ph.D. diss., Fielding Institute,

1993).

9. D. R. Spotanski, "An Assessment of the Leadership Practices Used by Agricultural Education Department Executive Officers (DEOs)" (Ph.D. diss., Iowa State University, 1991).

10. M. J. Stoner-Zemel, "Visionary Leadership, Management, and High-Performance Work Units: An Analysis of Workers' Perceptions" (Ph.D. diss., University of Massachusetts, Amherst, 1988).

11. P. J. Crnkovish and W. S. Hesterly, "Leadership Impact: An Empirical Test of a Predictive Framework," paper presented at the annual meeting of the Decision Sciences Institute, Mar. 1993.

12. A. M. Troudt, "Transformational Leadership in Home Health Care Administrators" (master's thesis, University of Wisconsin, Oshkosh, 1994).

13. S. A. Carless, A. J. Wearing, and L. Mann, "Transformational Leadership: Does It Make a Difference?" paper presented at the Western Academy of Management International Conference (Brisbane, Australia), 1994.

14. J. C. Berumen, *Applicacion del inventario de practicas de liderazgo en gerentes y empleados de empresas Mexicanas* ("Applying the Leadership Practices Inventory on Managers and Employees at Mexican Companies") (master's thesis, Universidad Intercontinental, Mexico, 1992).

15. C. H. Riley, "Superintendents' Leadership Behaviors Which Promote the Instructional Leadership of Principals" (Ph.D. diss., University of La Verne, 1991).

16. For example, Riley, "Superintendents' Leadership Behaviors Which Promote the Instructional Leadership of Principals"; F. L. Nolan, "Ethical Leadership and School Culture: An Exploratory Study of Nine Middle-Level Schools" (Ph.D. diss., University of Minnesota, 1992); and W.F.A. Truby, "Correlational Study of Transformational Leadership Characteristics and Perceived Stress of Christian School Administrators" (Ph.D. diss., Kent State University, 1992).

17. J. T. Roundy, "Hospital Administrator Leadership Practice Before and After the Implementation of Federal Cost Containment Policy" (Ph.D. diss., Arizona State University, 1991).

18. Ottinger, "Differences in Leadership Practices and Selected Demographic Characteristics of Women Executives in the Top Three Positions of Higher Education and Banking."

19. T. D. Zook, "An Examination of Leadership Practices in Large, Protestant Congregations" (Ph.D. diss., Indiana University of Pennsylvania, 1993).

20. M. E. Okeefee, "Leadership Practices in Family Support Programs" (Ph.D. diss., Seattle University, 1992).

21. For example, Bauer, "Are the Leadership Practices of College Presidents in the Northeast Distinct from Those of Leaders of Business and Industry?"; and Herold, Fields, and Hyatt, "Using Leadership Instruments in a Management Development Context."

22. Herold, Fields, and Hyatt, "Using Leadership Instruments in a Management Development Context," 10.

23. It should be noted that because of the very large sample sizes involved, even when statistical significance is determined, it may have very little *practical* significance. This is especially true at the individual level. A case in point: note that while there was a statistically significant difference between Self and Observer scores on challenging the process, the difference was only .43.

24. See, for example, R. J. Plowman, "Perceptions of Presidential Leadership Behavior and

Institutional Environment by Presidents and Vice Presidents of Selected Four-Year Colleges and Universities in Florida" (Ph.D. diss., University of Mississippi, 1991); Mactavish, "Toward a Leadership Model in Corrections"; and Riley, "Superintendents' Leadership Behaviors Which Promote the Instructional Leadership of Principals."

25. J. V. Aubrey, "The Principal's Leadership Role in Effective Site-Based Managed Elementary Schools" (Ph.D. diss., University of Bridgeport, 1992).

26. G. P. Erickson, "Leadership Development in Higher Education for Public Health" (Ph.D. diss., College of William and Mary, 1992).

27. N. L. Snyder, "Empowering Leadership and Achieving Style: A Study of Gender Differences Between Fraternity and Sorority Presidents" (master's thesis, University of Maryland, College Park, 1992).

28. Riley, "Superintendents' Leadership Behaviors Which Promote the Instructional Leadership of Principals."

29. Bauer, "Are the Leadership Practices of College Presidents in the Northeast Distinct from Those of Leaders of Business and Industry?"

30. Berumen, *Applicacion del inventario de practicas de liderazgo en gerentes y empleados de empresas Mexicanas.*

31. J. Long, "Leadership Practices of Elementary Principals and Parental Involvement in Their Schools" (Ph.D. diss., Eastern Michigan University, 1994).

32. C. L. Dunson, "Relationships Between Sex Role Orientation, Interpersonal Relations Orientation, Leadership Style Practices, and Fear of Success in University Faculty" (Ph.D. diss., University of Missouri, Kansas City, 1992).

33. Erickson, "Leadership Development in Higher Education for Public Health."

34. Ottinger, "Differences in Leadership Practices and Selected Demographic Characteristics of Women Executives in the Top Three Positions of Higher Education and Banking," reported that female executives in higher education engaged in the activities of challenging, inspiring, enabling, and encouraging significantly more than their female counterparts in banking.

35. E. W. Chance, "The BIA/Contract School Administrator: Implications for At-Risk Native American Students," paper presented at a meeting of the National Rural and Small School Consortium, 1990.

36. Berumen, *Applicacion del inventario de practicas de liderazgo en gerentes y empleados de empresas Mexicanas.*

37. Effectiveness was measured by a six-item scale with five-point Likert scales. The items asked about the extent to which this manager met the job-related needs of his or her workgroup members, had built a committed workgroup, and had influence with upper management, and they assessed the extent to which respondents were satisfied with the leadership provided by this manager, were satisfied that the manager's leadership practices were appropriate, and felt empowered by this manager. Internal reliability for the scale was .98. In Bauer's use of this same scale as a measure of college presidents' effectiveness, internal reliability was .93.

38. T. A. Larson, "Secondary Educational Leadership: A Study of Three High Schools" (Ph.D. diss., University of Nebraska, Lincoln, 1992), iv.

39. R. W. Brice, "Principals in Saskatchewan Rural Schools: Their Leadership Behaviors and School Effectiveness" (Ph.D. diss., University of San Diego, 1992).

40. Nolan, "Ethical Leadership and School Culture," 251.

41. Aubrey, "The Principal's Leadership Role in Effective Site-Based Managed Elementary Schools."

42. Long, "Leadership Practices of Elementary Principals and Parental Involvement in Their

Schools," 130.
43. L. Whatley, "The Relation of Vocational Administrators' Self-Esteem to Their Leadership Styles and Practices" (Ph.D. diss., Colorado State University, 1991).
44. S. J. Anderson, "Psychological Type and Leadership" (Ph.D. diss., University of Calgary, 1992).
45. Carless, Wearing, and Mann, "Transformational Leadership."
46. D. K. McNeese-Smith, "The Impact of Leadership Behaviors upon Job Satisfaction, Productivity, and Organizational Commitment of Followers" (Ph.D. diss., Seattle University, 1991); see also D. K. McNeese-Smith, "Leadership Behavior and Employee Effectiveness, *Nursing Management 24* (5) (1993): 38–39.
47. Roundy, "Hospital Administrator Leadership Practice Before and After the Implementation of Federal Cost Containment Policy."
48. Erickson, "Leadership Development in Higher Education for Public Health," 170.
49. Plowman, "Perceptions of Presidential Leadership Behavior and Institutional Environment by Presidents and Vice Presidents of Selected Four-Year Colleges and Universities in Florida."
50. N. L. Carlson, "Professional Roles and Functions of Presidential Assistants in Contemporary Higher Education" (Ph.D. diss., Vanderbilt University, 1991), 94.
51. M. E. Scott, "The Labyrinth of Challenge to Change: An Analysis of Community College Leaders' Thinking Styles and Behavioral Practices in the Current Environment" (Ph.D. diss., University of San Diego, 1989).
52. M. Lipton, "Leadership Characteristics of CDC Executive Directors: Preliminary Findings," paper presented at the annual meeting of the Urban Affairs Association, Charlotte, N.C., Apr. 1990.
53. Bauer, "Are the Leadership Practices of College Presidents in the Northeast Distinct from Those of Leaders of Business and Industry?"
54. Stoner-Zemel, "Visionary Leadership, Management, and High-Performance Work Units: An Analysis of Workers' Perceptions."
55. Crnkovish and Hesterly, "Leadership Impact: An Empirical Test of a Predictive Framework."
56. Zook, "An Examination of Leadership Practices in Large, Protestant Congregations," 173, 233ff.
57. J. L. Fulks, "Transformational Leadership and Its Relationship to Success in Development of New Churches" (Ph.D. diss., University of Texas, Arlington, 1994).
58. C. D. Koehler, "Personality Traits Associated with Transformational Leadership Styles of Secondary Principals in Christian Schools" (Ph.D. diss., Kent State University, 1992), 149–150.

ACKNOWLEDGMENTS

This book is the result of the loving, caring, generous assistance, advice, support, and encouragement of scores of people. If it weren't for them, there would be no book.

It's hard to pinpoint the beginnings of the project that led originally to this book. If memory serves us correctly, two people deserve recognition for giving us the kick-start we needed. Our earliest recollection is of a parking-lot conversation with Donna Kouzes about the characteristics of individuals who perform at high levels. We thought it would be interesting to apply this idea to leaders; and in her usual enthusiastic and energetic style, Donna began to collect the stories and cases that became the source of ideas and inspiration for this book.

Tom Peters gave us that important initial nudge up the mountain. Shortly after the publication of In Search of Excellence, Tom conducted a workshop with us at Santa Clara University. Tom led the first day of the seminar, and we led the second day. In an effort to help participants apply the excellence lessons to their own organizations, we utilized a technique we called the "personal-best leadership case." That was the genesis of the research methodology we've subsequently used to study and understand leadership. Tom's generosity of mind, heart, and spirit continues to overwhelm us. We deeply appreciate his kind and provocative comments in the Foreword to this book.

No book springs whole from the minds of the authors. Throughout the years, others have strongly influenced our thinking about leadership and organizations, and their ideas have found their way onto the pages you read. We owe an immense intellectual debt to these very special colleagues and friends: Warren Bennis, Dave Berlew, David Caldwell, Jerry Fletcher, John Gardner, Roger Harrison, Rosabeth Moss Kanter, Charles O'Reilly, and Warren Schmidt.

We were moved to laughter and tears, awe and inspiration, as we listened in on the uplifting experiences of hundreds of men and women who accepted the leadership challenge. They are the ones who taught us what it really means to get extraordinary things done in organizations; they are the real heroes of this book. You'll meet many of these courageous folks as you read The Leadership Challenge. We're forever grateful to them for sharing their lives with us, and we hope that we've represented them well.

One of the ways we tested our ideas about leadership was through workshops and seminars. Many people graciously agreed to be part of our experiments. They filled out questionnaires, asked others to do the same, participated in experiential exercises, and joined in on endless discussions. Ann Bowers, Boyd Clarke, Sue Cook, Ron Crossland, Michael Doyle, Randi DuBois, Paige Johnson, Peter Jordan, Marion Krause, Joan McIntosh, Ranny Riley, David Sibbet, Reno Taini, and Ricky Tam added great value to our initial designs. We also owe a special debt of gratitude to Tom Melohn and John Stanford, who not only served as leadership role models but took part in our early programs.

Moving from the realm of testing ideas to committing them to paper is always a test of teamwork. The first edition made it from ideas to print with the assistance of Liz Caravelli, Joy Congdon, Liz Currie, Judy Kasper, and Michael Malone. Anyone who has ever been involved in upgrading a product knows that a new edition really means starting over. We couldn't have written this second edition without the dedicated research assistance and case writing of Joan Carter. A great big thanks to Kathy Dalle-Molle for her expert fact checking, permissions work, and attention to detail. Jan Hunter was masterful in her role as developmental editor, weaving new material into the original, improving the readability of the book, and enabling us to come to consensus on material for the final text.

Contributions of new cases and examples for the second edition were graciously provided by Cal Atwood, Patrick Bedwell, Brian Biro, Shirley

Bunger, Saturnino Campoy, Patrick Carlton, Steve Coats, Angela Eaton, Verónica Guerrero, Steve Houchin, John Ivie, Janet McLaughlin, Carlos Moran, Darryl Roberts, Tony Rodoni, Jim Smith, Christy Svalstad, and Ching Yu.

Our colleagues at TPG/Learning Systems continuously uplift our spirits with their faith in and commitment to The Leadership Challenge Workshop™. They provide us with that enriching opportunity to test our work with practicing leaders. A special thanks for their years of stimulation, support, and encouragement.

The true art of editing and publishing is masterfully practiced by the family of professionals at Jossey-Bass Inc., Publishers. Their confidence in us and patience with us have been overwhelming. Without their support, there would be no book, only loosely connected ideas. Thanks to Cedric Crocker, Bill Hicks, Lynn Lukow, Trish O'Hare, Laura Simonds, and Terri Armstrong Welch.

We dedicate this book to our families. We had to literally close the door on them on countless evenings and weekends. If there was an aspect of writing that we hated, that was it. Our parents, Tom and Thelma Kouzes and Delores Gearhart and Henry Posner, were early role models of leadership and continue to encourage our hearts. Donna Kouzes was an initial collaborator and a frequent contributor of cases and suggestions. Jackie Schmidt-Posner provided perspective and balance as well as imaginative advice and laughter. Amanda Posner continues to be a delightful and stimulating distraction. Donna, Jackie, and Amanda are constant sources of love and warmth, inspiration and insight. We can't express enough our appreciation for their sacrifices, their steadfastness, and their support. They're living examples of what it means to care about and care for others.

Yes, as Don Bennett, the first amputee to climb Mount Rainier, told us, "You can't do it alone." We couldn't have done it without all of the folks mentioned above, and many others along the way. They made this book possible.

We love you all.

James M. Kouzes
Barry Z. Posner

THE AUTHORS

JAMES M. KOUZES is chairman and chief executive officer of TPG/Learning Systems, A Company in The Tom Peters Group, based in Palo Alto, California. In his association with The Tom Peters Group since 1987, he has personally experimented with the practices described in this book. With strategic business partners in England, Mexico, and New Zealand, TPG/Learning Systems offers such innovative educational programs as "The Leadership Challenge Workshop™," "Leadership Is Everyone's Business™," "Walking the Talk™," "The Tom Peters Seminar™," and "Service with Soul™."

Kouzes's interest in leadership began while he was growing up in Washington, D.C. In 1961, he was one of a dozen Eagle Scouts from across the United States selected to serve in John F. Kennedy's Honor Guard at the presidential inauguration. Inspired by Kennedy, he served as a Peace Corps volunteer from 1967 through 1969.

From late 1981 through 1987, Kouzes was director of the Executive Development Center (EDC), Leavey School of Business and Administration, Santa Clara University. Under his guidance, the EDC was awarded two gold medals from the Council for the Advancement and Support of Education for its unique leadership series. His career in academic administration began at the University of Texas School of Social Work in 1970 and continued in 1972 at San Jose State University, where he founded the Joint Center for Human Services Development.

Kouzes is the author of numerous articles and chapters in edited volumes on management education, leadership, and organization development. He received the Hubert H. Humphrey Award for the best article of 1983 from the *Journal of Health and Human Resources Administration*. He received his B.A. degree (1967) with honors from Michigan State University in political science and a certificate (1974) from San Jose State University's School of Business for completion of the internship in organization development. He is featured as one of twenty-five workplace experts in George Dixon's book *What Works at Work: Lessons from the Masters* (1988).

In September 1993, the *Wall Street Journal* cited Jim Kouzes as one of the twelve most requested nonuniversity executive-education providers to U.S. companies. He has conducted programs for such diverse organizations as Amoco of Canada, AGT, Apple Computer, AT&T, Boeing, Genentech, The Healthcare Forum, Honeywell, IBM, Imperial Oil Limited, Johnson & Johnson, Levi Strauss & Co., Nestlé U.S.A., Pacific Bell, Pacific Gas & Electric, McDonnell Douglas, Queen's University, Siemens Rolm Communications, Stanford University, and the Swedish Employers Confederation. Kouzes can be reached at (415) 326-5774.

BARRY Z. POSNER is professor of organizational behavior and managing partner of the Executive Development Center, Leavey School of Business and Administration, Santa Clara University. He served previously as associate dean, with responsibility for leading the school's MBA and undergraduate programs. Posner is an internationally recognized scholar and educator who has received both his school's and his university's highest faculty awards.

Posner's interest in leadership began as a student during the turbulent unrest on college campuses in the late 1960s, when he was participating and reflecting on the balance between energetic collective action and chaotic and frustrated anarchy. At one time, he aspired to be a Supreme Court justice, but realizing he would have to study law, he redirected his energies into understanding people and organizational systems.

Posner is the author or coauthor of more than eighty research and practitioner-oriented articles in such publications as *Academy of Management Journal, Journal of Applied Psychology, Human Relations, Personnel Psychology, IEEE Transaction on Engineering Management, Journal of*

Business Ethics, California Management Review, Business Horizons, and *Management Review.* In addition to his books with Jim Kouzes, he has coauthored *Getting the Job Done: Managing Project Teams and Task Forces for Success* and *Effective Project Planning and Management.*

Posner received his B.A. degree (1970) with honors from the University of California, Santa Barbara, in political science. He received his M.A. degree (1972) from The Ohio State University in public administration and his Ph.D. degree (1976) from the University of Massachusetts, Amherst, in organizational behavior and administrative theory. He is a member of the editorial review boards of the *Journal of Management Education* and the *Journal of Management Inquiry.* He has served on the board of directors of several start-up companies and currently sits on the board of Big Brothers/Big Sisters of Santa Clara County and the Center for Excellence in Non-Profits. He is a frequent conference speaker and serves on the faculty for executive development programs for such diverse companies as ARCO, Alcoa, Australia Post, Charles Schwab, Ciba-Geigy, Gymboree, Hewlett-Packard, Kaiser Permanente Health Care, Motorola, Novacor, Pacific Telesis, Silicon Graphics, TRW, and United Way. Posner can be reached at (408) 554–4634.

In addition to the best-selling and award-winning book *The Leadership Challenge,* Jim Kouzes and Barry Posner have coauthored *Credibility: How Leaders Gain and Lose It, Why People Demand It* (Jossey-Bass, 1993), selected by *Industry Week* as one of the five best management books of 1993. They have appeared in five video programs on leadership produced by CRM Films. Their Leadership Practices Inventory, available from Pfeiffer & Co., is one of the most widely used leadership assessment instruments in the world. Training programs based on their collective works are available from TPG/Learning Systems. To learn more about these products and services, call (800) 333–8878.

INDEX

ABOUT TPG/LEARNING SYSTEMS

TPG/Learning Systems was founded in 1987 by best-selling authors Jim Kouzes and Tom Peters. The work of these two men has provided the cornerstone for the company's pioneering management development work with many of the world's most successful and forward-looking companies. TPG/Learning Systems is committed to translating the work of Jim Kouzes and Tom Peters into dynamic and practical learning experiences that enhance individual and organizational performance.

TPG/Learning Systems offers a complete line of leadership products:

THE LEADERSHIP CHALLENGE™ WORKSHOP

Designed by and based on the award-winning book by Jim Kouzes and Barry Posner, *The Leadership Challenge*. An intensive two- or three-day program on the five leadership practices required to get extraordinary things done. Strengthens individuals' abilities and self-confidence to lead others in challenging situations. Implemented by some of America's most admired organizations, including Levi Strauss & Co., Motorola, and 3M.

THE CHALLENGE CONTINUES™

A one-day follow-up program to The Leadership Challenge Workshop that supports the transfer of leadership learnings into day-to-day reality. Provides feedback and reinforcement to the development of the five leadership practices.

LEADERSHIP IS EVERYONE'S BUSINESS™

Develops the leadership practices of individual contributors at all levels of the organization. Increases collaboration, trust, and involvement and creates a common language and empowerment culture. Heightens personal responsibility and accountability of all members to contribute to the organization's success.

VALUES IN ACTION™

Designed for organizations that want to strengthen individual commitment to shared values. Provides a forum for meaningful dialogue between employees and management about the values of the organization and their impact on daily actions. Builds a high-performing culture by aligning behaviors with organizational values. Increases trust and speed in decision making at all levels.

WALKING THE TALK™

A two-day program for managers on how to sustain commitment to shared vision and values. Enables managers to model and coach employees to close gaps between stated values and daily actions. Based on the award-winning book *Credibility*, by Jim Kouzes and Barry Posner.

Additionally, TPG/Learning Systems delivers powerful learning experiences to support key business objectives, including:

- Refocusing the organization on delighting customers
- Creating a strong competitive advantage
- Building teamwork and trust
- Energizing the curious and innovative organization

TPG/Learning Systems
A Tom Peters Group Company
555 Hamilton Avenue
Palo Alto, CA 94301
Phone: (800) 333–8878
Fax: (415) 326–7065

Also Available from Jim Kouzes and Barry Posner

	Price	Qty	=Total

CREDIBILITY
How Leaders Gain and Lose It, Why People Demand It

"'Credibility' may well move quickly into the lexicon as the next leadership buzzword." — *Fortune*

A personal, inspiring, and genuine guide to help us understand the fundamental importance of credibility for building personal and organizational success and for fostering trust within our work, family, and community. One of *Industry Week's* Top Ten Best Management Books.

Cloth   1-55542-550X $28.00 $28.00 x ____ = _____

Paperback   0-7879-0056-7 $16.50 $16.50 x ____ = _____

WHAT FOLLOWERS EXPECT FROM LEADERS
How to Meet People's Expectations and Build Credibility

A two-cassette audio program featuring stimulating interviews with successful business leaders, a "drop-in" conversation with executives participating in a leadership training session, and thought-provoking questions posed directly to the listener. 1-55542-908-4 $24.95 x ____ = _____

Available at fine bookstores, or order direct:

MAIL
☒ USE THIS ORDER FORM

FAX
800.605.BOOK (2665)
TOLL FREE 24 HOURS A DAY

Please send me the titles I have indicated above. I am enclosing $_____ , including shipping and appropriate state sales tax. (All payments must be prepaid in U.S. dollars only.)

❑ check/money order   ❑ Visa   ❑ Mastercard   ❑ American Express

Card no.: _____

Exp. date_____Day telephone _____

Signature _____

Shipping Charges for Prepaid Orders: $10 and under, add $2.50; $10.01-$20, add $3.50; $20.01-$50, add $4.50; $50.01-$75, add $5.50. CA, NJ, Washington, D.C., and NY residents add sales tax. Canadian residents add GST. Prices and availability subject to change without notice. Valid in the U.S. and Canada only.

Name _____

Address _____

City_____ State _____Zip_____

Jossey-Bass Publishers • 350 Sansome Street • San Francisco, CA 94104